D0437074

Just as I Am

My wedding day in December 1942, just after my eighteenth birthday. *Seated:* Me with my first husband, Kenneth. *Back row, left to right:* My mother, Fredericka; Kenneth's cousin, the best man; Reverend Jones, Kenneth's father, who married us; my sister, Emily, the maid of honor; my godfather; and my cousin, Sylvia Tyson, a bridesmaid.

COURTESY OF THE AUTHOR

Just as I Am

A MEMOIR

Cicely Tyson

with Michelle Burford

Foreword by Viola Davis

HarperCollins*Publishers*

First photography insert:
Page 1: Lord Snowdon, husband to Princess Margaret and an avid photographer, captured me in this Bill Whitten masterpiece of a dress—the one I wore to the New York premiere of *Sounder* in 1972. © *Snowdon/Trunk Archive.*
Page 2: My family, circa 1927. *Clockwise from left:* My father, William Augustine Tyson, holds my sister, Emily; my mother, Fredericka Theodosia Tyson (née Huggins); me, at age two and a half; and my brother, Melrose, whom our family calls Beau. *Courtesy of Cicely Tyson.*

Excerpt on page 70 from "Strange Fruit," recorded by Abel Meeropol in 1937.
Excerpt on page 351 from "Paul Robeson" by Gwendolyn Brooks.
Excerpt on pages 388–89 from "Ailey, Baldwin, Floyd, Killens, and Mayfield" by Maya Angelou from *I Shall Not Be Moved.* Bantam, 1991.

FIRST EDITION

Designed by Terry McGrath

Photograph on page 407 courtesy of Cicely Tyson

Library of Congress Cataloging-in-Publication Data has been applied for.

ISBN 978-0-06-293106-1
ISBN 978-0-06-307256-5 (signed ed.)

21 22 23 24 25 LSC 10 9 8 7 6 5 4 3 2 1

Contents

PART TWO: ROOTED

PART THREE: BOUNTIFUL

FOREWORD

A Mighty Seed

by Viola Davis

I WAS introduced to Ms. Tyson on a television set in my family's dilapidated apartment in Central Falls, Rhode Island. Oddly, it was a television that rested upon another broken one, a set with aluminum foil on its antennae for better reception. My sisters Deloris and Dianne sat beside me, cross-legged in front of the screen, and together we witnessed magic—an image that changed my life at the tender age of seven. There was Ms. Tyson in *The Autobiography of Miss Jane Pittman*, a made-for-TV movie based on the novel by Ernest J. Gaines. In the 1974 film, 110-year-old Jane Pittman reflects on her life, from her enslavement in her early twenties to the day nearly a century later when she defies Jim Crow by sipping from a whites-only water fountain.

I couldn't believe the same actress had played both the young woman and the elder one, but Deloris insisted she had. I stared at my sister, and then back at the screen, marveling at Ms. Tyson's mastery of her craft, the brilliance with which she had transformed herself. It planted in me a seed that immediately took root. She was the manifestation of excellence and artistry, a dark-skinned, thick-lipped woman who truly mirrored me. I can pinpoint the exact moment when my life opened up, and it was there, in front of that set, that mine did. With one mesmerizing performance, with one gorgeously poignant rendering of her character, Ms. Tyson gave me permission to dream.

I was no stranger to the wonder of dreams. For most of my life, dreams were all my siblings and I had. I was born in 1965, in a one-room sharecropper's shack on a plantation in South Carolina. My father was illiterate, and my mother had only an eighth-grade education. Desperate to support my siblings and me, my parents moved us north. My father was an equestrian who groomed horses and prepared them for racing, and in Rhode Island he found work. We settled in Central Falls, a mill town a single square mile in size. Though my father did all he could to piece together a living for us, we still lived in abject poverty, on society's lowest rung. Our deprivation far exceeded the financial. We were the only Black family in a town of white Irish Catholics, a family with no sense of ourselves, other than as invisible. There was no foundation of self-love or worth for us, no pathway to any kind of achievement.

We settled for a time at 128 Washington Street—or 128, as my sisters and I referred to it. That condemned building represented exactly how the world felt about us. It was the demon that sat on my chest during those years, the devil that still hangs over me as a painful memory of the trauma. Our third-floor, rat-infested apartment lacked heat, plumbing, and hot water because the pipes froze during the harsh New England winters. There was a single room with electricity, and from that room, a long cord stretched to connect us to the outside world through that foiled-antennae television. It was on that screen, in 128, that Ms. Tyson flickered into my world.

In Ms. Tyson I saw a dark-skinned woman with the same

'fro as my mother, an artist who carried herself with pride and poise. I was more than entertained by the story of Jane Pittman's life. I was mesmerized by Ms. Tyson's ability to transport me from my world to hers, to a place where I didn't have to wade through garbage bins in search of food covered in maggots, a place where the demon on my chest disappeared for a time. Even as a child, I knew I wanted more than 128, wanted more than the rat-infested existence we endured. Watching *Jane Pittman*, I saw my ticket out of poverty and shame.

Ms. Tyson, the daughter of immigrants, had herself risen out of poverty and onto the global stage. In her journey, I glimpsed possibilities for my own. For hours in our bedroom, my sisters and I would try to imitate everything about Ms. Tyson: her piercing gaze, those eyes brimming with memory and emotion, the way she held her jaw, how she so fully embodied her characters. By the time I was fourteen, I was so intent on following in her path that I took a bus to an acting class two hours away, since my family didn't have a car. There I was, a complete geek in my gaucho pants and my purple mascara, doing all I could to imbue my characters with the empathy Ms. Tyson brought to her portrayals. I wanted to be exceptional at my craft. And more than anything, I wanted to be like her.

Before I knew of her, Ms. Tyson had already made a name for herself as an accomplished actor, engraving our narratives into the storybook of the world. For six decades, Ms. Tyson has shown us who we are: vulnerable, magnificent, pain-ridden, and beautifully human. Time and time again, she has put our humanity on display, never compromising her dignity while creating a new chapter in Black history. In 1963 during the filming of the series *East Side/West Side*, she arrived on set rocking her 'fro, becoming the first Black woman to wear her natural hair on TV. Yet terms like "trailblazer" and "pioneer" don't fully capture what she means to so many of us who looked up to her as the epitome of Black strength. Ms. Tyson is the Master Truth Teller—a warrior with fierce courage and supreme artistry, her instrument precisely tuned to tell stories that capture our being.

Over the years, I've held close Ms. Tyson's brave spirit as I've admired her work from afar. Then, in 2011 on the set of *The Help*, I finally met my muse. There before me on a muggy afternoon in Mississippi stood the divine giver of gifts, the legend who had inspired me to act. I embraced her, tears spilling from my eyes as I stammered through a flurry of thank-yous, none of them conveying the depth of my gratitude. We had no scenes together in the movie, and I wasn't on set when Ms. Tyson filmed her segments as Constantine. But the director, Tate Taylor, recalled the dedication she brought to her work. She showed up on set in character and remained that way, insisting that she be called Constantine at all times. That's just who Ms. Tyson is: excellence personified.

Toward the end of 2014, I asked my role model to play Ophelia, the mother of my character, Annalise, on the ABC series *How to Get Away with Murder.* In life, Ms. Tyson had nurtured and mentored me. On the set, she would do the same, though in a way that initially caught me off guard. She'd just turned ninety years old then, and she strode in already steeped in the tense history between mother and daughter. As she entered, I stood there with an enormous smile on my face and my arms outstretched to hug her. She marched right past me, reprimanding me with her stern expression, a mother putting a child in her place. She knew that if she'd broken the moment by stepping out of character, her portrayal wouldn't be the same. Faced with that wall, I laughed and thought, *Well maybe I need to get working.* During our scenes in *Murder*, I experienced her ingenuity up close. With just her demeanor—with those lucid and revealing eyes, with traces of pain on her brow—Ms. Tyson often took viewers someplace you can go only if you've been there. That is because she does not simply act. She bares every corner of her soul. And in so doing, she accomplishes what all great art does: she makes us feel less alone.

A few years later when Ms. Tyson heard I'd been nominated for an Academy Award for *Fences*, she called to congratulate me. I clutched the phone, giddy like the seven-year-old I'd been watching her play Jane Pittman all those winters ago. "I know the road you're on," she told me. By that, she meant she understood the world that a dark-skinned actress not seen as conventionally beautiful was navigating. She knew the barriers in the industry, all the ways, explicit and covert, that someone with my nose and my lips and my hair is told she isn't enough. She was aware of how we Black women are expected to water down our complexity, how our pathology is seldom allowed exposure within the narratives written for us. She had confronted those obstacles. At the end of our call, she urged me to relish the path ahead, the accolades, all of it. Just as she'd once granted me permission to dream, she now nudged me to delight in the bounty. Here she was, offering me another gem, this time as a wise ally, lifting her lantern to light my way.

This book is Ms. Tyson's abundant treasure to each of us: her life, in her words, just as she is. She shares truths usually whispered between sisters and close friends in the dim light of a back bedroom, those candid declarations not often spoken aloud. And she tells her story the way only a Black woman can: in all of its dazzling authenticity, heels off and voice undulating, shifting between anguish and exuberance. The art of acting is the art of exposing, an emotional unveiling before others. Ms. Tyson is as revelatory on these pages as she has been on the stage. She is not just the performer who has so deftly captured the breadth of the human experience, with all of its unslicked edges. She is Cicely the woman, someone who has grappled with the fears and fragilities many of us carry. And during a season when so much in our culture is changing so quickly, she has now blessed us with a timeless jewel: her written legacy.

And what a heritage it is—one not gauged by her number of extraordinary roles, but by the countless lives, like my own, that she has lifted. "You'll never see a U-Haul behind a hearse," Denzel Washington often said as we worked together on *Fences*. "I don't care how much money you have or what level of notoriety you've achieved, you can't take any of it with you." There is a cap on earthly success, a ceiling on the amount of joy that possessions and awards can bring before disillusionment sets in. Our appearance, our prosperity, the applause: all of it is so fleeting. But a life of true significance has unlimited impact. It is measured in how well we've loved those around us, how much we've given away, how many seeds we've sown along our path. During her ninety-six years, Ms. Tyson has discovered the potent elixir: she has lived a life that is bigger than she is, an existence grounded in purpose and flourishing in service to others. That is her defining masterpiece. That is her enduring gift to us all.

INTRODUCTION

This Life

I NEVER intended to write an autobiography. Decades ago, after I presented an award to Barbara Jordan—the trailblazing civil rights activist and the first African American elected to the Texas Senate—I asked her, "When are you going to write your book?" A smile spread across Barbara's face. "When I have something to say," she told me. In that moment, I decided that if a woman as accomplished as Barbara could get away with such a reply, so could I.

Years later, a gentleman from *The Washington Post* interviewed me. "When are you going to do your book?" he asked. And just as I'd been doing for quite some time by then, I borrowed Barbara's response. "When I have something to say," I told him. "Well, I've been talking to you for three hours," he said, chuckling, "and it sounds to me like you've got *plenty* to say." I nodded and gave him the same wry grin Barbara had once given me, with no plan of ever committing my story to the page.

Back then I did not see an autobiography as personal. I thought of it as a written record of a public journey—for me, an account of my stage and film roles, the parts of my experience in view of the world. It would be my story through the lens of Miss Jane Pittman, through Rebecca in *Sounder* and Binta in *Roots*. To be sure, there are traces of who I am in every woman I have portrayed. In the tenacity of Harriet Tubman and the quiet strength of Coretta Scott King, I can be glimpsed. In the trembling fingers of Constantine in *The Help* and in the determination of Mrs. Carrie Watts in *The Trip to Bountiful*, my thumbprint is recognizable. Every one of these characters has left me with an emotional, spiritual, and psychological inheritance I will forever carry with me. But while each, in some way, reflected me, none could reveal who I am in my entirety.

A few years ago, my manager, Larry Thompson, started in on me again about writing a memoir. "You've got to do a book," he said one afternoon. "Yeah, you and the world think that," I told him, shaking my head. "No, I'm serious," he persisted. "It's time." I uttered the same refrain I'd been repeating to him for months: The lights and the trimmings of my career, the accolades—as far as I was concerned, none of it needed to be recounted. For me, the greatest gratification has come in refining my craft, not in gazing upon its merits. He stared at me for a long moment. "You're talking about a Christmas tree," he finally said. "What?" I asked. "Everybody thinks they know who Cicely Tyson is," he explained. "But what they see are the ornaments on the branches, the decorations. They know nothing about the roots."

That conversation is what planted the seed for *Just as I Am*. Larry's observation captured, for the first time, what I have felt for so many years. The glitter, the ribbons, the garnish—as wonderful as those things are, I have little desire to reflect on them solely. What I am far more interested in is how my tree, my story, first sprang into existence. How its roots, stretching far beneath the soil, have nourished and anchored me. How each tree ring whispers memories sometimes too troubling for me to recall. How its bark and rugged exterior have both guarded and grounded me. Every one of my experiences on the public stage has been rooted in my upbringing, those years spent at my mother's elbow and on my father's knee. That foundation, that rich earth, has given birth to who I am. Even now, in the winter of my life, I am just beginning to truly understand my identity.

Every holiday season in the heart of New York's Rockefeller Center, a spruce stands, proud and glistening, in a magnificent exhibition. And yet its display is but a snapshot of that tree's history, one brief and final episode in its lifespan. The thousands of lights adorning its branches disclose nothing about its path, about its nurturing and growth over decades. Only when that tree is stripped of its embellishments does it bare its scars and show its true nature.

Just as I Am is my truth. It is me, plain and unvarnished, with the glitter and garland set aside. In these pages, I am indeed Cicely, the actress who has been blessed to grace the stage for six decades. Yet I am also the church girl who once rarely spoke a word. I am the teenager who sought solace in the verses of the old hymn for which this book is named. I am a daughter and a mother, a sister and a friend. I am an observer of human nature and the dreamer of audacious dreams. I am a woman who has hurt as immeasurably as I have loved, a child of God divinely guided by his hand. And here in my ninth decade, I am a woman who, at long last, has something meaningful to say.

I stand amazed at this tree, this life. I stare up in awe at its branches, raising up toward heaven. I wonder about its origins, how a seed so minuscule could grow into a structure so vast and resilient. I'm still examining its genesis. To examine, to question, to discover and evolve—that is what it means to be alive. The day we cease to explore is the day we begin to wilt. I share my testimony in these pages not because I have reached any lasting conclusions, but because I have so much to understand. I am as inquisitive about life now as I was as a child. My story will never be finished, nor should it be. For as long as God grants me breath, I will be living—and writing—my next chapter.

PART ONE

PLANTED

Like a tree planted by the water,
I shall not be moved.

—NEGRO SPIRITUAL

I

The Vow

I KNOW instantly whether I should take a role. If my skin tingles as I read the script, then it is absolutely something I must do. But if my stomach churns, I do not touch the project, because if I did, I'd end up on a psychiatrist's couch. Either my spirit can take the story or it cannot, and my senses have never misled me. That is how I knew, with unequivocal assurance, that I was meant to act in *Sounder*, the 1972 film about a loving family's struggle during the Depression. What I didn't know is how *Sounder*'s tide would carry me toward a profound purpose—one spawned by comments from strangers.

The role offered to me in the film wasn't the one I would've chosen. "We want you to play the schoolteacher," the producers said to me as they handed me the script. Yet as I read the story, I felt certain I was meant to portray the mother, Rebecca, the wife of Nathan. Nathan was his family's backbone, Rebecca its robust and steady heartbeat. In that mom's devotion—in the tender way she cared for their three children even as she rested her palm in the small of her husband's back—I recognized my own mother. "But you're too young, too pretty, too sexy to play the mom," I was told. I was forty-seven then, though for years at the suggestion of my first director, Warren Coleman, I'd been claiming to be a full decade younger, with taut cocoa skin clinging to my secret. "What does my appearance have to do with acting?" I retorted, amused that I, a schoolgirl once called a skinny little nappy-head, was now being ruled out as too attractive. "As an artist, I should be able to portray anyone." But the producers wouldn't hear of it.

Three months went by and the team was still searching for an actress to play Rebecca. Meanwhile, feeling no less convinced that I was destined for the role, I had Rebecca's lines *down*, do you hear me? After another month had passed, I received a call from Bill Haber, my agent at the time.

"Well," he said, exhaling into the receiver, "you got the role of the mother." I didn't say a word.

"Did you hear me?" he pressed.

"Yes, I heard you," I answered calmly. "So when do we begin?"

"But aren't you excited?" he asked.

"About *what*?" I said. "I knew all the time that the role was mine. I was just waiting for them to discover it."

An actress the producers had gone after had wanted more money than they were willing to pay, and so she'd passed on the film. I could've saved them the trouble of their negotiation because the role was never for her. The money wasn't much, Haber explained; I'd earn around $6,000—a pittance even in those days. Yet I would've taken the role for half of that. It's how convinced I was that Rebecca was my character.

When filming began in Baton Rouge in spring 1971, the nation had teetered off balance. Dr. Martin Luther King Jr. was gone, his life sliced short three years earlier by a bullet thundering across a hotel balcony. On that fateful evening in Memphis, the Civil Rights Movement had lost not only its leader but also its way, wandering in search of a new path forward. It was in this America, one grieving and limping from a deep racial reckoning, that Blaxploitation cinema found a fertile audience. In a spate of films during the early 1970s depicting urban life, the Black man, muted over centuries by bigotry's cruel muzzle, at last got to play the hero in his own story line. But this newfound creative freedom came at a cost. In my mind, these films gave rise to a misery more harrowing than the realities they portrayed. The Black woman was often cast in a powerless supporting role, or as a hypersexual female eager to fall into bed. Ghetto life and vulgarity were glorified. Even still, theatergoers seemed ravenous for this movie genre, and directors, driven by profits, rushed to satiate that appetite. During this period, a producer had the gall to say to me, "Niggers want sex and violence, and we plan to give them both." He did not flinch as he spoke.

Given the box-office success of films such as *Sweet Sweetback's Baadasssss Song*, making a movie about a tight-knit Black family of Louisiana sharecroppers took some nerve. Marty Ritt, a gem of a director, clearly had plenty of it. With characteristic zeal, he forged ahead with filming *Sounder*, which was based on an award-winning children's novel and adapted for the screen by Lonne Elder. I did not know how the movie would ultimately resonate, nor was that my chief concern. I was focused on emptying my soul into Rebecca, my first lead role in a major film. Sharing the stage with me was Paul Winfield, who played Nathan, and Kevin Hooks, who portrayed David, the eldest of our children and the son who narrates the story. Paul, who'd already become known for his star turn in the 1968 NBC sitcom *Julia* with my beloved friend Diahann Carroll, was to be *Sounder*'s headliner. I, then in the infancy of my film career, wasn't slated to even have my name listed on the movie's poster. Circumstances would later have something to say about that.

Before *Sounder*'s release, I traveled across the country on a promotional tour with some of the other cast members. From San Francisco to Boston, Indianapolis to Richmond, reporters who'd previewed the film gathered to interview me about the production. It was during my stop in Philadelphia that the earth quaked.

Among the group of reporters stood a Caucasian gentleman, auburn-haired and around age thirty. He cleared his throat, lifted the microphone to his lips, and locked his gaze on me. "I have a confession to make," he said slowly, as if calculating the impact of what he would reveal. "I never thought of myself as being the least bit prejudiced," he said. "But as I watched the film, I just could not believe that the son was calling his father 'Daddy.' That is what my son calls me." Silence blanketed the room.

Well, child, I'll tell you: my mouth fell open like a broken pocketbook. As the man's words shuddered through me, I forced a smile. But all the while I was thinking, *My Lord, how appalling*. This man clearly knew nothing about our shared humanity. He had no understanding of God's multihued creation, of his place, next to yours and mine, in that colorful family mosaic. From his perspective, there had to be something radically wrong with a Black child calling his father "Daddy," a term he thought reserved for his own kind. How could Nathan, once declared three-fifths human by our Constitution, be worthy of such endearment? How could a fraction of a man stand forehead to forehead with him? That would put Nathan on par with all those born into the privilege of whiteness, as he had been. I don't know what stunned me more: the fact that the man believed what he did, or that he had the audacity to say it aloud.

After a lengthy pause, I regained my composure and my tongue. "I have to congratulate you, sir," I said, my tone tinged with sarcasm. "It takes a lot of courage to stand up here, in the midst of your peers, and admit you never thought you were prejudiced until you saw the film. Thank you." I was so disturbed by what I'd heard that, in that moment, this was the only response I could muster.

I left that press conference saying to myself, *Maybe it's just this one.* Surely, amid the shrill call for equality sounded during those years, there couldn't be many who shared this man's view. That is how I attempted to console myself.

Yet as I continued touring the country, I became acquainted with an America I'd seldom encountered up to then. At the time, I considered myself fairly knowledgeable about this nation I have always called home. I'd grown up in New York and lived either there or in Los Angeles, two culturally progressive cities. But outside of that bubble, in the many towns and communities I regularly flew over, the seed of Dr. King's dream might have been sown, but it obviously had not germinated. During a stop in the Midwest, another reporter's comment reinforced that notion.

"I didn't know that Black men and women had the kind of loving relationship that we see between Nathan and Rebecca," a young woman stated. "Their connection didn't seem believable to me." I was so taken aback by her assessment that I did not respond. So seldom had Black families been portrayed nurturing one another on-screen that, when art indeed imitated life, the truth of that narrative was met with deep skepticism. Embedded in this woman's observation was an assumption that lives at the center of all bias: *You are not like me. You are intrinsically different. And that difference deems you inferior.*

I recognized these comments for what they were: pure ignorance. Anger would've been the justified response, and for a time in private, I was certainly apoplectic. But as life has taught me more than once, resentment corrodes the veins of the person who carries it. These reporters' beliefs, however offensive they may have been to me, were not a bitterness to be nursed; they were a lesson to be heeded. So rather than recoiling in exasperation at the ideas expressed, I leaned in and listened intently at every remaining tour stop. Much of what I heard mimicked what those two reporters had dared voice. And the more aware I became of the bigotry that existed against Black people, what might've been reason to seethe became, for me, a reason to pursue my craft with new purpose. I returned home from the road saying to myself, *Sister, you've got some educating to do.*

It was at this juncture that I made a conscious decision: I would use my profession as my platform—a stage from which to make my voice heard by carefully choosing my projects and portrayals. I could not afford the luxury of simply being an actress. Yes, I was already selecting only those roles that gave me goose pimples, just as Rebecca in *Sounder* had. But as an artist with the privilege of the spotlight, I felt an enormous responsibility to use that forum as a force for good, as a place from which to display the full spectrum of our humanity. My art had to both mirror the times and propel them forward. I was determined to do all I could to alter the narrative about Black people—to change the way Black women in particular were perceived, by reflecting our dignity.

When I made the choice to pursue acting, the last thing in the world I intended to be was an actress for the cause. Like most artists, I expected to continually hone my craft by playing all types of roles, with little consideration for how those portrayals might impact the cultural dialogue. But the racial climate called for something more of me, and while traveling this great land, I resolved to answer in the one way I knew how.

Never once, during the billowing smoke of the Civil Rights

Movement, would I be spotted at a Woolworth lunch counter, braving a sit-in while hate-mongers hurled spit and spite. Never would I parade up and down the boulevards of Selma or Montgomery, a picket sign thrust high alongside my shouts. I admire the valiant freedom fighters who took to the streets, but it wasn't in my makeup to demonstrate in these ways. Nonetheless, I was set on speaking in the only place I felt courageous enough to do so—on the stage. I protested using not my own words, but those of the characters I inhabited. Fifty years after I made a silent pact with myself to play women whose legacies uplift us, that vow still guides me.

This life is something. When you've lived as long as I have, others always seem to be asking how you are. "I'm here—*still*," I'm fond of responding. "God must have more work for me to do that I haven't yet done." Over nearly a century, I've witnessed the times shifting even as I've watched them come swinging back around, full circle, to the moment we are standing in today. There is more of this glorious pilgrimage in my rearview mirror than there is up ahead.

When I think now on the promise I made all those seasons ago, I recognize it as a defining moment, one from which scores of others would flow. And what preceded that pivot was a miracle that confounds me: that a reticent girl, born in the slums and bathed in the mighty timbre of a church organ, ever stumbled into such a grand arena.

2

String Bean

My mother strolls along the sidewalk, pushing me, six months old, in a carriage. The South Bronx is just yawning awake, its wide boulevards not yet teeming with immigrant families scrambling toward their trains. Mom has risen early for some solitude before the day's responsibilities intrude. A Jewish woman, with short black curls framing her kind face, approaches. My mother's instinct is not to flee. It is 1925, an era in which neighbors are still more trusted than feared. The lady leans under the large hood of the carriage and studies my squinty face and bald head.

"Take care of that child," she whispers. Mommy scans the woman's eyes in search of what she means. "She has a sixth sense," she continues. "She's going to make you very proud one day—and she's going to take care of you in your old age."

The lady smiles and nods and then disappears down the sidewalk as my mother stares after her. The two had never spotted each other amid the factories and alleyways of the neighborhood. They will never again cross paths. Yet on this morning, during the daybreak of my life, providence sweeps them together for a singular exchange. And there I lay, swaddled and slumbering, as oblivious to the roar of passing locomotives as I am to the prophecy of a stranger.

My parents grew up together in Nevis, an island cradled between the Atlantic Ocean and the Caribbean Sea in the British West Indies. My mother, Fredericka Theodosia Huggins, was the only child of Mary Jane Sargent, a seamstress, and Charles Huggins, a fisherman who drowned when his boat capsized during a storm. Mary Jane and Charles were never married. My father, William Augustine Tyson, was one of eight children, or at least the eight he knew about. His dad, John Edward Tyson, the overseer of a wealthy family's estate, was said to have fathered twenty-four children. Eight of them were with my dad's mother, Caroline "Carol" Matilda Wilkes Tyson.

Carol—or "Kyar," as my mother mispronounced her name, along with nearly every other word she spoke in her thick Caribbean accent—was a wayfarer by nature, a spirit unable to tolerate stillness. Whenever Carol felt good and ready, she'd leave the house for weeks, with no indication of when she'd return. In would step Mary Jane, a dear friend of Carol and John's. My maternal grandmother had a heart more wide open than her embrace. She'd sweep those Tyson children into her long arms, caring for each with the same gentleness as she showed her own daughter. It was squeezed around her supper table, in a shanty the size of a thimble, that my mom and dad became acquainted. One evening as Mary Jane bowed her head, the sound of grace rising to mix with the smell of goat stew, my father winked clandestinely at my mother. He was just twelve years old then, already gregarious and rehearsing his mannish charms. My mother, one month his senior and more timid than I'd one day be, blushed and looked away.

Nevis is tiny, even when it puffs out its chest and stands tall alongside its big sister, St. Kitts. The entire island is about thirty-five square miles; you can drive its full length, from Newcastle in the north to Saddle Hill near its bottom edge, in less than a half-hour. The island's capital, Charlestown, on the western coast, was the birthplace of Alexander Hamilton. My parents' homes were on opposite ends of Nevis. Mom and her mother shared their two-room hovel on the northwest shore, in the village of Westbury in St. Thomas parish. My father was born in that same parish, but his father, then a laborer desperate to lift his low wages, moved the family from one village to the next. When my dad and his siblings weren't huddled around Mary Jane's table in Westbury, they mostly lived in the southern village of Gingerland, so named for the plenteous crops of the spice once grown there.

My parents' villages sat miles apart, but there was no distance at all between the values that governed each. My mother and father grew up in the Episcopal Church, under the watchful gaze and doting palm of the faithful. Rearing was done in the collective. With a side eye and an unsparing rod, a priest or parishioner could train up a child, be that youngster his own or another's. It was in this kind of spiritual community, one encircled by the guardrails of love and discipline, that my parents' heels were grounded. It is also where, on a Sunday when my mother was thirteen, her path in life was set.

On that morning, the congregation gathered for my mother's confirmation. In keeping with their tradition, every saint was dressed, head to toe, in ivory. After my mom received the Holy Sacrament, she and the other youth stood near an enormous window in the sanctuary. Through the opening flew a white dove, fully extending its wings before landing right onto my mother's head. Any other child would have shrieked and bolted, but not my mom. Even then, she was as steady as she was reticent. She just stared ahead as if such an unusual occurrence had been expected. "This child should not stay here," the pastor declared to the congregants. "She should go to America."

Years earlier, my mother's Aunt Miriam had moved from Nevis to the nation of dreamers. The dove, said the minister, was appointing Fredericka as the next in the family to follow. Soon after, Mary Jane wrote to Miriam about her special niece, this chosen child, and asked that she prepare the way for her. A decade later, once her papers were in order, she indeed made the journey. My father had arrived a year before her.

As my father grew through adolescence, he became more sweet on Fredericka. Her introversion was a perfect balance for his charisma. Love, invisible but palpable, lingered between them. And yet the relationship's strongest connective tissue was their shared sense of faith and family. My mom never told me how my dad proposed to her. I know only that, by the time my father set out for the United States, he'd made clear his intention to one day make Fredericka his bride. Years into their union, as my dad carried on during one of his raving fits, he told my mother he'd asked her to be his wife because Mary Jane had always been so good to him. Choosing her, he said, was his way of reciprocating that grace. My father's lips had been loosened that evening by whatever strife had prompted his rage. Still, his revelation bore a kernel of truth. Mary Jane's profound kindness had been part of what initially knit them together. Their care for each other and common values, and later, an abiding affection for their children, tightened the knot.

My father arrived at Ellis Island in the summer of 1919—just before his twenty-second birthday. The First World War's dust was still settling, and Jim Crow's cloud hung over the land. Woodrow Wilson was president. In 1918, the year before my dad sailed ashore on the S.S. *Korona*, Wilson screened, in the halls of the White House, *The Birth of a Nation*—a silent motion picture exalting Klansmen as saviors and depicting Black people as apelike, menacing degenerates. That is the America my dad entered, one with a legacy of assault on the heroes who tilled its soil. But my father and millions of others came here nonetheless, compelled by a force more powerful than hate: a hunger for opportunity. In his front vest pocket, my father held close the same resolve to better himself that still lures the most strident to our shores.

The throngs of West Indians flocking to New York in those years typically moved into either Hell's Kitchen or the Bronx. But my father settled first in Brooklyn, with my mother's Aunt Miriam (and her husband, Uncle Patrick), whom he'd met in Nevis. He divided his time between there and East Orange, New Jersey, in the home of his eldest brother, George, who'd transitioned to the United States before he did. My uncle and his family eventually moved from East Orange to nearby Montclair. My dad had honed a talent for carpentry in Nevis and brought the skill with him. In addition to handcrafting wood pieces, bureaus, and bed frames that drew squeals of delight from his patrons, he operated a fruit and vegetable pushcart. On the streets of Hell's Kitchen, as well as in Uptown Manhattan on the East Side—another neighborhood with a strong West Indian presence—he set up his cart, hawking everything from green plantains to fresh ginger for those yearning for a taste of home. He and a good friend, Mr. Benjamin Taylor, jointly operated the business.

As if those two jobs weren't enough to fill my dad's workdays, he enlisted in the 369th Infantry Regiment, the first all-

Black National Guard unit, famously known as the Harlem Hellfighters. Dad trained at Camp Whitman in New York but never served overseas. The men in his unit who did fight in the First World War were among this country's most gallant and well-decorated. After white American soldiers refused to perform combat duties alongside Blacks, the US Army assigned the Hellfighters to the French Army. The men spent 191 days in the frontline trenches—more combat time there than any other American unit. During their triumph in staving off the Germans, the troop also suffered the most losses, with fifteen hundred casualties. Despite their extraordinary valor and sacrifice, they returned home to the democracy my dad was navigating: a woefully prejudiced society that, at every turn, denied Black people equal citizenship.

My father and mother corresponded across the Atlantic, expressing, in hastily rendered cursive and without the luxury of a telephone, their longing to reunite. In 1920, the year my parents were both twenty-three, my mother at last joined my father in New York. On the afternoon she boarded the *Macedonia*, I can only imagine the brew of excitement and uncertainty she felt about leaving the world she knew and entering another, one unfamiliar to her. It was the last time she'd ever see her mother in this life, and as Mom tearfully waved goodbye from the ship's deck, her spirit surely sensed that finality.

Mom moved into Aunt Miriam and Uncle Patrick's brownstone. As she and my father resumed their courtship, Dad left Miriam's place. Living together before marriage, or "shacking up" as it was known, was frowned upon in their church community. So Dad stayed between the homes of his brother, George, and his favorite sister, Zora, who had settled in the Bronx neighborhood of Mount Vernon. My mom began work as a sleep-in nanny, taking care of a little white boy during the week and returning home to her aunt and uncle's place on the weekends. She and my father, elated to be near one another, picked up where they'd left off. They also squirreled away every nickel they could in preparation for an eventual wedding. Not long after Mom's arrival in the United States, she and my father became formally engaged.

In a cultural tradition known as the Calling of the Band, my parents' forthcoming nuptials were announced, three separate times, in Mom's home church in Nevis—in the same sanctuary where the dove had descended on her. "William Augustine Tyson and Fredericka Theodosia Huggins will be married on September 25, 1921," the reverend proclaimed. Mom, upon receiving news of the announcement in a letter from her mother, beamed as she read and reread the words. At the altar of St. Cyprian's Episcopal Church in Hell's Kitchen, my parents spoke their promises—vows that circumstances would test.

My parents began their married life together in a Bronx tenement before later relocating to Manhattan's East Side. The year after they wed, they welcomed my brother, Melrose, a name my father had loved since the day he spotted it on a street sign in the Bronx. Six days before Christmas in 1924, I arrived with my thumb poked in my mouth and nary a strand of hair. A year and a half later, my sister, Emily, came along to complete our family, crossing the "T" on the Tyson five.

I was born scrawny and with a heart murmur, twin liabilities in West Indian culture. When the doctors discovered the murmur, they told my mother and father that I probably wouldn't make it to three months old. My parents, who knew God and thus knew better, set out to prove medicine wrong. They got right to work on restoring me to good health and fattening me up, which, as they saw it, were one and the same.

Mom and Dad hovered over me constantly. If I whimpered in the slightest or my eyes fluttered awake, my mother pulled me close to her bosom and nursed me as she stroked my head. After we'd moved from the Bronx to the East Side, Daddy would put me in my stroller early in the mornings and walk me over to Central Park. "This child needs some fresh air in her lungs," he'd say on his way out the door.

After she'd weaned me, Mom kept on trying to put weight on me. Though my mother was naturally petite like me during her twenties, she wasn't about to have it on her parenting record that she'd lost a child to malnourishment. She'd mash up yams and shovel them in my mouth. I'd spit them out. As I got older, she'd push a bowl of oatmeal toward me at our breakfast table. I'd hardly even look at it. Everything about oatmeal disgusted me then: its lumpy texture, its drab color, the way it slid off the spoon. And if I didn't like what I saw, no way was I sticking it in my mouth. The fact that I love oatmeal now is a source of amazement to me, because for most of my early childhood, I was too enamored of my thumb to be bothered with oats or much else.

My murmur ultimately disappeared, but I was still skin and bones. So Mom trotted me all around town, to this physician and that one, seeking assurance that I was healthy. "Will you please leave this child alone?" a doctor finally told her. "She's not fat and she's never going to be." Mom was embarrassed. Not because she'd smothered me half to death, but because her suffocating had become noticeable enough to draw rebuke.

My mother had wanted to name me Miriam, after the aunt she treasured. By the time I was born, Aunt Miriam had passed away in a house fire, her body consumed by flames but her presence never more strong. My dad, though he also cherished

Miriam, insisted on another name. "I want my first daughter to be called Cicely," he said. An adorable girl who lived next door to them in the Bronx had the name, and the first time he heard it, he'd decided that he'd one day bestow it upon his daughter. That is the barefaced story he told my mother. Years later when I was grown, the truth would come spilling forth.

On the day I arrived home from the hospital, my father said to Melrose, "This is your sister." From then on, my brother called me Sister, or Sis for short. The rest of the family followed his lead, even as they added to my list of nicknames. My mother often referred to me as Father Face, because I'd inherited my dad's cheekbones. My father had two names for me: String Bean and Heart String. The former was because I was so skinny; the latter was because I was his first girl and therefore his most beloved. I could feel his affection for me. When I was a toddler, he'd scoot to the edge of the sofa, somehow balance me on his left knee while resting his guitar on his right thigh, and then belt out his favorite spiritual, "I'm gonna lay down my burdens . . . down by the riverside . . . and study war no more!" As he sang and strummed, he'd motion for Melrose, who sat cross-legged on the floor with his eyes dancing, to sing along. Up and down I bounced to the sound of Dad's booming baritone, his care for me reverberating between each note.

Most parents wouldn't dare admit to preferring one child over another, but in our home, that fact was not hidden. My father adored me and Emily. I don't know why, but Daddy just preferred girl children. Melrose, on the other hand, was my mother's heartthrob. No one called my brother by his given name. He abhorred the sound of it and insisted that his friends refer to him as Tyson. Our family mostly still called him Melrose (or Me'rose, for short), though Mom had her own term of endearment for him. "Beau, don't be gone too long," she'd say when he'd dart out our front door, his pockets bulging with a collection of marbles. Whenever Melrose was sick of being surrounded by two sisters, which was often, he'd scamper off to roughhouse with the neighborhood boys. Sometimes he wouldn't return for hours, long after dusk had descended. My mother would go out looking for her dear son, fussing at him the whole time as she dragged his behind up our stairs for an inevitable backhand from Dad.

In the streets, Melrose received more attention than my dad often paid to him. A faded family photo captures the spirit of their puzzling dynamic. My smiling father stands tall, dressed sharp as a Rockefeller with his shoulders squared. My brother, conversely, wears a somber expression and high-water pants. Whenever my mother would pass that photo on our living room wall, she'd shake her head and murmur, "Your father should've taken Beau to get a proper suit." Not only did my dad show little interest in grooming his son, he was also very hard on him. If Melrose cut up in class or brought home a less-than-stellar grade, my father's scolds were louder than his encouragements. I have no doubt that my dad cared for my brother as much as he did my sister and me. He provided for all of us just the same, and in our culture, provision speaks a love language that the tongue may seldom profess. But with me and Emily, my father's care manifested as an instinct to protect. With Melrose, it showed up as an urge to toughen him up by slicing him down, perhaps as a way to prepare him for a world that villainizes Black men. My brother's heart, soft and golden at its center despite his unflinching exterior, couldn't sustain the reprimands. It was why he so frequently escaped outdoors.

Emily was my father's other crown jewel. Dad borrowed my sister's nickname, Molly, from the Broadway show tune "My Blue Heaven." "Just Molly and me and baby makes three," Daddy would sing, "and we're happy in my blue heaven!" Emily's given name came courtesy of my father's cousin. When she heard that my parents' third child was to be born on her birthday, she said to my dad, "If you name the baby after me, it'll be the happiest birthday I've ever had." Though Mom called *me* Father Face, I always thought Emily looked more like Dad. My sister's face was a full moon, like his, whereas Mom and I had an almond shape; in my mind then, shape rather than color was the strongest marker of similarity. Over the years, I've come to recognize both of my parents' faces in my own, depending on the character I'm portraying. In *Sounder*, I spot Willie. In *How to Get Away with Murder*, I notice Fredericka. In *The Autobiography of Miss Jane Pittman*, I see both.

Emily was plump. When we were growing up, everyone always thought she was older than me, in part because her clothes were two sizes bigger than mine, and also because she was more forward and worldly than I was. In school, she gravitated toward classmates who were a year or two ahead of her, tilting her ear to catch any tea they spilled. The same was true when my mom's friends would stop by to visit. She'd crane her neck to overhear their grown-folk conversations until Mom urged her out of the room. My mother was often surprised at what tumbled from that girl's mouth. So was I. When my sister was still quite young, she heard a rumor that having sex keeps one from having headaches. One afternoon, she said to my mom, "Well I'm not gonna die from no headaches." Had my mother not been so shocked, she would've smacked Emily for that piece of sass, as well as for mentioning a subject never discussed in our religious household.

My sister possessed features celebrated in our culture: a full mane of hair, a thick and healthy body, and a gregariousness passed on to her from our father. I had none of those attributes.

When I was eight, I caught a glimpse of myself in a mirror on my way out of my cousins' house. I stood there for the longest time, studying my reflection. *Huh*, I thought. *I'm bowlegged.* I wasn't. But because I was so lanky, my stick legs had enough space between them to wedge a football in there. My hair, once I had some, was thin and wouldn't grow very long. Lord knows my mother attempted to both lengthen and groom it as she then saw best. While seated on our couch, Mom would clutch my head between her thighs as she greased my scalp with thick pomade before taking a hot comb to my tresses. I still have burn marks on my earlobes. And then there were my teeth. After arriving in this world with my thumb in my mouth, I kept it there for all of my early childhood. My mother did all she could to cure me of the habit, from wrapping my thumb with gauze to threatening that it would fall off. Her tactics were unsuccessful. As a result, my two front teeth turned to greet one another and have since held their positions.

As a child, I was quiet. My mother would take me and Emily with her to an outdoor market, one that stretched up Park Avenue from 111th Street to 116th. After his stop in Hell's Kitchen, my father usually parked his cart there. It was *the* West Indian meeting spot, our public square. The hub pranced to its feet on Saturdays, with women in vividly colored head wraps throwing back their heads in laughter and trading gossip about whatever was happening in church or in the news headlines. "Tyson!" someone would yell out at my mother across the stands. "Girl, where you been? I ain't seen you in two weeks!" As Mom and her friends cackled and communed, I'd stand silently at her side. "Oh, she's just so *shy*!" one of the women would say. Mom would glance down at me and smile and then go back to talking, until Emily had to pee so badly she'd contort her body into a pretzel.

It's not simply that I was shy; mostly, I was observant. I paid close attention to details, allowing the passing world and its peculiarities to seep into my pores. I was curious about all of it. When I did open my mouth to speak, my favorite word was "why." "You're too *jam noo-zy*," my mother would say, never able to pronounce "damn" or "nosy." Mom said I nearly *why*'d her to death. I now know that "Why?" is the most important question an artist can ask. But try explaining that to my mother, who threatened to knock the devil out of me when I'd pester her with my constant queries.

Even as a child, I longed to understand what motivated people to do and say what they did, why the sun opened its lids in the East and shut them in the West, why my battery-operated doll named Dolly, with her blond locks and white paint peeling from her face, was constantly crying. I was so inquisitive that I once took apart a wristwatch, determined to find out what made it tick. I studied everything. When we were out in the streets, I'd notice people's feet. I still do. In fact, my eyes fall first on people's shoes even before I look up at their faces. Our feet tell our stories. They carry us through this life, moving us from one sorrow and season to the next. Our gait can reveal us to be buoyant or bullish, dispirited or steadfast.

I was a deep chestnut brown in a nation that considers the darker sister the less attractive one. Colorism, which cut its teeth on slave plantations, thankfully was not nurtured among the Tysons. I grew up surrounded by cousins whose hues spanned the color spectrum, from lily white (there are a couple of albino children in my extended family) to jet black. My Uncle George and Aunt Beatrice in Montclair had five children who were like siblings to me: George, Helen, Robbie, Beatrice (aka Bette, who was every bit as spirited as Miss Bette Davis herself), and Emily. George was darker than me, just as his father and grandfather were, while Helen was quite fair. My favorite cousin, Robbie (when he'd visit us, I wouldn't let anyone else sit next to me—oh, how I loved Robbie!), was a shade darker than Helen. In my immediate family, my siblings and I had Dad's ebony complexion. Mom was café au lait. There was dazzling variety in our tribe and every color was embraced, if only because it wasn't commented upon. Our elders regarded us as God's most gorgeous creations. I could feel that.

And yet when it came to colorism in society at large, I was certainly not immune. No one had to tell me that the fairer your skin and the narrower your nose and lips, the more stunning you were considered. That belief permeated the atmosphere. Caucasian women were upheld as the standard of beauty while our features were denigrated. In print media, Black hair was portrayed as unkempt, a crop of wild, irascible wool that required taming. My mother and other Black women were mostly invisible to whites, and when they did see us, it was through the cracked and muddied lens of racial bias. In their view and in their advertisements, we were mammies and maids, subservient and ignorant, filthy and lazy—and yet somehow diligent, clean, and honorable enough to prepare their meals and rear their children. At best, our presence was tolerated or ignored. At worst, we were systematically locked out of homeownership and wealth creation, redlined into ghettos, and lynched. In no regard were we thought worthy of emulation. And not just our appearance was scorned. Our intelligence and very humanity were questioned, considered genetically unfit. The lie of Black inferiority was built right into America's infrastructure, and to this day, that framework remains stubbornly intact.

Given my dark complexion, I spotted no future for myself as a pinup girl. Much as my father in particular affirmed me, I did not feel pretty—and my classmates amplified that feeling.

On the playground, I heard a looping trio of insults: skinny, nappy-headed, and nigger. The latter truly stung me on the day an Italian boy in my class, my bosom buddy, called me that. He and I lived across the street from one another, so even when we weren't in school, we played together. That ended on the morning he came into our first-grade class with a grin on his face and a little poem.

"Hey, Cicely," he said, "you want to hear something funny?" I nodded. He cleared his throat and began. "God made the niggers, he made them at night, God was in a hurry and forgot to make them white."

I stared at the boy, refusing to let the devastation in my heart spill over onto my face, unwilling to give him the satisfaction of knowing his words had pierced me. In the life of every Black child, a moment arrives when he or she becomes wrenchingly aware of how we are perceived. This bruising recognition was among my first.

My earliest memory is a street address. On a Saturday in the spring of 1927, my mother took my brother, Emily, and me with her to visit some friends in Hell's Kitchen. We stayed out so long that by the time we got home, the sky was dark. We made our way up Third Avenue, crossed over to Second, and then rounded the corner onto our street. Melrose walked next to us as he kicked along a tin can. I, then age two and a half, had one hand clasped in my mother's right palm and the other of course in my mouth. Emily was holding Mom's left hand. As we approached the apartment, I stared up. At the top of our building stood a row of numbers, in large gold letters on the glass frontal: 219 East 102nd. The first chapter of my childhood unfolded at that address, the home we shared until I was nine.

Our area was called the East Side slums. Nowadays, it is known as East Harlem. Scarcity was and is the neighborhood's salient feature. We were poor, a reality I see most clearly in hindsight. When I was a child, it seemed we had much of what we needed, largely because my parents were so enterprising. Our food stamps and blocks of bright-orange government cheese were supplemented by the steady flow of vegetables my father brought home from his produce cart. We ate well. My mother, a masterful seamstress who created exquisite garments from mere scraps of fabric, dressed me and Emily like little princesses, because in her view, we were. Our community was largely Italian but also racially mixed, filled with parents who, like my own, toiled to lift their children's prospects. If I had any real inkling of our standing on the bottom rung of the country's socioeconomic ladder, it came when we walked through our neighborhood. Ladies of the night sashayed down the boulevards at sunset, hoping to capture the glances of weary shift workers crawling home. Broken bottles and cigarette butts littered empty lots. In deep winter, homeless people shivered beneath scaffolds, huddling together around trash barrel fires. Poverty has an odor to it, and in a nation then on the front porch of the Great Depression, it smelled at once of desperation and striving.

My parents worked relentlessly. Both rose before sunup, exhaustion sitting heavily on their eyelids. Mommy set out for the elevated train, known as the El. She commuted to the Bronx to work as a domestic for various white families, bathing and feeding their young'uns as a way to carve out a life for her own three. In addition to pushing their produce cart all around town, my father and his business partner, Mr. Taylor, also set up shop close to our home, at an open market between 101st and 102nd

Streets on Second Avenue. On Mom's "days off," she'd often walk over and help at the cart. Enter the woman we knew as our Nana, a neighbor my mother befriended. In those years when my siblings and I were too small to be at home on our own, Nana took care of us while our parents worked.

We never knew our grandparents back in Nevis, and Nana came to feel like one to us. So did a sweet woman by the name of Beal. On the day my mom brought me home from the hospital, Beal, an elder who lived close by, was standing at my parents' stoop. When she saw my mother approaching, she reached out her arms and said, "Give me that child." That same day, she insisted on becoming my godmother. From then on, there wasn't a weekend that Beal didn't visit us. Sometimes it'd be snowing or raining so hard that Mom would look out the window and say, "My God, I wonder if Beal is coming down here tonight." At that moment, there'd be a knock at our door. We'd open it to see Beal, standing there with joy on her face and her cute mutt, Bella, at her side. Between Beal, Nana, and my parents, the Lord kept four sets of eyes fixed on us.

The streets of the East Side slums stood in marked contrast to our home. My mother was spick-and-span about our apartment and required us to keep it immaculate. Near the building's top floor, we shared a three-room space. Mom and Dad had the bedroom. Up until I was nine, we three children slept together in the living room on a queen-sized rollaway bed, which we folded up and put away every morning. Across from the bed was the kitchen. In its corner sat the claw-foot tub where we bathed and where Mom washed our clothes by hand using a washboard. In another corner sat an icebox with a small mirror attached to its front and a top compartment for storing fifteen cents worth of ice that came wrapped in a canvas bag. When we returned from the market every weekend, we'd place our milk, cheese, and other perishables next to the ice. My siblings and I each had a Saturday morning chore. Mine was to sweep and mop the living room, and later, when I was older, to wash the windows. Melrose and Emily kept the kitchen and bedroom pristine.

When you're poor, two of the few realities you can control are your own appearance and that of your immediate surroundings. My mother exercised powerful jurisdiction in both domains. "Do not go out of this house with no dirty underwear," she stressed constantly. "If you fall down sick in the street and your underwear are dirty, nobody is going to touch you." Before bedtime, I removed my underpants, thoroughly washed them in the bathroom sink, and hung them up, using a wooden clothes-pin, on a line outside our kitchen window. The last thing my mother did every evening was check that line. If she didn't spot my panties out there, she'd wake me up. "What did you do with your underwear?" she'd press as I sleepily rubbed my eyes and tried to remember. I'd sometimes still have them on, or else I'd tucked them someplace random. No matter how late it was, she'd pull me from that bed to complete my duty. In our home, cleanliness wasn't just next to godliness; it was the heavenly Father personified.

Under the Tyson roof, respect for elders was sacrosanct. Children had not a say, but a mandate: to trust and obey, in the words of the old hymn. Sassing my parents or any member of the community was enough to draw ire and a belt. My backtalk took the form of willfulness. I might have been quiet, but I did plenty of rebutting in my head. I also did exactly the opposite of whatever my mother instructed me to do. "Sit down," she'd say. I'd stand up. "Walk," she'd command. I'd take off running. It was my way of asserting an independence I seldom experienced in the long shadow cast by my mother's lingering presence. She kept close tabs on all of us, but with me, her sickly child, Mom's vigilance was devout. I craved the space to move around without her always staring down over me, yet I was never afforded the same freedom as Emily and Melrose. If the two of them went out to play, Mom would find a reason to keep me at her side. "Sis, I think you're getting a cold," she'd say. Off my siblings would go, and there I'd sit, sulking and plotting my getaway.

The hovering didn't end as I grew. It continued long after that doctor assured my mother I was fine. There was the time I had the chicken pox and a high fever, and someone told my father to give me a spoonful of sugar with a touch of kerosene in it as a remedy. The minute it touched my tongue, honey, I began bleeding from every orifice in my body: my nostrils, my ears, my mouth. As Mom screamed, Daddy jumped down several flights of stairs to go summon Dr. Gatsby, a crippled physician who lived three blocks from us. I don't know how that doctor even made it up our stairs, given his limp, but he came hobbling through our door moments later to save my life. After that incident, my parents did not let me out of the apartment for a year. Another time, I got an infection under my right arm. Somebody told my mother to take some kind of brown soap, wrap it in a rag, warm it up in hot water, and put it on the bump, which was the size of a lemon. That didn't help. When my father came home and found me in bed screaming, he rushed to the drugstore and returned with a can of black salve and a roll of gauze. He applied both, and the bump burst open—yellowish pus oozing out to ease my throbbing discomfort. The fact that Dad had beat Mom to a remedy aggravated her. She accused my father of always trying to outdo her in their joint quest to ensure my health.

Try as my mother did to keep me within view, I often found my way outdoors and onto the subway, even when I was as young as eight. When Mom went to help Dad with the business on Saturdays, I'd wait fifteen minutes after she'd left the house and then I'd dash through the door. I'd make my way over to 103rd Street and Third Avenue, hop on the train, and ride it all the way up to the last stop in the Bronx. Once off, I'd stroll through the neighborhood, peeking into the windows of the beautiful suburban homes, savoring my freedom and alone time. Swearing Emily and Melrose to secrecy, I always managed to get back into our apartment five minutes before Mom returned. My mother never found out about my adventures. Yet she knew that even when she was with me, I'd dash off in a heartbeat if she turned her head. "As long as you're alive," my mom would often say, "Kyar Tyson will never be dead." My father's mother, Carol, was gone by then, but Mom believed my grandmother's restless spirit had found a home in me. By nature and by choice, I was a wonderer and a wanderer. I still am.

Even as a young child, I had a strong sense of autonomy, a feeling that I belonged first and foremost to myself. My mother begged to differ. When I challenged her authority, she'd pick up whatever object was near her, be it a wooden clothes hanger or an extension cord, and reassert her reign. In place of a time-out, there was a knockout, a single blow that could send you down onto your knees. Now such treatment would be called abuse, but in my era, it was called excellent child rearing. Mostly, my parents didn't even need to wield a switch in order to restore order. They had only to raise an eyebrow and we understood exactly what that meant.

Education was paramount. Each of us had a mission, and for my siblings and me, that was to excel in our studies. My parents viewed education as a passport out of poverty, a corridor toward a prosperity that hadn't been possible for them in Nevis. It's why Melrose caught hell from my father when he'd act up in class. I was a good student and loved our public school, which was integrated. Daily attendance liberated me from my mother's hawk-eye and provided a place where my curiosity could roam freely. Still, I rarely spoke in front of the other children. I enjoyed reading on my own, and I'd ask questions of my teachers one on one, but no way would I raise my hand to answer a question. Too bashful.

My third-grade teacher, Miss Sullivan, somehow spotted a potential in me that I didn't then recognize in myself. Prancing by my desk, she'd sing from the famous tune, "You oughta be in pictures, you're wonderful to see, you oughta be in pictures, oh what a hit you would be." I'm not sure what prompted her prediction. Perhaps I'd flashed an impish grin or cast a penetrating stare in her direction, because it couldn't have had anything to do with my speaking. All the time now, I remember her sidling up to me, with her navy suit and brunette bob, and I think, *Miss Sullivan, you were foretelling my future.*

Every afternoon when my siblings and I got home from school, we were met with a question: "Where is your homework?" That query was followed by a command: "Change out of your school clothes." We could never fool around the house wearing our nicest garments; we had to replace them with our old ones. Once we'd done so, the three of us would sit at our table and work on our lessons. Only after we'd completed our assignments could we huddle around the radio for an episode of *Amos 'n' Andy.* The radio series was all the rage during the 1920s and 1930s. In it, two white actors (Freeman Gosden and Charles Correll) portrayed a pair of poor Black farmers who'd left their land in Georgia and migrated north to Chicago, carrying just $24 and four ham-and-cheese sandwiches. In retrospect, I recognize how the show's characterizations covertly reinforced racist clichés. But in those years, we were hungry to hear or see any representation of ourselves in the mainstream, even if those depictions were stereotypical. It was an acknowledgment that our presence in this nation mattered—that we were *visible.* Following the nightly episode we ate dinner, did our chores, and then, of course, scrubbed our underwear before climbing into the rollaway.

We'd usually awaken to the aroma of Mom's cooking. My mother was some kind of cook. Though I lacked a voracious appetite, the smell of her okra and cornmeal mush always made my mouth water. Her macaroni and cheese has yet to be rivaled by any other I've tasted, though I'm sure my mother's version contained enough condensed milk to trigger a diabetic coma. On weekdays, she'd prepare our lunch before she went to work, stirring up a soufflé of creamy mashed potatoes, made all the more fluffy because she whipped in a soft-boiled egg. She'd slide a mound of those potatoes on a plate, put three pats of butter on top, wrap it up tight, and set it on our radiator to keep it warm. School was close by, so we had time to race home and eat at noon.

By 10 a.m. during math class, I'd already be dreaming of those potatoes. When I charged through our apartment door, they'd be there waiting for me on the radiator, the butter cascading down into a golden pool on the plate's outer rim. Lord have mercy, I can almost taste them. I'd be so eager to devour my lunch that I'd sometimes neglect to say grace aloud. *For health and strength and daily food*, I'd pray internally as I shoveled in the first spoonful, *we praise Thy name, oh Lord, amen.*

I never once saw my mother look at a recipe. She kept everything in her head, just as her mother had: a pinch of this, a dash of that, and all meals made from scratch. During the holidays, she'd weigh down our table with a royal feast: cookies, sugar cakes, coconut rum bread pudding, roasts, soups, curried goat, and potatoes—you name it. Friends and relatives traveled from all over town just to sample my mom's clear broth. Decades later, after she'd passed, none of us could replicate that broth. Emily came the closest. Emily's daughter, my niece Maxine, has now taken up the mantle. My mother's secret wasn't any one single ingredient. Her creations were a symphony of flavors, blended together perfectly with love immeasurable.

3

Church Girl

CHURCH was the cornerstone of my childhood. My mother was determined that our foundation be spiritual, just as hers had been. There was Sunday service, followed by Monday and Wednesday prayer. Friday was choir rehearsal. Emily and I were in the choir as young children. On Thursdays and Fridays, there were usher board meetings, youth meetings, elders meetings, and any other gathering the pastor could dream up. On Saturdays, my family cleaned the church. When I tell you we were in God's house all the time, I mean it.

We attended where many West Indians did, St. John's American Episcopal Catholic Church. In naming the church, our pastor clearly wanted to be inclusive, but our services followed the Episcopalian tradition. The original building, a storefront, was on 234 East Ninety-Ninth Street. The year I was eight, the congregation moved north to 1610 Lexington Avenue, near 102nd Street. I still recall the Sunday when our hundred or so members walked from the old spot to the new one, carrying lighted candles as we sang "Lead on, oh King eternal, the day of march has come." The second space was a four-story brownstone converted into a place of worship. The sanctuary was on the main floor, and down below, there was a cavernous basement for all those meetings. Reverend Joseph Byron, who grew up in St. Kitts, lived with his wife and their five children above the sanctuary. The very top floor was rented out, providing the church with an income stream. By day, Reverend Byron watched over his flock. As a side job, he managed a moving van and shipping business.

Emily and I were the best-dressed girls in church, as well as on the East Side, period. Mom made sure of that by sewing all our clothes, most of them from scratch, others using the Butterick and McCall's patterns she kept stuffed in a drawer. As she stitched together her magic on a hand-crank Singer machine, her wrist rotating 'round and 'round, she'd periodically yell out, "Sister, come try this on!" Mom poked and prodded us with so many stickpins as we tried on a dozen versions of whatever she was making. It drove me mad. Because of that, I still refuse to try on clothes in a store. I just buy an armful of outfits, test them out at my leisure at home, and return whatever doesn't fit. It didn't take Mom two minutes to whip out her creations. She'd finish our dresses, which were usually just alike, during the week leading up to service. Then on Sundays, Emily and I would step in wearing our matching organza numbers with soft layers that fell gently as a balloon, or colorful ones with elaborate smocking—finished off with black patent-leather Mary Jane shoes, shined to the hilt. When the Tyson sisters showed up in church or anyplace else, we didn't look like we came from any slum.

We sang a lot of the traditional hymns. Verse after verse of those songs will always live in my memory. I can still hear the congregation's thunderous chorus of voices rising up to the rafters with "Where He Leads Me, I Will Follow" and "Jesus, Keep Me Near the Cross." My mother's favorite hymn was "Blessed

Assurance." In the early mornings before service, she'd hum it in the kitchen as she cooked, the notes wafting through the air and settling over the peas and rice. Then in church, when the organ piped up with the song's opening line, she'd clasp together her hands and close her eyes. "Blessed assurance," she'd sing as she swayed, "Jesus is mine / Oh what a foretaste of glory divine." For my mother, that song was more than a hymn. It was a testimony of God's unremitting guidance along her spiritual path, a journey ordained by a dove.

Church was the one place where my timidity fell away. The deacons' wives often staged little plays, based on Bible stories, for the youth to take part in. More than once, I was cast in the leading role of Mary, mother of Jesus. For all of my reticence, I relished delivering my lines as the members encouraged me on with claps and amens. I wasn't at all nervous to take the spotlight. That's because in my mom's mind, and thus in my own, I wasn't performing. A performance is what happened in the secular world, that sinful place Mom referred to as "a den of iniquity." What we did in church was distinct from that realm and therefore sacred.

I'm blessed to have been raised in two rich spiritual traditions, Episcopalian and Baptist. On any Sunday when my parents couldn't make it to service, my siblings and I attended with Nana. Her Baptist church was right next door to St. John's, but a universe away stylistically. Order lives at the center of an Episcopalian service. Each follows a familiar rhythm: opening hymn, Old and New Testament readings, a couple of choir selections, a sermon, and a final prayer. Our worship began at 11 a.m. and always ended at 12:30. In Nana's church, the Spirit, not the clock, took the lead. As Reverend Hawkins whooped and wailed from the pulpit, the saints leaped from their pews and danced up and down the aisles to the staccato beat of the tambourine, the organ's vibrations providing the scene's musical score. Service lasted for two hours or more, until the Holy Ghost got ready to simmer down. I'd sometimes fall asleep next to Nana, my cheek pressed into the pew cushion as the fire around me raged on.

When I was seven, Nana said to me and Emily, "Wouldn't you girls like to sing for our congregation next Sunday?" Emily thought the idea sounded silly and declined. I, basking in the glow of a recent star turn as Mary in my own church, agreed. Mom, Emily, and Melrose went to St. John's, as usual, while Dad and I joined Nana in her service.

"Please give a warm welcome to little Miss Cicely!" Reverend Hawkins announced. As the congregation applauded, my father led me, in my emerald velvet dress and lace-trimmed socks, to the pulpit. The pastor handed me a microphone, and for a moment, I just stood there, not sure what I'd sing. In lieu of a plan, I belted out the opening line of a number I'd often heard and loved there in Nana's church.

"How do you do, my lovin' pastor, how do you do?" I hollered, half-singing and half-chanting. The room erupted as the organist quickly found my key and began accompanying me. A row of women in colorful wide-brimmed hats jumped up, lifting hankies and hallelujahs before I could launch into the next couple of refrains. "How do you do, congregation, how do you do?" I sang. "How do you do, choir, how do you do?" On and on I went until, moments later, something occurred that still makes me smile.

Four deacons made their way from the front pew to the pulpit and set me on a small wooden chair. Each of them clasped one leg of the chair, hoisted me heavenward in unison, and began parading me through the aisles. "How do you do, God's children, how do you do?!" I sang, increasing my volume and climbing an octave each time they lifted me higher. "How do you do, saints, how do you do?!" The congregation joined in, howling in disbelief that a child as young as me was singing with such fervor and conviction.

After service, my father couldn't get home fast enough to tell my mother how proud he was of his Sis. "She turned the place upside *down*!" he gushed. Before he could finish his recounting, others from church stopped in to give my mom the details as I stood by blushing. Honestly, I couldn't understand what the fuss was about. All I knew was that when I was up there on that chair, my Mary Janes dangling, my voice rising up from someplace deep within me, I felt a rush. The Spirit, twisting and flailing and arching its back, had shuddered through me. And as it did, my shyness vanished.

As far back as I can recall, I've known I have a sixth sense—an innate ability to see, feel, hear, taste, and smell events before they happen. Strong evidence of this prescience came in the winter of 1932, the December I turned eight.

On an afternoon when my parents were out working, I smelled smoke and thought the scent was coming from the building next door. Melrose and I went out to look around, as well as to check on our neighbor, a woman our family knew well.

"I smell smoke," I told her when she opened the door.

"What do you mean you smell smoke?" she asked.

"I think something is burning," I said.

She glanced at the living room and kitchen behind her and then stared back at me. "Well nothing's on fire in here," she said. "I don't smell anything."

That week, my mother had bought me a new pair of Sunday shoes. I felt so convinced of an impending blaze that I went into our closet, pulled out my box of Mary Janes, and cradled it close to my chest. I wasn't about to let my shoes go up in smoke. In fact, I even slept with that box next to me on the rollaway. When no sparks flew that evening, I forgot all about what I'd smelled.

Two days later, I awakened to the squeal of sirens slicing through the frigid air. In the building next door, there'd been an electrical fire—one that began in our friend's apartment. The fire crew thankfully arrived soon enough to evacuate the place and douse the flames before they spread. Later, when our neighbor came by and gave us that report, all I could think was, *Good Lord, I knew it.*

I had these premonitions frequently. Like the many times when I'd be talking about someone, and ten minutes later, that person would appear at our front door. Or those occasions when I'd tell my mother that someone in our church was quite sick. "How do you know?" she'd ask. "I saw it last night in a dream," I'd say. And sure enough, Reverend Byron would stop in with news that the person I'd seen in my dream had taken ill. In other instances, I'd overhear my parents talking in their bedroom. My dad would tell my mom that he'd run into so-and-so that day at the market. Mom would laugh and say, "I know." "What do you mean?" he'd ask. "Sister told me that yesterday," she'd say. "She dreamed it."

My mother also had this sixth sense. I don't know whether her parents were born with it as well, but there's no question that my mother possessed it. "Sister, come here and sit down," she said to me one morning before she left for work. I slid into a chair at our table and she locked her eyes on mine. "I dreamed last night that I saw you going through the window," she said. "Do not wash any windows today, you hear me?"

"It's a school day," I reminded her, "and I only wash windows on Saturdays."

"Did you hear what I told you?" she snapped. "Do not wash any windows today." I nodded and hushed my mouth.

That afternoon after school, Emily and I were playing in our apartment near a set of glass French doors that separated the living room from the bedroom. My sister flung open the two panels and then slammed them behind her. In an effort to keep her from closing me out, I lunged toward the doors. As I did, the glass shattered and sliced through my right arm, starting near my inside wrist and extending up two inches. Our neighbor, Miss O'Connor, heard the commotion and rushed over to find me lying in a pool of crimson. She wrapped my wrist in a towel and rushed me to a nearby drugstore. The pharmacist urged her to take me to the emergency room, where the doctors stitched me up. Nine decades later, the scar remains—a reminder of my mother's uncanny ability to predict, often with chilling accuracy, what would occur.

When I was small, my sixth sense did not seem odd to me or scare me. I had only my experience as a reference point, only knew what it felt like to live in my own body. And though that fire did get my attention (*What if our neighbor hadn't made it out of her building in time? How could I have lived with myself for not insisting that she clear the premises?*), I didn't give most of my premonitions much credence or thought. That began to shift as I grew older and my insights increased in both number and significance. One incident in particular spooked me.

I was eleven when my Aunt Beatrice passed away, a few years after we'd lost my Uncle George. Before the memorial, our family stayed overnight with my cousins in Montclair. Mom and I slept together on the second floor. My aunt's casket was already there in the house. In those days, it was common for a loved one's body to be transferred from the funeral parlor to the family's home on the night before the service.

At 2 a.m., I made my way downstairs to the main floor to use the bathroom. While in there, I heard the front door to the house creak open and then slam shut. I thought little of it. With so many relatives around, folks had been going and coming a lot.

"Who came in?" my mother asked when I returned upstairs to bed.

"I don't know," I answered.

"What do you mean you don't know?" she pressed. "Weren't you just downstairs?"

"Yeah, but I didn't see anyone," I told her.

I drifted to sleep. And in my dream, Aunt Beatrice appeared and spoke to me. "I hope I didn't frighten you this morning," she said. "I wanted to say goodbye to all of my loved ones, and I was trying to make it back into my casket before anyone missed me."

The second my eyelids slid open later that morning, I sat up straight and announced to my mother, "It was Aunt Beatrice who slammed the door."

Mom didn't say a word. She also didn't seem surprised by my revelation and didn't quiz me about it. She just grinned, shook her head, and rose from the bed to begin preparing for the day. Maybe Aunt Beatrice had also shown up in my mother's dream. Or maybe Mom thought I was talking some foolishness. Or maybe my mother's smile was one of recognition as she recalled the woman who'd once predicted my clairvoyance.

Unlike my earlier extrasensory perceptions, this one unnerved me. It's one thing to have an ability to foretell the future; it's a completely different matter to actually be visited by a ghost. The vision was so brilliantly lucid: I could see my aunt in all of her color and dimensions, could practically reach out and take her hand. It seemed as real as if she'd actually been there in the room with me, and in the world of my dream, she was. The experience of her presence, even in the reality of its absence, truly spooked me. *Why was I the one sensing these spirits and hearing these voices? Why didn't other children, or even my own brother and sister, have these intuitive insights?* In place of answers, I had only my fear to contend with.

During my whole childhood, my mother and I never openly discussed her sixth sense or mine, nor did she tell me then about the stranger's prophecy. Like a great many other topics in the Tyson house, Mom simply chose not to address my third eye, even amid irrefutable evidence of its presence. Years would pass before I'd view my ability not as a burden to be frightened of, but as a rarity to be embraced.

We each have many faces, various ways of appearing and behaving. In one moment, we may show remarkable steadfastness, and in another, an aching vulnerability. We can be at turns tranquil and belligerent, jubilant and despairing. We are inherently multifaceted and yet marvelously complete. This was true of my mother and father, two human beings as nuanced and complex as any of us.

As I grew up, I became acquainted with each of my mother's faces. There was her reserved nature, the quiet girl once known as Dosha. Whenever I heard someone call my mother by her childhood nickname—which was short for Theodosia, her middle name—I knew the person had known my mom since her days in Nevis. Dosha nodded more than she spoke; if a cashier greeted her in a store, she smiled sheepishly. That face of my mother reflected all that was innocent and generous and good in her, all the warmth and care her own mom once bestowed. Mom seldom talked about her Mu-ma, as she called her, but my mother's kindness across the miles said plenty. She did not have the financial resources to visit Nevis, but every chance she got, Mom would pack a large barrel with food and clothes and have Reverend Byron ship it to her mother. During holidays, she'd also send a large ham. Before she closed the barrel, she'd round up a few dollars, tie the bills in the foot of an old nylon stocking, and stick it someplace in between the other gifts.

Then there were Mom's other sides. At times she was joyous, like when she sang while preparing supper. As she stirred one pot and lifted the lid from another, she'd have her head tied up in a scarf, her cotton Hoover apron over her house clothes, and her bare feet slid into my father's old shoes, which she'd turned into her slippers by smashing down their backs. In those moments, she was carefree. In other instances, she revealed her fiery streak. Feisty Fredericka would blurt out "Damn it to hell" if she was tested, which life and my father ensured she was. It was this Fredericka who thought nothing of throwing a hairbrush in my direction when I defied her.

In public, my mother wore yet another demeanor: proud and unwavering, a sturdy oak refusing to be uprooted. She had the same rigid back she passed on to me. No matter what she was struggling with or how short on money she found herself, she held her head high and marched onward. She had the pocketbook of a pauper but the posture of a queen, exuding a regality that prompted others to regard her as such. "We may be poor," she'd often say, "but once you leave your house, people don't have to know whether you've got a pot of tea or a back door to throw it out of." She was what I call *swelegant*, a combination of "swell" and "elegant"—blessed with a model's figure and a wardrobe she'd tailored so precisely to her frame. When she and my dad strode into St. John's—Mom in her rayon frock, high heels, and straw hat cocked to one side—a hush fell over the sanctuary. She and my father were the most handsome couple in church. They dressed to maim and to kill.

My father was a study in contrasts. Even as a boy, he brimmed with the vitality that drew my mother to him. Magnetism coursed through his arteries. "Your father is a star," my cousin Bette would often say. She was right. Dad was artistically gifted, like all of the Tysons. My father's cousin, Donald Walbridge Shirley, was the renowned classical and jazz pianist whose life is depicted in the 2018 Oscar Award–winning film *Green Book*. My dad himself wasn't a trained musician, yet he played the guitar and sang with perfect pitch, enchanting all who heard his robust yet smooth vocals. And like my mother, he was a dresser and a stepper. Talk about a Dapper Dan . . . that man had swagger! Like many soldiers, he wore metal heel taps on his shoes, and boy, you could hear him coming long before you saw him. Even when operating his produce stand, he strutted through town in a stylish suit to go along with his air of confidence.

My father also had an unpleasant face, one I'm still trying to reconcile with his other, more admirable ones. When he was good, he was very good—a man so committed to us that he often pushed around that cart fifteen hours a day to keep our rent paid and our stomachs full. But when my father behaved badly, he was horrid. He was a womanizer. He never drank alcohol, but ego was his strong tonic. Throughout my childhood, he carried on illicit affairs around town. Maybe these sexual escapades allowed him to temporarily escape the burden of his circumstances, to forget the indignities of being Black and poor. To be colored in early-twentieth-century America was to brave an existence even more fraught with anxiety than our current times are. Whatever forces might have lured my father into the arms of women, he did not resist.

Word of my father's liaisons snaked through our community

and slithered onto my mom's doorstep. Even before she heard tell of his infidelity, she'd spotted it in my father's every gesture, in the flecks of remorse on his brow. Dad had been brought up to respect his vows and his spiritual values, but he cast both aside when temptation turned his single roving eye into two. Beneath Dad's charisma lived an underbelly of compulsiveness, a tendency to allow his passions, virtuous and vile, to overtake him. Those passions rose to the top surface when he and my mother argued bitterly about his philandering. He sometimes struck her.

Much of the conflict between my parents happened behind closed doors. In the late evenings as I lay huddled next to my brother and sister on the rollout, I'd hear Dad's footsteps as he stomped home after hours of revelry with various women. He wore his emotions on his feet. I knew by the thumpity-thump of his heavy steps, that loud tapping of his heels, that war was imminent. *Bang. Bang. Bang. Ba-dang.* He'd bound over our threshold and onto the battlefield, the flames of his coming antagonism toward my mother stoked by his own guilt. Mom, who'd be up waiting, stood ready to confront him. So as not to wake us, they'd take their brawl into the bedroom. Through sobs, Mom hurled shoes and accusations, demanding that Dad end his trysts.

I don't know how Emily and Melrose slept through these ordeals, but they always seemed to. I'd overhear everything. I'd pretend to be knocked out as I quivered beneath my blanket, nursing my thumb in an effort to soothe myself. Occasionally, their discord would spill over, like smoldering lava, into the kitchen and across the living room where we slept. When my parents' arguments there became physical, I'd leap from bed and wedge my body between theirs, pleading for my father to lower his voice and his hand. "Stop, Daddy!" I'd wail, hot tears flooding my face as I banged on my father's chest. "Please stop!

Leave my mother alone!" That interrupted the fighting but seldom ended it. My parents would put me back in bed, disappear into their room, and carry on with their ruckus.

Just as we each have more than one face, we also carry an array of conflicting emotions. I revered my father, then and now. At the same time, I could not stand how his infidelity humiliated my mother, how his outbursts frightened me to my core. When he'd pound up those stairs, ready for a fight, the Daddy I so admired became the one I resented, the one who raised a fist to my mother and to his own wife. And yet this was the same devoted father who'd balanced me on his knee, the man who'd celebrated me, his little String Bean, every chance he got. This was the Willie who'd courted Dosha from across an ocean and forged a life for his family in their new homeland. But he was also someone who, at times, fell devastatingly short in demonstrating his love.

Even with my childhood long behind me, I find it difficult to lay bare my parents' blemishes. My instinct is to protect their legacies in a world where we are too often demonized. My mom and dad, with all of their frailties, are part of a centuries-long story, a narrative setting that hangs behind myriad Black lives. That story harkens back to when our foreparents were herded onto ships, their naked bodies stacked, row after row amid vomit and sewage, for the treacherous Middle Passage. That tale continued as more than two hundred years of enslavement pressed its foot down on our necks. Our men were emasculated and thrashed, our women raped and brutalized, our families ripped apart and auctioned off like cattle, our grueling labor uncompensated. We still bear the emotional and economic scars. The assault on us, and its resulting trauma, spans generations. Our traditions, our communities, our dignity—all of it has endured barbarous attack. And when someone makes an assassination attempt on your tribe, you adopt a posture of self-defense. You fold in on yourself as a way to cover your wounds. And you dare not hand your assailant another weapon, another piece of shrapnel he or she will use to further shame and dehumanize your people.

This is the painful history my parents were born into. And it is only against this backdrop that their many choices and faces can be understood. Two human beings whose ancestors were declared savage beasts. Two imperfect souls loved by a perfect God.

In the days after my parents clashed, I'd often notice another of my mom's dispositions—the reflective one. She would sit in her rocking chair in the bedroom, shaking her head and repeating under her breath, "This life, this life." A canvas bag filled with peanuts was her sole companion during those times. Every weekend, she'd buy a pound of them. She'd give Emily, Melrose, and me a handful, and then she'd take to her wooden chair, shelling those nuts one by one and peering out the window. I could feel her anguish. That is why I found it so bewildering when she'd occasionally chuckle.

"Why are you laughing, Mom?" I'd ask.

"Child," she'd whisper as she pulled another nut from the bag, "I am laughing at my own calamities."

As Mom rocked herself back and forth, I now imagine she was tucking away her sorrows, relegating them to the farthest corner of her heart, concealing them the way she did her Muma's bills in those barrels. Dosha, the shy island girl, must have been secretly weeping over the abuse she withstood. But Fredericka, the immovable oak with three children whose survival rested upon her courage, kept much of her agony hidden.

4

Transitions

I WAS nine the autumn my world cracked into two. One early morning in 1934, I awakened still a child. When the sun closed its eyes on that day, my girlhood, like a fragile vase, had toppled from a table ledge and smashed onto the floor.

The previous year, the pungent smell of my father's adultery had drifted into our church. Dad began secretly carrying on with a woman who shared our pews, and from the onset of the liaison, Mom had sniffed it out. For months, she insisted that my father end the affair, and for months, he ignored her. One Saturday evening, Dad stomped up our stairs, raring to go for one of his and my mother's usual rounds of acrimony. The next afternoon, Mom got the last deafening word in their argument.

After service, Emily and I stepped outdoors and into an altercation. There, at the foot of the church stairs, my mother was right in the face of the Other Woman. "I want peace in my household!" Mom screamed with such force that a shower of spittle landed on the woman's cheeks. Melrose watched from nearby, holding my mother's hat and pocketbook amid the group of church members who'd huddled to witness the feud. "Get away from my husband and my family!" my mother yelled.

I cannot recall whether the woman had been in church with us that day, but I will always remember what occurred next.

Melrose, out of an instinct to defend our mom, picked up a pebble and threw it at the woman's leg. The shouting ceased. A second later, the scene stirred back to life when Emily and I barreled down the stairs, collected several rocks from the ground, and hurled them at the woman's back. "Get away from our mother!" I squealed in unison with Emily. My mom, perhaps emboldened by our show of solidarity, resumed her shouting and added shoving. The woman pushed back. That's when Reverend Byron came outside and leaped toward them.

"Calm down!" he said, attempting to pry them apart. Mom kept on shoving and swinging. "Mrs. Tyson, that's enough!" the pastor shouted. Once he'd managed to squeeze his body between the two, that lady could hardly stand. She slowly backed away, straightening her blouse and inhaling deeply as she did. I tell you, boy, my mother whipped that woman's behind. Thank the Lord none of our stones hit her in the head.

Just as the embers were settling, my father strode out of the church doors. Everyone froze and peered at him, our gazes delivering a judgment that needn't be uttered. My father had lit this fire, and all those gathered realized it. The rumors of his infidelity were, by then, commonly known, even if rarely acknowledged aloud. Dad was silent. He stood there with shock on his face, stunned that his wife had done something he hadn't predicted she'd do: allow their marital animosity to ignite into a spectacle. Right there in our spiritual town square, the privately fierce Fredericka had made her grand public debut, intent on defending her honor and her territory. This was more than my father had bargained for, and by his countenance, I knew it had frightened him.

And yet it did not scare him enough to alter his course. My

dad and the woman set aside their relationship for a time, but by that spring, they were back at it. That turned up the heat on my parents' tension. In the evenings, Dad would sit at our table and share dinner with us. Almost before the last plantain had touched his tongue, he was out the door with hardly a goodbye. Mom realized where he was going. We all did.

With each passing month, my mother's resentment rose. She no longer prepared his supper plates. She'd make our dinner, feed us early, and leave the remaining rice and peas on the stove for him to spoon up for himself whenever he came home. She also refused to wash his clothes. She'd throw his soiled shirts in a tin pail and let them soak in water for days, the washboard resting on the pail's side, beckoning him to pick it up. As Mom saw it, Dad's dirty laundry, cotton and otherwise, was his alone to deal with.

One morning when my father was on his way out the door for work, he said to me, "Sis, when you come home from school today, I want you to wash these underwear for me." He nodded toward the pail overflowing with his long johns, the heavy flannels my mother had sewn for him. On those days when my father set aside his cart to work at painting the Triborough Bridge, his thermals kept out the cold.

"Yes, Daddy," I said.

I had every intention of laundering the underwear. But that afternoon, I got so caught up in my homework that I never made it around to the chore. I climbed into bed with absolutely no memory of what my father had asked me to do.

Early the next morning, Dad awakened me, Emily, and Melrose. Mom, who had a rare day off from work, was still in her housedress and headscarf.

"Sister, didn't I ask you to wash out these underwear for me?!" he shouted.

"Yes, Daddy," I said as I rubbed my eyes, "but I forgot."

My mother, stone-faced, stared at him from across the living room. Melrose and Emily dropped their eyes to the floor. My hands began to tremor.

"Well I'm going to show every damn one of you something!" he shouted.

Daddy tore through the apartment, smashing the washboard in half, knocking over the pail of long johns, emptying Mom's freshly made stew out of a cast-iron skillet and into the sink. As we looked on in horror, my father stormed into the bedroom and toward a chest of drawers where my mother stashed her earnings. He picked up an iron, propelled its sharpest edge toward the bureau's top drawer, and punctured the lock with such power that the drawer could no longer be opened.

Mom said nothing. She was as astounded as we were by my father's rampage. "Come on, children, get up from here," she finally urged us. In silence, we put away our rollout as we glanced around our apartment, surveying the damage, calculating the impact on our family. Once we were all dressed, Mom ushered us outside. She took me by one hand, Emily by another, and the three of us walked, alongside Melrose, to my father's pushcart on Second Avenue. Mr. Taylor, who managed the cart with my father, was already there working.

"Keep an eye on these children for me," my mother told him. He read in her eyes that there'd been trouble with Willie, heard the anxiety in her tone. "I'll be back shortly," Mom said. He nodded and we gathered near him around the cart as my mother walked off. No one spoke. In my head, I was still trying to make sense of what was unfolding, replaying the reel of Dad's explosion.

Mr. Taylor reached into his pocket, pulled out a quarter, and handed it to Melrose. He'd sensed Mom's desperation and wanted to help our family, in some small way, financially. That gave enterprising Melrose an idea. Just as he'd done so often when he was out working the cart with my father, my dear brother scurried off to the corner store and returned with two enormous armfuls of brown paper shopping bags. He'd talked the merchant into selling him the bags for half a cent each, with the hope that we could resell them for a profit.

"You might be able to get two cents apiece for these," said Mr. Taylor as he inspected the square bags, clearly pleased with my brother's initiative. "Let's go out and see how we do." Melrose handed each of us a stack.

We made our way up Second Avenue, offering bystanders our wares. "Two cents a bag!" Melrose yelled. Within minutes, he'd sold three. Emily and I, initially glued to Mr. Taylor's side, sold a few as well. As the sidewalks swelled with passersby on their way to work, we eventually decided to divide up so we could cover more territory. Melrose and Emily wandered up the avenue together. Mr. Taylor kept me in sight from across the street. Near the corner of 105th, a middle-aged white man strolled by.

"Mister," I said shyly, "care to buy a bag for two cents?" I held up a bag.

He looked first at the bag, and then he lowered his eyes onto my bustline. His lips spread into an eerie grin. "No," he leaned in and whispered as he ogled my chest, "but I will give you five cents for it if you let me touch your breasts."

I dropped the bags. With adrenaline surging through me, I scrambled to the ground and gathered the totes into a jumbled heap. I darted away, escaping across the street to reunite with Mr. Taylor. The man went on about his business, looking back at me over his shoulder as he walked off.

"Everything all right?" said Mr. Taylor, who'd seen me dropping the bags.

"Yes," I lied.

"Was that man bothering you?" he asked.

I shook my head from side to side as my insides screamed otherwise.

At nine, I was still quite skinny. But developmentally, I was ahead of schedule: my breasts had come in early. Still, they couldn't have been any bigger than apricots. And yet on my petite frame, they appeared to be the size of peaches that this man believed were his to pick. I hadn't yet begun wearing bras, had only my shirt as a barrier between my chest and that man's animalistic gaping. As he'd undressed me with his eyes, my knees buckled, my spirit revolted. It was the first time I'd ever been approached in a sexual manner. It was the last time I felt truly safe. With his hungry gaze, this stranger had stolen from me a sense of security. That is what violation does: it wrenches away one's God-given freedom to exhale, to feel relaxed and unguarded in this world. You don't have to be physically touched to be emotionally robbed.

For the rest of that morning, I stayed two inches from Mr. Taylor's elbow. Down the avenue and back we walked, holding up our bags as I prayed inwardly for my dear mother. I felt fearful about continuing, but I knew Mom needed our help. We stayed out on that street for three hours, until every one of our fifty bags was sold, earning us a one-dollar return on Mr. Taylor's twenty-five-cent investment.

Before dusk, Mom arrived at the cart to pick us up. Mr. Taylor presented her with the dollar as he proudly told her about my brother's resourcefulness. She thanked Mr. Taylor and Melrose profusely and we left. But instead of returning to our apartment, Mom led us to Ninety-Eighth Street and Third Avenue. We stopped at a building marked 234 East Ninety-Eighth.

Mom led us up a rickety staircase to an apartment on the

fourth floor. She pulled out a large silver key, turned it inside the lock, and pushed opened the heavy wooden door. Emily, Melrose, and I darted into the two-bedroom space, peering at our possessions scattered across the living room and wondering how they'd gotten there. Mom rested her pocketbook on the radiator and said to us, "This is our new home."

True to Mom's nature, she let a decade pass before she told me all the distress that day had held for her. After leaving us with Mr. Taylor, she returned to our apartment. By then, my father had gone off someplace. Mom yanked up the bottom corner of her mattress, dug into an open slit she'd made with her sewing scissors, and fished out the wad of cash she'd been hiding there for months. She counted out $500. She then dashed to the corner store and purchased some boxes. Back in our apartment, she singlehandedly packed up the few things we owned. Near the doorway, she stacked her boxes alongside her sewing machine, our beds, and the broken bureau. She did not touch my father's things. Over the next hour, she walked all over our area in search of vacancy signs. She discovered one at 234 and inquired about it. The landlord offered Mom a price she could afford for a place that would still be within walking distance of our school. Within hours of my father's fit of rage, she'd put down a deposit on our new lives.

Once she'd secured the apartment, Mom went to see Reverend Byron. "I'm leaving Willie," is all she said, her speech steady. He nodded in recognition, requiring no explanation beyond the steadfastness etched on her face. The Reverend offered her one of his moving vans, as well as some extra hands. Soon after, he and several deacons arrived at our apartment and helped my mother load up everything. As they hauled boxes, my father returned home. He stood in the doorway and gaped at the scene before him.

"The children and I are leaving," my mother said plainly. "I've already found a new apartment." He did not attempt to stop her, nor did he question her choice. And particularly in the presence of Reverend Byron, whom my dad respected, he did not dare argue. He knew by Mom's sternness, that nothing he could say would change her trajectory. He could sense her resolve, could feel his own fault in the matter. He gathered his belongings and packed them, and then he poked through Mom's boxes to be sure none of his effects had been inadvertently mixed in with ours.

To this moment, I am in awe of how my mom made it through that day. Please don't tell me anything about Black women, about our extraordinary fortitude and resilience, because I know precisely who we are. Beneath the burdensome weights of abuse and degradation, my mother straightened her spine, summoned the strength of God and her ancestors, and bravely stepped ahead. She felt as frightened as any woman would, felt her stomach climbing into her throat. But when circumstances called on her to rise, she answered with nary a quake in her voice.

By jamming that lock on the bureau, my father thought he'd rendered my mother financially helpless. But never once during their relationship was he able to rupture her resourcefulness. Like so many in our world do, my father gravely underestimated a Black woman's ingenuity. He hadn't counted on Mom creating a second stockpile of cash, just as he hadn't anticipated she'd teach the Other Woman a lesson amid a whirlwind of dust. And what had been true on that autumn day was undeniable on this one: my mother had had enough. That morning, Dad had unleashed an inferno that prompted Mom to move her children out of his destructive path. Without realizing it, my father had crossed a red line of demarcation, the one labeled Maternal

Instinct. And when he blazed his way out our front door, my mother found a way to march us through a new one. That is power. That is tenacity. That is an oak.

Our father showed up at the new apartment that evening. *How did he know we were here?* I wondered as he casually entered. He must have seen the question in my eyes because he said, "Sis, I came to put a new lock on the door." My mother had been the one to give him our address and had even asked him to come and install our old lock on the new door. Her intent hadn't been to ban him from our lives, only to put some distance between their children and his tirades. *I wonder if he is going to stay here*, I thought. *Maybe they made up.* They hadn't. But they did put a peace treaty in place. Dad would be present in our world. He just wouldn't permanently reside with us. After leaving our old apartment that morning, he'd rented his own place a few streets away.

As Dad unscrewed the lock, his hands shook ever so slightly. Tears welled up in his eyes and threatened to escape. He was absolutely broken. He knew he was to blame, that his womanizing had provoked the rift. In the following years, Mom would often say that the Other Woman had splintered our home, that she'd created so much misery for our family. But in the quietest chambers of their hearts, my mom and dad must have known the reality. That woman spotted a crack in my parents' connection, a fissure that had been forming for quite some time. She simply slid her way into a deep crevice that was already in existence. My dad had been the one most culpable for fracturing our family. On that Sunday when we children cast our stones, we struck just one of the two Goliaths. My father, the taller and more accountable giant of the pair, initially went untouched.

I lingered near my dad's side as he installed the lock. When he finished, he leaned in close to me and whispered, "I threw away all the things your mother used to beat you with." During the long months of his latest affair, Mom's tongue had dripped with more and more venom. When she called me Father Face, she did so with a sneer. Given how much I resembled my dad, as well as how much my mom detested his unfaithfulness, my dad feared I'd pay a blistering price in the coming years whenever my appearance reminded my mother of his. So when Mom's back had been turned that morning, he'd removed some wooden hangers and extension cords from her boxes. He also took her jump ropes. If I, Emily, or Melrose disobeyed our mother, she'd sometimes sit on the edge of her bed and braid three of those ropes together as she warned, "This is for you."

I didn't know what to think about my father's attempt to spare me a beating. In one respect, I was relieved that Mom would have fewer weapons to use against me. But in another regard, I understood it was my dad's conduct, not my mother's belt, that had created this upheaval in our home. His comment left me feeling as if I were somehow in the middle, just as I'd been on all those nights when I'd crammed my body between theirs, begging them to surrender. And from my place at the center, I vacillated between my tremendous love for my father and my anger at his behavior.

After Dad had gone, Melrose set up our pullout. Until Mom bought each of us a bed, that is where we slept. As the sun set on the most painful pivot of my childhood, I lay there quietly weeping next to Emily. Much as I knew my father's affairs were the true reason for our family's dissolution, I also felt deeply responsible. I had been the one to forget about what my father had asked me to do, had been the child who'd left his underwear sitting in that pail, soaked with water, heavy with enough proverbial kerosene to spark flames. It was my forgetfulness that had catapulted him into the fury that overturned our world. However untrue I now know that is, it is what I felt as a girl.

For some, childhood innocence slips away in small increments, over years, with the steady ticktock of a metronome. I lost my wide-eyed naivete in one frightful pendulum swing, in the cadence of a single day. My space and spirit violated. My family irreparably broken.

5

The Other America

I SAW two horror films as a child—one in a theater, another on a sidewalk in the Bronx. The first frightened the daylights out of me. The second vexed my spirit.

The sanctified and the secular were not mixed in our home, so Hollywood films, as part of the latter world, were mostly absent during my upbringing. Emily, Melrose, and I did sometimes watch movies at church. In the basement, the youth leaders would string a sheet onto a wall, set up a small projector, and play films they felt were appropriate for us, like *Little Rascals* or any other show with Black children in the cast. They wanted to instill in us a pride in our heritage. Reflecting back to us, on the screen, those who shared our features was a way to affirm us, even if the characters available to us then sometimes reinforced racial stereotypes. (*Little Rascals*, for instance, was ahead of its time in featuring cross-cultural friendships, but the clueless Buckwheat, with his wildly spiked hair, spoke very little, and when he did, he often mumbled incoherently.) Church films aside, never once had my mom taken us to see a movie in a theater. That changed in 1935, the year I turned eleven.

Though my mother and father had been separated for quite

some time by then, they would occasionally still go at it, especially when Dad came by our apartment talking some nonsense. One Saturday during spring, Mom had heard enough and hastened my father out the door. Soon after, she blurted out a sentence that hadn't ever passed her lips. "Children, we're going to the movies," she said matter-of-factly, as if we regularly took part in that activity. My sister, brother, and I exchanged looks of disbelief and scrambled to put on our shoes. Mom needed to lay down her burdens on this afternoon, and for reasons unknown to me, she chose to lower them in the aisles of a darkened theater.

We walked to the Eagle Theatre, a movie house then at 102nd Street and Third Avenue. *King Kong* was playing. We settled into our seats as the lights dimmed and the curtains parted. The moment that massive gorilla pounded onto the screen, my throat closed. I eventually caught my breath, only to lose it again when Kong thrust his eight-foot hand into the apartment of the blond starlet (portrayed by Canadian actress Fay Wray). I gasped, burying my face in Mom's shoulder.

As the monster snatched the lady from her bed and pulled her from the window, she flailed her arms and screamed bloody hell—and for months after that, so did I. In all of my childhood, *King Kong* was the only film I saw at the cinema, and Mom regretted choosing that one. At nights, I'd wake up howling from a nightmare. I didn't step foot in a theater again until the 1972 premiere of *Sounder*. That's how disturbing I found that beast. I seem to recall my mother putting me between her and my father in bed, attempting but failing to pacify me, but I'm not sure how that could've been because they'd already split.

The year of *King Kong* brought with it an even more frightful drama, this one from the real-life chronicle I call Being Poor and Black. After my parents separated, Mom took on more work.

By then, she'd moved on from her nanny job but continued as a housekeeper. Between her permanent shifts, she also sought out daylong cleaning jobs. Her clients were well-to-do Jewish families. She'd come home loaded down with shoes and clothes, as well as food left over from the portions she'd made for her employers. That is how I came to enjoy matzo ball and borscht soups. Particularly with her regulars, Mom was embraced as a family member, though one of course not completely in the fold. Yes, she was treated with great kindness and felt strongly attached to these families, but at the end of the day, she was still "the help." As long as she and others like her dared not stray outside the bounds of their status, love overflowed. Therein lies the dynamic in which Black people can be seen and even welcomed by whites, but seldom genuinely known by them, rarely viewed beyond the limited, one-dimensional role we play in their narrative—a saga in which a blond woman, not a Black one, is nearly always the beauty to be saved, the damsel in distress deserving of rescue from a monster like Kong.

That same year, on a Saturday morning a few weeks before Easter, Mom said to me, "Take the train to the Bronx this afternoon and we'll go to Alexander's together." Though she'd already made my dress for our most sacred religious holiday, Mom wanted me to pick out some new shoes and a pocketbook to complete my ensemble. She scribbled down the address where I was to meet her and handed me the paper. Nomad that I am, I couldn't get myself out of our apartment fast enough.

It was raining when I got off at my stop, near the busy shopping district where Third Avenue and East 149th Street intersect. In those days, Alexander's, one of the city's most prominent discount clothing store chains, was in a sprawling building called The Hub, which I spotted upon exiting the El. From there, I began searching for the address Mom had given me, checking the number on every building, pulling the hood of my raincoat down over my forehead to guard me from the drizzle. I finally glimpsed the street name Mom had given me. As I turned onto the block, I spotted a group of about twelve Black women along the sidewalk. *What are these ladies doing here?* I wondered, scanning the faces and recognizing none. *My mom wouldn't be here. She doesn't know these women.* I paced onward. And then suddenly, just as I was walking off, I heard someone say, "Sister." I spun around and there, among the women, stood my mother.

I looked again at the women surrounding Mom, struggling to make sense of why they'd all be gathered there in a group. Right then, a white woman approached. She tilted back her umbrella, scanned one of the Black women from head to toe, and said to her, "Can you start now?" The woman nodded and followed her. A few more white women strolled past and repeated a similar exchange. On the street, a couple of Buicks slowed down alongside us as motorists peered out their windows at Mom and the others.

I took in the sight as an awareness jolted through me: these women were lined up to be considered for work, inspected as if on an auction block the way enslaved Africans once were. Who was the strongest? Whose teeth were cleanest? Who among these apes was least likely to stir up trouble? Which one was worthy of purchase? The scene was reminiscent of what Black people had experienced time and again during the most shameful chapter of America's history. One by one, strangers waltzed up to survey them with a sweeping glance, hardly looking into the women's eyes as they determined who seemed decent or tidy or docile enough to cross their thresholds and clean their homes.

I obviously knew my mother worked as a domestic, but I'd grasped that fact only in concept, the way I'd theoretically understood, through reading, the ruthless brutality my ancestors withstood. But on that sidewalk, as onlookers stopped by to evaluate my mom, the agonizing truth of her situation settled over me. I'd never imagined that my own mother, a queen who wore her dignity as a splendorous, flowing silk cape, could be in such a position. I'd never imagined that someone so majestic would have to put up her labor for sale while casting her gaze downward in deference to white strangers.

That reality cut me deeply, sliced through the raw flesh of my insides. It stung me in the same way that my Italian classmate's words once had. And just as I'd done then, I shoved down the hurt, locked it behind an unmarked door in my heart where griefs unimaginable reside. The experience was yet another discovery of how my people were viewed. It was a reminder of our true position in this nation, like a map with an enormous red dot labeled "You are here." Black children learn where they stand in this world by recognizing the spaces where our people can and cannot enter, and if granted access, whether our presence and humanity will be regarded as equal.

Earlier that day, Mom had finished her usual work shift. She'd stopped on this street, the known pickup location for housekeepers, only in hopes of booking another job for after we'd shopped. But she didn't linger on that sidewalk long enough to be chosen. She'd noticed my disbelief, seen how I'd hesitated to walk toward her after she'd called to me. There was a flicker of shame in her eyes. Her embarrassment wasn't about seeking out the kind of work she could get as a Black immigrant in 1930s America. It was about my reaction. "Come on," she said, taking me by the hand and leading me from the huddle. "Alexander's is over there."

"I don't want to go anymore," I mumbled.

"What's the matter with you, child?" she asked.

"Nothing," I said, my expression betraying my claim. "I just don't want to go."

We went anyway. And as we navigated the packed store in search of my Easter accessories, I replayed in my head the scene I'd witnessed. All of these years later, I have not gotten over the horror of what happened on that street. I may never.

The era I grew up in both deepened my racial wound and soothed it with the healing balm of the arts. My childhood spanned the 1920s and 1930s, two of the most economically memorable and culturally rich decades in US history—a period when Negro literature, music, and culture flourished. The Roaring Twenties rollicked joyously with jazz, decadence, and illegal whiskey, while the thunderous market crash of 1929 rattled nerves throughout the thirties. What these shifts meant to daily life, or whether they had any noticeable consequence at all, depended upon where you lived and how much you were able to earn—both of which were inextricably tied to the color of your skin.

The United States has never been "one nation under God" but several nations gazing up at him, dissimilar faces huddled beneath a single flag. In white America, the twenties may have roared, but in my Black world—in what has been called the Other America—the decade also moaned. Then, when stock prices plummeted, catapulting the nation into its worst economic downturn, Black people knew what we still know: communities of color are always grappling with financial despair. The fact that the Great Depression was given a name just meant that enough whites were now suffering alongside us to warrant an official title.

For the majority culture, the twenties can be summarized in

two words: flamboyant excess. The First World War, then the bloodiest in human history, had at last come to an end, however unsatisfying its conclusion. Americans moved on from their sorrows by throwing a decade-long soiree. When I came along in 1924 (the same year, by the way, that the famous Macy's Thanksgiving Day parade began), the wartime economy had already ushered in unprecedented financial prosperity. In short, Americans had more money than ever, and it was burning a hole in their pockets. Materialism grabbed ahold of the zeitgeist and would not stop squeezing.

Though the abundance mostly benefited middle- and upper-class workers, it lifted the tide for all, buoying spirits and replenishing bank accounts. Wall Streeters strutted through Manhattan with extra millions in their portfolios and greater confidence in their strides. In 1920, Prohibition banned the sale and import of liquor, giving rise to bootleggers who smuggled booze across borders and into speakeasies. As the good times shimmied, hemlines rose. Young flappers, with their bobbed hair and rebellious streaks, showcased their opulence with mink stoles at lavish parties in a *Great Gatsby*–style existence. During the architectural boom, skyscrapers soared in Midtown, with construction commencing on the Art Deco–style Chrysler Building in 1928. Affluence was the new American goal, and for many, the extended Bull Market put that aspiration within reach for the first time.

As spending power increased, consumers laid out cash for all manner of luxuries and appliances: cars (Ford's Model T had its heyday), automatic washing machines (however, those as poor as we were continued to rely on manual washboards—we never got a machine), electric refrigerators (we also never replaced our icebox with a fridge), and phonographs and radios (the day my father brought home a small RCA set and turned it on, I thought, *Now why is there a voice coming out of that box?*). Americans also had more to spend on leisure, flocking to see the rash of both silent films and "talkies" released during those years. The antics of Charlie Chaplin, with his mustache and baggy pants, drew millions to the box office. In 1927, the first talkie, *The Jazz Singer*, lured theatergoers into enormous movie palaces, as cinemas were then called. The movie business grew into big business.

New York City earned its wings during the twenties. The five boroughs overflowed with more than five million residents, moving the city ahead of London as the world's most populous. By boat and by rail, by foot and by any means necessary, immigrant families flooded in, carrying with them the same dreams my parents had clutched. During phase one of the Great Migration, millions of colored folks, as we were then called, moved from the rural South to New York City and other urban centers around the Northeast and Midwest. The Ku Klux Klan had raised its burning crosses with increasing height and frequency, signaling it was long past time for us to flee. Like Rebecca and Nathan in *Sounder*, many had worked as sharecroppers whose efforts and earnings were exploited. They escaped in search of civic and economic parity. Those who came to New York mostly settled in Harlem, then the largest Black community in the nation. Uptown West was the place to be—a cultural epicenter for the United States and the Western world.

The nation began tapping its toes to bebop during the Jazz Age. If jazz was America's first musical superstar, then Harlem was that star's grand arena, the twenties its golden hour. The avenues and alleys vibrated with the sounds of improvisation, of trumpet and piano and syncopated rhythms seemingly delivered scattershot and yet masterfully arranged into a sophisticated whole. The nightclub scene was exactly that—a scene. Anyone eager to cut a step while relishing big-band brilliance stopped by the Savoy Ballroom (birthplace of the Lindy Hop and land of the Charleston and Fox Trot) or the Back Room (the speakeasy's entrance was hidden behind a bookcase).

The Cotton Club, then on 142nd Street and Lenox Avenue, was the ultimate hot spot. Night after night during that decade and beyond, greats such as Duke Ellington, Fletcher Henderson, Cab Calloway, Billie Holiday, Louis Armstrong, Fats Waller, Bessie Smith, and Jelly Roll Morton delivered hankie-lifting performances, riveting audiences with their artistic genius. Hits like "Ain't Misbehavin'" and "Sweet Georgia Brown" reverberated from nightclub venues and onto boulevards. Late-night jam sessions extended into the early morning hours, with revelers in zoot suits and feather boas stumbling home at daybreak. As Americans of all racial backgrounds fell under the irresistible spell of the hip new sound, jazz radically altered the musical landscape. The music's electrifying spirit could not be contained, even amid a strictly religious upbringing like my own. The city pulsated with revival, and as a child, I could feel the fervor. Exuberance danced its way up and down 125th, Harlem's bustling main street.

Jazz stirred at the center of a broader cultural movement, the Harlem Renaissance—a profound social, intellectual, and artistic awakening in Black America that spilled over into all facets of society. Renowned philosopher Alain Locke, who penned the movement's definitive text, *The New Negro* (1925), called the era "a spiritual emancipation." James Weldon Johnson had his own description for it, "a flowering of Negro literature." A historically shackled and voiceless community now demanded its full freedom and its say. It was our first opportunity in this country to define ourselves, to express our unique identity and declare our humanity.

The chorus of gifted literary voices Locke gathered in *The New Negro*—which includes essays, poetry, and fiction by writers such as Zora Neale Hurston, Langston Hughes, Countee Cullen, and Claude McKay—delivered the movement's rallying cry for Black autonomy and self-respect. Locke—who earned his doctorate at Harvard University, was the first Black Rhodes Scholar, and served as a philosophy professor at Howard University—encouraged artists to look to Africa for inspiration. The path to Black progress, he understood, began with self-determination and a regard for our homeland heritage. "The question is no longer what whites think of the Negro," he wrote in his anthology, "but of what the Negro wants to do, and what price he is willing to pay to do it."

Locke and his contemporary W. E. B. Du Bois, one of the most distinguished scholars of the twentieth century and the author of *The Souls of Black Folk* (1903), held differing views about Black aesthetic expression and its role in the movement. And yet the two shared the conviction that the arts were essential to forging a new Black identity. Du Bois founded and edited *The Crisis*, the flagship publication of the NAACP that gave voice to artists and intellectuals during the Harlem Renaissance and beyond. With the Black elite at its helm, the Renaissance shined its light into every corner of the artistic community, from literature and music to the performing and visual arts. *Shuffle Along*, which was produced, written, and performed entirely by African Americans, debuted on Broadway in 1921, showcasing the talents of Josephine Baker, Paul Robeson, and Adelaide Hall. Aaron Douglas, the eminent painter and graphic artist who produced the illustrations for *The New Negro*, created hundreds of images that evoked Black pride and captured the Renaissance spirit.

When the financial markets collapsed on October 29, 1929,

the Roaring Twenties sobered up and whimpered to a close. According to the Library of Congress, the unemployment rolls during the Great Depression swelled to 24 percent for white workers. Black workers sustained double that blow: in 1932, 50 percent of us were unemployed. "These white folks are jumping out of windows, falling out like paper in the wind," my mother observed during that era. Bread lines and soup kitchens formed as Americans struggled for their next meals in a nation where, a few short years earlier, surplus had abounded. My own parents and thousands of others relied on government assistance to close the gap between what they could earn and what they needed for basic survival. Over and over in our world, we have witnessed how today's riches can become tomorrow's scarcity. We'd do well to heed the lesson. In times of plenty, paucity sits by, licking its lips and awaiting its next grand appearance.

The Depression was just one of a series of devastations Black people endured during the thirties. In 1931, long before the innocent Central Park Five were deprived of justice, the Scottsboro Boys, nine Black teenagers, were falsely accused in Alabama of raping two white women on a train. In a case of blatant racial bias, an all-white jury convicted the boys and sentenced eight of them to death. The following year, the US government sanctioned the Tuskegee Syphilis Experiment, a forty-year-long health assault on our community. Biomedical research doctors recruited impoverished Black men with the promise of free medical care. These physicians claimed to be treating the men for so-called bad blood, but in fact, they were using Blacks as guinea pigs to study the long-term effects of syphilis. Scores of our men, knowingly left untreated with syphilis long after penicillin had been discovered as a cure, suffered blindness and death.

The attack on our humanity continued in 1934. That year, the Federal Housing Administration established redlining, a set of racially discriminatory real estate and bank-lending practices that barred Blacks from purchasing homes in white neighborhoods—and thus set the stage for the wealth disparity between Black and white households that remains to this day. Home and land ownership are the primary means by which Americans have historically amassed wealth, and when Blacks were locked out of bank loans and segregated into slums, we were robbed of the potential to build fortunes. President Franklin D. Roosevelt's New Deal brought a measure of relief for poor Blacks, but some of its policies, such as redlining, made the New Deal a raw one for us.

It's no wonder that many African Americans carry a lingering distrust of whites, even those we sincerely love and embrace. Given the horrors of our abuse in this nation, we are understandably wary. To ever heal these deep racial traumas—and seldom has it felt more urgent that we do—we must acknowledge that they indeed still exist, throbbing and tender beneath the surface, spilling over, like molten rage, into the streets. As difficult as it is to recall this country's atrocities, it is essential that every American of every color does. It is critical that we connect that centuries-long ugly history with, in our times now, a cop's knee on George Floyd's neck and bullets riddling Breonna Taylor's body. The line from our nation's original sin to its present heartache is not faint and dotted; it is solid and direct. And even when the impulse arises to cringe and look away from a system predicated on Black oppression, a system that is still doing precisely what it was designed to do, we must stare into the face of our past and examine what happened here, on our soil, much of it less than a lifetime ago, a lot of it happening now. Turning a blind eye to our history has not saved us from its consequences.

My early years played out during these two wildly different

decades—the first a cultural resurrection and the next a painful reckoning. In 1939 during the last days of the Depression, Billie Holiday stepped bravely up to a microphone at Café Society in New York's Greenwich Village and sang, for the first time, "Strange Fruit," a lyrical protest anthem:

Southern trees bear a strange fruit
Blood on the leaves and blood at the root
Black bodies swingin' in the Southern breeze
Strange fruit hangin' from the poplar trees.

A bitter crop, battered and dropping. The bruised and blood-stained carcass of the Other America.

The nation's shifting times paralleled a spirit of change in our house. After my family fell apart, the basic rhythm of our existence returned, but it swayed to a more sorrowful tempo. Melancholy hung in the air, hovered over our soup bowls at dinner, settled into the cracks of our wood floor. When my mother and father weren't arguing, they didn't talk much. Dad was around a lot, often stopping by our apartment two or three afternoons a week. When he was there, he and Mom looked past one another, mostly remaining cordial and always maintaining an emotional distance. Much as I wished my family had remained intact, I was relieved to have the late-night battles in our rearview mirror. Alongside our gloom lived an uneasy peace for which we'd all paid dearly.

Mom thought Dad would eventually move in with the Other Woman. He didn't. The two continued their relationship for several months after my parents split, but they ultimately ended things. It perplexes me that, given the freedom to do as he pleased, my father chose not to be with that woman. I've often wondered whether she regretted her affair with my father given that, in the end, he did not stay with her. Perhaps Dad never truly wanted to build a new life with someone but rather craved pursuing the forbidden.

Mom did not file for divorce. In that era, West Indians weren't too into the whole divorce business. Some would live separately for fifty years and still say "my husband" this and "my wife" that. For one thing, many couldn't afford the legal fees. And in my mother's case, all she'd wanted was to get her children out of the way of a man who'd suddenly gone berserk. But years later when I was in my teens, my Aunt Zora, Dad's sister, said to me, "The day your mother opens her bank vault is the day she'll get a big surprise." Following their split, my parents continued to share a safe deposit box. My aunt had reason to believe that my father had assembled divorce papers, and rather than having them served on my mother, he put them there for her to find. Mom heard the same story from my aunt but didn't believe it. I have no idea whether my mom ever saw those papers, or if they even existed. My dad did marry another woman around 1940, but perhaps he did so illegally, without ever officially severing his first marital ties.

After my parents parted ways, Mom took Dad to court for striking her. I was with my father one afternoon when he went to city hall to review some papers Mom had submitted. Before we boarded the train, we stopped at a five-and-dime store. My eyes fell on a gorgeous cameo pin. Dad, noting my desire, said to me, "Do you want that pin?" I nodded yes. He purchased it, in part because he relished delighting me, and probably also because he wanted to show the judge what a wonderful father he was. He fastened the pin on my collar as I beamed. On the way out, he bought me a ring with three faux rubies, one so popular then that practically every little white girl had one. As we walked up the stairs to the train, he took my hand and escorted me, as if I were ascending the stairs to my castle. Later, in court, I glided in as the prima donna I felt like.

Despite how much taller I'd grown, I was still my father's little String Bean, his first girl. He constantly bought me small gifts—bracelets, trinkets, toys. When I'd return home and show Mom my bounty, she'd muster a half-smile. Then later if she got angry with me, she'd spew her resentment: "This man who thinks so much of you, when I was going to the hospital to give birth to you, he had something else to do. And you're supposed to be his favorite." She often threw that one in my face.

I realize now that Mom's rage had little to do with my dad's tenderness toward me and everything to do with how deeply he'd hurt her. Still, my mother's words blistered me as much as her beatings always had. Once Dad left, she didn't whip us as frequently, mostly because she didn't have the energy. After all of her many work shifts, she'd lumber through our door too exhausted to do much beyond prepare our dinner. My father contributed what money he could, but my mother bore the lion's share of the financial responsibility. Dad would often complain about how gnarly his fingertips had become from painting WPA war posters around town, another job he took on. Never once did Mom breathe a complaint about her duties. With sealed lips and persevering hands, she just got up every day and did what she had to do.

The year my parents separated is the year my brother, then eleven, began running away from home. Mom often said that Melrose, like me, was born restless, led by a spirit that called to him. He'd sometimes be gone for days at a time, long enough to frighten the hair off my mother's head. She'd walk the streets searching for her firstborn, her Heart String. She'd find him sitting out on a bench, staring off as if something in the distance had captured his attention. "Where you been all this time?" my mother would ask him as she led him home. He'd shrug and continue gazing. "And what did you eat?" she'd prod. He once mentioned that a kind man in our neighborhood would often spot him outdoors and then return to hand him a cup of milk. For years into his adulthood, Melrose wouldn't touch milk, probably because he associated it with those distressing times. He was a troubled child, my brother. We each had our way of handling the misery of our situation, and Melrose drifted out into the streets even as he drew inward.

Emily dealt with our new reality by blaming my mother. My sister, though seldom one to withhold her opinions, said little to me then about our family's tearful transition. But years later when we were grown, she revealed that she'd mostly held our mother accountable. She and Melrose had slept through much of the conflict I'd witnessed. What Emily did see had been enough to unnerve her. And yet, however poisonous our family dynamic was, she still desperately wanted our father there with us, at the center of it. She faulted my mother for walking away, not understanding that my father had long since made an emotional departure. In retrospect, I understand Emily's assessment not as an indictment of my mother, but as a way to cope with her own anguish. When your heart has been sliced wide open, you tend to haphazardly hurl rocks in every direction. You want someone, anyone, to ache and bleed as badly as you have. You cast stones and aspersions the way we children once did at the Other Woman.

After my mother left my father, we moved to a different church. Mom wanted a fresh start away from the public disgrace. She couldn't stand the idea of my father's infidelity following her through the pews of St. John's as her fellow parishioners traded whispers and knowing glances. My mother called Ms. Weeks, a dear friend she'd grown up with. "What church do you attend in Harlem?" she asked her. Ms. Weeks welcomed us to join her congregation, St. Andrew's Episcopal. In practice, Reverend Byron would still serve as our spiritual shepherd, as the friend and reverend Mom could call upon if any of us so much as sneezed. But our new church became St. Andrew's, then still a small parish, but now one that stands as a stunning neo-Gothic sanctuary near 127th Street and Fifth Avenue. Though the congregation was predominantly West Indian, the minister, whose name I cannot recall, was white. The Episcopal Diocese of New York had appointed him to that parish, and the church is now a city landmark.

As we settled into our second church home, we were just as involved as we'd been at the first one. Mom attempted to groom Emily as a pianist, hoping she might one day play in church. She also wanted to imbue all of us with some culture, as well as keep our minds and hands productively occupied. After purchasing beds for us, the next thing Mom bought was a ramshackle upright piano, which we scooted against a wall in our living room. Mom bought it from a Black lady from the neighborhood, Mrs. Wilson, who gave Emily lessons at twenty-five cents per session. But Emily didn't take to the keyboard. "I want to play the violin," she told my mother, backing up to evade the dotted eye she knew was coming. "When you get old enough to go to work and can buy a violin," my mother retorted, "then you can get one yourself." Since my brother had no interest in the piano (he would pick up any items he could find and turn them into drumsticks . . . I tell you, if my mother hadn't steered him away from what she thought was too worldly of an artistic passion, Melrose might've been a great drummer), I was the last remaining potential pianist in the house. After Emily quit within weeks of her first lesson, I began my lessons with Mrs. Wilson when I was ten. At twelve, I could play every hymn in our church hymnal. At fifteen, I was accompanying both our congregation and the choir. I had such a knack for it that I also taught myself how to play the organ.

The piano provided me with the consolation I needed to at last give up my thumb. One day when I was around twelve, I stuck it in my mouth, pulled it out again, and stared at it for the longest time. *Wait a minute*, I thought. *What happened to you? . . . You don't taste so good anymore.* From then on, the piano served the purpose that my thumb always had: it became my solace. During long afternoons as the sun's mango rays painted shadows on our walls, I'd sit hunched over those chipped keys, soothing myself with the message of the hymn that has become my daily meditation:

Just as I am, without one plea
But that Thy blood was shed for me
And that Thou bid'st me come to Thee
O Lamb of God, I come! I come.

In a home and family uprooted, that song became my safe haven, my grace note. There, in the measures of that musical prayer, I find comfort still.

6

Unspoken

PARENTS lie to their children. They misrepresent their painful truths and their personal histories. Concealing is the human way of pretending that we are who we imagine ourselves to be in the fairy tales we invent, that our lives have unfolded as we wish they would have rather than as they so wrenchingly did. My mother's falsehoods were not outright fabrications but lies of omission. She spoke little and withheld much, a restraint every bit as damaging as a barefaced falsehood. Her silence cost us both.

My first menstrual period arrived the same way most things did in the Tyson household—without much mention. It also arrived quite early—when I was just nine years old. In those years, Mom had her way of keeping us entertained when school and the sun were both out. On summer weekends, she'd often take us on the El from our place on the East Side all the way down to Battery Park. I lived for those rides. I'd poke my head out the train window to watch the world whiz by, savoring the breeze on my cheeks, gazing into the high-rise windows, and wondering about the families I spotted. Parks, museums, zoos: Mom shuttled us all over the city and the tri-state area. One

Sunday afternoon, the four of us even enjoyed an annual boat excursion, organized by our church, out at Keansburg Beach in New Jersey.

Early the next morning, Mom awakened me. "Go to the bathroom and wipe yourself," she said. I sleepily rubbed my eyes as she held up a square cotton rag and two long strings, each with a large safety pin attached to its end. "Put this on," she said. "Where?" I asked. She motioned for me to tie the strings around my waist and pin them onto the rag. Moments later in the bathroom, when I stared down at my scarlet-soaked underpants, I was sure I was dying. I don't know how Mom even knew I'd started my period; she'd probably dreamed about it or sensed it. I'd once overheard my sister mention something about menstruation and bleeding, and though I was older than Emily and should have known more than she, I wasn't at all clear what was involved. Nowadays, I cringe and shake my head in disbelief when I recall just how ill-informed I was. *Maybe this is it*, I thought as I wrestled with the strings and positioned the rag between my thighs. When I emerged from the bathroom, walking like a zombie, Mom was standing there with her uniform on and her pocketbook in hand, ready for work. "Stay away from the boys," she told me. "I will talk to you when I come back." She hasn't gotten back to me yet. In the following months, when my flow kept returning for a curtain call, I eventually figured out the whole period business on my own.

A few years later, my breasts joined the puberty party. The budding chest I'd had at nine was in full bloom by my twelfth birthday. That year, Mom had moved us from our place on Ninety-Eighth to 178 East 101st Street, into a two-bedroom railroad apartment near my school, Margaret Knox Junior High. One afternoon when I was playing in front of our building, procrastinating on practicing the piano, I saw my father approaching from down the street. I sprinted up a hill to meet him, and as I ran, my boobs bounced downward and upward, jiggling and screaming for support. After Dad and I embraced, he turned to me with a serious expression and said, "Go upstairs and tell your mom to put a bra on you."

I stared at him and then down at my sandals, mortified that Dad had noticed that my boobs needed harnessing. I didn't mention his observation to Mom, but he must have said something to her, because soon after, she arrived home from Alexander's holding an acknowledgment of my adolescence. "Put this on" is all she said as she handed me a white B-cup corset. I don't know why my mother hadn't purchased a bra for me before then, or whether she'd planned to talk to me about this mysterious corridor I'd entered. My guess is she was too embarrassed to speak about it. Also, discussing my changing body would've meant reckoning with the inevitable: her firstborn girl, the once-sickly child she'd for so long kept close, had grown out of her arms and into a new season.

We did not talk about periods or breasts. We did not talk about sex. We did not, in fact, talk about much of anything regarding adolescence. The little I knew I learned from Emily or from my friends. That left me struggling to cobble together the truth, the whole time running for the hills whenever a boy came near me. *What will happen if he touches me? Why did Mom tell me to steer clear?* I got one clue from Fannie Lou, a neighbor a few years older than me. One afternoon when a pregnant woman walked past us, Fannie Lou nodded toward her and then looked back at me. "You know where babies come from, don't you?" she asked. I nodded, not prepared to admit my ignorance. "Well a baby is going to come out of that woman's stomach, from where you go pee-pee," she said. I gazed at her in horror, trying to make sense of what she'd revealed. *A baby is coming out from between that lady's legs*, I said to myself, *but how did the baby get* in *there?* No clue. And no mother willing to sit me down and explain.

Dating came late in our house, and it's a miracle it arrived at all. My mother was wary of strangers. Only family could be trusted, she reasoned. "If anything ever happens to me," she'd often say in the years after she and my father split, "I know I can rely on those two men to look after my children." The men she referenced were a couple of my father's cousins whom he'd grown up with in Nevis. I was around fourteen when my mother discovered her faith had been grievously misplaced.

One evening when brimstone spilled over between Mom and me about God knows what, I blurted out a secret I'd been too fearful up to then to expose: one of those men had put his hands on me when I was eleven. During a moment when Mom had turned her attention toward supper, he'd brushed his palm along the backside of my dress, robbing me of a sense of safety just as that white man on the street once had. Upon hearing my revelation, Mom hadn't yet picked up her jaw before Emily exclaimed, "And me too!" Until then, I hadn't known my sister had been touched. As outgoing as Emily was, she and I shared remarkably little about our interior worlds in those years, adopting the same code of silence our mother lived by. Mom's eyes filled with horror and she disappeared into her bedroom. She never mentioned our disclosure. I've often wondered whether she privately confronted that cousin, because after that day, we rarely saw him. From then on, she became so adamant about protecting us that she wouldn't even entertain male friends. She couldn't take the chance that another man would mess with her girls.

Emily got an early start with the boys, long before Mom granted us official permission to court. My sister might have been a year and a half younger than me, but when it came to awareness, she stayed five paces ahead. From age fourteen on, she was out there living her best life. I don't think she was having sex, but she had boyfriend after boyfriend. She'd meet them wherever she went. Down the sidewalk she'd waltz, with her Coke-bottle curves and her beaming smile, drawing stares from young men. My mother, who was away a lot working, had no idea Emily was running around. Also, Mom was so busy worrying over me that she took her eye off Emily. "I went to see Miss Taylor this afternoon," my sister would fib when Mom questioned her whereabouts. Or "I went to the store with my friend Ruby," she'd claim. In actuality, she'd have her tail down at the park, carrying on with her newest heartthrob. I'm surprised word never got back to Mom.

When Emily and I each turned fifteen, Mom at last allowed us to begin socializing with young men. She didn't refer to it as dating. She also didn't reconcile her previous insistence that I stay away from boys with her consent for me now to keep company with them. She had her reasons for loosening the reins. Her dream for Emily and me was that we'd meet and one day marry nice church boys—a desire made clear by her parameters. My mother's first commandment: Thou shalt go out only with a young man who is the son of a minister. All other socializing had to be with family members she'd vetted. The Dores family and their four teenage boys (cousins on my mother's side of the family) were on the approved list. So were our other cousins who were around our age, the Tysons and the Swanstons, all of whom were brilliant musicians. Schubert Swanston, the eldest of four, was a piano prodigy who eventually worked with Louis Armstrong. He and his siblings played at least two instruments each, from the cello and the violin to the bass fiddle and the organ. After dinner on Sunday evenings, our family would gather for a concert at the Swanstons' place near us on the East Side.

Church, school, cousins: that was our protected world. Emily's parallel universe, invisible to Mom, was twice the circumference of my own.

Horace Chenery was my first crush. He was a year older than me and as tall as heaven, with kind eyes. He lived a few doors down from us on the same street and attended my school. Horace didn't go to church (strikes one, two, and three in Mom's book), but Horace's mom, Miss Violet, was an usher in our congregation. Violet's mom, Miss Lawrence, was half-white and half-Black, and she'd passed her honey complexion on to her grandchildren. Though Miss Violet was my color, Horace was quite fair, with a dreamy smile and dimples. On the day when Horace and I caught each other's eye in our neighborhood, I blushed and quickly looked away.

It wasn't just Horace's appearance that gave me goose pimples. As we got to know one another on long walks home from school, I felt drawn to him because of how he made me see myself, through the soft light of his adoring lens. "You know," he'd often tell me as we walked home from school, "your face is shaped like a heart." He'd then gently trace his thumbs around my face as I snickered. I couldn't get home fast enough to study my reflection in the bathroom mirror. *Could I be cute?* I thought, as "nappy-headed nigger" memories reeled through my head. *What's he talking about, a heart?* I didn't see any such shape. Yet there was no mistaking the flurry of monarchs flapping inside me when I was with him. I told no one about our budding romance, if it can be called that. We never even held hands or kissed. But Horace was the first boy who made me feel like I might be attractive, just maybe.

I also fell for his brilliance. In those years, I was an admirer of the mind. That is true even now. If you can tell me something I don't know, you've got me. Horace was intuitive and smart, an

A student who shared my curiosity and affirmed my inquisitiveness. When I'd ask "Why?" he'd meet my question with another. "Have you been to the Empire State Building?" he once asked me. Even with all of our family's traipsing around the city, Mom hadn't yet taken us to view the Midtown marvel, completed in 1931. With his eyes dancing, Horace recounted every detail of the structure, which was erected in a race to build the world's tallest building (an honor it held for forty years, until the World Trade Center's North Tower soared higher in 1970). And he was as sensitive as he was bright, his eyes often brimming with tears of emotion when he'd share stories from his boyhood. Our puppy love might've become a full-grown poodle if Mom hadn't cut off its nourishment.

One afternoon, Melrose saw Horace and me walking down our street together. I realized he'd noticed us but thought nothing of it. That changed when, later that evening, Mom approached me with a sentence I knew meant trouble. "Come here, I want to talk to you," she said. I took a place at our kitchen table and she sat down across from me.

"Now this Horace Chenery business," she said, "it has to stop. I don't want you seeing him anymore."

"I'm not *seeing* him," I retorted. "What do you mean?"

Right then, my brother rolled into the kitchen with his public service announcement: "You and Horace were on 101st Street together today," he said.

I glared at Melrose, not sure why he'd ratted me out to Mom, perhaps out of some (annoying) instinct to shelter me the way our parents always had. "Well I live on 101st Street and so does Horace," I said. "Where else was I supposed to walk?"

"You're supposed to walk anyplace but next to him," Mom shot back. "I don't ever want to see you talking to that boy again."

Horace may not have been a minister's son, but he was an upstanding young man—which, as I saw it, should've earned him boyfriend clearance. Mom saw it differently, and in a house more dictatorship than democracy, I knew not to question her mandate. Also, giving her lip would've led to further restriction on my social agenda.

I spotted Horace from my window the next day, just as he swung around the corner onto our block. Mom was at work and Emily and Melrose weren't around, but my neighbor, Elizabeth, was visiting me. When Horace got close to my building, he looked up and waved at us. Elizabeth, who didn't know Horace and I were sweet on one another, waved back at him and grinned. "You know him?" I asked her. "No," she said, "but I've seen him around here and he's cute." That's when I got an idea.

I called out to Horace, shouting for him to wait. Elizabeth and I dashed downstairs and met him in front of the apartment. Out of breath, I scanned our surroundings to be sure tattlesnitch Melrose and Mom were nowhere in sight. I then turned toward Horace.

"I have to tell you something," I said.

"What is it?" he asked.

"My mother and my brother don't want me to see you anymore," I said, hardly pausing between each word.

He frowned. "What do you mean?" he asked.

"I can't really explain it," I told him. "I just can't see you anymore."

I stared at the ground and then looked up at Elizabeth. "But I want to introduce you to my friend," I said to Horace. "She's really nice. You'll like her."

For a long moment, none of us said anything as the awkwardness of the situation hung in the air. Horace, befuddled and yet clear that there was no more information to be gathered from me, finally spoke. "Well look," he said to me, "this has nothing to do with us." Then as the perfect gentleman he was, Horace warmly greeted Elizabeth. I'm sure she'd been standing there wondering what the devil she'd walked into.

That was in the summer of 1939. Horace and Elizabeth dated throughout high school and eventually married and raised a family together. Both of them, my maiden crush and my neighbor, are long gone now. And all of these years later, I am left with questions, with specks of wistfulness and regret in the spaces between them. How might my life have turned out if I'd stayed with the beau who'd stolen my heart even as he traced its shape with his thumbs? What if I, rather than my friend, had been the one to marry Horace? What would have happened if I'd defied my mother and secretly followed my inclination? I can only ponder.

After Horace had been forced from my world, there entered another young man—someone who, in the view of my mother, was an ideal match for me. Our team of pastors often hosted gatherings in their homes for members, and you'd better believe Mom ensured that Emily and I turned up at all of them. "I'd like you to meet someone," one of the ministers said to me one evening during the party. I stared at the pastor as if he'd just announced the Second Coming. I was seventeen then, but I was no less reserved than I'd been a decade earlier. The pastor nodded in the direction of a young man who approached. "This is my son, Kenneth," he said.

I'd of course seen Kenneth around church, but in our large congregation, he and I had never been formally introduced. I smiled and straightened the collar of the velvet dress Mom had sewn for me, just for this occasion. I didn't know what to say, which is why I stood there and gawked. Kenneth had a close-cropped 'fro and dewy chocolate skin, with a smile stretching from ear to ear. He wore a three-piece suit, with a row of gold buttons lined up vertically along the vest. At more than six feet tall, he towered above me, just as my dear Horace had. While sipping soda, we traded stories. He'd just completed his last year of high school. I was still a student. He was working as a security guard and planned to become a police officer, and his older brother, a lieutenant, was already stationed overseas ahead of the Second World War. I knew absolutely nothing about war, aside from the one that had destroyed my household. Years earlier, Kenneth's mother had died in childbirth, and he'd been raised by his father. He now had his own apartment on Morningside Avenue in Harlem. I still lived under my mother's roof and rulership.

Days later, Kenneth came by our apartment. The pastor had told Mom that he'd introduced the two of us, and Mom met him at the door. "So I hear you're the son of a minister," she said with a smile bright enough to light up Times Square. "Yes, Miss Fredericka," he said, beaming. And I, recognizing the absolute delight on their faces, knew an unspoken understanding had been reached—an agreement not requiring my consent.

I may not have had much of a voice during adolescence, but I did have aspirations. Given my talent for the piano and organ, I initially thought I'd become a concert musician, a dream my mother birthed on my behalf. My goal shifted the year I was fifteen. By then, I was taking lessons from a lady by the name of Miss Mann. Her eldest son was the organist at Convent Avenue Baptist Church in Harlem, and I'd sometimes accompany the choir or play for the congregation there. During a concert one

Sunday, I played, from memory, "Poet and Peasant," a fifteen-page overture composed by Franz von Suppé. At the close of the piece when I stood and bowed at the warm applause, I said to myself, *I will never ever do this again.*

Sure enough, on that afternoon I walked away from the piano, and it was the last day I set my fingers on ivory. Not only had the Franz piece worn me out, the piano demanded far too much of my time. I'd wake up early to rehearse for two hours before school, only to return to that hard bench before bed. "All that money wasted!" my mother fussed. In hindsight, I'm stunned she let me quit, however insistent I was. Mom continued in her mission to rear us with some culture, and by then, I felt I'd soaked up my share.

By age sixteen, I'd moved on to hairdressing. For years, Mom had her hair pressed by a woman who lived two blocks from us, Miss Jones. (How on earth can I remember these names? No wonder I have a headache . . . so many details in my head!) After Miss Jones passed, her hot comb got handed down to me. I was good enough at pressing and curling that I turned it into a little business, a way to earn my own money in a house where cash was scarce. On Friday nights, I'd pack my bag with the hot comb and bobby pins and curling irons and begin making my way around to the homes of all the sisters in the church. My road show continued on Saturdays. Then on Sundays, I'd peer out across the sanctuary to see my handiwork on display, in pew after pew of fresh presses and pin curls.

Horace had convinced me I was cute, and my hot comb contributed to my vanity. I stayed by the bathroom mirror, running between there and the stove as I laid down my edges and pressed out my bangs. All that primping made me constantly late for class, because no way was I showing up at school with my hair all over the place. I had a different style for every day of the week, from deep waves on Monday to a chignon on Friday. I pressed the life out of my strands every morning, restoring them to order after I'd slept them into a mess the night before. Once when I strode into French class, tardy as usual, my teacher, Miss Byrnes, lifted an eyebrow. "Cicely, why can't you get here on time?" she asked. I pointed to my hair. "Well," she said, smirking, "one day that hair is going to put you on the top of the world." Neither of us could have known just how prescient she was.

My shyness began melting away during junior high and high school, but only a touch. In eighth grade, I served as secretary of the student body. I also auditioned for the class opera and was somehow chosen, but I sang so softly during rehearsals that I got fired because I was too reticent to project my voice. Even now, I find it impossible to speak from my core until I find a character's voice within myself. In high school, I was slightly more outgoing, thanks to Horace's loving perception of me. But even in my brief moments of extroversion, there lived a quiet, questioning girl inside. At one point during my teen years, I thought I'd become a psychologist because I was fascinated by people, by what made them do and say the things that they did. I wanted so badly to get inside their minds. But then, clutching a pressing comb, I gradually became more interested in what grew out of their pores. Everyone, including me, predicted that I'd become a professional hairdresser. This was years before acting got ahold of me—and boy, has *that* allowed me to get inside some heads!

Emily also earned her own money. Having inherited our mother's skill as a seamstress, she landed a job at a lingerie factory, sewing gorgeous and expensive slips, underwear, and bras. That's when our arguing began. I'd sneak into her bureau and pull out one of her lacy camisoles, tie it into a knot so it would fit me (or string a ribbon around my waist to cinch it up), and wear it beneath my clothes. After school, I'd race home to shove the camisole back in the drawer before Emily could discover it was missing. She usually caught me, and when she did, an explosion ensued. "Stay out of my things!" she'd yell. I'd smile and scamper off, with no intention of keeping my hands to myself. That lingerie was far too pretty to lie there unworn. Melrose worked as well, at any job he could hustle up on the streets. For a time, he had a job at a bagel shop, and in the evenings once his shift was done, he'd come through our apartment door carrying fresh-baked bagels, with an aroma tantalizing enough to pull us out of bed for a taste.

In addition to our side hustles, we of course had our chores. My job as resident window washer remained intact throughout my teens. Every weekend, I'd climb through each window opening and balance myself on the ledge, with no fire escape or guardrails to prevent me from toppling onto the pavement five floors below. Decades later when that building was named after me, I returned there and stared up at that window in disbelief. I still get chills thinking about all those Saturdays I risked my life in service of spotless glass. *Lord Jesus, how did I do it?* I could have easily fallen into an urban grave. God literally had my back, just as he does now.

My father still lived close by, and I saw him frequently. The year I was sixteen, my Aunt Zora, Dad's sister, hosted a party with her social lady friends and some family. Dad took me along. The two of us were off in a corner, catching up. He had his back up against a chest of drawers, with his arms loosely draped around me as he stood behind me. "Cicely," he said, "why don't you come over here?" I swiveled around and looked at him. "Dad, why are you talking to me like I'm on the other side of the room?" I asked. "Oh, so you think you're the only

Cicely in the world?" he said, laughing. He nodded toward a tall, elegant Black woman in a far corner. "That's the lady you're named after," he said.

As soon as I stepped through our apartment door that evening, I gave Mom the news. "I met my namesake today," I announced.

"What kind of foolishness you talking, child?" she said.

I told her about my father's confession. "I always knew I wasn't named after no little girl next door," I told her. "I just had a feeling."

Mom stared in my direction but did not speak. "Did you hear me?" I said. "I met the lady I was named after."

My mother remained silent. Even after she and my dad had separated, even after he'd raised his palm and bruised her spirit, she never spoke negatively of him to us, other than her occasional reminder that "Willie Tyson," as she always referred to him, had refused to accompany her to the hospital when I was born. Despite how my dad had hurt my mother, he was still our father, still the man she insisted we respect. When she did mention my dad's shortcomings, she usually did so indirectly, by folding in his transgressions with all those of his gender who'd been unfaithful. "These mens," she'd say in the plural. "They no damn good."

When I recounted the day's happenings for a third time, Mom leaned back in her rocker and uttered a phrase she used often. "You do well," she said, shaking her head. "You do well." That was her way of saying, "So you finally know something you didn't know, huh? Well good for you. What you're claiming might be true, but I'll never admit it." It was also her way of urging you past an uncomfortable conversation and back to the Land of Mute. You're dismissed. The end. A period and a closed subject. You do well—and you'd do best to move on.

Kenneth had been on my mother's approved list even before she'd seen him. He checked the only box that seemed to matter to her: he was the offspring of a reverend. At the party, when Kenneth had asked whether he could take me out, I'd agreed, knowing in my heart that he wasn't for me. He was respectful and attractive, but in his presence, I felt none of the magnetism that had pulled me toward Horace. That much I knew. All else, my mother would decide.

Urged on by Mom, Kenneth and I began officially seeing one another. One afternoon, he showed up, unannounced, for a visit. Because I hadn't been expecting him, I was wearing one of my mother's old housedresses. I'd also just unbraided my hair, and it was scattered all over my head. After Kenneth greeted me, I quickly excused myself to tidy up, feeling embarrassed that he'd seen me in such a state. When I returned, Emily had turned on the radio for our daily episode of *Amos 'n' Andy*. An announcer interrupted the program: "Pearl Harbor has been bombed," he said. I stared at Kenneth, who sat expressionless on the couch. "Did you hear that?" I asked him. "We're at war!" Kenneth looked straight ahead, his eyes dazed. "At war?" he finally said. He'd heard the announcer as clearly as I had, but the news didn't immediately sink in: the conflict overseas had at last thundered onto our shores.

Not long after, my personal world was likewise overturned. I don't remember everything about the day that permanently ended my childhood, that finished it off with a painful and lasting punctuation mark. The moments I do recall, many of them now dim and faded, unfolded in slow motion. It was late spring, toward the end of my junior year in 1942. With Mom's permission, I'd planned to see Kenneth at his apartment around four o'clock that afternoon, following school. "I want you home by seven," she said. I nodded and left.

This wasn't my first visit to Kenneth's place. Over the months, as he'd charmed my mother with his impeccable manners, with his "Ms. Tyson" this and his "Ms. Tyson" that, she'd been increasingly permissive of our spending time together on our own. I think she was more smitten with Kenneth than I'd ever likely be, in love with the idea of our possible future together. Our evening progressed pleasantly, like many others before: we sat on his living room sofa, talking about the news of the day and listening to the radio. After we'd been together for a while, I glanced at my watch: 6:20. "I have to go," I said, imagining the hell I'd catch if I returned home even one minute late. I pulled on my jacket and walked to the door. He followed me.

"Why do you have to leave so *soon*?" he said playfully, resting his hand over mine. "You should stay a little longer." I smiled and he slid my palm off the knob. He turned me around and pulled me toward him, my back resting against the door. He slowly unbuttoned my coat. He then gently began kissing me, first on my forehead, then on my neck, and finally on my lips. As our tongues intertwined, he pulled me even closer, pressing his aroused body into mine, running his palms along my breasts, breathing heavily with desire. Our caressing grew more intense and he lifted my dress. I recoiled slightly, but before I could back away, he was inside me. He immediately exploded.

With my thighs trembling, I looked at my watch again. It was 6:40. "I really do have to go now," I said, straightening my dress and rebuttoning my coat. As I grappled internally with what had just occurred, he and I said nothing, and I left. On the bus ride home, I replayed the scene in my head. *Did we just have sex? Is that what that was?* I honestly was not sure. Like my period and all other topics of a sensitive nature, Mom had never had a forthright conversation with me about intercourse.

I thought of the pregnant woman my friend Fannie Lou had pointed out on the street. *Was this how a baby got inside of her stomach?* Maybe, but I was not certain. I thought of a photo I'd once seen in a book of a naked couple having intercourse on a bed. *Kenneth and I couldn't have had sex*, I reasoned. *We were standing up with most of our clothes on.* And though I didn't fully understand the mechanics of sex, I did sense we'd done something my mother would have prohibited. Maybe this is what she'd meant when she'd told me, at age nine, "Stay away from the boys." A small part of me felt scared that perhaps we'd stumbled across a red line I hadn't known was there. But a much larger part of me exhaled, grateful that I'd stopped short of engaging in what I imagined sex to be—an act carried out horizontally. *Nothing could've happened*, I kept telling myself. *You cannot have intercourse standing up.* By the time I arrived home exactly at seven o'clock, I'd convinced myself I had nothing to be concerned about.

Nature had a different take. A few weeks later when my period went missing, Mom, fearing the likely but praying for the improbable, booked a doctor's appointment. After I'd been examined and given a pregnancy test, the doctor pulled my mother aside in the hallway. "Your daughter is pregnant," I heard him tell her through the half-open door. "She's probably almost a month along." *Silence.*

In the exam room, my heart hammered away in my chest as my brain raced. *Pregnant? How could I be pregnant? Kenneth and I didn't do anything for me to get pregnant. We didn't even lie down!* Mom returned to the room and stared at me, aware by my stone face that I'd overheard the doctor. A tear escaped down her cheek. "If only you'd waited," she whispered, her voice trembling. "And now, dear God, Willie Tyson is going to kill me for his child." After Mom and Dad had separated, my father had often said to her, "If anything bad ever happens to my Sis, I'll kill you." My circumstance, in the view of my religiously raised parents, indeed qualified as something bad. Their seventeen-year-old daughter, herself still a child in many ways, was going to become an unwed mother.

I sat numb in the cold exam room, vulnerable in my thin blue paper gown and sock feet. I could not comprehend what I'd just been told, just as Kenneth hadn't been able to process that our country was under attack. I'd heard the doctor. And yet the reality of what he'd said felt inconceivable to me, entirely surreal, as if he was talking to some other girl in some other life, while I simply listened in. I dressed as Mom waited in the lobby. Sitting side by side on the number 6 train toward home, neither of us spoke.

7

Ground Shifts

NEAR the close of my senior year, the principal called me to her office. "What is this?" she asked, holding up a folded paper. I instantly recognized it as an invitation to my daughter's christening and wondered how she'd gotten hold of it. I shrugged.

"So is it true?" she pressed. "Do you have a child, Cicely?"

Seeing no end run around the evidence, I nodded. "Yes," I whispered. "It's true."

She lowered the invitation and sighed. "Well then I'm sorry," she said, "but we cannot allow you to graduate from this school."

I stood there staring blankly at her, hoping she'd amend her ruling with an exception. But her judgment was final. Only four weeks before I was to receive my diploma, just one measly month before graduation, the secret I'd carried beneath my dress had now somehow made its way onto my principal's desk. And as a result, she and the school's administrative staff disregarded my whole senior year and made me repeat that coursework at the school's night program.

The year before, when I first learned that I was expecting, the resulting torrent of emotion nearly took me under. I was confounded about how I'd ever gotten into such a predicament and fearful about my path forward. Yet amid the confusion about how I'd become pregnant, amid the immense sadness I felt about how I'd let myself and my parents down, there emerged in me an unmitigated resolve: I would earn my diploma. That was, for me, as much a matter of practicality as it was of honor. I wanted to complete my course and stand proud at the finish line. If I had to keep my belly undercover in order to march across that graduation stage, I was determined to do so.

The concealment turned out to be effortless: I had no discernible baby bump at the start of my senior year, nor did I ever develop a large stomach. Before the pregnancy, I'd been a stick at five feet four inches and around ninety-seven pounds. Six months into gestation, my belly had grown only to the size of a small cantaloupe, one mostly unnoticeable beneath my clothes. My principal and teachers had no idea I was pregnant, nor did my classmates. My own mother could hardly tell. "That baby must be standing up inside of you," she'd often say. I wore the same A-line, button-down dress to school that fall as I wore to the hospital on the day I gave birth the following February. If Emily and Melrose noticed I was pregnant early on, they did not mention it, and frankly, I did not want to talk about it, did not want to acknowledge my shame aloud. Even once they eventually overheard the news from our mother, my sister and brother and I never discussed it. Their sorrowful gazes, from my eyes to my stomach and back to my eyes, said plenty.

When you get pregnant during adolescence, you grow up in the space of two minutes. In minute one, your feet are dangling from an exam table as you hold your breath and wait. In minute two, all wondering is replaced with reckoning, all equivocating with the definitiveness of the doctor's words. And in that instant, you are no longer a girl, wandering and curious and innocent. You are, by proof of a urine sample and by declaration of a physician, ushered to a doorway labeled "Parenthood." Through that entrance is an uncertain future, filled with adult anxieties and responsibilities. All at once, your center of gravity shifts from *me* to *us*. Your existence is no longer just about you, but rather about this defenseless child who will rely on your strength as a source for his or her own. That is the state I found myself in on the day of my appointment: half-clothed and glassy-eyed, seated at the corner of life as I'd known it and a frightening forever.

Upon learning I was pregnant, I spent two full weeks just trying to figure out how it had happened. Sex, as I'd misunderstood it, necessitated pleasure. What I'd experienced was the swift ascent of my hemline and a three-second burst of warm liquid. Years later, my friend Maya Angelou would describe her own pregnancy this way: "When I was sixteen, a boy in high school evinced interest in me, so I had sex with him, just once," she wrote. "And after I came out of that room, I thought, *Is that all there is to it? My goodness, I'll never do* that *again!*" Next thing she knew, she was expecting—which is precisely how I felt. I hadn't even lain down, for God's sake, much less experienced any kind of euphoria. I'd been cheated out of intimacy's pleasure ride, yet I was still required to pay its full entrance fee. That is what happens when parents think they're protecting their children by withholding the truth. They are in fact exposing them to heartache.

There was never any question I'd keep the child. In my family and church community, abortion was not even a thought or conversation. With that consideration off the table, I moved right along to the next: whether Kenneth and I would marry. In many ways, that question had also already been answered, because Mom had long since decided that Kenneth was the One for me.

The fact that he and I now had a child on the way simply accelerated that eventuality. Just as my mother had pressed me to go out with Kenneth, she likewise demanded that we marry that December. "I'm not signing any papers for you to marry before you're grown," she murmured. "We'll wait till you're eighteen."

When Maya had first told her mom she was expecting, her mother asked her calmly, "Do you love the boy . . . and does he love you?" When Maya answered no, her mother said, "Then there's no sense in ruining three lives." If only things had gone that way in the Tyson house. At the time, I experienced my mom's insistence that I marry Kenneth as an extension of her autocracy, her maintenance of a control she felt slipping away. Looking back on it, however, I recognize her behavior for what I believe it was: an attempt to redeem herself, as well as to redirect the plotline of our family's generational narrative.

"No unmarried daughter of mine is going to bring a child here," my mother said to me repeatedly. And yet her mother, Mary Jane, had done exactly that. She and my grandfather, Charles, were not married when they became intimate, and by the time Mary Jane discovered she was pregnant, Charles had been killed at sea, his fishing boat overturned by a violent storm near Nevis. Years later and a world away, my parents of course traded vows, and I'd always assumed they'd done so long before welcoming Melrose. Emily, who sat down one day and did the math, eventually steered me to the truth: my dad and mom married *after* conceiving my brother. And then, to my mother's heartbreak, her daughter had unknowingly repeated the very familial pattern she'd longed to end. I think now that my mom pressured me to marry not just to spare me a public disgrace, but as a penance for her own and her mother's choices. Her adamance was a kind of peace offering—a way to restore her purity in the eyes of a heavenly Father she felt she'd disappointed.

I don't remember Kenneth's reaction, or even my own, when I first told him I was pregnant. I'm sure I mumbled it and then devolved into tears, probably backing out of the room as he absorbed the news. My mother's conversation with the pastor, her confrontation of Kenneth, her declaration to him that we must wed—it all feels as illusory to me now as it did in the summer of 1942. Our spirits have a way of dulling the traumatic, of blunting painful memories to lessen their ache. I do recall that Kenneth wanted our child, however unexpected her arrival. I also remember that he never proposed to me. He didn't need to. Our future had been cemented on the evening he'd lifted my dress. Following my pregnancy, the only thing left to do was repent of our unholy act by embracing holy matrimony. I held both of us responsible for our situation, but truthfully, I blamed him more than I did myself. He hadn't exactly forced himself on me, but he had asserted his will in place of mine, let loose on the fertile ground of my ignorance. That is how I felt then. I see now that my perspective was my way of coping with a world upended for us both.

I wasn't there when my father heard about my pregnancy. That whole summer, I was so busy hiding from him, as well as from all of the nonsense I knew might occur, that I didn't know who was saying what—or whether Mom broached the topic with him. In an extended family as large as ours, where news spreads more easily than butter on hot cornbread, I knew he'd eventually hear it from someone. If Mom didn't tell him, one of his siblings or cousins certainly would, which is what happened. I managed to avoid seeing my father for the entirety of my pregnancy. Given that his previously frequent visits came to an abrupt end, it was clear he was avoiding me as much as I was him. Perhaps he was attempting to spare his heart the dagger that would eventually have to land.

My first trimester was excruciating. I did not suffer from morning sickness, yet I could not escape a burgeoning sense of remorse. My mother had her way of deepening my regret. Whenever we'd pass a department store window, she'd repeat the refrain she'd first spoken in the doctor's office. "If only you'd waited, Sis," she'd say, shaking her head as she eyed the ornate white gowns. "If you'd just waited." *If only you'd told me the truth*, I'd be thinking. For years, Mom had dreamed of hosting a big wedding for Emily and me. Yet she'd been so consumed with the notion of a day, of an elaborate one-time affair, that she'd neglected to explain the basic facts of life.

My eighteenth birthday arrived on December 19. Just after Christmas and just before the start of my last school term, Kenneth and I took our places at the altar for a small ceremony in our church. His father officiated. My own father did not attend. I learned later that Mom hadn't invited him, and if I'm honest, I was relieved he wasn't there, thankful to escape his mournful gaze. From the pews, a small group of our family members looked on and wept throughout the service. Everyone cried, tears of lament disguised as those of happiness. It felt more like a funeral than a wedding.

As I stood at the altar in my pale blue gown, my pregnant belly still hardly perceptible, I cried because I did not want to be married. It didn't matter that Kenneth loved me. It didn't matter that he was a respectable young man, which he was. He had not shirked his responsibility to me, to us, to our unborn child. He'd even welcomed our nuptials. And yet despite how he might've felt or behaved, plain and clear, I was not ready for the commitment. Repeating my vows felt like surrendering my freedom. Just as I was beginning to find out who I was, this marriage placed a chokehold on the discovery. With the exchange of our gold bands and the declaration by the reverend, I was no longer Cicely, the autonomous. I had become a wife, an underling to be commanded and shepherded.

The day after the wedding, I moved out of my mother's apartment and into Kenneth's place. Though I'd relocated, I never truly left Mom's home. Kenneth worked the night shift as a security guard. Since I was so close to delivering, my mother insisted I stay with her in the evenings. She wanted to keep close watch over me, just as she'd been doing since the day I was born.

One day in February after arriving at Mom's apartment, I felt unusually energetic. Powered by my burst of vigor, I cleaned her apartment from stem to stern, pulling down the drapes and pulling off the sheets, throwing everything in the bathtub so I could scrub it clean on the washboard. By the time my mother arrived home from work, I was wiped out. "I think I'll go home now," I told her. "Kenneth is off tonight." "No you can't go home now," she said, glancing at the clock. "It's after nine. It's too late for you to be out in the streets. You should stay here." Practically before she could complete that sentence, I was laid out on her bed.

A couple of hours later, I got up to use the bathroom. When I lumbered back to bed and groaned, Mom awakened. "What's the matter?" she asked.

"Well I have to pee," I told her, "but I can't seem to go."

She sat up. "Put on your clothes right now," she said. My sudden urge to clean and to nest, along with the inability to urinate, told her my labor could be imminent.

"For what?" I asked.

"I *said* put on your clothes," she snapped.

I did as she instructed, and moments later, we were out on a steep stretch of Lexington Avenue, trying to hail a taxi in snow that felt like it was up to our waists. On the icy uphill sidewalk, my mother slipped. There I was, with my pregnant belly and my freezing palms, struggling to pull her up off the ground. Once I did, we still could not find a cab. In the pitch black, we walked for the longest time before finally finding a ride to Metropolitan Hospital. We walked through the doors at 4 a.m.

Thus began the wait. Hour after hour, nurses paraded in and out of my room, checking to see how much I'd dilated, as I lay there, wishing I'd stayed home a while longer. Finally, at 6:30 that evening when my water broke, doctors began debating the best method of delivery. My birth canal was so tiny, they feared I'd be ruptured when the baby came out. "Let's cut her," I heard one of them say. That was my cue to faint. I regained consciousness just in time to see them taking my daughter out of me. Even before I saw her face, I heard her, because boy, she was already sucking away on that thumb! As the nurses stitched me up, the doctor laid my six-pound, three-ounce angel on my chest, her body warm, her head as bald as mine once had been, her heart pattering in sync with my own.

Upon hearing I was in labor, Kenneth scrambled from work to the hospital but didn't make it in time for our daughter's birth. When he did arrive, he came in holding a red tin can of celebratory chocolates, handing them to me with a kiss and then cradling our baby girl in the crease of his elbow. I stayed in the hospital for five days, with Kenneth at my side for much of it. Mom was there as well. "When you were born," she fondly recounted, "those nurses waited on me hand and foot for an entire week. It was the best Christmas I'd ever had because I didn't have to lift a finger to cook for anyone." As I lay there in bed, nursing my sweet newborn, I likewise relished the sacredness of the pause, the stillness at the start of this thrilling yet terrifying passageway.

Mom encouraged me to call my daughter Miriam, the name she'd wanted to give me. I instead gave her a name that I chose, and in these pages, I will call her Joan. Kenneth wanted us to take our daughter home by taxi, but I refused, knowing just how little money we had saved. He'd been working back-to-back shifts, socking away all he could for our family. Yet even with his diligence, we were barely making rent.

Soon after Kenneth and I brought Joan home, I finally saw my father. He stopped by our apartment when my husband was at work. One look at my dad's face told me that, without question, he'd known about the pregnancy for months. In his eyes, I noticed not a glimmer of judgment or reprimand, but one of recognition. His String Bean, his heartthrob, was no longer a baby girl but a mother herself. He never addressed my unwed pregnancy outright, abiding by the same rule of silence that had always governed our family. And surprisingly, he also never confronted Kenneth about getting me pregnant. I think my father was more sad than angry; the pain of the situation rendered him silent, not combative. On the evening of his visit, he just looked at me for a long moment, the unspoken truth permeating the air between us. "So what's her name?" he said, smiling and reaching for his first grandchild. "Joan," I said. Subject forever closed.

Two weeks after I'd given birth, I returned to school, my breasts heavy with milk, my resolve to graduate undiminished. By day, I kept my head in a math textbook while Kenneth cared for Joan, until I could race home during my lunch break to nurse her. I'd then pump fresh milk to leave for her in the refrigerator. As soon as the last bell of the school day sounded, I was out the door again, eager to get home to my sweetheart as Kenneth prepared to leave for work. I continued that routine for weeks, until the afternoon in May when my principal cut short my momentum with her discovery.

I hadn't planned to christen my daughter right away. I wanted to wait until summer, after my schooling was complete. But of course, my mother replaced my desire with her mandate: Joan would be dedicated during a service at our church that May. My mother planned the whole ceremony and even mailed out the invitations, one of which landed in the hands of a woman my father had previously had an affair with. That woman's son happened to be a fellow student in my science class. He'd been the one to disclose my secret to the principal.

On the day I was summoned to her office, it made no difference that I stood within shouting distance of my diploma. What mattered was the school's strict policy: students were not permitted to indulge in what was considered adult behavior. I'm sure some of my classmates were sexually active, but the proof was in the pregnancy. And once it was revealed that I was a mother, that revelation immediately revoked my status as a student and made that year's credits null and void. Devastating as this news was, I felt undeterred in my quest to earn my diploma.

For me, those months were the most painful of my young motherhood. The night campus was all the way down on Eighteenth Street, an hour's ride by train. As much as I yearned to move beyond my mother's rule, I was also desperate for her help, especially since Kenneth worked nights. Together, he and I decided that Mom would watch Joan in the evenings while I attended classes.

In the fall of 1943, when Joan was about seven months old, our grand rotation commenced. I took a job as a part-time clerk, working from 9 a.m. to 2 p.m. while Kenneth cared for our daughter. I'd then hurry home to feed and change her before carrying her off to my mother's apartment, where she'd stay until I returned in the late evening. The moment I walked through the door, Joan would begin wailing for me, her arms outstretched from the edge of her crib. How agonizing it was for me to be away from my baby, to hear her weeping when I returned, to see her little face flooded with tears. It is why I often now tell young people to slow down and think, to use protection, to consider what's involved when you bring a human being into this world. It is a heartbreaking thing for children to have children. These kids, they just go off and have babies, and they have no idea of the commitment involved, how their paths will be as irrevocably altered as mine was. Until you are standing in the responsibility of parenting, you cannot truly understand how it shifts your life's terrain.

At the close of 1943, I earned my diploma. My precious Joan was nearly a year old, with a full head of thick hair and a laugh that melted me. I had a child I cherished in a life I never planned on. And by God—and by perseverance—I had completed high school.

As Kenneth and I settled into married life, a road of tedium and regret stretched before me. And when I peered ahead at that path, extending miles into the distance, I felt an enormous urge to retch. The ending to my life story, it seemed, had already been written, before I'd even had a chance to live it. I hadn't ever been in love with Kenneth. Our union did nothing to change that. In fact, I had no desire to be married, period, and I'm sure he could feel that. My resentment pervaded our every exchange, spilled over into the long bouts of silence between us. I wanted to do right by our daughter, as well as to be respectful of my husband and our vows. And yet the thought of pretending, of living out my mother's dream instead of discovering my own, felt utterly soul-destroying.

When Joan was two years old, I left Kenneth. And following the afternoon I cleared out of the apartment, I never saw him again. He of course called over to my mother's place, looking for me, desperate to know how he could mend whatever was broken between us. I'm sure she must've told him what my actions had made apparent: I was done.

Ahead of my departure, I did not tell Kenneth I was leaving the marriage. I knew it would shatter him, and it did. Yet it was a choice I felt strongly I needed to make, and if I'd told him, he would've tried to dissuade me. We did speak by phone after I left, and he pleaded for me to reconsider, begged me to allow him to remain part of our daughter's world. But I was firm in my decision that we separate entirely. Kenneth was a good man, but it wouldn't have done either of us a favor for me to languish in a relationship my spirit could not take. Maya Angelou's mother had it right: I would've ruined three lives.

Even as I fled, I knew I was trading one metaphorical prison for another. With no place else to go, I had to return to my mother's apartment. I could not yet stand on my own financial feet, and to Mom's credit, she graciously welcomed me back. But once that short honeymoon wore off, we began clashing. She wanted to do things her way, to raise Joan as she saw best. And I, newly emboldened by my role as mother and head of my family, resisted her domination. Yet because I relied on Mom to look after Joan while I worked, there was only so much arguing I could do. That left me seething internally.

Our family doctor recognized my rising blood pressure and mounting stress and mentioned it to my father. "Cicely is going to have a nervous breakdown if she stays in that house," he told my dad. "You need to get her out of there." After I'd been with Mom for two years, Dad heeded the doctor's warning and moved me in with his sister, my Aunt Zora, in Mount Vernon.

Between my aunt and other nearby family, my village rose up to help me care for Joan while I pieced together a living for us.

On the weekends or anytime I could manage to get off work, I took my daughter everywhere with me, wheeling her around in the carriage I'd splurged on. In the newspapers, I'd seen images of well-to-do London mothers with their fancy buggies, complete with oversized hoods. Though such strollers became scarce during wartime, I would not rest until I hunted down a used one. My determination was not about necessity. It was about gifting my beloved princess with royal treatment—the same sense of nobility and worth my parents had bestowed upon me.

When Joan was around four years old, I began work as a legal secretary at Sapinsley & Lucas, a law firm at 551 Fifth Avenue. The following year, when she was old enough for kindergarten, I enrolled her in the Little Brown Schoolhouse, a small private school in the Bronx founded by Helen Meade. I could not truly afford it, but I worked overtime and took on side jobs, emptying my financial cupboards in order to cover the cost. I wanted the comfort of knowing my daughter was in excellent hands, that she'd receive an education superior to my own. Nearly all parents I know can sum up their aspirations for their children in one word: *better.* That is what my mom and dad wanted for me, Emily, and Melrose when they eked out a life for us in the slums, and it is what I wanted for Joan. It is why I rose before sunup to prepare her for school and walked with her, our fingers intertwined, to the bus stop. It's why I worked steadfastly to keep her in that school.

The notion of *better* was the bedrock for my every choice during Joan's earliest years. From the time she was a baby and into her toddlerhood, I treated her like a real-life doll, decking her out in frilly dresses, doting over her as my father had me. No item was too luxurious for my princess, no bedtime story spared. In the land of make-believe child rearing, that world of pretend parenting ever on display in the media landscape, dressing Joan up was my way of being the Good Mom, the ever-present and adoring nurturer. I realize now that it was also my attempt at atoning, of blotting out my past choices with the fresh ink of redemption, just as my own mother had sought to do.

8

Divinely Guided

I AM a firm believer in divine guidance. Above all, I am God's child, cradled in his unfailing arms, guided by his infinite wisdom. Everything that is happening in my life is unfolding exactly as God has intended. There are no coincidences. Rather, there is a loving Savior who holds my future as securely as he does my life, and at every juncture, he is whispering his will, showing me the way. In 1954, the year I turned thirty, I followed the Father's voice down a path that both thrilled and unnerved me.

Much on the planet had changed by then. The winter after I had Joan, the Second World War raged on overseas, with Allied forces eventually knocking the opposition to its knees during the Battle of Stalingrad in 1943. That same year, the Tuskegee Airmen, the all-Black group of pilots who defied Air Force leaders' belief that Blacks were intellectually incapable of becoming aviators, bravely flew their first combat mission in Italy. Here in the United States during that era, the color line showed the slightest sign of fading: in 1944, Reverend Adam Clayton Powell Jr., then the pastor of Abyssinian Baptist Church, became the first Black from New York elected to Congress, standing tall for his Harlem community in the House of Representatives. Then in 1947, Jackie Robinson scored a home run for history when he joined the Brooklyn Dodgers as the first Black athlete to play in Major League Baseball. Full equality for our folks was still way off in the distance, but if you squinted real hard, you could see it taking shape.

My family had likewise shifted. After Emily finished high school, she'd kept one toe under the roof of our mother and another out on the town with suitors. Her godmother, Miss Cole, eventually introduced her to Reginald, a young man whose family hailed from Nevis. One afternoon when Reggie stopped in to see Miss Cole's niece, whom he had taken out a few times, he spotted Emily's picture on the wall. "Who is this young lady?" he asked. "That's my goddaughter, Emily Tyson," she said proudly. Noting his salivation, Miss Cole arranged for the two to meet, and I was there on the evening of Reggie's visit. *Knock. Knock. Knock.* "Who is it?" I called out, grinning across the living room at Mom and Emily, who already knew, courtesy of Miss Cole, that Reggie would come calling. "It is I, Reginald," he announced in his most proper, put-on-a-show English. I opened the door and in he strode, shoulders square, beret cocked to the left. Lord, have mercy, it was the funniest sight. It took all my might to squelch a snicker.

Next thing I knew, Miss Cole's niece had gone the way of all flesh as Emily, the charmer that our father had been, swept in and took over Reggie's heart. They courted for a year or so and married. I served as Emily's maid of honor, as well as the resident hairdresser who styled the manes of the entire wedding party. I also designed the bridesmaids' gowns. As Reggie and my sister spoke their promises before a congregation of more than a hundred, my mother's countenance radiated joy: she had her fairy tale. At last, she had a daughter who'd done things the right way—*her* way.

No one in our family would've predicted that Emily, with her fresh self, would turn out to be the Good Daughter, the wholesome one, the girl who married before bringing my mother her grandbabies in God's time. There at the altar, by her side, I stood balancing my sister's bouquet, forcing a smile for her sake while shoving down my sadness. However naive I'd been in becoming a teenage mother, however ill-equipped Mom's silence had ensured I was, however enraptured I felt by the miracle of Joan, a part of me still mourned falling shy of my mother's great hope for me. My spirit longed to give her the storybook ending she had craved, the fantasy Emily was now handing to her. We are our mothers' children, every one of us. And that umbilical cord connection makes you and me, in ways unconscious and profound, their dream keepers. Though I'd done so unintentionally, I'd allowed my mother's dream, delicate and treasured, to slip from my grasp and shatter at her feet. The fact that we never spoke forthrightly about her disappointment, never dragged that truth out onto the scaffold of our relationship and stood there with it, in no way diminished the pain of its existence for me.

Emily's husband, Reggie, was no minister's son. But after the precedent I'd set, Mom had revised her expectations to include *any* respectable Christian gentleman, whether or not his father was a man of the cloth. Like my father, Reggie earned his living as a produce salesman, overseeing a thriving business selling watermelons door to door. In the summers, Reggie would load his truck with a crop and drive up and down the boulevards of Harlem and the Bronx, scouring for customers while yelling, "Fifteen cents a melon!" So admirable was his ambition that it once drew the notice of a prominent businessman, who stopped by to make a purchase. After Reggie had talked his new customer into buying not one melon but three, the man offered Reggie his card. "Why don't you give me a call sometime?" he said. As it turned out, the man was one of the owners of Filter Queen, a burgeoning vacuum-cleaner company. "You seem like quite a salesman," he told Reggie. "How would you like to sell some vacuums?" "Sir," Reggie said, straightening his posture, "I can sell *anything*." Less than a year later, Reggie had become a top-earning salesman. He did so well that he and Emily traded their apartment in the city for a home in Mount Vernon. She lived close to our Aunt Zora, making herself and my brother-in-law part of my village in rearing Joan.

By the early 1950s, my brother had also settled into a new season. During high school, Melrose had been expelled for fighting and sent to a campus for troubled boys. With the same clenched jaw that powered me through my studies, my brother earned his diploma. Soon after, he moved to Montclair, near our cousins there, and he eventually married a lovely woman by the name of Bernice. For years, Melrose earned a living as a clerk for the post office. If there'd been an award for penmanship, Melrose would have garnered the gold: he had the most gorgeous cursive I've ever set eyes on, with each loop and swirl gracefully rendered. Just as no one would've pegged Emily as the Tyson traditionalist, few would've foreseen that my brother, a restless soul of the streets, would grow into an impeccable scribe. For that matter, only God could've foretold that I, the gullible girl with no idea how periods and pregnancies were connected, would become an unwed mom. I tell you, this life doesn't simply come with its share of unpredictability; surprise is its most conspicuous feature.

Joan sprouted up fast. In those years, I marked time by how well my darling grew. Her care became my singular priority, my all-consuming point of reference. Blurry-eyed and breathless, I sprinted from one daybreak to the next, scrambling to keep the paychecks coming and Joan's tuition covered. During back-to-back shifts at various clerical jobs, I kept my fingertips glued to a typewriter, click-clacking my way to solvency. Late every evening, I'd then crawl my way back to my aunt's place and tiptoe into Joan's bedroom, sitting at her side, witnessing her lost in her dream world, watching her chest rise and fall. Before turning in myself, I'd lay out Joan's clothes and prepare her lunch for the next day. Such was my life's tempo until the year Joan was nine—the year when my dear aunt craved a respite and I, reluctant yet clear that I needed consistent child care, returned to Mom's place and purview.

I truly did not want to move back in with my mother. And yet the heavenly Father, in his omniscience, obviously saw fit to keep drawing us together, perhaps because he knew I had some spiritual business to complete. When you ask God for strength, as I do daily, he doesn't usually just drop it from the sky. He often answers by placing you in a circumstance that requires you to build fortitude while relying solely on him. Motherhood had thrust me into adulthood prematurely, and yet emotionally, even by my late twenties, I was still a child in some ways—still a girl guided by the rise and fall of my mother's brow, by her approval and displeasure. While living with my aunt, I towered in my sense of autonomy, wrapped myself tight in the cloak of my position as an independent parent. But back in my mother's apartment, I found myself regressing into the voicelessness of my earliest years, cowering beneath the reign of the woman who'd always steered me. By voiceless, I do not mean mute. I bickered weekly with my mother, railed against her rule more than I dared to during childhood. I see now that I wasn't fighting against her, but for myself. Defying her voice was my way of making space for my own, however feeble and uncertain. At the heart of our disputes lived my struggle for womanhood, my yearning to trust God's whispers and tune out all others.

A year after I'd been with my mother, the Father's whisper crescendoed into a shout. After work late one evening, I returned home to find Joan out on the street in front of the apartment, hop-scotching with another girl from the block. I peered around. On one shadowy corner sat a row of old men, slamming down dominoes on a fold-up table and swigging beer. Across from there, a group of women balanced themselves on crates, cackling and carrying on as a radio blared. I then looked up. There, near the top floor of our building, my mother sat on the ledge of her apartment's window sill, gazing down at the scene. I glanced at my watch: 10 p.m. *What on earth is my child still doing up?* I approached Joan, who skipped over into my arms when she spotted me.

"What are you doing out here at this hour?" I asked her.

She smiled. "Playing," she said, oblivious to the worry on my face.

"Do you know what time it is?" I said. "You have to go to school in the morning."

Upstairs, my mother had no reasonable explanation for why she'd allowed Joan to linger in the streets. "Mom, why is this baby outdoors so late?" I asked, my voice rising by the syllable. She shrugged. "Don't come in here fussing," she snapped. "I had my eye on that girl all evening. I could see her from where I was sitting."

Joan was ten at the time. When I was that age, the earth would've had to topple off its axis for my mother to allow me outdoors after dark. *What was she thinking?* I did not know. The one reason I conjured had to do with my tense dynamic with Mom since I'd returned to live with her. Our disputes were vociferous and constant. In fact, that very week, we'd had a doozy of a quarrel. I cannot recall what triggered the clash, probably because it wounded me so. *Our strife must be spilling over into her treatment of Joan*, I thought. Or maybe, after raising her own three children, Mom had understandably grown weary with caretaking. Whatever had prompted her strange behavior, I knew our arrangement had to end. I did not discuss this with my mother, nor did I ask for her opinion. I simply made a grown-up decision, one markedly absent of her input: I would secure my baby's care. I didn't know how I would do so, but I was convinced that I must.

The next morning, I began researching boarding schools. With the fifty- and sixty-hour workweeks I was clocking, I knew I could not be there for my daughter in the way that I wanted, the way countless working mothers long to be. And yet if I was going to partner with others in caring for Joan, I had to be sure I could trust the palms I placed her in. When you don't know what to do, you do what you know—and all of my life, I'd been taught to trust those guided by the same God who led me. That is why, when my eyes fell on an advertisement for a Christian boarding school in upstate New York, I immediately became interested. Upon calling, I learned that the school was run by a minister and his wife, a couple who once had presided over a church in Harlem.

The next week, I traveled to meet the couple. I toured the middle-school campus, talked with some of the teachers and students, and inspected the all-girl dormitories. My spirit said yes. But you can never be too careful when it comes to your child, your treasure, which is why, weeks later, I visited again, to be sure all was in order. I returned home carrying both a greater sense of certainty that this was the right place for Joan and a financial arrangement with the school that put the cost within reach for me.

When I revealed my plan to my mother, with nary a stutter as I spoke, she of course protested. "Why are you taking that child up there?" she pressed. I stared at her but felt no urge to explain, no desire to reveal how her behavior had prompted my choice. I knew what I had to do, and nothing she could say would unbutton my resolve. I would stay on with my mother and continue working in the city, I told her, but Joan's care could not be compromised. That was that. In the fall of 1953, at the start of my daughter's fifth-grade year, I packed her belongings and took the train with her upstate.

Joan was more excited than hesitant about her adventure. But that changed the farther north we rode. An hour into our journey, she folded her palm into mine and leaned in to my shoulder. "Mommy, why can't you come with me?" she asked. I squeezed her hand. "Sweetie," I whispered, "I promise I will visit you as often as I can. But Mommy has to work." How do you explain to your daughter, the center of your existence, why you must separate from her? How do you tell a child, one you love to the stars and beyond, that a long stretch of sunrises will live between you? You don't. In place of clarifying, you weep inside, your lips trembling as towns and pine trees and colors blur by your train-car window. You wish it did not have to be, this distance between your worlds. You cringe as you hear your baby's plea and grip her hand more tightly.

And yet you know. You know with the same immutable assurance that rose up in me on the day I walked away from my marriage. By all outward appearances, there was a decision to be made, a lever to be pulled: stay or go. But inwardly, the only true choice for me was onward. I understood that to my core, knew it with the same certainty I'd once known our neighbor's apartment would go up in flames, knew it as surely as I know there is a Creator. And yet the truth, however irrefutable it is, does not spare its pursuer the accompanying anguish. On that fall afternoon when I waved goodbye to my child, the red-orange leaves above us lowering their heads in lament, every part of me ached.

I kept my promise to visit frequently. In the following months, I traveled north any time I could yank my fingers away from my typewriter. I also brought Joan home for spring break and holidays and sometimes on weekends. I missed her as much as I knew I would, multiplied by far more than that. Whenever Joan was in the city with me, I whisked my angel around town, loading up shopping bags with more dresses and shoes and coats than my checking account could bear. Our eventual partings, our eyelids brimming with sadness and adoration, were no less excruciating than the first had been. That year of long division flowed seamlessly into 1954, the year I turned thirty and was still living with my mother, still finding my way. That's when God cleared his voice and again spoke. His message, undeniable in its clarity, penetrating in its delivery, came in several spine-tingling installments.

9

Shoulder Taps

SHOW me a West Indian woman, and I'll show you an enterpriser holding down three jobs. Years before the arts swept me up in its gale winds, I strung together a living by adding multiple side gigs to my main one. I wielded my hot comb all over the five boroughs, leaving a trail of charred scalps in my wake. After my primary job at the law firm was finished each day, I staggered over to my second gig, what was then known as a typing pool: a group of work-for-hire secretaries who transcribed shorthand notes for (male) executives who did not have their own administrative staffs. I worked nights.

Typing pools were not for the feeble. In a cavernous warehouse space, row after row of ambitious young women, with their tie-neck blouses and ruler-straight postures, swiftly churned out documents on mammoth Imperial typewriters. Just to break into most pools, you had to accurately type eighty words per minute. Repeated mistakes, which cost the employer both time and paper in a world still absent of correction fluid, could get you dismissed. I can still feel the brush of my fingertips against the cold steel keys, can hear the cacophony of taps and dings wafting to the ceiling. I'd thankfully mastered both stenography and shorthand in high school, and by graduation, I could deliver pristine copy at one hundred words per minute.

Aside from that graveyard shift, I rounded up scores of other jobs over the years. One summer, I worked as a transcriptionist for Save the Children. The next, I took a spot on the assembly line of a nail factory. Toward the end of the war, I was hired as a secretary inside the Navy Purchasing office, a sprawling edifice at 90 Church Street. That job put a spring in my father's gait.

"After you finish high school," Dad would often tell me when I was a youngster, "I want you to go to work in one of those tall buildings downtown." Mind you, he did not care what position I held. My mere presence in a soaring structure, one representing upward mobility, was accomplishment enough for him. In his mind, earning a living in a skyscraper where few Blacks were ever spotted meant I'd made it, that his offspring had fared better than he could've when he arrived in America, empty-handed and hopeful. On the day I landed the job, I called him. "Well Dad," I said, "you got your wish. I'm in one of those tall buildings downtown." That week, he took the number 6 train south to see it for himself. Arm in arm, the two of us stood together on the sidewalk, gazing up in awe. He looked over at me, then skyward again, and then back at me. "Congratulations, String Bean," he said, planting a kiss on my cheek as he beamed.

The year Joan went to boarding school, I renewed my search for temporary gigs I could fit around my position at the law firm. In those days, everyone at the employment office of the Urban League in Harlem knew me by name; I was in that office more than I was in my mother's apartment. One afternoon, I pranced in, my short hair freshly pressed and precisely styled. Audrey Hepburn, with her pixie cut and her delicate pearl earrings, was the golden girl to mimic in that era, and my family, noting my take on the icon's cut, began calling me the Black Audrey. Even strangers would often proclaim, "Oh, you look just like Audrey Hepburn." Not quite, but I embraced the compliment.

"What kind of position are you looking for?" asked a young woman I hadn't yet met.

"Anything," I said.

"How fast can you type?" she asked.

"Over a hundred words a minute," I said.

She nodded approvingly, picked up the receiver on her phone, and dialed one of her contacts. Afterward, she scribbled something on a sheet of paper and handed it to me. "Go here," she said. I eyed three words at the top of the paper—American Red Cross—with the address, in Midtown near Thirty-Eighth and Lexington, scrawled beneath. That afternoon, I was hired as a fill-in secretary to the vice president, Ms. Ruben. The part-time position, which involved typing case histories for the organization, eventually morphed into full-time work. It also became the vehicle for God's strong tap on my shoulder.

It was 1954. I'd been at the Red Cross for about a year when Ms. Johnson, a sweet older Black woman who sat three feet from me in the office, retired. She'd spent most of her career at the company, hunched over a typewriter, producing hundreds of case histories. A farewell party was organized, complete with a sheet cake and well wishes from those who'd worked with her. Ms. Johnson's longtime supervisor gave a sentimental speech about how much she loved this woman, how noble her service had been over many decades. As she closed, dabbing at her eyes with a white hankie, she presented Ms. Johnson with a parting gift: a gold wristwatch. Everyone around me clapped. I did not. I stood there feeling dumbfounded, observing all the tears and grins and applause while a thought gripped me: *A watch? You mean she spent nearly all her adult life in this place, and all she gets is a measly watch?* It seemed absolutely pitiful to me. It also seemed like an opinion best kept to myself.

Which is why, later that afternoon when my perspective came sputtering forth, it stunned me. As Ms. Johnson said her final goodbyes around the office, the rest of us clerks settled back at our typewriters, eyeing the wall clock to calculate the number of click-clacks till quitting time. That's when, seemingly out of nowhere, a proclamation tumbled out of my mouth. "I'll tell you one thing," I said loudly enough for everyone to hear. "I'm not gonna be any place for no thirty years until somebody hands me a wristwatch and says, 'Thank you very much.' I'll *buy* myself a watch." *Silence.* If a strand of my hair had fallen to the carpet, you would have heard it. That's how quiet that room got.

Two of my co-workers glanced over at me and another giggled nervously, peering around to see whether our boss had heard me. The girl closest to me stared at me like I'd plumb lost it. In a sense, I suppose I had. As life has taught me time and again, you often have to lose your present circumstance to make room for your forthcoming one. A moment later, I went back to typing even as the sentiment lingered. *I'm never going to be in Ms. Johnson's position*, I said to myself. *Not me.* Some might call it a thought, or perhaps a quiet resolve. I firmly believe it was the voice of God, presenting itself in the form of my own instinct.

Leading up to that declaration, God had already planted a seed. For months, I'd been feeling an increasing sense of dissatisfaction, an uneasiness born of the query buried in the bosom of all humanity: *Is this all there is?* That question had been gnawing at me for quite some time. The party, and the gift to Ms. Johnson, simply prompted its expression. To be clear, there is nothing disgraceful about how this woman had chosen to spend her working years. For all I knew, Ms. Johnson had fulfilled her grand vision for herself in a perfectly honorable pursuit. When she'd entered the workforce in the 1920s, this sister would've been considered quite fortunate to have office work, never mind a job steady enough to sustain her through the Depression and beyond. And yet I had a powerful sense that my journey would be less stationary and more adventure-filled, that it would wind and bob its way through a landscape devoid of steno pads and number-two pencils. I couldn't imagine spending decades at a desk, all for someone to congratulate me, in the end, with a watch from a department store. My life, my service, my time—they were worth far more to me than a hundred-dollar timepiece.

Not long after, that feeling intensified. I was given a new case history to transcribe, one involving a young Black wife and mother. In her consultation with my supervisor, the woman confided that her husband was having sex with their eight-year-old daughter. When I got to that line, I stopped typing and picked up the paper, rereading and praying I'd seen it wrong. I hadn't. "Why didn't you report him?" Ms. Ruben had asked the mother. Her answer still sends a shiver through me: "I was afraid he would lose his job," she had said.

I'll tell you, I was no good for the rest of that week. *Your child is being molested by her father, and you won't go to the authorities because you're scared he'll be fired?* It sickened me to my core. It also served as a painful reminder of what it meant, and still often means, to be Black in this country. So precarious has our financial position been that too many of us have been forced to choose between economic security and safety for our children. Even now, all these years later, recalling that transcript makes me want to retch. No way could I, year after year, bear witness to such agony, memorializing heartache with ink-stained iron keystrokes. After typing up the full case that afternoon, I pushed myself back from the desk and made another major proclamation. "I am sure God didn't put me on the face of this earth to bang on a typewriter for the rest of my life," I said. "There is something else for me to do. I don't know what it is, but I will find it." From my lips to God's ears—or, as I see it now, the other way around.

The next week, I received another love note from heaven. During my lunchtime, I shot out of the office and headed straight for nearby Lord & Taylor. Oh, how I loved that department store! During the holidays, its windows along Fifth Avenue featured the most breathtaking Christmas displays, lavish and sparkling, casting a spell and glow over the entire block. Admirers traveled from all parts of the globe just to stand before those windows in all their twinkling glory. I frankly had little business in a store, given what I earned, but that never stopped me from roaming the aisles, dreaming about a new pocketbook or a scarf for Joan. It broke my heart when, decades later in 2019, the store closed its doors after a century in business. Anyway, on that day, I flounced out to shop, feeling attractive in my wraparound pinstripe dress and patent-leather pumps, eager for my midday routine. What happened next was anything but.

Just as I was rounding the corner onto Fifth Avenue, a Black man decked out in a business suit and a scarlet bowtie tapped me on the shoulder. I swiveled around.

"Excuse me, Miss," he said, "are you a model?"

"No," I said, searching his face for where this was going.

"Well if you aren't," he said, "you should be."

I blushed, not sure how to respond. I never saw myself as beautiful. My first crush, Horace, had convinced me I was somewhat cute, at least in his eyes, but beyond that, I thought I was plain. When it came to appearance, what I felt certain about was my ability to *dress*, thanks to the elite fashion education afforded to me by my parents, known in our church as Mr. and

Mrs. Beau Brummell. Stylish? Yes, darling, and please pass me my mink stole. Slender? Absolutely. But beautiful? That label did not live at the heart of my self-identity. In the view of whites in this country, one's Blackness—characterized by the tiniest drop of melanin or the faintest trace of a Negroid feature—has historically nullified one's gorgeousness. And yet despite that, others always seemed to be telling me I was pretty, particularly in my twenties as I grew out of my lankiness and into my face and figure. So when this stranger stopped me on the street, the surprise wasn't just that he thought I was attractive. It was that he nudged me toward a universe that was foreign to me.

"How do you go about becoming a model?" I asked him.

"You connect with an agent and you go to modeling school," he explained. "Once you've finished your training, the agent sends you out on interviews for jobs." He paused and looked me up and down, as if to be sure his original assessment had been accurate. "You really should give it a shot," he said. I smiled, politely thanked him, and went on about my way to the store.

I initially disregarded the stranger's comments. *Me, a model?* The idea seemed outlandish, given that I was almost thirty years old and presumably well past a model's prime time. And yet our conversation curled up in my spirit, the way certain notions do when they're set on residing permanently. And right alongside that *hmmm* was the feeling I'd been grappling with, the sense that my work as a secretary was not the end of the career road for me, but rather a milestone along an alternate route. So acute was this feeling that one week after that businessman stopped me on the sidewalk, I pulled out the Yellow Pages. I flipped to the section labeled "Modeling Schools" and scanned the list of agencies. All of them, based on the names and locations, seemed headed by white folks. *They're not going to take me for no modeling job anyhow*, I thought. I slammed the book shut.

Yet I continued to ponder the idea and even mentioned it to my longtime friend Thelma Jack. The two of us had met years earlier during our young teens at a summer camp upstate. Thelma's face lit up when I told her what the man had proposed. "You know, there's a woman in Harlem who runs a modeling school," she told me. "Her name is Barbara Watson. She's the daughter of Judge Watson"—as in James S. Watson, the first Black judge elected in New York City, and husband to Violet Lopez Watson, a founding member, along with Dr. Mary McLeod Bethune, of the National Council of Negro Women. In 1946, Barbara Mae Watson, the eldest of four, founded the first agency for African-American models. Emboldened by my friend's encouragement, and armed with this fresh data, I called the school. Ms. Watson herself answered. I stammered my way through a conversation, and she saved me from my bluster with a concluding request: "Why don't you come in for an interview?"

I got right to work on preparing. I may have known nothing about a catwalk, but I was confident I could put on a fashion show, one I prayed would impress this well-spoken, Barnard-educated lady who'd been gracious enough to invite me in. My favorite color was light blue, and my closet teemed with the hue: blue tea-length hoop skirts, blue pocketbooks, blue everything. Years later, I grew into purple, but it never stole blue's spotlight. "Don't you know any other color?" my mother would ask me. I never wearied of its soothing quality, its ability to transport me to a wide-sky, cloud-dappled tranquility.

So for my inaugural meeting with Ms. Watson, I of course fished out my finest powder-blue cotton dress, one gathered at the waist, with a row of glistening gold buttons stretching down its left side. I completed the look with black suede pumps and silk thigh-high stockings, minus garters. Like many working-class West Indian women, I secured each stocking with a top knot tight enough to cut off one's circulation. I was blessed to even have silk nylons. During the war, silk and other commodities had run in short supply, and as a result, nylon repair shops sprang up. My spot was a little cleaners in a basement, around the corner from the Red Cross. Before my interview, I took my nylons there, and child, once they fixed my two runs for five cents each, those stockings looked brand new. People then took such pride in their workmanship.

On the day I stepped my suede toe over Ms. Watson's threshold, I strutted in like I was working a Paris runway. She scanned my outfit, smiled, and offered me a seat.

"So have you done any modeling at all, Miss Cicely?" she asked.

"No, ma'am, I have not," I said, carefully pronouncing each word.

"I see," she said. She then asked me a few questions about my background, as well as how I'd learned about the agency. I gave her the short story as she jotted down notes on an intake form. "Well," she finally said, leaning back in her seat and laying down her pen, "what would you think about having some photos taken?"

I nodded. "That would be, I mean . . . yes, Miss," I said, trying to contain my glee.

"Excellent," she said, standing up to show me out to the lobby. "And in the meantime, I hope you'll sign up for our course."

Nearly before she'd completed that sentence, I'd enrolled. The evening course, which included about twenty-five women, spanned several weeks. Ms. Watson taught us the fundamentals of charm and poise: how to perfect our postures, how to hold our bodies as we glided across a room with effortlessly supple movement, how to pose for photographers, how to pivot and curtsy and smile. At five-feet-four-inches tall, I wasn't runway material, so I kept my ears widest for the catalog and magazine model training. Meanwhile, I began work on my portfolio. I arranged for a photographer to take three images of me: a head shot in a (navy) suit, a body shot in a (baby blue) dress, and a swimsuit shot in a (teal) two-piece suit. The latter was quite modest—nothing like today's dental-floss bikinis that leave one's derriere hanging out. If I'd been required to don such a suit, this church girl would've ended her modeling career before it began. But I was comfortable in my portfolio bikini, one cut just below the navel—and one just like those I wore to the beach.

Once I'd received the photos, I scheduled a session with Ms. Watson to show her the spread. Her business partner, Mildred Smith—who also served as an editor at *Our World* magazine, a lifestyle publication catering to Black women—attended the meeting. The two looked through my photos, closely studying each. Neither said a word. "Can you please give us a few moments to speak?" Ms. Watson finally said. "Yes, of course," I said, my heart hammering away in my chest. The women then stepped off to the side and out of my earshot—likely so they could decide how to run me out of that office, I feared.

After what felt like hours but was probably three minutes, they turned to me. "So how many copies did you have made of each of these photos?" Ms. Watson asked.

"Well I didn't know what you would expect," I said, "so I just got a few."

"Well," she said, "we'd like to order a few hundred more on your behalf."

I gulped. "Really?" I said, my eyes widening.

"Yes, really," she said, smiling.

While I'd decided I was about to be banished from modeling schools the world over, the women had been discussing my strategic launch: how to saturate the market with my photos. In my class of potential models, only two were ultimately chosen. I, daughter of a housekeeper, child of the Most High, was astoundingly one of them.

I did not resign from the Red Cross, at least not right away. In the early days of my new modeling career, I had no reason to believe this little venture of mine would be anything more than a leisure pursuit. A hobby wouldn't pay Joan's tuition. Still, I poured my soul into the project. Ms. Watson, of course, rounded up opportunities for me. And I, rather than high-tailing it to Lord & Taylor at noon, scoured the avenues of the city, turning up cold at magazines and women's catalog companies and offering my portfolio. Every one of us bears the wounds and characteristics our parents unwittingly pass onto us, and likewise, we receive their most admirable tendencies. Willie and Fredericka, bare-knuckled and unremitting, handed their work ethic to me.

I booked a few catalog gigs immediately, bolstering my excitement that modeling might be my ticket out of a years-long sentence as a secretary. The jobs were small, but I loved the work, just loved it: the posing and the grinning, the rapid-fire *click-click-click* of the camera, and of course, the bottomless well of beautiful clothing. I suppose to be truly successful at any pursuit, you have to fall in love with it, surrender to its gravitational pull, allow it to carry you off to that world of giddy sleeplessness.

Speaking of shut-eye, I got little. I pecked my way, nine to five on weekdays, through my work at the Red Cross before making my evening rounds with portfolios spilling from my satchel. Then after my 10 p.m. to 6 a.m. shift in the secretarial sweatshop two nights a week, I dashed home with just enough time to shower, brush my teeth, and limp back out the door.

From the start, I viewed modeling for what it was—a business, an income generator. The fact that I saw it as such is why the bashfulness of my youth naturally fell away, because believe me, I have never been shy about making money. The most potent antidote to reticence is survival.

The gigs at first trickled in, and then flooded. In the beginning, I modeled anything and everything: shoes and handbags and hats and swimsuits and even wigs for local hair salons. Those entry-level jobs put me on the map in the modeling community, and before long, I was landing covers and spreads for major magazines such as *Ebony*, *Jet*, and of course the publication where Ms. Mildred Smith worked, *Our World*. It was there, one afternoon in early 1955, when God breathed in my direction yet again.

On my way out of a meeting with Ms. Smith, I spotted a woman in the waiting room. As I passed, she gave me the once-over and I, thinking nothing of it, nodded courteously and hurried back to the Red Cross. I didn't know it at the time, but that woman happened to be Evelyn Davis, an actress. When Evelyn went in to see Ms. Smith, she asked her, "Who was that young lady who sashayed out of here?"

"She's a model working with Barbara Watson," she said. "Why do you ask?"

"Because I just came from an interview for a movie," she said, "and they are looking for a young lady who looks just like her to play the lead."

I hadn't been back at my work desk for more than three minutes when the phone rang. "I think I got you a movie," said Ms. Smith, hardly breathing between each word.

"A movie?" I said. "What are you talking about, a movie?" She explained what Evelyn had mentioned and then concluded with, "And can you believe you look just like the young lady they're looking for?! Evelyn can arrange for you to meet the director."

I paused and glanced around, concerned that my supervisor would overhear me on the phone. "Listen," I said, "I don't know anything about making no movie. And I'm not going any place to make a fool of myself." *Click*. I'd been to see one film during my lifetime, and as you know, the experience scared the spit out of me. *A movie?* No way was I going to get involved with the film business.

But God clearly saw it another way—and he sent Ms. Smith to deliver his opposing viewpoint. The next morning she called me again, begging me to reconsider. "Why don't you just go over and meet the director?" she kept saying. I declined. Finally, after she rang me three days in a row, I almost burst a blood vessel.

"Look, do me a favor," I said, trying and failing to whisper. "You're going to make me lose my job. Please . . . don't call me anymore."

"Then tell me that you'll go see this man after you get off work today," she urged.

"Yes, yes, yes!" I said, rushing her off the phone. Just as I was about to click down the receiver, she said, "But wait—you don't know where I'm sending you!"

"Well then you'd better talk fast," I told her. She gave me the address, an office down in Carnegie Hall. The director's name was Warren Coleman.

I wasn't at all nervous to meet Mr. Coleman—whom I eventually came to call Warren. I had no expectations and therefore no stakes, other than to get Ms. Smith off my back. I sat there, relaxed as could be, while Warren, with his velvety-smooth voice and easy smile, led me on a tour of his professional ascent. As one of theater's most gifted operatic baritones, Warren had created and played the roles of Crown in Gershwin's *Porgy and Bess* and John Kumalo in Kurt Weill's *Lost in the Stars*. He became a Broadway fixture throughout the 1930s and 1940s, which was long enough for him to recognize how Black artists were mistreated, how our creative brilliance was overshadowed by our social rank, how the same white audience members who applauded Black performers publicly wouldn't allow them to scoot up to their private dinner tables. Those realities had prompted him to form his own production company and create films reflecting African-American life, in all of its resplendent intricacy. He was just beginning work on his first independent movie, *The Spectrum*, a film about color consciousness in the Black community.

As he spoke, I feigned interest, nodding at the appropriate junctures, the whole time thinking: *This is nonsense. I am not going to be any actress.*

"How much do you know about acting?" Warren asked me.

"Nothing at all," I said.

"Well I have the script of the film right here," he said. He rummaged through a stack of papers and notebooks on his desk and handed me a spiral-bound book. "Why don't you take this home and read it?"

I flipped through it, just to be polite. "I've never done anything like this, sir," I told him. "I just don't think I'm the right one—but I appreciate your time." I then sat the book on the desk, picked up my pocketbook, and walked toward the door.

"No wait a minute . . . wait," he said, retrieving the script and following me toward the entrance. "I really want you to take this script with you. Can you just read it and see what you think? Will you do that?"

I looked back at him. "I suppose," I said, thinking, *What harm could come of it?* "I guess I could have a look."

"Excellent," he said, giving me the book. "I'll give you a call in a couple weeks."

I carried the script home and tossed it into my bedside drawer. I prefer my humiliation private, thank you very much, and as ambitious as I was to earn money, I had no interest in making a public spectacle of myself. I promptly forgot about the script until, a couple of days later when I was searching in that drawer for a hairbrush, my eyes fell on the book's cover. I pulled it out and read the first page. An hour later, I was still reading.

The story gripped me. Autumn, the female lead and a blossoming writer, came to New York with aspiration in her eyes, hoping to sell an article she'd penned. She was my dark complexion. The magazine editor she approached was light-skinned, as was the man she eventually fell in love with. The two began a courtship, and the man's mother, determined that her son maintain the privilege of their honey-tinged heritage, protested mightily. "If you marry her," she warned him, "you'll destroy your career." I found the plot captivating, yet I still could not see myself in it, especially as the lead. If Warren succeeded in making the film, I told myself, I'd be the first to line up at the cinema to see who played in it and what this whole acting thing was about. And yet, much as I had no vision of myself as Autumn, my curiosity had been awakened—another shoulder tap, another whisper from on high.

At two weeks to the day, Warren rang me. "I'd like you to come to the studio and meet someone," he said. I agreed. When I arrived, he introduced me to an actor by the name of Hal DeWindt, who was to play the male lead in *The Spectrum*.

"So what did you think of the script?" Warren asked me with hope in his voice.

"I think it's great reading," I said, chuckling. "I enjoyed the story very much."

"Good," he said. He looked over at Hal, and then back at me. "I'd like the two of you to read a scene together," he said.

"Cicely, you read Autumn, and Hal will read his part." I paused, slowly reached into my bag, and pulled out the script.

The reading flowed seamlessly. Our voices fit together naturally, weaving and swaying in step, as if we'd been rehearsing with one another for weeks. Magic operates as such. When a pivot is predestined on the stone tablet of your life story, there is often an inexplicable ease to it. It feels otherworldly, from an Almighty source beyond your frail humanity. That is how reading that scene felt to me—supernatural. When I completed my final lines and looked up, Warren was staring at me and grinning.

"So do you want to be an actress, Cicely?" he said. "Seems to me you already are."

I lowered the script and looked down at the floor, giving doubt a chance to resurface. "I don't know anything about making a movie," I told him.

"Well," he said, laughing and sidestepping my reluctance, "I guess you'll find out."

Warren asked whether he could call me again. The part of my spirit that understood the moment's transcendence, the power of the precipice I was dancing along, agreed. Even when we humans are busy shaking our heads no, shoving down our fears and shoving off our blessings, the Father has a way of propelling us forward, of moving us toward his way. Warren indeed called and pleaded with me to play Autumn, only to be met with another round of my misgivings. And just as Ms. Smith had, he called a second time, refusing to be shunned. By his third call, I'd finally aligned my will with the Father's. I told Warren yes. And he not only persuaded me to play the role; he insisted that he manage me.

"How old are you?" he asked me early on.

"Thirty," I told him.

He gazed at me incredulously. "Really?" he said. I nodded.

"Well you certainly don't look it," he said. "You could pass for ten years younger, my dear, and from now on, you should claim to be." Nature has bestowed Black people with one of its most prized gifts, melanin, and in a society where we are seldom allowed an advantage, Warren understood the importance of utilizing mine. Six decades would go by before I let the public in on what was frankly never any of their business.

By the time I agreed to portray Autumn, filming had paused. Warren was leaving shoe tracks all over Manhattan, trying to raise the necessary capital to complete the production. That didn't stop Hal and me. We began rehearsing during my lunch breaks, as well as any time I could wedge a session into the cracks of my packed schedule. As we practiced our scenes, gone was the apprehension I'd felt about acting, and in its place was the passion that had powered my rise as a model. I may initially waver before lunging toward a new experience, but once I do, I grow unrelenting. I rehearsed my lines with the frenzy of a capsized sailor, gasping for air, desperate to stay afloat. And even while Hal and I worked, Warren began sending me out on small auditions. I mostly floundered, but that didn't matter because at least I was in the room. One failed audition at a time, I was learning the business, dipping my toe in its frigid waters.

It was Warren who introduced me to the flurry and bustle of New York theater and, in many ways, to life beyond the walls of the church world I'd been reared in. Given his long-standing success on Broadway, he had access, which he leveraged to offer me a crash course in both craft and sophistication. I became fast friends with the affable Diana Sands, another young actress in *The Spectrum*, and Warren whisked us from one play and concert to the next, where we met performers backstage, soaking in the chaos and the costumes and the color of their behind-the-curtain artistry and antics. Afterward, he exposed us to some of the city's finest cuisines (in the rice-and-plantains existence of my youth, escargot had absolutely no place). Into the wee hours of the morning over such purported delicacies, we'd talk scripting and technique and plot. I had no idea what I was gibbering about, of course, but Warren insisted I had potential. "You've got natural talent," he assured me. I'd smile and think, *What does that even mean?* A raw slab of marble also has so-called potential, but only when a sculptor chips away at it, piece by piece, does a face emerge. Raw talent does not a fine actor make.

Which is why, even as I zealously rehearsed with Hal, I prioritized my modeling work. Before I knew it, I was earning enough money to finally leave the Red Cross, three decades shy of a gilded watch, and feeling grateful for the stepping-stone that job served for me. From the start, I'd told my mother about my modeling work, and surprisingly, she voiced no objections, especially after she began spotting me in the center spreads of the magazines she read. She soaked it up: she had a famous daughter, child, one with accomplishments worth displaying, one she could now be proud of again after a season of a lowered head. My work qualified not as an ungodly undertaking, but as a point of family and community pride. But the same could not be said of her perspective on my film work, which I hid from her.

One night Warren asked me, "Have you told your mother about the movie?"

I shook my head. "She would not approve," I said.

"Well maybe I should talk to her," he offered.

"That's not a good idea," I shot back. "I would rather her not know right now."

My work on *The Spectrum* was easy to conceal. Mom was used to my coming and going at all times of the day and night, so that did not raise suspicion. But things changed soon after my conversation with Warren.

Late one evening, after Warren and I had seen a mesmerizing production of *My Fair Lady* at the Mark Hellinger Theater, he walked me home. My mother happened to be sitting at her window, looking down and watching the world go by, like the old folks often do. She spotted Warren and me. When I got upstairs to the apartment, the grand inquisition commenced.

"Who was that man you were with?" she asked me.

"He's a producer, Mom," I said. "He's doing a movie, and he would like me to be a part of it." I stopped short of revealing I'd been rehearsing for months.

"You can't do that," she told me.

"Why?" I said.

"You're going to leave this good job you have for this damn foolishness?" she said, referring to my typing pool and modeling work.

"I didn't say I was leaving anything," I retorted. "I just said I was going to go do this movie."

She stared at me for a long moment. "Well you can't stay here and do that," she said. Her statement jarred me so, echoed through me, that I could not even look at her. Without a word, I rose from the couch and disappeared into my bedroom.

There was no sense in arguing with my mother. What she was forbidding me to do I was already headlong into doing, with no intention of reversing course. God himself had pointed my suede pumps in this new direction. I'd come to believe that, even as I was still making sense of the film industry and wondering whether I had any place in it. And while I'd known instinctively this disagreement with my mother had been postponable, I'd also realized it was inevitable. I'd dared to enter the den of iniquity, Lucifer's workshop as my Mom saw it. Anything to do with entertainment or theater was pure sin, the devil's territory, an express train to Hades. My apparent transgression, as well as the temerity I'd shown in mentioning it within my mother's earshot, was grounds enough for her to promptly dismiss me.

The next day, I called Thelma Jack. She was working for the telephone company and had her own place downtown at 112 East Seventh Street. It had two bedrooms. "May I come live with you?" I asked her after explaining my situation. She enthusiastically agreed, eager not only to share her apartment, but also to halve the rent. I'd have my own private space there, one large enough to have Joan with me during her school breaks. Another upside that made Thelma the consummate roommate candidate: she and I wore the same dress size, a 4. That was important to me because, in between rehearsing and modeling, I was still constantly interviewing for clerical temp jobs. When I'd go out on interviews, I could borrow Thelma's dresses—and borrow I did.

When I left my mother's apartment, we did not speak for nearly a year. We did not see each other for almost two. As devastated as I was by her choice, as deeply as her words had sliced through me, I knew she'd made the only decision she felt she could. It was her way of loving me, of trying to redirect my steps and shift my affections away from the strivings of this world and back toward the kingdom of heaven. And yet even those who care deeply for us cannot always see our big picture, the Grand Story Line that is destined to unfold before us. They are on their own journeys. And though their paths may run parallel to ours, each is singular in its curves and mileposts, unique in its destination. As much as others want the best for us, they do not necessarily understand God's best. He alone does.

My liberation from my mother's rule created in me a newfound fervor. Mom had hoped to douse my burgeoning dream with her condemnation, prayed she could snuff it out with a stinging decree. But she'd inadvertently lit a match beneath me.

Up to then, enamored though I was with the notion of acting, I was still secretly grappling with my fears, my uncertainties about whether I'd ever be good enough for the stage. My mother's disapproval became my liquid fuel, my requisite source of strength. Before she put me out, I'd been attempting to prove to myself that I could excel as an actress. Afterward, her displeasure pushed me, if nothing else, to prove her wrong.

I tell you, boy, God certainly kept me in his sight line. I couldn't have dreamed up a script more compelling than the one that played out for me during those years. Who just happens to be approached on the street by a total stranger, only to have that man propose modeling, only to have that modeling work become a footbridge to the stage? To some, this might look like happenstance, a sequence of coincidences, a string of disconnected flukes. As I see it, my tide shift, my sharp turnaround, had the Savior's handprints all over it. His sovereignty was apparent to me. It still is. The same Master who holds the firmaments in the crease of his palms, who commands oceans to recede, who maintains humanity's entire existence with the mist of his breath—that God, the Source of time itself, the Creator of all life, has forever been directing mine.

10

Center Stage

IT'S NOT every day you find yourself seated next to Marilyn Monroe. Such a day arrived for me in 1956, not long after I'd devoted myself to acting.

By then, *The Spectrum* had become an afterthought. Once Warren's coffers had run dry halfway through filming, he never could replenish them, even once he'd left skid marks all over Manhattan trying to raise capital. Rather than simmering in that setback, he linked arms with director Harold Young and screenplay writer Charles Gossett for *Carib Gold*, a maritime movie about a shrimp boat crew that discovers a sunken treasure. Diana Sands, who'd become a dear sister-friend to me, was cast in the film. So was I, though not as the lead. I was to play Dottie, wife of a deckhand. Perhaps strangely to some, I felt relieved not to play the principal role. With my career still in its infancy, my preparation had yet to catch up with my passion. By the time Warren connected with Harold and Charles about the script, the inimitable Ethel Waters, the 1920s blues singer who, by that time, had begun lending her artistic deftness to the stage, had already been tapped as *Carib*'s headliner.

"Do you even want to be in the film?" Warren had asked me,

having observed my periodic vacillations between euphoria to be in the industry and murmuring about how ruefully ill-prepared I felt. I shrugged. During one particularly low valley, I'd even threatened to go back to the Red Cross. What stopped me was the stubbornness passed on to me from a certain Fredericka Theodosia Huggins, the woman I was set on rebutting.

"Well what do you want?" Warren pressed, aggravation in his tone.

"I want to learn what it's all about," I said, sighing. "I don't know what I'm doing, Warren. I don't understand it. I need to study."

Thus began my months-long quest for formal training. Warren persisted in his belief that my innate gifts would be enough to carry me, that the well of emotion stored up during my childhood, formed by my wail amid strife in my family's East Side home, shaped when I witnessed my mother up for auction on a Bronx sidewalk, was all the training necessary for me to infuse my portrayals with authenticity. It wasn't. Trauma may give rise to intense feeling, but to refine one's artistry, an actor must be taught to channel the unbridled rawness of that emotion, to effectively use it in service of a character's every groan and grimace. Rather than placing me in a course for total beginners, Warren instead sent me to a downtown studio for actors with some experience, albeit limited. The course gave me a migraine. I'd sit in class wondering, *What are these people talking about? How do they know how to gesture, whether to speak, when to emote?* I couldn't grasp it. I don't remember the instructor's name, but I do recall becoming friendly with his wife.

"You know," I told her after class one day, "I really don't like this."

"Why not?" she asked. "What's the matter?"

"Because I don't understand what's happening," I said. "I need someone to explain this whole thing to me."

"Don't worry," she said, smiling, "it'll come."

It didn't—even after I'd stayed on for several more classes. She and Warren kept claiming, counterintuitively to me, that I was lost because I had *too* much skill. "The problem is that you're so far ahead of your classmates there's nothing there for you to learn," Warren said. That assertion made no sense to me. As far as I could see, I had plenty to learn, whether or not he acknowledged it.

The next experience was significantly better but still no bull's-eye. Warren connected me with Miriam Goldina, the Russian-born stage actress and drama coach who'd studied under Konstantin Stanislavski, the grandfather of method acting—a technique requiring a performer's full immersion in the emotional realities of the character to be portrayed. Miriam taught me some tangibles. For one thing, she made me acutely aware of the importance of words: how to listen closely to them, how to read the spaces between them, how to become cognizant of the intent behind each. When you're in conversation with someone, why might that person be saying what he or she is saying? What is that person trying to elicit from you? We examined those questions and many others, making me conscious of how critical it is for an artist to do more listening than speaking, a skill I'd been unknowingly practicing since my earliest years. What Miriam and I did not explore was what she likely assumed I already possessed—the fundamentals of acting, Theater 101. More than anything during that time, I craved a foundation.

That is exactly what I told Lee Strasberg on the day I enrolled at the Actors Studio, then the most prestigious theatrical collective in the nation. Lee, who'd refined and further developed Stanislavski's approach to method acting and introduced it to the West, was training greats such as Anne Bancroft and Jane Fonda. Surely he could guide me through my labyrinth of confusion and give me the basics.

"Please," I begged him, "I don't want to be put in a class with professionals. I want to start from the beginning."

Lee nodded as if he agreed, but he apparently took Warren's word over mine and placed me with the pros. That's how I ended up an elbow's length away from the blond and beguiling Marilyn Monroe, then fresh off her run in the blockbuster romantic comedy *The Seven Year Itch*. I, too, had an itch—an instinct to flee the second I spotted her: *Lord in heaven, what am I doing here!?* "Hello," she purred in my direction. That was my first time in class with Marilyn. It was also my last.

I huffed my way out of there and over to Warren's office. "When I tell you I want to start at the bottom," I said, "I mean the *very* bottom, not in a class with a big star!"

Warren, as amused by my tantrums as he was accustomed to them, just laughed. "Well all right, Cicely," he said. "Maybe it's time I send you over to Lloyd Richards."

I knew the name. Diana had mentioned the distinguished acting coach to me on several occasions, most notably when I'd fallen into one of my steepest stupors about my inexperience. I'd uttered another (empty) threat that evening: I was one melancholic episode away from returning to my day job.

"You know, you really should go down to Paul Mann Actor's Workshop," Diana had told me. "Lloyd Richards, Paul's business partner there, is supposed to be one of the best. Try it. And if, after you go, you find that you still can't make sense of this business, then you can quit. But please give yourself a chance."

Paul, an accomplished theater actor who'd founded the workshop in 1953, was Caucasian. Lloyd—a renowned African-American actor and director who, years later, went on to serve as dean of the Yale School of Drama—had created a nurturing environment for Black artists. Sidney Poitier had studied with Lloyd. So had Harry Belafonte, Ruby Dee, and Billy Dee Williams. That was résumé enough to get me across the threshold to the school.

My initial appointment was with Paul, whose introductory course was required for incoming students. Our meeting began as such encounters do, with handshakes and smiles and niceties. It ended traumatically.

"So Cicely," he said after we'd been chatting for a few moments, "where do you see yourself going in this industry?"

As I thought about his question, his gaze traveled down from my eyes to my chest. My heartbeat raced. Paul rose from his desk and walked over to shut his door. I stood, as did every hair on my neck.

"Well, I mean," I stammered. Before I could continue, Paul, a menacing tower of flesh, thrust himself toward me and began manhandling my breasts, attempting to remove my blouse as I shoved him away. "No!" I yelled. "Get off of me!" He tried to jam me against the wall and shove his hand under my camisole, but I somehow managed to break free. Once I'd pried myself loose, blouse untucked from my skirt, hair scattered in every direction, I grabbed my pocketbook and fled to the door. As I reached for the knob, Paul spoke. "Class begins next week," he said in an eerily calm voice, as if he hadn't just attacked me. "You are welcome to come." Without looking at him, I opened the door and disappeared down the hall, holding back tears long enough to make it out the front door. Once home, I collapsed into sobs on my bed.

A week later at the start of his introductory course, I showed up. Paul had already gathered with the group of students who'd enrolled in it, and when I entered, he stopped speaking and stared at me. "I thought I'd never see you again," he said, incredulousness in his tone. I breathed not a sentence and took a seat.

Life is choices, and as I saw it, I had two. I could've fled from that man's office and never returned. Many, understandably, might have chosen that route. And yet the alternative option, the less obvious of the two, was the one I settled upon. I had arrived at that studio with the singular purpose of training with Lloyd. And though Paul, in a show of flagrant lasciviousness, had attempted to thwart my mission, I was not to be deterred. When someone sees you headed in a direction, and that person throws a brick into the road, that is the precise moment to forge onward, with greater velocity, toward your destination. I had a purpose, one that, despite all of my wavering, I had witnessed God orchestrating. And I refused to have some man, with his hot breath on my neck and his pasty fingers on my nipples, impede my plan.

It had never been Paul's name that had been spoken to me. It was Lloyd's. And whatever it was that Lloyd had to offer me, I intended to get it. If that meant enduring Paul's course so I could move on to Lloyd's permanent tutelage, so be it. If that involved swallowing the recollection of his brazen assault, of forgetting what he'd stolen from me in the same manner a passerby once had, if that was the price to be rendered, I stood ready to pay. All these years later, what Paul did to me that day—the way he put his hands on me—the trauma is emblazoned on my memory. When someone violates you sexually, it does not simply haunt and aggrieve you; it alters the very shape of your soul.

And altered I was. Contrary to the mythology surrounding the unflinching nature of African-American women, we, too, experience trauma. Black women—our essence, our emotional intricacies, the indignities we carry in our bones—are the most deeply misunderstood human beings in history. Those who know nothing about us have had the audacity to try to introduce us to ourselves, in the unsteady strokes of caricature, on stages, in books, and through their distorted reflections of us. The resulting Fun House image, a haphazard depiction sketched beneath the dim light of ignorance, allows ample room for our strength, our rage and tenacity, to stand at center stage. When we express anger, the audience of the world applauds. That expression aligns with their portrait of us. As long as we play our various designated roles—as court jesters and as comic relief, as Aunt Jemimas and as Jezebels, as maids whisking aperitifs into drawing rooms, as shuckin' and jivin' half-wits serving up levity—we are worthy of recognition in their meta-narrative. We are obedient Negroes. We are dutiful and thus affirmable.

But when we dare tiptoe outside the lines of those typecasts, when we put our full humanity on display, when we threaten the social constructs that keep others in comfortable superiority, we are often dismissed. There is no archetype on file in which a Black woman is simultaneously resolute and trembling, fierce and frightened, dominant and receding. My mother, a woman who, amid abuse, stuffed hope and a way out into the slit of a mattress, is the very face of fortitude. I am an heir to her remarkable grit. However, beneath that tough exterior, I've also inherited my mother's tender femininity, that part of her spirit susceptible to bruising and bleeding, the doleful Dosha who sat by the window shelling peanuts, pondering how to carry on. The myth of the Strong Black Woman bears a kernel of truth, but it is only a half-seed. The other half is delicate and ailing, all the more so because it has been denied sunlight. On the day I went back to Paul Mann's school, I was unswerving in my resolve to study with Lloyd. I was also vulnerable—as traumatized by Paul's behavior as any woman might have been.

My decision to return became a defining one, a choice that

sent a resounding echo through the decades of my career. After I'd endured Paul's course, eyes averted, nose in my notebook, I went on to train exclusively with Lloyd, one of two genius coaches who molded me during those years. I managed to completely avoid Paul, showing up at the studio only when Lloyd was teaching. By the time Lloyd and I connected, I'd begun work on *Carib*, flitting between New York and Key West, Florida, where the movie was shot. When I returned to the city during breaks in filming, I couldn't get over to Lloyd's office fast enough, ready to soak in all he had to teach me—about exploring my character's emotional truth, about enhancing my understanding of her given circumstances, about making artistic choices commensurate with that awareness.

At the school, I got to know Ruby Dee. She was also in training then, though alongside my shade of bright green, Ruby and her husband, Ossie Davis, were already deep-emerald sages of the stage. Ruby, diminutive yet spirited, was as much a firecracker then as her decades of civil rights crusading, in front of the curtain and beyond it, would reveal her to be. "Girl, I'll tell you," she'd often say to me then, "if you can be Black and live in this world, you can be anything you want to be." Ruby, who by 1956 was nearly two dozen stage and film credits into her career, had experienced the humiliations that come with Acting While Black, of having nearly every available role be that of a domestic, of loaning her talents to directors who, away from the lights, sneered down at her as genetically and intellectually subpar.

Ruby had cut her thespian teeth amid such insults. She, Ossie, Harry, Sidney, Isabel Sanford, Alice Childress, Hilda Simms, and scores of other then-unknown artists had come up through the American Negro Theater, a 1940s community theater group founded by Black actors, in part as a response to the dearth of roles illuminating the breadth of our experience, and in part to create a warm cocoon for Black actors confronting bigotry in the shadows of the Great White Way. In the group's early years, actors rehearsed in the basement of the Harlem branch of the New York Public Library and performed at Harlem's Schomburg Center for Research in Black Culture. Ruby and the rest of them understood that the most difficult part of our work happened not in studios and rehearsal spaces, not on stages and sets. Just walking through this life as a Black person, and actually surviving that, was and still is an ovation-worthy performance.

During those times, I knew Ruby and the others not as the theatrical giants the world would come to regard them as. I knew them as human beings, first and foremost, grappling with their private insecurities and frights, struggling to breathe air into their characters' lungs. I knew them as waitresses and as dishwashers, as clerks and as survivors, as dreamers moonlighting their way to some semblance of solvency. The introverted Sidney Poitier, who began work on *A Raisin in the Sun* in the late 1950s, was always more confident on film than he was before a live audience, when nerves, at times, got the better of him. Such tremors had arisen during Sidney's 1946 Broadway debut in *Lysistrata*, when his preshow peek at a packed house sent his teeth to chattering. When he walked out onstage, he forgot his first line and skipped straight to his eighth. But still, his talent shone through. The show was critically panned, yet Sidney received favorable reviews, enough of them to untie his tongue and put fresh wind at his back.

It was Sidney who connected Lloyd and Lorraine Hansberry—the soft-spoken revolutionary who had penned *Raisin* as a head-nod to Langston Hughes's poem, and in memory of her own childhood marred by flagrant prejudice. Sidney had a long-standing pact with his friend and director. While a student at Paul Mann Actor's Workshop, Sidney once said to Lloyd, "If I ever do anything on Broadway, I want you to direct it." So when Lorraine's scintillating script landed in his possession, he knew exactly where to take it. In Lloyd's gifted and nimble hands, and with the prowess of an all-Black cast headlined by Sidney as Walter Lee Younger and Ruby Dee as his wife, Ruth, the play lit Broadway ablaze, even as it reordered theater's playbook. Before *Raisin*, the prevailing wisdom among the industry's power brokers was that white audiences would support an all-Black show only if it was a musical, with us shimmying and guffawing our way toward an enduring stereotype. The rapturous applause and repeated curtain calls, with a verklempt Lorraine urged by the roar to take her bow of validation, demonstrated otherwise. "Never before," James Baldwin commented of the play, "had so much of the truth of Black people's lives been seen on stage." And it was Lloyd, God rest his soul, who had, in one way or another, molded every performer in that trailblazing production.

For months before I connected with Lloyd, Warren often asked me, "What are you looking for in a teacher?" I never quite knew how to answer. Once Lloyd and I began training together, I realized I'd been looking for a rock, which Lloyd provided. His method acting approach was not substantively different from what I'd become familiar with up to then. But his manner of delivery, the patience with which he illuminated the tenets, the haven he created for actors—he became the Gibraltar that I and countless others stood upon.

Stylistically, Lloyd was more copilot than captain, more laissez-faire than commander, a teacher who preferred his student to fly solo as he, reservedly in the wings, whispered cues during the route. He was less apt to deliver a sermon, more likely to raise a thoughtful question. "Who is she?" Lloyd would ask me about a character I was preparing to depict. "What are the moments that have shaped her?" He understood that meeting a character on the page was akin to making her acquaintance in life. To study that character—to insatiably pursue her backstory, to dissect her memories and her motivations—was to begin the process of becoming her. That is why, to this day, I read a script a hundred times over, steeping myself in the nuances of the character, searching for the silence between the notes in the melody of who she is. By the time I get on that stage, I've lived in my character's skin so continuously that she often takes over my physical being. *Where did that come from?* I think when a gesture, a head tilt, or a smirk distinct from my own emerges. Lloyd laid the foundation for that to happen. These days when I talk to young people aspiring to the stage, I tell them, "You can spend half your life trying to find the right teacher for you." Lloyd and I were simpatico from day one.

Had I allowed Paul Mann to short-circuit my dream, I might have missed out on the blessing of Lloyd, whose artistic skill was eclipsed only by his kindness. In contrast to his business partner, he was, for me, a torchlight of integrity. In 1984, decades after my experience with Paul, eight actresses accused him of sexual assault. In a civil suit that landed in the State Supreme Court in Manhattan, the scales of justice leaned in the direction of the women. Paul was issued a guilty verdict and ordered to pay his victims $12,000 in total, a paltry $1,000 to $2,000 for each of them. Before his death in 1985, Paul had given much of his life to the theater, training artists and accruing accolades. History has recorded him as a celebrated teacher, one who prepared numerous luminaries for the stage. Yet in my book, he will forever be regarded as the man who, along my path toward Providence, hurled a brick—one I picked up and threw aside.

As I dedicated myself to honing my craft, my baby arched her back toward adolescence. When Joan had left for boarding school at age ten, her period had not yet arrived. Given that my own had shown up when I was just nine, I thought her first sign of womanhood might be imminent. One thing I knew: I could not allow silence to do my teaching for me, as my own mom had. So ahead of her departure, I had pulled Joan close to me on my bedside, and together, we read through a book about menstruation. She listened intently and nodded, but she did not speak—until a year later when she was home on Christmas break.

"Mommy," she said to me while we were on our way to the hairdresser, "I got that thing you told me about." Her lips spread into a smile.

I looked over at her. "What thing, darling?" I asked.

"You know," she said, "that thing we read about in the book—my period."

"Really?" I said, embracing her.

"Yes, really," she said. In that moment, I couldn't help but feel like I'd in some way traced over my mother's blunder, her costly restraint, with an improved way forward for Joan. My daughter needn't stumble her way through adolescence, piecing together nature's truths without the benefit of a narrator. At the end of Joan's break, I sent her to school well supplied with all that she needed to care for herself.

And yet, I realize now, Joan needed far more than that from me. Our separations were gut-wrenching for both of us, but most especially for her. She longed, as any child would, to linger at my elbow, to be there for the nightly suppers, the homework sessions around a kitchen table, the impromptu mommy-daughter conversations. I will always remember the summer I traveled to Key West to film *Carib Gold*. Joan, then on break from school, wanted to accompany me on the road. I considered it, of course, yet in my heart, I knew the experience would be wholly unsatisfying for her and might force an even sharper wedge between us. The job of a professional actor—the script memorizing, the dashing to and fro on set, the disappearance into a character's interior world—demands an enormous intensity of focus. Joan might have been there with me in the flesh, but with my head somewhere beyond the heavens, she would have missed me all the more. So I arranged for her to stay with my sister, Emily, during that break—and it was yet another parting that bowed her head.

"Mom, why can't I come back to New York and go to school here?" Joan often asked me. With remorse lodged in my throat, I did not always know what to say to make her understand. Any explanation I gave sounded to Joan like an attempt to relegate her to the sidelines of my world, to prioritize my career over her.

Joan viewed our situation the only way she then could, through a child's eyes, whereas I observed it under the unsparing light of adult pragmatism. As grievous as our distance was, I was doing what I felt I had to do in order to provide. Provision, in my mind, was the barometer that bested all other gauges, the litmus test by which my parenting would ultimately be measured. *Am I able to give Joan everything she requires? Does the life I make possible for her improve upon the one my parents could offer me?* I know now that Joan pined more for my presence than she did for my pocketbook. She needed my provision, yes, but decidedly more of the emotional sort, a cheek-to-cheek coexistence. I do not regret that I chose to earn a living in the manner in which I did, or that I arranged for Joan to attend school in a world miles north of mine. But I do mourn that my child, during the years she hungered to have me close, felt my absence so profoundly. My utmost, well intentioned as it was, fell short of her needs and desires.

Joan began her freshman year of high school in the fall of 1956, around the time *Carib Gold* was released. I rarely view my own work and have watched only a handful of my own films. The gratification for me comes in the doing of the work, the creation—the embodying of a character so fully that the audience comes to believe, feel, see, smell, and taste her existence, climb into her reality, understand her humanity as a means for reflecting upon their own. That is where my satisfaction comes from. Once I've played a character, that portrayal no longer belongs to me. It is an offering to those who witness the unveiling. The joy, for me, comes in the crafting of that gift, the choosing and the nurturing of it, and then in giving it away. Art, in a sense, is the transference of pleasure. And also, once I've poured myself into a performance, I can't do anything more about it—which is why I do not torture myself by viewing it.

And yet, out of curiosity and excitement as a newcomer to the industry, I did see *Carib*. Words fall short in conveying the pure exhilaration you feel, as an artist, of watching your work flicker to life for the first time, of seeing this strange likeness of yourself crackling across a screen in Black and white. I will always remember the row of words at the bottom of the opening credits, recall how it sent chills through me to see my name there, standing tall and majestic: "And introducing CICELY TYSON." Dubious as I'd been, at moments, that this endeavor of mine would evolve into anything more than a recreational pursuit, there it was, indisputable in all caps, a confirmation that I was actually doing what I'd set out to do.

When an audience views a film, they experience the story on the screen. As an actress, I also recall the moments between the plotline, the occurrences off set. There were the myriad hours I spent tutoring with Lloyd, the trembling lips that brought me, over and over, to his doorway for help in developing Dottie.

There was the weekend, while filming in Key West during Christmas, when Warren arranged for us to visit Cuba, before Fidel Castro wrested control from then-President Batista. That holiday was the first I'd ever spent away from New York and family, and my scowl was evidence of that. In an effort to buoy my spirits, Warren accompanied me from Key West to Havana on a day-long sail, the breeze playing patty-cake with my hair, the smell of the sea, for a time, vanquishing my wistfulness for home. Ashore, we were welcomed by the sounds of "Silent Night" and "Feliz Navidad" floating between row houses, pigmented in an array of pastel façades. Gorgeous as the island was, the ninety-degree temperatures failed to put me in the holiday spirit. At my insistence, Warren sent me home for New Year's. Such memories are what flooded to mind when I saw *Carib.*

Piercingly, what I also recalled was my child's sadness during my months of filming in Key West, how much we missed one another, how conflicted I often felt about our separation. When Joan finished middle school, I did move her back to the city to live with me for all four years of high school. When I needed to travel for work, such as during my time away filming *Carib*, she stayed in Mount Vernon with Emily and Reggie. By then, my sister and her husband had three children of their own, Maxine, Reginald, and Verna. Joan's cousins became like siblings to her.

Having Joan close slathered consolation on the wound created by our years apart. On weekends, we attended concerts and plays together. One of her favorite memories is the day I took her to see the film *Madame Butterfly*. And yet decades would pass before the bruise of our earlier separation received the light and air it needed to begin healing. I ache in reflecting upon it now; I ache that, though my choices were planted in the soil of my deep love for Joan, she nonetheless felt cast aside. I live with that sorrow. It is why, in part, I write so scarcely of her. Joan felt, as a child, that she had to share me with the world. I give her now, in adulthood, what my heart has always longed to bestow—my undivided focus, along with the full measure of her privacy.

The first time I wandered into a Broadway show, I was mesmerized. I was still new at the Red Cross then, long before the gold-watch epiphany. During the holiday season, we office clerks took to the streets, shaking coin-filled tin cans at passersby, hoping to collect donations for the nonprofit. I don't know why, but I was a nervous wreck rattling that darn can. Late one afternoon, I was assigned to raise my ruckus out in front of the Martin Beck Theatre on Forty-Fifth Street. *The Crucible*, Arthur Miller's fictionalized drama of the Salem witch trials, happened to be in previews there. At the end of my shift and near the show's last act, I slipped through three sets of double doors and into the back of the theater. I've never gotten over what I saw.

Lord, what is this? I thought. I had no concept then of a professional stage production, had never even been inside of a playhouse. In my mind's eye, I can still envision it: the eerily darkened amphitheater, the 1690s garb and the elaborate set, the lights shining down to dance upon the actors' expressions, the row upon row of audience members, staring ahead in rapt attention. "You misunderstand, sir," declared Walter Hampden, portraying the play's villain, Deputy-Governor Danforth. "I cannot pardon these when twelve are already hanged for the same crime. It is not just." The whole scene felt, at once, deeply haunting and wondrously magical. Which is why, years later, when Warren pressed me to step toward such magic, my goose pimples made a comeback.

"Vinnette Carroll is planning to direct a play called *Dark of the Moon*," he told me a few months after *Carib*'s release. "She's staging it at the Y in Harlem, and she's looking for a lead. You would be perfect."

I stared at him perplexed, the same look I always give when I'm scrambling to come up with reasons to decline.

"I can't do any play," I said. "I've never been on a stage in my life." Though I knew more about film than about live theater, I'd glimpsed enough, while racing 'round town with Warren to shows, to be frightened I could not deliver. Movie filming involves take after take. In theater, there are no do-overs, no second or seventh chances. You either get it right in real time or you flounder and make a laughingstock of yourself. Warren, accustomed to my waffling, nonetheless insisted I meet Vinnette.

Everyone in my circle knew of Vinnette. Even then, decades before her gospel-infused production of *Your Arms Too Short to Box with God* thundered onto Broadway in 1976, I regarded Vinnette as theater royalty, a Black female innovator amid a sea of white male faces. She'd grown up in a well-heeled Jamaican family, with a dentist father who pushed her toward medicine rather than the arts. She obliged him to a point by earning a doctorate in psychology from Columbia University, but her tug toward the stage proved too powerful to overcome. After studying with Stella Adler and Lee Strasberg, she acted for a time, even creating and touring her one-woman show. Yet amid a paucity of good roles for Black actors, she turned toward directing and teaching, joining the faculty of the prestigious High School of Performing Arts in New York. Her production of *Dark of the Moon*, Warren explained, would be a revival of the 1945 Broadway folk play about a witch boy, John, who yearns to become human after falling in love with a mortal girl, Barbara Allen. Vinnette would assemble an all-Black cast as part of the Harlem Y's "Little Theater" program. The dance numbers in the play, set to spirituals, would be choreographed by a young Alvin Ailey, then also in the middle of creating what would become his signature work, *Revelations*.

Warren jotted down Vinnette's phone number and address and handed it to me. "Go see her," he said. "She's expecting you." At the time of our appointment later that week, I arrived at Vinnette's townhouse at 864 Broadway in Flatiron. What happened next makes me shake my head at myself.

As I entered the four-story building, I was so nervous to meet the director that I began yelling her name. "Vinnette Carroll!" I screamed like a squealing cat. "Vinnette Carroll!" On and on I shouted, one wooden staircase after the next, until I finally reached her doorway at the top. There she stood, tall and elegant with saucer-round eyes, hand on her hip and half-grinning as she searched my face. "What's the matter, Miss Cicely?" she said in that robust voice of hers.

"Nothing," I responded.

"Well then why on earth are you screaming?"

I shrugged and snickered. "Because I didn't know where you were," I said. It's a wonder she didn't send my silly tail back down those stairs and right out the door.

I did not audition that day. Vinnette and I simply chatted, about this play and that one, about my experience in *Carib*, about that moment I'd first encountered theater magic in Midtown. At some point I must have done a script reading for her. I don't recall. But soon after we connected, my misgivings melted away, as they were prone to do in Vinnette's affirming presence. Before I knew it, she and Warren had persuaded me to make my theater debut as Barbara Allen. She'd coach me, she promised, and supplement Lloyd's guidance of me. I agreed—and little has been the same in my life since.

Lloyd and Vinnette were both theatrical masters, but they

shepherded me in markedly different ways. Whereas Lloyd preferred a minimum effective dose of intervention, Vinnette took an interactive approach, one that included homework and built upon my childhood tendency to ask "Why?" During one of our sessions, Vinnette said to me, "I want you to observe someone from afar and then create a backstory for her. People don't come out of nowhere. They have roots." Someone's appearance and demeanor, she reasoned, offer clues to those beginnings, to the *whys* and *hows* of that person's present state. That notion becomes applicable when analyzing a character, when noticing how his or her story may manifest in every tic and sway, every lurch forward. Infusing a portrayal with such layers of truth is an actor's greatest aspiration.

I put my own handprint on that assignment by attempting what I'd been doing since my earliest years: staring at people's feet. On the train that week, I observed a Jewish woman, immaculately coiffed and manicured, with a lavish mink stole draped around her shoulders. I looked down. She had on saddle Oxfords, tattered around the edges, scuffed at the toe, with a bunion the size of a golf ball butting its head against the leather interior, threatening to break free. In that moment, I decided her wealth had to have been acquired. Perhaps she was a refugee who'd escaped to the United States, seeking a better life as my parents once had. If she'd been someone born into privilege, no way would she have donned such footwear or, for that matter, even boarded a subway car. I created a whole probable history for this woman based on those shoes, and submitted it to Vinnette. "Very good, Miss Cicely," said Vinnette, using the name she always called me. I beamed.

Vinnette taught me to learn technique and then to forget it—and to resurrect it only if it served my portrayal. Technique is important, to the extent that it is undergirded by emotion. I once knew an actress who was a brilliant technician, but her portrayals fell flat. She could create a moment and bring it to fruition, yet it was apparent she wasn't feeling anything, and as a result, neither was her audience. What is required for such a moment is what Warren had been claiming I had naturally. Vinnette trained me to mine the quarries of that childhood emotion and offer the riches onstage. When you're a novice, it's so important that whoever coaches you at that juncture knows what he or she is doing. Actors who find one great teacher in this business are blessed, do you hear me? God saw fit to smile on me twice.

Once Vinnette gave me the script for *Dark of the Moon*, it did not leave my hands. I ate with it, bathed with it, slept with it, slow danced to its tune during every hour of every day. "I want you to come for a table reading at the Y," Vinnette told me after we'd been studying with one another for a time. I was such a theater rookie that I'd never heard of a table read—a gathering of the cast for a script run-through. On the afternoon I turned up, my fellow actors had already assembled—and I didn't yet know a soul among them. Richard Ward and Isabel Sanford were on one side of the table. Clarence Williams III, Lea Scott, and Louise Stubbs sat on the other. I drew in a breath, clutched my script toward my chest, and took a place next to Roscoe Lee Browne, who'd been cast as a preacher. The previous year, he'd made his stage debut in a New York Shakespeare Festival production of *Julius Caesar*.

When my turn came, I picked up the script, held it three inches from my face, and began muttering my lines. Roscoe smiled, reached over, and gently pulled my hands down. I returned his grin but then moved my hands back up and perched the script on top of my nose again. On and on this went for most of the reading: me burying my fears into the pages, him encouraging me to reveal my face. Finally, near the end of the reading, Roscoe pulled my hands away once more, touched the bottom of my chin, and tilted my head upward. "You are going to be marvelous," he said in his deep baritone. "Just marvelous." I giggled, partly because I felt awkward—and partly because I hoped God had heard Roscoe.

As my stage debut grew closer, Emily told our mother I was to star in a play. "Huh, she goin' up there and make a fool of herself," Mom said in her thickest accent. Upon hearing this report from Emily, I called my mother and asked her to come to the show's opening night. At the time, I did not fully understand what compelled me to reach for the phone and dial my mom, particularly amid the gulf of unspoken hurts that had separated our worlds. Yet something in me wanted her there. Acting is, in part, about laying bare a character's soul, about allowing someone's secret hopes and frailties to be, at long last, *seen.* I realize now, in reflecting upon it, that I longed simply for my mother to see me. That is all. I needed to know that this left turn I'd taken, this calling I'd followed, was worthy of her acknowledgment. To be seen in this life, truly observed without judgment, is what it feels like to be loved. Whoever else might have shown up at my play, there was no gaze of pride, no measure of applause that would have mattered more to me than that woman's approval. That is why I invited her. And, perhaps because she was so stunned to hear from me, my mother immediately agreed to come.

On opening night, boy, I was a heap of nerves. Before the show, I made sure I knew exactly where my mom and the friend accompanying her would sit, which was at the center of the theater and about ten rows back from the stage. If I so much as glanced in my mother's direction, if our eyes inadvertently crossed paths as I was performing, that would have been the end of me. Knowing her precise location, I reasoned, would allow me to avoid her stare. It would not, as I soon discovered, put her on mute.

The lights faded and a hush swept the theater. The moment I emerged and took my place on the set, I could hear Mom's voice instantly. "Oh my God!" she said to her friend in what she thought was a whisper. I assure you it was not. "There she is! There's my String Bean!" The whole way through Act One, as I attempted to stay focused, I could hear her oooing and cooing, pointing out this prop and that one, and, as if creating a soundtrack to go along with the story line, laughing and drawing in deep breaths with her palm pressed over her heart. It just about drove me crazy.

Still, I somehow managed to concentrate, and by Act Two I'd even disappeared into my secret kingdom, that magical realm I withdraw to when a character's spirit washes through me. Barbara Allen's words, the sentences and scenes I'd rolled around on my tongue for so long, flowed effortlessly from my lips that evening. Acting, like every art form, is meant to transport its beholders, and the artist is frequently the first to make the journey. On my trip as Barbara Allen, I could speak. I could utter sentiments that I, Cicely Tyson, might never dare express. Revealing her interior world felt like unburdening my own, like emptying my soul of its every weight and care. It felt the way it did when I, playing a battered upright piano as a girl, moaned the words to old hymns that soothed my insides. It felt the way it had on that Sunday in church, decades earlier, when the saints had thrust me heavenward while I bellowed. On my first theater stage in a Harlem Y, I was that child once more, feet dangling from a chair, Holy Ghost sweeping through me. It felt like finding a sense of freedom I hadn't known I was in search of.

To the very last scene, Mom kept right on talking. After the audience bathed me in warm applause, I eventually found my way to the exit where the crowd was filing out. There stood my mother, with her pillbox hat and Sunday pocketbook, beaming as she accepted congratulatory remarks on my behalf. "Yes, I always knew, ever since she was a little girl, that she was going to be an actress," she claimed. "She liked to sing and to dance, and . . ." *Now wait a minute,* I thought. *This is the same mother who put me out of her house, the woman who would not speak to me because I wanted to act. And now she's out here telling this barefaced story to these people?* I found it so unbelievable that I stared at her and burst into laughter. All these years later, I'm still shaking my head.

I think now that my mother's pivot had nothing to do with a shift in her perspective. The devil, as she saw it, lived not just in the details, but also along the boulevards and byways of my business. Her view had not changed in that regard. Still, whether my mother admitted it to me forthrightly, which she did not on that evening, her behavior had rendered her opinion, handed down a verdict of validation. As she'd observed me from her place in the audience, open-mouthed and spellbound, she'd seen me as she could not have before, in that way you can see a thing only when you pull back from it, when you step away so you can marvel at its entirety. In panning out, she'd recognized me, for the first time, not just as a daughter to be lorded over, but as a vessel bearing a gift. And the heavenly Father, for reasons then unknown to both of us, had chosen to grace me with the seed of it.

PART TWO

ROOTED

A race without the knowledge of its history
is like a tree without roots.

—CHARLES C. SIEFERT,
The Negro's or Ethiopian's Contribution to Art

11

Riverside Park

Miles Davis could play that horn, I'll tell you—blew echoes of his brilliance right down through the centuries. That trumpet was his voice. In every riff and timbre of *Kind of Blue*, his 1959 album, you can hear his longing, feel his sorrow between the notes. A mother once took her eight-year-old daughter to see Miles in concert, and when it was finished, the girl said, "Mom, when he plays, it sounds like a baby crying." Through his trumpet Miles told his story, found his solace, spoke his truth. And long before I met him in the flesh, he'd already spoken to me.

I'd been curious about Miles for some time, especially once I heard he lived in Diahann Carroll's building. I'd first crossed paths with Diahann during my earliest days in theater, when Warren was still trotting me all over Broadway. She and I met backstage in 1955 at *House of Flowers*, the Harold Arlen–Truman Capote musical she starred in with Pearl Bailey. Diahann had a wicked sense of humor, and after our first laugh that evening, we never stopped cracking up. We became such good friends that we'd often go bike riding together all over Manhattan, a giggle punctuating each turn of the pedals. When I stopped by her apartment on Tenth Avenue, she mentioned that Miles and his wife, Frances Taylor, the dancer, lived on her floor. Diahann and Frances were close, so she knew all about him: the good, the bad, the genius and the drugs, the roving eye and the running around. She never let me go without telling me how talented he was. "Why does he play with his back turned to the audience?" I asked. Around town, I'd heard others remark that he seemed arrogant. "Who knows, child," Diahann said. I thought I'd show up at one of his concerts and see for myself.

Miles was playing at Lewisohn Stadium, the West Harlem amphitheater where so many of the greats performed. There in 1952, Marian Anderson, alongside the New York Philharmonic, lifted her contralto to the heavens. Ella Fitzgerald, Louis Armstrong, Leontyne Price—they all came through Lewisohn. I took the number 1 train up to 137th Street and found my way to the back of the open-air stadium. I had no intention of Miles seeing me. I climbed up to the last seat in the last row so I could take in the scene widely, observe Miles and his quintet from afar. There he was onstage, short 'fro, sculpted cheekbones, skin so velvety dark that it almost looked unreal. And boy, was he sharp: Brooks Brothers blazer, coolness personified. He blew that horn with such tenderness, such passion that it gave me goose pimples, the way it still does. He indeed turned his back to the audience; years would pass before I understood why. When the concert was over, I got back on the subway, returned home, and thought little more of him. Until the day, months later, when Miles showed up at Diahann's apartment while I was visiting her.

Diahann and I were sitting in her living room, laughing and carrying on, when we heard her front door creak open. "Diahann," said a raspy voice from down the hall. Before either of us could move, Miles, still in his housecoat, rounded the corner.

He was holding a measuring cup in his hand. "I need some sugar," he said. Miles, Diahann had told me, was quite a cook. As Diahann nodded and rose, Miles stared over at me. "Who's that?" he asked Diahann. "That's Cicely Tyson," Diahann said, chuckling. He never said a word to me. Once he had his sugar, he went on about his business.

Sometime in 1965 is when I spotted Miles on a bench in Riverside Park. By then, I'd moved from my place with Thelma up to Seventy-Fourth Street on the West Side. Miles lived nearby, in a brownstone at 312 West Seventy-Seventh Street. He and his close friend, Corky McCoy, the illustrator, were sitting side by side on the bench that morning, taking in the sun. I spotted Miles before he saw me and decided I'd sashay on by.

"Hey you," he said. I kept right on walking. *I am not "hey" or "you,"* I thought.

"Ms. Tyson," he said, "how are you?"

I smiled and turned around, but only part way. "I'm fine," I said.

"Come here," he said. "I want to talk to you for a minute."

I hesitated, not sure I wanted to be bothered. He was still married, and I had no interest in messing with no married man. When I told him that, he laughed.

"Frances and I have been separated for a while," he said.

"Well I have never heard that," I said, "so have a good day." I then walked off.

A few months later, I saw Miles again: same bench, same park, same glimmer in his eye as I strolled past. This time, he at least started out right, by addressing me by my name. We chatted briefly. He was just back from playing in San Francisco, I think, and I asked him about his time there. Just as I was wishing him well and turning to leave, he said, "Why don't you come see me sometime?"

"See you for what?" I said, stalling as I do when I don't know what else to say.

"Why don't you come by the house," he said. "My housekeeper, Burlina, is a good cook. She'll fix us a good lunch. Just come."

I shrugged. "Maybe . . ." I said, trailing off into shyness. "I'll think about it."

I knew of Burlina. She was a cousin to Harold Melvin, then a prominent hairstylist. For years, Burlina had kept house for Harold, and when he heard that Frances had fled the marriage in 1965 and moved out to California (and once they split, they never reunited), Harold sent his cousin over to take care of Miles. Around then, I got an earful from Diahann: Miles had apparently overdosed while he was in California and was found unconscious in a gutter. The friends who discovered him had cleaned him up, fed him, made sure he got plenty of rest, and then sent him back to Burlina's care in New York. On the day he invited me to come see him, he didn't look like any drug addict. He was a shiny penny, Black as me and then some, bright and glistening as the sun kissed his forehead. He didn't appear to be someone who'd known such troubles, and I couldn't imagine he'd ever hurt a woman.

As time went by, I'd occasionally see Miles on that bench. In those years, I routinely walked from my place clear up to 125th Street in Harlem. And when I'd run into him, every one of our conversations would end the same way: "You know, you'd like Burlina," he'd say. "She's a good cook. You should come see me." Curiosity at last got the better of me, so I called Harold.

"Miles invited me to come over and have lunch with him and your cousin," I told him. He laughed. "I don't know about Miles," he said, "but you'll love Burlina." That was enough to slow my stride for another few months.

I then ran into Miles again, this time on my street late one afternoon. I was walking up to my apartment when I heard footsteps behind me. I swiveled around. "Oh this is where you are?!" he said. "What are you doing here?" I said. "I just wanted to know where you live," he said, laughing, "but you wouldn't tell me." He asked to come in but of course I wouldn't let him. So we sat out on my front stoop and talked for the longest time until, by sunset, he'd persuaded me to come by and have that lunch with him. Soon after, I finally did.

Burlina, a plump older Black woman, answered the door. "Come on in!" she said, arms outstretched as if I were one of her own. Over smothered chicken and collards, we laughed and talked, her kidding Miles the entire time. She was as funny as they come, Burlina was, would laugh as easily as she embraced; you couldn't be Miles's friend and not be humorous. She also knew Miles better than just about anyone, I came to realize. To truly know that man, you had to see him away from the lights.

That day's lunch turned into more, and before long, Miles and I were seeing one another frequently. He'd invite me over any time there was cooking. First of all, that man loved to eat. And second, he did not like to be alone. Every time I'd come by, the house bustled with folks coming in and out, the smell of oxtails mixing with the sound of laughter. If Burlina wasn't cooking, Miles was. "Hey, got some chili in the pot, come over," he'd call his friends and say. Soon after, a house full of guys would be sitting at his table, with or without spoons and forks—didn't matter, he was going to feed them. I loved his oxtails in those days, but that chili, it was way too hot for me. His okra, however, was like none other. I used to hate okra, but when he made it, I began loving it. This was the way of things for a long while between Miles and me. He'd cook, I'd show up, and long after the others had gone, we'd linger in the shadows, lying across the foot of his bed with the aroma of black-eyed peas hanging over us.

When the world speaks of Miles, the legend, they have no idea who the man really was. The Miles I knew was sensitive and ailing, bruised by the hurts this life metes out. With trembling lips, he told me of the years during his childhood in East St. Louis when he'd been called Blackie by his friends and even some of his family, gazed down upon as a nobody, rendered invisible by his dark hue. He told me of the time, at age thirteen, when he'd been seduced by a grown woman, forced into his first sexual encounter with a friend of a relative. He spoke of the years when his father, a well-to-do dentist, had wanted him to follow in his career path, until a teacher who'd recognized Miles's gift intervened. "Forget it. Little Davis is not going to be any dentist," that teacher told Miles's father. "He's going to be a musician."

The first time Miles blew that horn, he'd found his consolation. In playing that trumpet, he did the only thing he knew how, the one thing that made him feel worthy. That is the Miles I knew and, in time, grew to cherish. Our conversations rippled with honesty, with depth of understanding. There is a love that gently guides your palm toward the small of another's back, a care that leads you to ensure no harm ever comes to that person. From the beginning, that is the love I had for Miles. That is the soft place where our connection rested its head. I'd been wary to get involved initially. But once I glimpsed his innards, and once it became clear that he and Frances had truly moved on (and I was with him on the day in 1966 when Miles received her divorce papers), my misgivings were swallowed whole by the warmth between us.

One night as I was leaving Miles's place, he asked me to stay the night with him. I blushed. "But I left the lights on and the

windows up at my place," I told him. "I've gotta go lock up."
"No you don't," he said teasingly. "Nobody's going to bother that place." When I insisted, he walked me around to my apartment to close it up. He then led me back to his place, pulled me close, and for the first time, we made love. It was beautiful. It was gentle. It was an expression of our deep care, our bodies undulating gracefully in the shadows of dusk. It was also everything I'd imagined it would be—and all that my connection with Kenneth had lacked. There was love. There was devotion. There was understanding. And in our embrace, there lived an enduring connection.

That was in 1966. As my heart fluttered to life for Miles, the nation's conscience stood at a crossroads. Just more than a decade earlier, in 1955, fourteen-year-old Emmett Till was accused of flirting with a white woman in Mississippi. The woman's husband and his half-brother brutally beat Emmett, shot him in the head, and hurled his corpse in a river. They were acquitted. Months later that same year, Rosa Parks, weary after a day's work and no doubt tired of her second-class relegation, refused to give up her seat for a white passenger and sit at the back of a segregated Montgomery bus. Dr. Martin Luther King Jr., then a young local pastor, helped organize the Montgomery Bus Boycott during 1956, which turned her stance into a rallying cry for justice and sent shudders from shore to shore.

That protest swelled into the Civil Rights Movement, a stewpot of agony and aspiration. In 1957 at Central High School in Little Rock, Arkansas, the Little Rock Nine, determined to live out the 1954 promise of the US Supreme Court decision of *Brown v. Board of Education*, braved their way through violent mobs spewing spit at their stone expressions. Then in 1960, the Greensboro Four—students emboldened by Emmett's murder and steeped in the tenets of peaceful protest—scooted up to a whites-only Woolworth counter and staged a sit-in. Dr. King, the face and pulse of the Movement, gave voice to their dream during the 1963 March on Washington. On that muggy August day, a quarter of a million souls crowded onto the National Mall in Washington, DC, to hear Dr. King declare a hope that, up to then, had eluded us. The country, as it does now, faced a choice—to peer over its shoulder at a wrenching past and continue along its trajectory, or to march toward a different season, a powerful new beginning. The summer I began seeing Miles, I faced that very decision.

By the time I met Miles, my career had taken root. Warren had introduced me to the theatrical world, and my role in Vinnette's production widened that world's scope and sphere. Every year in those times, directors pulled together a variety show including some of Broadway's powerful scenes, a festival to showcase up-and-coming actors. For the Talent '59 festival, a scene from *Dark of the Moon* was selected. My castmate Hal DeWindt and I were chosen to perform. I was absolutely blown away by the experience. Everybody in the theater world, it seemed, was there to see us, and because of the exposure, my phone started ringing. "Can we get Cicely Tyson to come to this audition?" they'd ask Warren. Things were happening, boy, and I could feel the shift in the air, the electricity. I'd do a little part here, another there, and before I could finish, there'd be more requests: "We want Cicely Tyson." Honey, the moment I heard, I was down my apartment steps and out of there. I'd sometimes go to three auditions in a day.

I can still feel the exhilaration of that time. I tried out to portray a girl from the slums in the film *12 Angry Men*, a courtroom drama starring Henry Fonda. "You're too chic for the role," I heard from the casting director. That was my cue to regroup. I scurried home, fished out an old skirt and ripped its hemline, scattered my hair all over the place, and topped it off with a dirty raincoat. When I turned up again, the secretary, who didn't recognize me, attempted to block my entrance. But once I got through to the casting director, I read the part again and was hired on the spot.

Around that time, I was also called in to audition as an understudy for the intrepid Eartha Kitt, as Jolly Rogers in the play *Jolly's Progress*. I landed the role but never performed. Still, it was thrilling just to be there, alongside a star who played veteran to my rookie. Eartha never spoke to me or even glanced in my direction, and no way would I have approached her. So you can imagine my surprise when I overheard her on the phone in her dressing room. "Who, Cicely?" she said. "Oh my goodness, she's a fantastic actress." You could've tipped me over with a feather. I didn't think Eartha even knew my name, much less regarded me as talented.

During this whirlwind of opportunity I'd moved to the Upper West Side. In many ways, I and a handful of other Black artists integrated that neighborhood. Eartha Kitt, who was already there when I arrived in 1960, added one of the first dabs of color. After I'd settled into my place on Seventy-Fourth, Diahann came to visit and loved the area. She was married then to Monte Kay, the music entrepreneur and agent, and the two of them moved around the corner from me, near Seventieth and West End. Then Harry Belafonte, who was being managed by Monte, moved a few blocks north of their place. Brock Peters of *To Kill a Mockingbird* fame soon followed. So did Lena Horne, who moved into the same building where Harry lived. (And by the way, it was Harry Belafonte's hit 1957 song "Mama Look a Boo Boo" that led to another of my nicknames. I loved the tune, and when Emily's youngest daughter, Verna, would come toddling over to me, I'd call out "Boo! Boo!" She assumed that was my name and began calling me that, and now three generations of Tysons know me as Aunt Boo Boo.)

We were still "colored" in those years, so just renting an apartment required an act of God. To supplement my feast-or-famine stage work pay, I'd taken a secretarial job at Save the Children. During my lunch break one day, I scoured the classifieds in the *New York Times*, looking for apartments. I found one, and when I turned up, a white woman answered the door. "I am inquiring about the apartment you have vacant," I said. She slammed the door before I could even finish my sentence. I found another place, and this time, I called first. The woman explained that she was about to vacate the apartment, to which I replied, "I am Black. And if you have feelings about allowing your apartment to be rented by someone of that race, tell me now." She laughed. "You don't have to worry," she said. "My husband is Black." That's how I ended up as the lone Black person in an all-white building, a few streets away from a love story.

The Blacks—the critically acclaimed play written by French dramatist Jean Genet—became the defining role of my blossoming career. I am not one to feel as if I have arrived, for even at age ninety-six, I am still arriving. But being cast in that show was the closest I've come to experiencing that delight. From the pen of a provocateur flowed a masterpiece of racial reckoning, an incendiary visual display meant to cajole. The spectacle unfolded nightly, down at St. Mark's Playhouse in the Village, and marked the beginning of avant-garde theater.

For Genet, *The Blacks* was a commentary on prejudice, a play within a play urging white audiences to gaze upon themselves. For me and a cadre of other rising Black actors, it was also sustained exposure and steady earnings. The show became the longest-running off-Broadway nonmusical of the 1960s, debuting in May 1961 and not lowering its curtain until September 1964. I played Stephanie "Virtue" Diop, an impish streetwalker, and a steadily paid one, thank you very much. The show lasted so long that I came and went over its three-year, 1,408-show run, squeezing in other work where I could. The same was true for much of the cast. Dignitaries filed through the audience regularly, and in 1962, Dr. King and his wife, Coretta, took their seats in the audience. I wasn't performing on that evening, but his attendance demonstrated the show's importance. It was more than a play. It was a landmark cultural moment, an indictment of white supremacy and a theatrical pivot point.

Just about every young actor of note was, at some point, connected with *The Blacks*. The grand ensemble included James Earl Jones, Roscoe Lee Browne, Lou Gossett Jr., Billy Dee Williams, Charles Gordone, and Maya Angelou. The circle of Black actors was then fairly small, so I knew several of my castmates. Others, like James Earl Jones, I met for the first time. He was painfully shy in those years, reticent enough to make my own bashfulness seem like extroversion. He kept to himself backstage, but boy, once that curtain rose, he spoke plenty. Maya, who played the queen—both in *The Blacks* and in real life—intimidated me at first. At six feet, she towered over me, and she had the confidence and booming voice to match her stature. She walked around like she owned the world, whereas I always sat in a corner and waited for Gene Frankel, the director, to shout, "Come onstage!" before I moved a hair. At the read-through for the show, I first spotted Maya alongside Abbey Lincoln, the actress and jazz vocalist, who was also in the cast. Maya and Abbey were quite close then, before they later had a falling-out. Recalling it brings me to tears, because they had been such good friends.

Maya was larger than life, a force of nature, and every other cliché inadequate for capturing her essence. Over the years, we'd often debate about when we met, with me insisting it was during *The Blacks*. "No, I met you two years before that," she'd claim, but she could never recall where. "You are the one friend I've known the longest." I'd deny her recollection, and back and forth we'd go. It didn't matter to me when we met, because we became so close. Maya was many things to many people, but perhaps one of her greatest roles was that of a hostess. That woman's home, then at Park West Village near 100th Street and Columbus, was always full! She seemed to know everybody, from Duke Ellington to James Baldwin, as well as the scores of artists she'd connected with through the Harlem Writers Guild, part of the Black Arts Movement of the 1960s: Rosa Guy (the guild's cofounder, along with John Oliver Killens), Audre Lorde, Sarah E. Wright, Douglas Turner Ward, on and on. For Maya to pull out her finest cutlery and Baccarat crystal, there needn't be a holiday or special occasion, other than the blessing of still breathing. She was always welcoming people, throwing pots onto the stove, lending her generous spirit and constant laughter to her Southern home-cooked recipes, just like Miles did.

I was precisely the opposite. Once I retreated into my apartment after a show, my home became my haven. "I don't know how you have any friends," my mother would often say. "You never have anyone over." I didn't need to. I did plenty of socializing at Maya's place. My friend Roxie Roker—who in *The Blacks* eventually replaced Maya as the queen before going on years later to play Helen in the TV sitcom *The Jeffersons*—was often over at Maya's. Roxie and I clicked from the first hello. She's also Caribbean (her father was from Andros in the Bahamas), and when we'd get together, we'd yammer back and forth in a heavy West Indian dialect. It was very funny.

The Blacks cast did everything together: we dined, drank, gossiped, and even traveled with one another. One summer we were invited to perform our show at a festival in Venice, my first time in Europe. I loved Venice, but my eagerness for adventure lured me beyond. "Why don't you just stay here?" Roscoe asked me. "You can stay," I told him, "but I'm going on." I took the train to Rome and then to Munich. Lex Monson, who played the bishop in *The Blacks*, came with me. Lex hopped off in Germany, but I boarded a sleeper train on to Barcelona. I found it thrilling to be on the road by myself, wandering and wondering as I'd done in childhood, taking in the smells and sounds and rich history of each passing city, storing away the experiences in that place where I keep all my sense memories. I relished my time in Spain in particular. Having grown up in an integrated neighborhood that included Puerto Ricans, I enjoyed the warm spirit of the Latin culture. The Spaniards greeted me with open hearts.

Home in New York, the crew got back to talking smack. On most nights after the show, a bunch of us would gather at Sardi's, an Italian eatery on West Forty-Fourth Street in the theater district. Child, we talked about each other like *dogs*! If you weren't in attendance on a particular evening, boy, you can be sure you were being bad-mouthed. Everybody gathered there, even those who weren't in the show. Lonne Elder came through a lot. So did Diana Sands, Bobby Hooks, and of course, Diahann and Sidney. That show not only kept us employed, it also kept us laughing. Those were some fun times.

Everyone, and especially me, knew that Sidney and Diahann

had eyes for one another. The two of them went to France to work on the movie *Paris Blues* in 1961, and while they were there, they must've forgotten they were both married. From the beginning of their relationship, I never believed Sidney would leave his wife to be with Diahann, but next thing I knew, Diahann was divorcing Monte so she could be with Sidney. She even bought a place and furnished it, waiting for him to come, but he never did. She set that record straight herself in her own book, *The Legs Are the Last to Go.*

Not long after Diahann separated from Monte—and was waiting on Sidney to divorce his wife, as he'd said he would—I ran into Sidney near Carnegie Hall. As usual, he came over and hugged me. "Hey, Cic!" he said, beaming. "How are you?" "I'm good," I told him. After we'd caught up, I said, "Well congratulations . . . I hear you're finally going to take the walk again." He looked down at the pavement and started kicking around a can, and in that moment, I knew: Sidney wasn't ever going to marry Diahann. He didn't have to say another word. His body language did his speaking.

During the years to follow, Diahann carried on with her life and career, earning a Tony for *No Strings*, an Oscar nomination for *Claudine*, and a Golden Globe for her lead role in *Julia*, the 1968 sitcom that was the first to defy Black female stereotypes on television. I'm not sure whether she ever got over Sidney. But through her portrayals and an extraordinary six decades on the stage, the swelegant, elegant Diahann Carroll surely spoke a resounding word.

I had my own share of romances before I met Miles. After my brief marriage to Kenneth, I hadn't wanted much to do with

In the romantic comedy *Bustin' Loose* (1981), Richard Pryor and I scored a box-office hit with our first on-screen pairing.

MICHAEL OCHS ARCHIVES/STRINGER/GETTY IMAGES

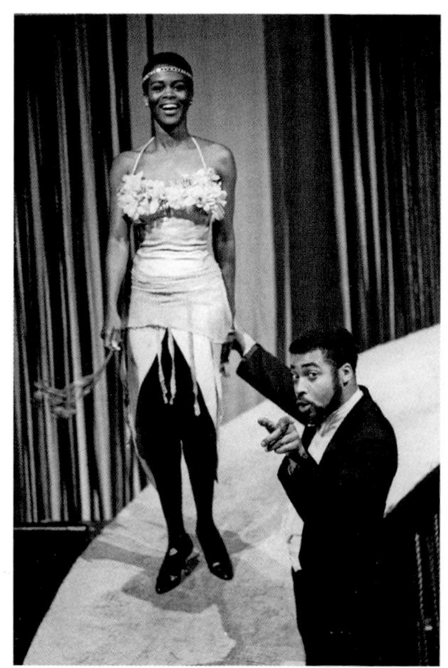

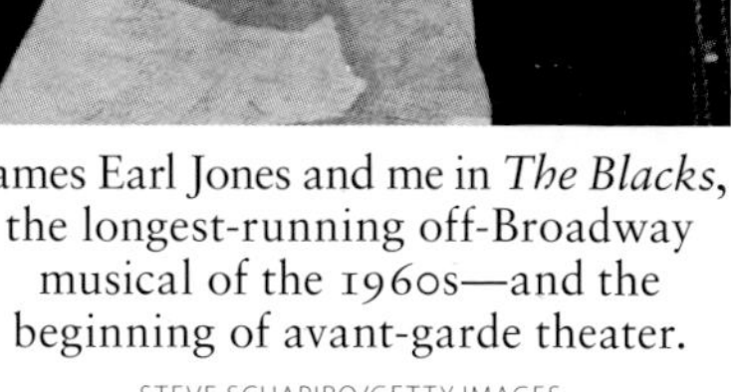

James Earl Jones and me in *The Blacks*, the longest-running off-Broadway musical of the 1960s—and the beginning of avant-garde theater.

STEVE SCHAPIRO/GETTY IMAGES

Alongside my costars in the 1966 musical drama *A Man Called Adam*, (*clockwise from my right*) Ossie Davis, Frank Sinatra, Sammy Davis Jr., and Louis Armstrong.

SILVER SCREEN COLLECTION/GETTY IMAGES

The Trip to Bountiful—a ride across the stage, courtesy of my castmates during the show's final performance.

WALTER MCBRIDE/GETTY IMAGES

In 2015, James Earl Jones and I costar in Broadway's *The Gin Game*—our first onstage reunion since 1966.

JEMAL COUNTESS/GETTY IMAGES

In the 1972 drama *Sounder*, I played Rebecca, devoted wife to Nathan (Paul Winfield). For my performance, I earned an Oscar nomination.

PARAMOUNT PICTURES/HANDOUT/GETTY IMAGES

I'm with Maya Angelou in the opening scene of *Roots*, the 1977 television miniseries that revolutionized the culture.

WALT DISNEY TELEVISION VIA GETTY IMAGES

In the 1974 television drama *The Autobiography of Miss Jane Pittman*, I played the 110-year-old Jane, defying Jim Crow by drinking from a whites-only fountain.

AFRO NEWSPAPER/GADO/GETTY IMAGES

In 2016, President Obama awarded me with the Presidential Medal of Freedom—the nation's highest civilian honor.

NICHOLAS KAMM/GETTY IMAGES

In 2015, I was chosen as a Kennedy Center honoree, alongside (*clockwise from my right*) Carole King, Seiji Ozawa, Rita Moreno, and George Lucas.

POOL/GETTY IMAGES

In 2020, I was inducted into the Television Academy Hall of Fame.

JORDAN STRAUSS/INVISION/AP/SHUTTERSTOCK

In 2018, Turner Classic Movies honored me with a hand-and-footprint ceremony at the TCL Chinese Theatre in Hollywood.

EARL GIBSON III/GETTY IMAGES

In 2010, the NAACP honored me with the Spingarn Medal, its most prestigious award. Here, I'm with fashion designer B Michael and Mark-Anthony Edwards at the event in Kansas City.

COURTESY OF B MICHAEL

Accepting an honorary Oscar in 2018—forty-five years after the Oscar nod for *Sounder*. I was the first Black actress to receive the award.

KEVIN WINTER/GETTY IMAGES

For my portrayal of Jane Pittman in 1974, I earned two Emmys—for Best Lead Actress in a Drama and an unprecedented Emmy for Actress of the Year.

MICHAEL OCHS ARCHIVES/STRINGER/GETTY IMAGES

In 2013, *The Trip to Bountiful* culminated with a trio of honors: a Tony, a Drama Desk Award, and the Outer Critics Circle Award for Best Actress.

MIKE COPPOLA/GETTY IMAGES

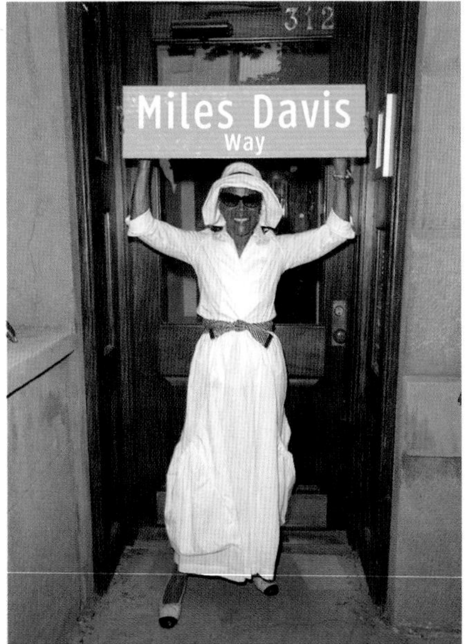

In 2014 in Manhattan, I joined with revelers in renaming West Seventy-Seventh Street "Miles Davis Way"—a tribute to my late husband, who once lived there.

EARL GIBSON III/GETTY IMAGES

In 2018, my hat turned heads and set Twitter ablaze at the homegoing service of my dear friend Aretha Franklin.

PAUL SANCYA/ASSOCIATED PRESS

A former model, I was working the runway at 2009's Fashion Week in New York City.

BEBETO MATTHEWS /ASSOCIATED PRESS

Sass on display during my early modeling days, circa 1956—with the sense of style I inherited from my parents.

COURTESY OF CICELY TYSON

Oprah and I are the proud godmothers to Tyler Perry's son, Aman. Here, in 2015, we celebrate Aman's christening at Tyler's home in Beverly Hills.

COURTESY OF TYLER PERRY STUDIOS

In the years since my school opened its doors, I have relished attending every graduation. Here, seniors listen in as I commemorate their accomplishments.

MUSTAFA HOOTEN, D1 MEDIA PRO, LLC

At the 2015 Kennedy Center Honors, I gathered with my family (*clockwise, from my right*): my great-nephew, Devin Grandison; my niece Maxine Grandison; Maxine's husband, Louis Grandison; my dear friend Arthur Mitchell; and my great-niece, Rebecca Grandison-Akinyooye.

RON SACHS-POOL/GETTY IMAGES

In celebration of civil rights icon Rosa Parks's birthday in 1990, I gathered with Coretta Scott King, Everee Ward (Parks's aunt), and Rosa Parks.

ROBERT SHERBOW/GETTY IMAGES

I'm with writer James Baldwin, dancer Arthur Mitchell, and actor Harry Belafonte at the *To Be Young, Gifted, and Black* gala at New York's Cherry Lane Theater, 1969.

RON GALELLA/GETTY IMAGES

In 2012, I reunited with longtime friends Harry Belafonte and Sidney Poitier at the 43rd NAACP Image Awards in Los Angeles.

CHRIS PIZZELLO/ASSOCIATED PRESS

Diahann Carroll, my close friend who introduced me to Miles Davis.

© ANNIE WATT.COM

Arthur Mitchell, the first African-American dancer with the New York City Ballet—and my closest friend. Here, we're on the red carpet of the Oscars in March 1973, when I was nominated for *Sounder*.

LOS ANGELES TIMES PHOTOGRAPHIC ARCHIVE, LIBRARY SPECIAL COLLECTIONS, CHARLES E. YOUNG RESEARCH LIBRARY, UCLA

In Tyler Perry's 2006 film *Madea's Family Reunion*, I share a scene with longtime friend Maya Angelou. We first met while playing in *The Blacks*.

PHOTO 12/ALAMY STOCK PHOTO

I'm with Elizabeth Taylor and producer Zev Buffman at the premiere of the Broadway revival of *The Corn Is Green* in 1983.

RON FREHM/ASSOCIATED PRESS

In 1974, First Lady Betty Ford chats with me at an event in Birmingham, Alabama.

MARK FOLEY/ASSOCIATED PRESS

At the 25th anniversary Essence Music Festival in New Orleans in 2019, with Forever First Lady Michelle Obama.

COURTESY OF B MICHAEL AMERICA

At the 1995 grand opening of the Cicely L. Tyson Community School of Performing and Fine Arts, I celebrated with former New York City mayor David Dinkins, Angela Bassett, Nick Ashford, Valerie Simpson, George Faison, Tamara Tunie, and other friends.

BRIAN KILLIAN/STRINGER/GETTY IMAGES

I'm flanked by friends Shonda Rhimes and Ava DuVernay at the 2019 *Vanity Fair* Oscar Party in Los Angeles.

KEVIN MAZUR/VF19/GETTY IMAGES

Escorted on the red carpet by my beloved godson, rocker Lenny Kravitz, at the 2013 premiere of *Lee Daniels' The Butler*.

JAMIE MCCARTHY/GETTY IMAGES

My decades-long friend Aretha Franklin.

FRANK MICELOTTA/INVISION/ASSOCIATED PRESS

At the 43rd NAACP Image Awards in 2012, I share a light moment with Viola Davis—my on-screen daughter in ABC's *How to Get Away with Murder*.

ALBERTO E. RODRIGUEZ/GETTY IMAGES

I'm with distinguished designer B Michael, my couturier of nearly two decades, at the 2019 *Vanity Fair* Oscar Party in Los Angeles.

STEVE GRANITZ/GETTY IMAGES

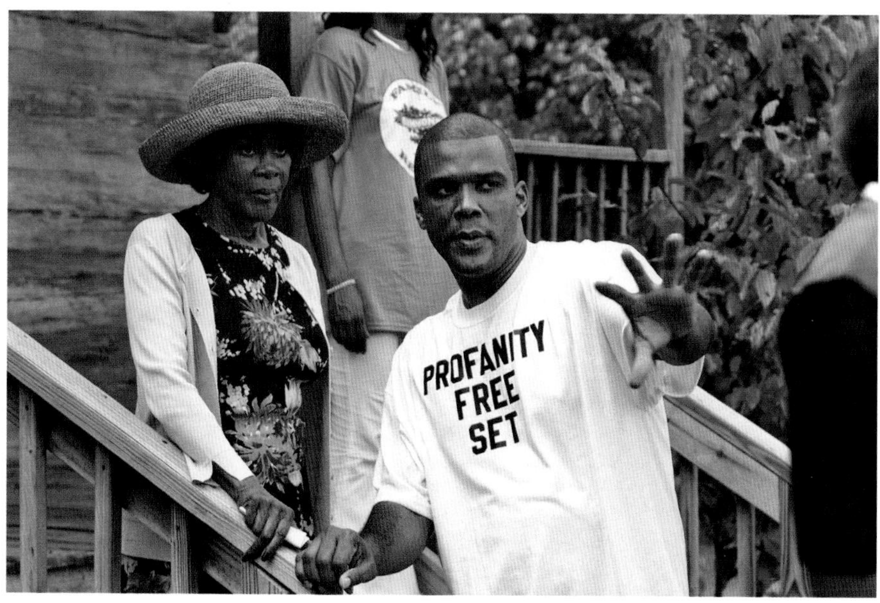

In 2006, I worked with filmmaker and close friend Tyler Perry for the first time, here on the set of *Madea's Family Reunion*.

PHOTO 12/ALAMY STOCK PHOTO

Miles and I were married for eight years. Here, we're sashaying through the Copenhagen airport in 1982—the year after we traded vows.

JAN PERSSON/GETTY IMAGES

Miles and me, at the premiere of *The Heart Is a Lonely Hunter* in July 1968—a few months after Dr. Martin Luther King Jr. was assassinated.

RON GALELLA/GETTY IMAGES

In a 1983 star-studded tribute to Miles Davis, I joined him onstage at Radio City Music Hall.

GARY GERSHOFF/GETTY IMAGES

men. My priorities were my daughter, Joan, and the stage. Still, a few relationships sprang up, some of them lasting the length of my pinkie finger. I dated a disc jockey for a time, a man I met at a jazz club. That went on for only a few months. After he'd worried me half to death with too much talking, I dumped him by calling into a radio station and dedicating the Billie Holiday song to him "You Ain't Gonna Bother Me No More." Another man, a dancer, lasted just weeks before I let him go. I don't even recall why. But anytime I'd break up with someone, my mother would start asking about him. Men loved to charm her with gifts and flowers, and she gladly accepted the bounty. "Why you didn't marry so-and-so?" she'd lament. "He was such a nice man." "Look, get out of my business," I'd retort. "If he's so nice, why don't you marry him?" That was enough to close her mouth.

Even when I wasn't dating, others always seemed to be speculating that I was, or else trying to get in on the action. Backstage at *The Blacks*, someone once cut a peeping-Tom hole in the curtain covering my changing area. "Who did this?" I asked, grinning. A few of my male castmates snickered but none of them said a word. I later found out it was Godfrey Cambridge, who admitted he'd been trying to catch a glimpse. I didn't pay him any mind, especially after I made a discovery off set. I once went to the library to do some research on Jean Genet, and there it was in black and white: the playwright and I had the same birthdate, December 19. I decided then that I, too, must be an artistic genius. Well, sir, the next day, I strode backstage with my head up in the air, never looking to the left or right. I stepped into my changing area and yanked closed my holey curtain. "It doesn't matter what tricks any of you all try to pull on me," I blurted out, "because I know I am a genius." We all got a good laugh out of that one.

Godfrey wasn't the only suitor trying to sneak a peek. Once I became known around town as Cicely Tyson the promising young star, my phone never stopped ringing. I got calls from just about every Black man in theater. "Can I help you?" I'd say. "This is so-and-so," I'd hear, "and I just want to welcome you to the business. How about dinner?" One man would call and then say nothing once I picked up. Another actor, one who was married, would call and try to disguise his voice. James Earl Jones, after he'd moved past his shyness and gotten to know me well (in 1962, we did *Moon on a Rainbow Shawl* together), once said, "All of the guys in all of the plays around town were just trying to take Cicely out." I didn't go out with any of them. I wanted to keep my stage life and my personal one separate.

It was during these years that I met my closest friend, Arthur Mitchell, the acclaimed dancer. One night when I was leaving *The Blacks*, walking over to the Hotel Albert, I heard someone behind me say, "Ms. Tyson." I turned around to see him, tall and beaming. "My name is Arthur Mitchell," he said. "I know who you are," I said, chuckling. A few years earlier in 1955, Arthur had already cemented his place in history as the first African-American dancer with the New York City Ballet; soon after, he went on to become the principal dancer. He'd just seen *The Blacks* that evening, and he told me how much he'd enjoyed the play. That topic led to another, and Lord knows how long we stood on that corner and talked! Finally I told him, "I've gotta go." "Okay," he said, turning to leave, "but we're gonna work together someday." *He's crazy*, I thought to myself. *I'm an actress, he's a dancer. How in the world are we ever going to work together?* Time would prove me to be the crazy one.

We ran into each other again, this time on the Upper West Side. He, too, had an apartment there, a few blocks away from mine. He walked me from the number 1 train at Seventy-Ninth

Street to my front door. Thus began a ritual: when I'd return from *The Blacks*, Arthur would meet me at the train, escort me to my place, and then walk to his own. And every single night, he'd stop by a candy store and buy himself a pint of vanilla ice cream. Once home, he'd call me, as if years had passed since we'd last connected, and we'd talk as he scooped up his dessert. We'd laugh and carry on for hours, talking about everything and everyone. That conversation went on for sixty years.

In those times, I did have one romance that survived longer than five minutes. Just as I was hobnobbing my way into the business, I crossed paths with Bert Andrews, the photographer. I still marvel at how destiny's gossamer strings pulled us together. Sometime around 1956, I was walking down Seventh Street when I spotted a gentleman on the other side of the road. His eyes lit up as if he knew me, and he made his way over to my side of the avenue. With a camera around his neck and a leather bag overflowing with film, he introduced himself. "Ms. Tyson, my name is Bert Andrews," he said, extending his hand. He was working for the *Amsterdam News* at the time, he explained, but he once had worked with the photographer Chuck Stewart, who'd photographed me for the cover of *Our World*. "If you ever need some more photos for your portfolio," Bert offered, "I'd be happy to take them." The whole time he spoke, I stood there staring at him and thinking, *Where have I seen this face before?* I couldn't place him. And suddenly as he was leaving, it came to me, clear as crystal: *This is the man from the wedding.*

Several years before, I'd attended a wedding with my family. I was seated at a table with my mother and Emily, enjoying the meal and the celebration, when a man walked into the ballroom.

He was there to take photographs, and a host greeted him. I was so taken with this man—the kindness in his expression, the depth in his eyes, the gentleness of his manner—that I could not look away. That is how arresting I found his face. The two of us were never introduced that day, and moments after he arrived, he disappeared into another room to take pictures of the wedding party, I'm sure. And here he was, a decade later, as drawn to my face, from across a street, as I'd once been to his. Isn't that something? I told him what I'd recalled, and after a round of amazement, he handed me his card. "Give me a call when you are ready," he said. "It would be my pleasure to photograph you."

Bert began shooting me, and eventually, we started seeing one another. We were two young strivers, he poring over photos in his darkroom in the wee hours after midnight, me making relentless rounds to build my modeling career. In was in that commonality of dreams, as well as the warmth I first recognized in him, that our relationship flourished, both personally and professionally. After I'd landed the lead in *Dark of the Moon*, Vinnette said to me, "I need a photographer." "I have one for you," I told her. Bert came to a rehearsal and met my mentor, and after looking through his portfolio, she hired him. In the years to follow, Bert became the foremost photographer of Black theater, his work featured in a book I cherish and still purchase by the dozens, *In the Shadow of the Great White Way: Images from the Black Theatre*. The 1950s and 1960s were a momentous era in Black theater, and through his wide lens and open heart, he captured and memorialized all of it.

Bert and I dated for a few years, and even once life moved us on, we remained good friends. "Whatever happened to 'Buhk'?" my mother would of course ask, mispronouncing his name. "He was such a nice man." I'd just smile and shake my head. I saw Bert frequently around the business, and while I was in *The Blacks*, he once came by to show me some photographs he'd taken. During the show's run, I'd sometimes stay at the Hotel Albert down on Tenth Street and within walking distance of St. Mark's Playhouse. Bert met me there and as we looked through his shots, he noticed a review I'd just clipped out of the *New York Times*. The piece was about Paule Marshall, the renowned Barbados-born writer. In 1959, she'd penned her first book, *Brown Girl, Brownstones*, a novel about a Trinidadian immigrant family eking out an existence in 1940s Brooklyn, while confronting the dual scourges of racism and poverty. "Some day they are going to do a movie of this book," I told Bert, "and I am going to play the lead character."

"Oh, do you know Paule?" he asked.

"No," I said, "but I am *going* to know her."

A smile spread over his face. "We did our first job together," he told me, "she as a writer and me as a photographer. I'll call her up and arrange for you to meet her."

On the appointed day, Bert and I, along with Paule and her husband, gathered at the couple's home. Over dinner, Paule and Bert, who hadn't seen each other in the longest time, caught up about everything under the sun—but no mention of the book. When it came time to leave, Paule leaned in to talk with me. "You know," she said, "this book that I've written . . . CBS is talking about turning it into a television movie. But I don't have any confidence it will happen." She then handed me a copy of the book. "Read it—and when I return from Barbados in a few weeks, I'll let you know if anything comes of it."

I inhaled the book in one sitting. Paule didn't just write a novel teeming with authenticity of the immigrant experience. We know now, in hindsight, that her writings became what scholars have called a "critical bridge" between early Black female writers like Zora Neale Hurston and later ones such as Toni Morrison. She also did what so little art, then and now, manages to do: shine a light on the interior world of Black women, and in so doing, render us fully human. The novel features two characters, sixteen-year-old Selina Boyce, and her sister, Ina, nine. As I read, my skin tingled as it does when I absolutely know I am meant to take on a project. Soon after, Paule called me. "Yes, CBS is going to do it," she told me, "and they want you to play Selina." I paused. "Well I don't want to play the older sister," I told her. "I want to play Ina." God knows I was nowhere near age nine, and playing Ina would strain credulity for the audience, but that is the role that resonated with me. That child was in me.

Still, when I showed up to meet the casting director, I read for Selina. And as I was leaving, the director said to me, "Ms. Tyson, come back here. Why don't you read Ina." When I was done, he reached over, took my script, folded it, and tucked it under my arm. "Call me after six o'clock this evening" is all he said. As it turns out, he'd been prepared to bring in a young girl to play Ina, but once he heard me, that plan vanished. I did call him that night, and to my astonishment (I was thirty-five at the time!), he offered me the role of Ina. Benita Evans, then twenty, played Selina. Ossie Davis played our father. The CBS Repertoire Workshop marked my first role on a TV show, and it all came about through a fortuitous reconnection with Bert. This life amazes me.

Between Bert and Miles stretched a long canyon, one filled with no serious romance to speak of. The loves of my life then were Joan, who I kept at my side whenever I wasn't working, and the stage. I dated here and there, of course, but had no intention of marrying, not in the years when I was building my career. My friend Roxie went a different way.

When we weren't cutting up over at Sardi's, Roxie and I would sometimes meet at the Carlyle, near Seventy-Sixth and Madison. During her run in *The Blacks*, she began dating Sy Kravitz, then a news producer at NBC. "I've got something to tell you," she said one evening when we met for dinner. She smiled. "What?" I said, leaning in. "Sy asked me to marry him," she said. My eyes widened. "Oh really?" I said. She nodded. "Well my guy hasn't asked me to marry him," I said with a smirk, "so you better hurry up and marry that one." I of course had no desire to tie the knot then, nor do I recall whom I was even seeing. Yet I was thrilled to witness the joy on my friend's countenance. Roxie and Sy indeed married in 1962 and soon moved around the corner from me on the Upper West Side. Two years later, they welcomed their son, little Lenny. Lenny Kravitz is my beloved godson, and I'll tell you, I am so proud of that man.

Years later when Lenny was grown, I was still living on Seventy-Fourth Street. I heard some loud music in Riverside Park. I opened the door to the terrace and spotted a group out there carrying on. So I put on my shoes and went down to see what all the commotion was about. As I entered the park, there stood Lisa Bonet, Lenny's wife at the time and then playing Denise Huxtable on *The Cosby Show.* "Ms. Cicely!" she said, hugging me.

"What are you all doing over here in my neighborhood?" I asked her. "We're cutting Lenny's record," she told me. When I made my way back upstairs, I called Roxie.

"You hear all that noise?" I said, raising the phone's receiver out on the terrace. "That's your son and daughter-in-law making all of this noise in our neighborhood." We both just fell out laughing.

During my years in *The Blacks*, and as winds of dissent bristled through the nation, I once considered relocating to Atlanta, the cradle of the Civil Rights Movement. My castmates—and especially Maya, who'd been quite involved with the Movement and knew Dr. King well—talked me out of it. They feared for my life.

My sister, Emily, had traveled down South several times. A girlfriend of hers was married to a minister, and he was from Georgia, I think. After visiting there, Emily would come back raving about how wonderful it was to be surrounded by Black people who had their own schools, their own churches, their own cultural events and communities. She had a ball. Visiting a loving Black family in Atlanta provided my sister with one vantage point, but driving through the small towns and byways of the South gave me a different one.

During the 1950s, I took a road trip with a friend of mine, a musician by the name of Eddie. He and I drove from New York to Georgia, winding our way through Virginia, North Carolina, and Tennessee. Somewhere along the back roads of Alabama, we stopped at a small restaurant, more like a shack, to get something to eat. He parked and went around back to put in his order. I stayed in the car. Moments later, he jumped back in the car, out of breath and gripping a brown paper bag containing his food. He shoved the key into the ignition.

"What's the matter with you?" I asked him, laughing a little. "Why can't we sit here and eat?"

"Shhh!" he said, starting the engine. "Don't laugh. We gotta get out of here."

After we'd driven a distance, he exhaled and I started in with my questions.

"Why did we leave there so fast?" I asked him.

He looked straight ahead at the road. "We're in the South, Cicely," he said.

"What does that mean?" I asked.

"It means it wouldn't take them but a second to pull me out of this car and lynch me right here."

I will never know what happened around back outside of that restaurant. Eddie never revealed it to me. Perhaps, while he waited for his order, someone had shot him a look that sent shivers through him. Perhaps he'd dared to breathe in a white person's direction. Perhaps, thinking of Emmett Till, he feared the imminence of death, his own lifeless body floating down a river.

That experience piqued my first deep interest in the mistreatment of our people in this country. I began reading, taking in all I could about our history, about the assaults that tested us but could not break us. It stung me even as it flung open my eyes. America has our blood on its palms, our flesh between its teeth. When you come to understand what we have endured, when you let the barefaced savagery of it all truly penetrate, you are forever haunted by the horror.

Years after my journey south, when I mentioned to Maya that I wanted to temporarily leave acting to become part of the Civil Rights Movement, I thought I had a fairly good idea of what I'd be getting into. Maya disagreed. "You can't go down there," she insisted. "You'll end up dead." The quiver in her voice, one I'd never once heard up to then, persuaded me she was right.

12

Going Natural

I NEVER set out to start a natural hair craze. On the day I showed up at Shalimar barbershop in Harlem, I simply wanted a haircut. What came next stunned even me.

The year was 1962. I was in *The Blacks* by then and had also been asked to take a role in *Between Yesterday and Today*, the CBS Sunday morning drama. In a single live episode, I was to play an African wife, a woman who, once in the United States, wished to preserve her cultural heritage. The cast rehearsed the day before the show, and like many Black women in those times, I was then wearing my hair relaxed. *This character wouldn't have worn her hair straightened*, I kept thinking as we ran through the script. So adamant was this woman about embracing her native culture, there was no way she would have chemically processed hair. It didn't feel right to me.

So I took myself up to Shalimar's, the place where Duke Ellington used to get his hair cut. A barber greeted me and introduced himself as Streamline. "How may I help you today, Miss?" he asked.

"I would like to have my hair cut," I said, "and I want it as short as you can possibly get it."

The man stared at me as if I had a unibrow. "Excuse me, what do you want?"

"You see my hair?" I said, pointing at it. "I want it cut. And then I would like to have it shampooed so that it goes back to its natural state."

He coughed. "Are you sure that's what you want?"

"I'm sure," I said.

He put me in his chair and draped a cape around me. He then turned on his clippers. As he proceeded to cut, I closed my eyes, mostly because I didn't want the sight of my neck-length hair to deter me from my mission. He cut for fifteen minutes or so before saying, "Well . . . how do you like it?" I flung open my lids.

"It's not short enough," I told him. My hair then was probably eight inches, and he'd cut it down to about five. "I want it as close to my scalp as you can get it," I told him. "Okay, Miss," he muttered. "Whatever you want."

I closed my eyes again and let him buzz away. Even once he turned off the clippers and said, "Okay, let's go to the shampoo bowl," I kept my eyes closed as he led me to it. He shampooed me once, twice, and a third time. He then took me back to his chair, blow-dried my hair, rubbed some pomade through it, and patted it down. "What do you think?" he said. When I opened my eyes and saw myself in the mirror, I said, "That's her!" My half-inch 'fro looked exactly to me like the one my character would've worn.

The next morning for the show, I strode onto the set with my head tied in a kerchief. I got my makeup done, my costume on, and heard the director yell "Places, please!" Just as I walked onto the stage, I pulled off my scarf. The room stopped. By the dumbfounded look on the director's face, I was sure I was about to be fired. "Cicely," he said, walking slowly toward me, "you've cut your hair." I nodded. "You know," he said, drawing in a breath, "I wanted to ask you to do that . . . but I didn't have the nerve."

My character is who gave me the audacity. Anytime I've changed my hair over the years of my career, it has had nothing to do with me personally. It has always been about being authentically in character, about staying as true to her essence and appearance as I can. That has always been my sole intention. And yet when that episode aired, all anyone could talk about was this actress who showed up on television with a nappy head. That was only the beginning.

The next year, the actor George C. Scott saw me in *The Blacks*. He asked my agent to send me over to audition for *East Side/West Side*, the CBS drama series he starred in. I'd heard they wanted Diana Sands for the part, but my agent insisted they had always had me in mind. So soon after, I read for the role of Jane Foster, a secretary to an unflinching New York City caseworker (Scott). As I left the audition, I asked the casting director, "What should I do with my hair?" Again, I wanted to ensure my hairstyle would reflect the character. "Leave it the way it is," he said matter-of-factly. I played on the series for one season and was the first Black woman to star in a television drama. I also was the first Black TV actress to reveal my hair in its bare-naked state.

Within weeks of my first appearance, letters began pouring in. All over the country, hairdressers wrote to the network, claiming I was impacting their business. "My clients want to have their hair cut off like the Black girl on your show!" they wrote. Episode after episode, the letters continued arriving by the bushels. I now wish I'd had the sense to save some of them, just so I could read them again and laugh as I remember. "This actress has all our customers chopping off their hair," the salon owners noted. In that sense, their business was thriving: never had there been such demand for female barbers, some said. But their earnings for chemical services? Gone, or at least noticeably curtailed. That is how the natural hair trend of the 1960s began.

I loved wearing my hair natural. I felt beautiful with it, like the real me, which is why I continued with the style long after *East Side*. It was also incredibly freeing since, for the first time in my life, I could wash and go, minus any scalp abrasions from chemicals. Maya, of course, loved my new look. "We always wore our hair natural on the road," she said, recalling earlier days when she'd traveled abroad with the touring company of *Porgy and Bess*. Overseas, no one was mixing lye or heating hot combs, so you had to wear it the way God gave it to you.

The first time my daughter saw me with my 'fro, she gasped. She then called my mother and told her I'd cut off my hair. "What do you mean she cut off her hair?" my mom breathed into the receiver. "She wouldn't be so damned foolish." She was something else, that Fredericka, and certainly never one to clamp her tongue when it came to her children's choices. For a while, she wouldn't even let me come to her apartment. "You're not gonna embarrass me in front of my neighbors," she said. God help that woman.

While I was on *East Side*, a Black organization in DC flew me in for a big award, to recognize me as a pioneer in the emerging trend toward natural hair. When the splendorous celebration was over, the leaders got down to the root of what they actually felt. They whisked me into a side room and told me how I was degrading Black women by wearing my natural hair onstage, for the entire country to witness. "You're in a position to glorify our beauty," one said, "and you're doing the opposite. You're wearing your hair nappy on live television!" Can you imagine the hypocrisy? Child, I set down the award they'd given me, marched right out the door, and never glanced back. *How is it degrading to walk through the world displaying the hair I was born with?* It wasn't. It's still not.

And yet, over centuries, we've been taught to be ashamed. It did not begin that way. Our ancestors, long before they were sold from their homeland, took great pride in the appearance of their hair. Our foremothers created the world's most ornate, intricate, and diverse hairstyles, squeezing their young'uns between their thighs, swapping laughter with every braid and twist. In our communities, to be groomed was to be loved. With our mothers' hands down in our scalps, in the tenderness present in their palms, we felt cared for and connected. Hair, for us, was the opposite of disgrace. It represented intimacy. During the Middle Passage, our untended locks became matted, our rituals and unique hair tools were stolen from us. In the new land, European traders often cut off the tresses of their "cargo," their animals covered in "wool," not human hair.

The dehumanization did not end there. In European narratives, our hair has been presented as mangy and unmanageable, dirty and rough. The American-born English writer Florence Kate Upton was among the first to degrade our appearance, with the creation in 1895 of her character Golliwog. Then in 1899, Scottish author Helen Bannerman published *The Story of Little Black Sambo*, which became widely popular around the world for more than a half-century. Both Golliwog and Sambo were presented as dark-skinned pickaninnies with big red lips and frizzy hair. Upton described her character as "a horrid sight, the blackest gnome." The British golliwog doll carried over into a 1944 storybook by English writer Enid Mary Blyton, who formed the trio "Golly, Woggie, and Nigger." (Blyton peddled her beliefs far and wide, selling more than six hundred million of her various books around the globe.) In the late 1800s all the way through the 1950s, B. Leidersdorf Company sold a product called "Nigger Hair Smoking Tobacco" in a metal tin can bearing the picture of a Black person's head with an enormous afro and nose ring. White folks have been Other-izing us for hundreds of years, initially because that served their purpose in justifying our enslavement. Brutes, or those labeled as less than human, needn't be accorded respect. Just as they have policed our bodies, they have criminalized our tresses while attempting to extinguish our very existence. In minstrel shows, in books, on television, in kitchen-table conversations, our natural hair has always been under siege in a calculated campaign to devalue us.

In hindsight, I do not fault my mom, or even the leaders at that awards banquet, for decrying my natural hair. The crusade to hide our crowning glory, to consider its texture somehow inferior to that of whites, has hooked its claws into all of us in one way or another. It is as insidious as it is pervasive, like dust particles in the air. You breathe in the toxins without recognizing they're even present. Moreover, a Black woman's hairstyle in this country has often been linked to her survival. In the color hierarchy set up by slave owners, the closer you were to looking white—fair skin, loose curls rather than tightly coiled ones—the higher your status in their eyes. Over centuries we were taught to disregard ourselves, a habit we are still unlearning.

How I hope that we can. And while striving to do so, I also pray we can begin defining ourselves *for* ourselves, dismissing the three hundred years of a Eurocentric beauty standard hovering over us. As gorgeous as our locks appear, as powerfully as they express our artistic genius, as often as they've been used as a barometer of our politics, our hair is not truly who we are. We are defined not by what grows from our heads, but what flows from our hearts. That is our greatest testimony. Our hair may be our crown, yet a life of love and service is our real glory. So as we navigate our journey, let us graciously make space for one another. Whether you relax it or coil it, weave it or dread it, cover it with a wig or cut it plumb off, the choice is yours. Good hair is your hair—however you decide to wear it.

The 1960s, for me, were filled with a spate of roles, some forgettable, others leaving an imprint. Most of the time I was just happy to be working, bringing in a steady income to support Joan. In the years following her birth, I had a sense that I would not have more children, and I didn't want my one child to ever go without. After landing roles in *The Blacks* and *East Side/West Side*, my first two steady income sources, I immediately took out a life insurance policy for $500,000. By then, Joan had finished high school, and her passion for social justice had led her to become a mentor with a church-affiliated organization based in the Village. For years, she both worked and lived in that community, growing close to her fellow mentors as they together supported children. Though Joan was no longer at my side daily, I still wanted to be sure she'd always be financially secure. Later on as I started earning more, I eventually increased the insurance policy to $1 million. And if I got a per diem on a show, I would not spend it. I'd instead take my lunch to work and set aside the money for her. I was sometimes surprised at how quickly those small amounts added up.

Following my 'fro debut in *East Side*, I had some other television firsts. In 1966, the year Miles and I began seeing one another, I got a role on *Guiding Light* as Martha Frazier, a registered nurse known for handing out advice to her comrades (and the first Black character to appear on a soap opera). I never watched *Guiding Light*, even after I landed the part. That wasn't the case for my mother and sister, however. They followed every single plot twist. My mother, who by then had loosened her entertainment-is-evil beliefs in favor of some daily amusement, would sit on her living room couch while shouting at the TV screen, telling so-and-so how wrong he was to steal someone's wife. These conversations would go on for hours, do you hear me? And just about every time they saw me on an episode, they'd call me, saying, "You shouldn't have done such-and-such."

Miles even got in on the conversation. After work when I'd see him, he'd meet me at the door with a smirk and his input: "Who do you think you are, giving these people advice? You've got some nerve getting on television and telling people what to do and how to do it. It's none of your business." Between hours-long sessions on his horn in the basement, he somehow also found the time to tune in to *Guiding Light*.

In those years, I also played Princess Amara in *I Spy*, the NBC series starring Bill Cosby. That's where I first met Bill. Years later, he and I costarred in *The Bill Cosby Show* (1969–1971), the first of two to bear his name. I portrayed Mildred Hermosa, the blind date and first girlfriend of Bill's character, Chet (and for this role, I wore a bouffant afro wig). I'll never forget the blind-date scene. The sun was out, a gorgeous day. For a costume, they had me in a full-length colorful silk dress that hit at my hips. I had to take this long walk to get over to Bill's character. When I drew close, I walked into his arms, and we kissed. Right after we'd acted it out, the soundman yelled "Cut!" He'd heard some kind of ambient noise, he told us. We did it all over, and when he heard the same thing, we did it a third time. The commotion, it turned out, was Bill's heart thumping away in his chest. In all of our years working together, he never laid a finger on me off set, but for that scene, I did get his ticker going.

I got to know Bill and Camille well during that era. We all

became close. Bill, jazz connoisseur that he is, worshipped the ground Miles walked on. From time to time, we'd all have dinner at their place. Bill was constantly laughing, always the comedian. You could never have a serious conversation with him, because whatever you said, he turned it into a joke. Camille was always wonderful to me, polite and kind, with impeccable manners. I remember her as innocent, and fairly reserved, in the early years of their marriage. Her parents hadn't initially wanted her to marry Bill. I once noticed a piece of paper posted over Bill's office door. "What is that?" I asked him. He told me it was a letter young Camille had once written to him while they were dating, explaining that she had to break off their relationship because her family did not approve. Bill of course went on a campaign and changed their minds, and he wanted everybody to know he'd won. The posted letter was proof of that.

A few months after Miles and I got together, my third eye started blinking. My sixth sense had never gone away. Since that year in my childhood when I'd foreseen the fire and heard whispers from my deceased aunt, I was constantly having premonitions. Much of the time, my clairvoyance showed up in the form of vivid dreams. I'd dream of someone, and then the very next hour or day, that person would either pass me on the street or show up at my door. Other times, I'd hear a voice, clear as if someone were standing in the room with me. As a child, this did not rattle me. But as I got older and the foresights came with greater frequency, they began upsetting me. With all these voices and visions, I truly started wondering whether I'd gone stark raving mad. A turning point came on an evening in 1967.

I was staying at a hotel in Midtown, to be near whatever show

I was working on then. My cousin, Don Shirley, had been on my mind all week, so I decided to call him. When I picked up the phone to dial, his voice was already on the line. "Hello, Cic?" he said. It startled me so that I slammed down the receiver and began crying, upset that such occurrences always seemed to be happening to me. Moments later, I heard a knock on the door. I didn't answer. A key went into the lock and in stepped a hotel housekeeper.

"Get out, get out, get out!" I yelled. "What do you want?"

"Ms. Tyson," she said, "somebody downstairs is trying to reach you. He said you hung up on him."

I stared at her. "Who is it?" I said.

"Mr. Don Shirley," she said. "He's in the lobby. Shall I send him up?"

I told her to first put him on the phone from downstairs, and when he'd confirmed it was indeed him, I asked him to come up. By the time he arrived at my door, I was hysterical.

"Cicely, what on earth is the matter with you?" he asked, laughing a little.

"I think I'm losing my mind," I told him. I revealed everything: the dreams, the premonitions, the eerie experiences, like his already being on the phone when I tried to call him. My cousin, whose story was shared with the world in the movie *Green Book*, was not only a legendary pianist and composer; he was also a trained psychologist who'd earned his degree at the University of Chicago.

He sat on the edge of the bed next to me. "Okay listen, Cic," he said. "Let me tell you something. What you have is ESP—extrasensory perception." I'd never heard the term, so I gave him a puzzled stare. "I believe everybody has ESP to some extent," he continued, "and a few have a more developed intuition than others. Obviously you are very developed to be able to pick up things. Come with me and let's take a walk." Don took me by the hand, led me through the hotel lobby, and walked me over to a bookstore on the corner of Fifty-Seventh and Seventh Avenue. He bought me several books on ESP. "Read these," he said, handing me the bag. "And if you have any questions, call me and I will explain it to you."

I scoured every page of every book he gave me, and one paragraph at a time, I began to understand this gift, this strange ability I'd been born with. The more I learned about it, the less frightening it seemed. Reading about it helped normalize it for me. If someone had given it a name and written an entire volume about it, this clearly wasn't something I'd dreamed up. This was a known ability, and perhaps even one I could use to my benefit. A premonition I had not long after reinforced that.

During the first months of my relationship with Miles, we'd grown quite close. In general, it took Miles a long time to trust others, fully let them in, but he'd opened his soul to me early on. Between Miles and me, there was never any pretense; what I saw is what I got. Miles was as true to his emotions as I was to my hair texture, and in the case of the latter, he preferred me that way—plain and natural, no wigs, no extensions, no nothing. When Miles asked me to be on the cover of his 1967 album *Sorcerer*, the Columbia team layered makeup on my face. "Wipe that shit off," Miles said when he saw me. "I want you just as you are." The resulting profile image reflects me, sans foundation, exactly as he loved me.

In keeping with Miles's desire for the real, he displayed the full spectrum of his emotions. I'd seen him act crazy as a loon, and I'd seen him cry like a newborn. Not long before we met, he'd lost his mother. He was also still grappling with his separation from Frances. The first time I saw him in tears was in 1966. One day when I was at his brownstone, he went out to get the mail, and when he returned, he bore an envelope and a dazed expression. Without a word, he went straight upstairs to his bedroom on one of the floors above. He stayed up there for the longest time, as I sat in the living room, debating whether to go up and see about him or to let him have his privacy. I finally went up.

When I cracked open the door, there he was, lying across the bed on his stomach while holding a letter, sobbing and trembling. "What's the matter?" I asked from the doorway. He did not even look up at me, so I closed the door and left him alone, figuring that whatever he was struggling with, he wanted to do so privately. A few days later, I asked him about the letter. He sat silent for a while and stared ahead. He finally told me he'd received divorce papers from Frances. "I failed," is all he said before he cupped his head in his hands and cried once more. After that day, he never again spoke of the wound, at least not with words.

In those early days of our relationship, everyone seemed to have an opinion about Miles, and especially about why I was with him. Rude. Arrogant. Mean. Enigmatic. Those are the terms others often used to describe him, as a person and as a performer. But I came to see Miles otherwise. He was always refining himself, always pushing the boundaries of what was musically possible, never settling. I eventually found out why he turned his back to the audience while onstage. "Because I can hear the orchestra better," he told me. When you're downstage, he explained, the notes float directly your way, and Miles, perfectionist that he was, positioned himself to take in each measure. He cared deeply about the creation of every tone, whether it came from his own instrument or from those of his guys. Turning his back had nothing to do with disdain for his audience. Yet in the eyes of some, it made him a "bad boy," a man who gloried in insulting his fans. How wrong they were.

And yet like all who walk this earth, Miles had his imperfections, one of which became abundantly clear a few months into our courtship. Miles took as much pride in his cars as he did in his dress and appearance. He drove nothing but a Ferrari or a Maserati. But back when I'd met him, when he'd been in one of his heaviest drug periods, he'd lost both his driver's license and the right to buy a car in his own name. So one afternoon Miles, who knew I did not drive, said to me, "I want to buy you a car."

"For what?" I asked. There must be something about this face of mine that makes people think I'm stupid.

"I just think we should have a car," he insisted, "and we can put it in your name."

We? I thought. "Well if you want a new car," I told him, "you can put it in your own name. I'm not going to be the one driving it."

Somehow over the next few weeks, he managed to get himself both a license and a car, probably through his managers. He told me it was to be delivered at some point during the following month, but he did not mention the make and model of the car, nor did he know precisely when it would arrive. A few days later, I was walking around Midtown when, in my mind's eye, I saw Miles in a white Ferrari, top down, speeding up Seventh Avenue in Harlem. Next to him was a fair-skinned Black woman with her hair blowing in the wind. I found my way over to a phone booth, fished out a dime from my pocketbook, slid it into the slot, and called Miles at his house. He answered.

"Oh," I said, "so you got the car today." *Silence.* Miles, not yet aware of my sixth sense, often swore to God that I'd had a detective spying on him. "Why don't you stop hiring people to follow me around?" he'd yell. Frankly, I didn't need to hire anyone. He almost always gave himself away with his reactions. That time, his silence told me I'd hit a nerve.

"Did you hear me?" I said again. "I see you got your car today."

"Where are you?" he asked.

"I'm on Sixth Avenue and Forty-Second," I told him.

"Meet me at the house," he said. *Click.*

When I arrived, he was sitting on the windowsill in the living room. "Come here, darling," he said, drawing me into his arms. "So where were you today?"

"I was just out and about, doing a little shopping," I said.

"How did you know I got the car?" he asked me.

"A friend of mine told me she saw you driving up Seventh Avenue in a white Ferrari with the top down," I said. He stiffened and loosened his embrace. I hadn't even mentioned the girl I'd seen in my vision, yet his body language told me everything I needed to know. "What friend?" he said, anger in his tone. "What's her name?" His fury rattled me, which is why I made up a fake name: Tina.

"Where does Tina live?" he pressed. I had an aunt-in-law who then had an apartment on St. Nicholas Avenue in Harlem, and in my fluster, I gave him her address. "I'm going out for a few minutes," he told me. "I'll be back."

I'm sure Miles must've gone straight to Harlem. I'm also sure that, if he'd turned up at my aunt's address and asked for "Tina"—and I never heard that he did so—no one there would've answered to that name. All I can be certain of is that he'd indeed gotten his Ferrari that day, and that he didn't return until hours later. We never discussed where he'd been, nor did I ever tell him about the woman I saw in my head. I forgot all about my vision until, years later, that very woman turned up.

I didn't need a vision to confirm Miles's tendencies. There

was real-world evidence. He once claimed he had to drive out to Long Island for a dental appointment at eight o'clock in the evening. "What kind of dentist takes patients at this hour?" I asked dubiously as he darted out his front door. He shrugged and left. It was a nice summer evening, and soon after he'd gone, I went for a walk. Miles always kept his cars parked in a garage on Riverside near his place. As I made my way down Seventy-Ninth Street, who did I see pulling out of that garage? Miles Davis. Next to him was a young white woman. I wish I had a photograph of the shock on that man's face. I just swiveled around and marched back to the house. He later came in, saying something or other about the woman being a friend he knew through a friend. I guess she must've needed dental work on Long Island as well.

I spoke not a word to Miles. As far as I was concerned, there was nothing to discuss. What could he have said to change what I'd witnessed with my own eyes? Not a thing. We were living together then, but I'd never given up my place on Seventy-Fourth. After listening to his explanations, I went back to my apartment, got in my bed, and fell sleep. When he called me a while later, I did not answer then, nor for days after. I felt deceived and hurt, most of all because he lied to me. Children lie out of fear they will be punished in some way. But adults, as I see it, have no right to lie. If you do something wrong, just fess up and say, "I did it and I'm sorry"—or you did it, and you're not sorry. Sooner or later, the truth will come out, and the deceit, for me, can be as damaging as the offense. If he wanted to traipse around town with some white woman, so be it. I had no right to stop him. But I also didn't need to stay around and watch him do his dirt.

Miles and I did not argue about the woman I caught him with, or anything else during those years. I detested arguments. I grew up in a home fraught with them and the palpable tension they create. When my father pounded home after his nights out on the town, he and my mom went at it, forcefully enough to draw me, wailing, from my bed. So when I was upset at Miles, he could not drag a solitary word from my lips. That made him even more furious. He wanted to provoke an argument with me to ease his conscience, but if I'd let him draw me into his wrath, it would not have ended well. The years ahead would prove that. When I wouldn't give him the satisfaction of a response, he'd blow off steam by boxing. He had a punching bag in his backyard, and he'd be out there for hours, grunting and swinging like he was Joe Louis.

And then there were the drugs. He did not use in front of me. In fact, in all my years with Miles, never once did he shoot up, snort cocaine, or even smoke a reefer in my presence. I'm sure Miles must've shot up or snorted in his bathroom, but he left no sign of it, clearing away any paraphernalia. He knew how much I despised drugs. Also, my religious upbringing ensured I had nothing to do with them. I still don't.

One night after Miles had played at a club in Midtown, he and I, along with some of his band members, drove uptown toward his place. One of the guys lifted a small bag, presumably filled with drugs, and offered it to me. Miles pushed away his hand. "Man, are you kidding me?" he said, laughing. "I can't even get Cicely to smoke a cigarette." Yet that didn't stop him from getting his fixes privately. On many other evenings when we were on our way home, he'd pull up and park at a building near Eighty-Second and Amsterdam, then a known dope house. "I'll be out in a few," he'd say. I might've been naive about drugs, but I came to recognize the dazed, faraway look in Miles's eyes whenever he stumbled out of that building. "I'll be out in a few" became my cue to take a cab home. I wasn't crazy enough to sit in his car and wait for him to drive me home in that state.

"Why didn't you wait for me?" he'd come through the door slurring. "I was tired of sitting in the car," I'd tell him. Whatever he smoked or shot up, he usually reeked of it. I knew the scent of marijuana, but other than that, I couldn't tell the difference between coke or heroin or any other drug. On many occasions, he emitted a distinctly powerful scent, like the smell of burnt iron. It permeated his pores. He'd try to cover it with cologne (he loved his collection), but I could still smell it. And when I did, I stayed as far away from him as I could, because I knew I wouldn't have been talking to Miles anymore. I'd be having a conversation with the person he became when a substance had taken him over. The drugs. The wandering eye. The outbursts. I dealt with it then by not engaging it. I suppose it was my way of reconciling the Miles I knew, the porous soul bearing a hurt-filled past, with the Miles he became in quelling his pain.

After I'd been mute for a while following the white-woman sighting, Miles apologized the way he always did: by showering me with gifts. It was his way of attempting to win me back. Down on Fifty-Seventh Street was a women's clothing store, a haberdashery that Miles knew I loved. He'd go in there and buy a whole rack of dresses for me. And he couldn't find enough jewelry and flowers to present to me. On many occasions over the years, my place would be filled with so many peonies, roses, lilacs, and hydrangeas that you would've thought someone had just passed. I kept the clothes but never wore them, and I'd let the flowers die in their vases. My affections could not be bought, and I wanted Miles to understand that. Most of the time I did not even acknowledge his gifts, which drove him insane. And yet his presents—along with his pleas for me to return to him, and his promises that he'd sit up straight—did eventually soften me.

I could have left Miles. He clearly had his sharp edges, jagged shards that pierced and injured me and, at times, drove me away.

And yet when I looked up from my own agony and over at him, there stood a man who did not care whether he lived or died. Beneath his so-called bad boy exterior, I saw a man who was ill at his core, a tormented soul who used drugs to anesthetize his sorrows. When people attempt to destroy themselves, even if unconsciously, they have a handgrip on a knife, make no mistake. Self-injury is a statement regarding one's own worth or its glaring lack. Miles played fast and loose with his life far too frequently to have known his value. And even while grappling with my own anguish, I could not stand by and watch this man waste the rare gift he came here to share. His behavior at times disturbed me greatly, even humiliated me. And yet more than anger, I felt compassion, and pity for his sad state. It is possible to be at once hurt by a man and heartbroken for him. I could not allow Miles to throw himself away. The loss, I felt, would've been too great—for me and for the world.

One evening near the end of 1967, Dizzy Gillespie, granddaddy of bebop and a longtime friend of Miles, came by for dinner with us. On his way out, Dizzy pulled me aside. "You know, Cic," he said, "I've never heard Miles talk more lovingly of anyone than he does of you." "Really?" I said with a smile in my eyes. He nodded. "All you really need to do is take him in your arms and cradle him like a baby," he said. "That's love for him"—and that, in those years, is what I extended.

13

1968

MILES could make me laugh so hard I'd nearly choke to death. Every time we'd sit down for dinner, he'd start up with his crazy stories. I never knew where his tales would go. A few made me cringe (like the one about a friend he called Third Story Joe, so named for his skill in scaling buildings to rob them), while others made me curious (during Miles's childhood, his mother, when hosting ladies' lunches, counted out her guests' peas before serving them). Regardless of the memory shared—whether it was relishing his early years as Little Davis in Charlie Parker's quintet or recounting how his beloved father once locked him in his guesthouse in an effort to help Miles break his drug habit, cold turkey—every one of his accounts, by the end, had me doubled over. There was something about Miles's storytelling, peppered with color (the F-word took up residence on his tongue) and lacking in pretense ("Jazz is a nigger word that white folks dropped on us," he'd say), that inevitably choked me up. One evening, after semi-successfully avoiding the bones in his fish soup, I slammed my spoon down and yelled, "You're trying to kill me! Why don't you tell me these stories when I'm not eating?" He was so full of the devil, that Miles. What an incredible sense of humor.

And style. Miles, like my father, was a Dapper Dan, a certified stepper. He had an Italian tailor, Mario, who dressed him to the hilt. In the 1960s, men's fashion was exactly as I prefer it: slim-fitting suits complemented with thin ties, thin lapels, thin collars—clean, and perfect for Miles's svelte figure. Wherever the two of us turned up, boy, we turned some heads. I beamed at his side, glamorous in my couture, showing off looks by style mavens such as Arthur McGee, the first Black designer to ever run a studio. I felt proud to stand alongside Miles, loved folding my silk-gloved hands into his strong ones. "I knew, sooner or later, one of the big boys would sweep you off your feet," Warren would tease me. Like Ossie and Ruby, Miles and I were among a handful of Black power couples of the sixties, an artistic duo that drew stares. Once when he and I were out at a dinner concert, a well-known singer I won't name glided over to our table after she'd performed. "You've got the prize, Ms. Cicely," she told me. Around town, everyone knew she'd been salivating over Miles for years. She then turned to him and said, "And I can't tell you how lucky you are." I smiled and pulled my sequin wrap more snuggly around my shoulders.

One of my most cherished fashion staples was a gift from Miles. He once called up a renowned designer and said to him, "I want you to make Cicely a fur coat." "I don't make fur coats," the man told him. Miles repeated his statement, the second time adding "and I want it here on December 24th." Sure enough, by noon on Christmas Eve, an enormous brown paper bag sat in the middle of Miles's living room floor. "What's *that*?" I asked. "Well open it and see," he said, a glint of mischief in his eyes. I lifted out the floor-length stunner and gasped. In the following years, I wore that mink out, do you hear me? And whenever

I donned my Cadillac of coats, others gawked and exchanged glances. I basked in the glory and the gaze.

Hair was central to the fashion show. I learned to style my 'fro in every manner known to Black womankind: shortly cropped, twisted out, pulled into a poof, cornrowed. For versatility, I reached for beehive wigs, clip-on chignons, and goddess braids created using extensions. In those years, Miles and I frequented Casdulan, the upscale beauty parlor on 125th Street in Harlem. Camelo Casimir, the French-Haitian owner and stylist we all called Frenchie, offered premiere hair and makeup services to the stars. Many in our circle came through there. Our friend Harold Melvin rented a booth at the salon in those days (and years later, after Frenchie passed, Harold opened his own salon on Seventy-Second Street, where it still stands). James Finney, in the era before he became Miles's personal hairdresser, also hung around Casdulan a lot. Finney, notorious for his braiding talents, created mane masterpieces on Valerie Simpson of Ashford & Simpson and others. We all gossiped at Casdulan as much as I did at Sardi's, exchanging scuttlebutt amid the sounds of Sam Cooke, promising us, over the salon loudspeaker, that a change was gonna come.

That was the sixties, a peculiar combination of fashion and frivolity, protest and profound social turmoil. The decade, in our America, bore varied expressions, each seared in my memory as deeply as those of Miles's many faces. The era radiated with ethnic pride, as Black Panthers donned kente cloths and proclaimed "Black Is Beautiful." It spat back at its oppressors, with the Black Power Movement insisting upon change by any means necessary. It throbbed and ached, drooping its head low after the church bombing in Birmingham and the assassinations of JFK and Malcolm X. It clenched its jaw and clutched its fist, chanting "Mississippi Goddam," Nina Simone's anthem in response to Medgar Evers's murder. With Freedom Rides and demonstrations, Watts riots and urban uprisings, the sixties raised its voice even as it stiffened its spine. And then, in the spring of 1968 as the decade screeched toward its close, it let out a primal wail.

That April, Miles and I were on a tour stop in Seattle. Anytime Miles was on the road, he never wanted to go out for lunch or dinner, preferring always to preserve his energy for his performances. So in the kitchen of the apartment we stayed in, I fixed us something to eat while he sat in the living room, talking on the phone with his attorney, Harold. When their conversation ended, he laid down the phone and looked over at me. "Harold said they shot King," he said. I continued stirring my pot of broth, feeling sure that, as usual, Miles was joking. I was just about to blurt out "Now that's not funny!" when he delivered the remainder of his sentence: ". . . and he's dead."

I folded like an accordion, my body turning in on itself as I faltered to my knees. The words, a penetrating dagger, stabbed me right in my solar plexus. "What?" I asked. "What did you say?" "King has been assassinated," Miles told me. "He's gone."

I will always be amazed at how a singular occurrence can break open the soul of the world. One moment you're stirring your wooden spoon through a saucepan, lost in the aroma of savory bouillon, oblivious to what awaits. The next moment, a simple turn of the spoon later, you are down on the cold linoleum, arms cradled around yourself, numbed into silent weeping. On the evening the Reverend Dr. Martin Luther King Jr. was gunned down on the second floor of the Lorraine Motel in Memphis, the earth rocked and quaked, and then, all at once, splintered in two. The suddenness of the shift, the wrenching pain of it all, was, for me, soon followed by a personal gut punch.

After Dr. King's passing, life carried on, but with a low hum of melancholy beneath it. The loss rearranged the air's molecules, made the atmosphere heavy. Living, in those times, felt like trudging forward in the slowest of motion, more sluggish by the step. Every movement and task, even the most mundane, took on a kind of lethargy. That is how grief sits down on you. It closes in, presses your chest with all its might, and makes it difficult even to breathe.

A few years before King's death, life sent me another hard lesson in surviving as a Black actress. I received a call from Elia Kazan, a renowned Greek-American theater director. He and Robert Whitehead cofounded the Repertory Theater at Lincoln Center, which, in 1964, opened in its temporary home in Greenwich Village, while its permanent home, the Vivian Beaumont Theater at Lincoln Center, was being constructed. Even before Elia called me, I'd heard that he and Robert were casting for their upcoming productions. I'd also heard that some of the industry's Black organizations had been pressuring Elia to cast at least one African-American actor. He'd relented by bringing in two light-skinned performers, men so pale you had to squint to even know they were Black. "Can't you find a Black female actress?" Elia had been asked. He claimed he didn't know any—which is when he was given my number. He rang and invited me to come by his office.

The meeting started out pleasantly enough. "I've heard quite a bit about you," he said, smiling. "Tell me more about yourself." I explained how I'd gotten into the business, where I'd studied, and what I'd enjoyed most about my work in *The Blacks*. The conversation flowed easily, and before we knew it, an hour had gone by. "I find you very interesting," he said, "but unfortunately, I have to leave for an appointment. Can we meet again tomorrow?" I agreed and returned the next afternoon for another equally delightful chat. "You know something?" I said near the close of our meeting. "I'd like to ask you a question." He nodded and sat up at his desk. "Why aren't there any Black women in the company?" I asked. "Cicely," he said bluntly, "I have to tell you this: when a Black woman walks across the stage, the audience's mind turns to sex."

I stared at him, absolutely dumbstruck by what he'd told me. To this moment, I cannot believe that, even if he believed what he was saying, he'd be insensitive enough to actually say it to a Black woman. And not only did he say it. He uttered it casually, without even a hint of self-consciousness. This man was considered the foremost director of his time, and he was admitting—openly professing—that he'd deprive me of a job because of a long-held stereotype. Well you know something? I got up from my chair, I walked out of that man's office, and I never returned. I later heard that the company eventually brought in Ethel Ayler, the talented and gorgeous Black actress who'd once replaced Abbey Lincoln in *The Blacks*. I can only imagine what that poor woman endured. Elia was eventually fired from his post and replaced, amid rumors that he'd clandestinely blacklisted actors during the communist Red Scare of the 1950s.

Three years later, in 1967, I auditioned for a role in *The Heart Is a Lonely Hunter*, a beautiful film about a deaf-mute man, a story based on Carson McCullers's novel. Alan Arkin was to play the lead. I read for the role of Portia, daughter of a physician who is disappointed that his well-educated child has chosen to work as a domestic. For the audition, I was asked to put on a Hoover apron, the kind my mother used to wear around the house. I did so and began reading. Afterward, the producer, Thomas Ryan, stared at me, and then over at a colleague. "No one's gonna believe she's a maid," he said. "She looks like a model." *Here we go again with this nonsense*, I thought. *What is this fool talking about?* With my petite figure, I didn't fit the well-worn trope of the buxom mammy, so I was constantly told I wasn't quite right. *Why even call me in for the part?*, I'd stand there thinking as the casting crew members murmured among themselves. *Before I got here, you knew what I looked like*—which, as I saw it, had little to do with whether I could convincingly portray a character. "Can we put her in a different costume?" Thomas called out to someone on his team. *I'm playing a maid and this is my body*, I said to myself. *What more do you want from me?* He obviously got over the misgivings because I eventually landed the part.

I was on set filming when the country suffered yet another body blow. A lone gunman shot Robert F. Kennedy, then running for president. The world gasped in unison, as it did a day later when he died at Good Samaritan Hospital in Los Angeles. Only two short months before, we'd lost King. Most Black folks in the country saw RFK as the remaining hope: a candidate intent on extending King's quest for civil rights. Here was a man who promised to end a deeply controversial war overseas in Vietnam and who promoted equality for Black Americans, who had not yet been granted first-class citizenship here. (This was precisely Muhammad Ali's point when he refused, in 1967, to serve in the war and said, "I ain't got no quarrel with them Viet Cong.") King's murder had been devastating on its own. But when Bobby was assassinated, that devastation morphed into delirium. There was a sense, as there is in our times now, that the country had come undone.

In July 1968, right after that one-two punch, *The Heart Is a Lonely Hunter* premiered in New York. Miles and I showed up on the red carpet together. An image of us, yellowed by time but forever stashed in my box of memories, brings to mind the feeling of that era. Miles's arms are folded across his body, his eyes covered with sunglasses. I, wearing a simple sleeveless dress, stand near him, with one hand clutching my pocketbook, the other resting on his hand. A pair of silver chandelier earrings swirl from my lobes toward my shoulders, like two large teardrops. We both peer blankly into the camera lens, our bodies present in the room, our spirits far away. When I look at that photo now, it reminds me of the stillness of those months following Dr. King's and RFK's murders, of the quiet and the questioning that befall you once a casket has been lowered into the ground. We were there to celebrate the opening of a film, and still, we were inwardly weeping.

A few weeks after the premiere, Miles gave me yet another reason to grieve. One afternoon I was relaxing in his living room on the ground floor while he was upstairs in the bedroom. The doorbell rang. When I opened the door, there stood a light-skinned young Black woman, with straight hair cascading down her back. She stared at me. *This is the woman*, I thought. I immediately recognized her as the lady I'd seen in my vision months before—the one who sat at Miles's side as he sped up Seventh Avenue in his white Ferrari. Before I could speak, Miles, who'd heard the bell, came down the stairs and to the door. He looked at her, and then at me, and then back at her. He pushed past me, ushered the woman away from the entrance, and shut the door behind him. I stood there, jaw on the ground, scrambling to make sense of what had just occurred.

I'd heard the talk that Miles was fooling with some woman by the name of Betty Mabry, a model and musician nineteen years younger than he was. The circle of Black entertainers was tiny in those days, and even smaller in the world of Casdulan, our parlor. Two seconds after juice had slipped from someone's lips, that OJ had slid its way out the door and across town. I'd never seen the woman, but both Finney and Frenchie had spotted her. She'd had the nerve to start having her hair done at Casdulan, and on several occasions, she and Miles had been seen sniggling and giggling as they left there together. "She struts in here acting like she's Mrs. Miles Davis," I'd heard. I never asked Miles about the rumors, in part because I did not want to believe they were true, and in part because I loved Miles so. But I never forget a face, and once Betty stood across from me in Miles's doorway, one truth was irrefutable: this was the woman I'd foreseen.

I stood there for only a moment. Miles and this woman were hardly down the block by the time I stormed from his place and back to my own a few streets away. Once home, I pulled out a large suitcase, lifted it onto my bed, and opened it. I packed up everything Miles had ever given me: the dresses, the shoes, the jewelry, the mink coat, the items reeking of the guilt that had prompted their purchase. An hour later, I hailed a taxi and loaded the suitcase in the trunk. "Please take me around the corner to 312 West Seventy-Seventh," I told the driver. Upon arrival, I hauled that suitcase to Miles's door and rang the bell. I didn't know whether he'd be back home and I did not care; either way, I had a message to deliver. He opened the door. I pushed past him and hurled the suitcase into the air. It landed, with a thud, a few feet from Betty, who stood there looking dumbfounded, like she'd just witnessed the Second Coming. Before either of them could speak, I bolted off.

The next week at the salon, word of our split had of course made its way to Frenchie. He'd heard that after I'd thrown that suitcase and marched away, Miles had gone absolutely berserk. Betty, upset that Miles had been giving me lavish gifts while secretly courting her, told her friends that she'd never seen Miles more angry. *Angry?* If anyone had a right to fury, it was me.

Miles had been strutting all over town with this woman, obviously with no care about mortifying me, and plainly with no fear of reprisal. As much as I cared for Miles, as deeply as I understood the hurt-filled past that plagued him, I would not allow him to blatantly disrespect me. Still, in those days after I discovered his affair, I felt more numb than indignant, more wounded than furious, more somber than upset. If he wanted this woman, then he could have her. But he could not have us both at once. And clearly he did want her. Because soon after our debacle, and around the time Miles's divorce from Frances became final, he married Betty in the autumn of 1968.

Yes, Jesus loves me, because he sent me an exit ramp out of the country. That fall, with my emotions still raw, I landed a small recurring role in a Canadian television series. I don't recall the show's name, only that it became a lifeline for me. I packed my sorrows alongside my toiletries and flew to Toronto, channeling my sadness into my role, soothing myself the way I had during my childhood, over the keys of a piano. For most of autumn, I was away. Away from the salon chatter. Away from the misery swirling around the situation. Away from Miles, whom I did not speak to after I flung that suitcase into his world. Years later we'd again cross paths for Act Two of our story.

When the clock struck midnight into 1969, the country exhaled. The agony of 1968, one of the most turbulent years in US history, was at last behind us, even if our collective anguish lingered. For me, the new year marked a time to move onward even as I continued healing. Back from Canada, I dove into more work. That April, *Trumpets of the Lord*, a show I'd played in during 1963 (and a musical based on James Weldon Johnson's book of poems titled *God's Trombones*), returned to Broadway. I reprised my role as Reverend Marion Alexander.

Following *The Blacks*, I'd played in a string of such productions, some of which have now fallen from memory, others of which bring a smile or a grimace. People are always telling me that I've had an illustrious career, but when I look back at some of the show titles, I think, *Did I even play in half of these?* Apparently, I portrayed an upstanding maid opposite a spiteful snob (*The Blue Boy in Black*, 1963); performed poetry and song as part of an ensemble cast curated by Roscoe Lee Browne in his directorial debut (*A Hand Is on the Gate*, 1966); and played Myrna Jessup in *Carry Me Back to Morningside Heights* (1968), the first—and only—play directed by Sidney Poitier. Not only was the latter a flop, but it also marked the first time I was fired. The story centered on a guilt-ridden liberal Jewish man who insisted on becoming a slave to a Black law student, as penance for whites' mistreatment of Blacks. During rehearsals, and frankly away from them, I don't say anything unless I have some reason to say it, and when I do so, I tend never to shout. Well, the other actors kept complaining that they couldn't hear me, which is one reason I ended up getting fired. The other is that I didn't get along with one of the actors, though I don't recall what the nonsense was all about. Someone on the production crew, but not Sidney, sent me on my way, and Sidney and I never spoke about it or let it get in the way of our friendship. I don't remember who took my place, but it didn't matter. The show lasted mere days before the curtains crashed down.

Trumpets of the Lord, the 1969 show I played in as I still mourned Miles, didn't fare any better. It ended after only seven performances. Seven! Sidney, who could certainly sympathize, took me out for a drink after the final show. "I'm finished," I told him. "This is it. I can't do this anymore.'" I of course was not done with acting but was just expressing the angst we artists feel when a show ends so abruptly. You work, you carry a child for nine months, and then your baby miscarries. "I'm just going to leave this business," I told Sidney. He stared at me for the longest time, with that arresting gaze only Sidney can give, and he said to me, "And do what, Cicely?"

I forged ahead, ever clinging to the wisdom my mother had once passed on to me sometime in the early sixties. I'd auditioned for a role I truly wanted but did not get, and around that time, I went by to see my mom. I was sure I'd wiped the disappointment from my face, but she spotted it. "What's the matter with you?" she asked as soon as I walked in the door.

"Nothing," I told her.

"Don't tell me 'nothing,'" she said. "Sit down here and let me talk to you." I took a seat at her kitchen table, and she repeated her question.

"I didn't get the job," I admitted in a mumble. She stared at me intently and then leaned toward me.

"Let me tell you something, girl," she said. "What's for you in this life, you will get. And what is not for you, you will never get. Do you hear me?" I nodded, the whole time thinking she'd gone mad. But as the years wore on, her words carried me through some things. My mother understood what I didn't yet at the time, that there's a path in this life with your name on it. What God means for you to have, no one can take away from you. It's already yours. Our mission, as God's children, is to surrender to what he has ordained—and to freely let all else just pass us by.

What God had in mind for me was a new chapter. In 1968, I'd suffered another devastation when Warren Coleman died suddenly. He'd always had a major ambition to build a thriving Black film company, which is what had led him to direct *Carib*

Gold. Once that effort floundered, he moved back to his hometown of Boston where his brother, Ralf, was directing the Negro Federal Theater of Massachusetts. He worked alongside Ralf even as he applied for an endowment to fund his own dream. When he opened the envelope and read that he'd received the substantial endowment he'd requested, he found the news so astonishing, so unbelievable for a Black man during that era, that he suffered a massive heart attack. While still reeling from that stunning tragedy, I found another agent but didn't take to her too well (she was always cutting me off in meetings). I moved on quickly. Somehow or another I found my way to Bill Haber, whom I call Haber for short. Haber was based in California, the place where my path next carried me.

Jimmy Komack, the actor and producer, asked me, through Haber, to star in an episode of *The Courtship of Eddie's Father*, an ABC sitcom Jimmy created. The episode, titled "Guess Who's Coming for Lunch," involved a setup between my character, Betty, and Tom, a Latino character played by Brandon Cruz. Jimmy flew me to Los Angeles for filming. I stayed with Haber and his wife, Carole, in the Hollywood Hills. Each morning, he rose early and slid the call sheet under my door, and after a few days, I'd done what I had to do. On my last afternoon in town, I stopped by the ABC lot to thank Jimmy. He must have been impressed with me, because he said, "Don't go. You don't belong in New York City. You belong here." He then mentioned that he'd seen a Black woman on the lot that day, "and that must mean they're looking for a Black character," he said. "Come with me." He walked me to an adjacent studio, where he disappeared down the hall as I waited. A half-hour later, he returned with a director who was casting for the hospital drama *Medical Center*. The series's first episode was to feature O. J. Simpson, and the director was looking for an actress to play O.J.'s wife for the one episode. I auditioned that very day and landed the part.

Even before I could ring Haber with the news, Jimmy had already called him and persuaded him that I should remain in town. "But where will I stay?" I asked Haber when I returned to his place that evening. "You can stay here with us," he said without hesitation. I didn't know it at the time, but Haber hadn't yet informed Carole, whose second son, Quinn, was still an infant. Haber walked me into the kitchen where Carole was feeding little Quinn in his high chair. "Carole, Cicely is going to be staying here with us for a while," he told her. She nodded and forced a half-smile, but she didn't say much. And can you blame her? The nerve of Bill Haber to march me in there without first talking to his wife! Haber showed me to my space downstairs in their multilevel home. I'd have a private floor with its own entrance, he explained. I thanked him profusely.

Haber's invitation for me to stay for "a while" turned out to be nine years, on and off. I never gave up my apartment or life back East. New York will always be my home, my foundation, the place where I feel rooted by loved ones and community. But starting in 1969, I became bicoastal. I'd fly in to Los Angeles, do a role, and then fly back to New York City. The Habers became my second family. In fact, even when they moved to the Pacific Palisades during the 1970s, they asked me to move with them. Given the rumors that swirled during my time there, it's a wonder they let me stay.

While I was living with the Habers, the world seemed convinced that Haber and I were having an affair. I can assure you we were not. For one thing, the idea of it was just plain ludicrous. And for another, he wasn't my type. I have always preferred Black men. Yet in those years, if I so much as breathed in the direction of any man, it was assumed I was seeing him.

Even back when I was in *The Blacks*, folks seemed sure I was carrying on with Sidney Bernstein, one of the producers, though the two of us were just friends. One night when he was walking me home, he said, "You know, someone asked me whether we're having an affair." I screamed. Sidney was as old as Jesus then, probably around eighty. "Well what did you say, Sidney?" I asked him. "I said, 'Of course!' Do you think I'm going to say no?" I cracked up.

A few years into my time with the Haber family, Bill took me to dinner. "Carole thinks we're having an affair," he said bluntly. I laughed, not just because I was amused by such foolishness, but also because they'd both witnessed the steady parade of suitors arriving at their home to take me out during that era. "That's not true," I said, smirking. He laughed and nodded. "And she says her girlfriend heard the three of us were having a ménage à trois." I put down my fork and stared at him. "Oh Bill, stop the nonsense," I finally said as we both burst into laughter.

That summer, I mentioned this to Carole. She and Bill had a place in Paris, and every August, they'd invite me and a guest to join them there. "Carole," I said as the two of us were preparing dinner one evening, "I hear you've always thought Bill and I were having an affair."

She glanced over at me. "Yeah," she said.

"Carole, look at me," I told her. "Why in God's name would I be living in your house with you, Bill, and your children and having an affair right under your nose? What is the matter with you, huh?"

She smiled and shrugged. "What was I supposed to think?" she said, chuckling. "That's what everybody was saying all over town." Can you believe that? People's minds work in the strangest ways.

Looking back on it now, I still shake my head when I recall that

Haber had the audacity to ever waltz me into his house without first asking Carole whether I could live with them. Guess who's coming for lunch and then staying for nearly a decade? Me.

Around New York, everyone I knew had been talking constantly about how to carry on Dr. King's legacy, how to move his dream from rhetoric to reality, asking ourselves the question that hovers above our nation now: *What will be our part in the revolution?* We were also easing the ache caused by King's tragic loss, attempting to replace the emptiness and dream with a new sense of hope. Our leader had planted the seeds for change. We, those left holding his grand vision, were charged with ensuring its growth for future generations. Arthur Mitchell and I would talk on the phone for hours, trading ideas. "Let's do this or that," we'd say. "No, that won't work." Early one morning a few weeks after we lost King, my phone rang. It was Arthur.

"I've decided what we should do," he said excitedly. I rubbed my eyes and looked over at the clock: 3 a.m. "I'm going to form my own dance company," he went on, like it was noon, "and I want you with me." The fervor in my friend's voice, the passion with which he spoke, dragged me from my bed. I washed my face, pulled on a trench over my pajamas, and took a cab over to his place a few streets away. On Arthur's living room floor, amid papers and photographs he'd assembled while brainstorming, we sat talking about how we could move his vision forward.

"Wait a minute," he said after we'd been talking for an hour. "We need one more person to be in on this."

"Who's that?" I asked.

His face brightened. "Let's get Brock Peters," he said.

Out the door we went over to Brock's place a few streets

away. Arthur pressed the buzzer, but nobody answered. We rang again. Finally, we heard Brock's sleepy voice over the intercom. "Who is it?!" he asked.

"It's Arthur and Cicely," Arthur announced.

"What's the matter?" Brock asked.

"I'm going to form my own dance company," Arthur explained, "and I want you and Cicely to join me." Brock lumbered downstairs moments later. Once Arthur had persuaded him of the urgency of his idea, Brock threw on his coat and walked with us to Arthur's apartment. There, with his eyes dancing, Arthur shared with us his vision. He dreamed of opening a classical ballet school, a place where Black children—toes pointed, horizons expanded—could learn the rigors and discipline that had lifted him toward prominence. He wanted to pass on to them the same gifts, the same dedication and unassailable work ethic that had carried each of us to that moment. More than anything, he wanted to awaken in them a dream, strong and pulsating, of a world beyond their own. Though poverty and prejudice surrounded them, it need not define them. A few hours later when the city stirred awake, the three of us were still talking, still huddled in that circle with our hearts wide open.

That is how Dance Theatre of Harlem began more than five decades ago—in the wee hours, with a trio of visionaries clustered together on a living room floor. All those years earlier when I'd first met Arthur, he'd assured me we'd one day work together. That morning as the sun peeked up over the horizon, my friend's dream took both flight and root.

Arthur, ever a doer, got right to work clearing a path as Brock and I stood close, handing him his shovels. Dorothy Maynor at Harlem School of the Arts, near 141st and St. Nicholas Avenue, had been asking Arthur to teach classes there, and when he visited, he spotted potential in the school's bare-bones gym.

He used his personal savings of $25,000 to remodel the space, installing a dance floor and ballet barres. More funding trickled in—along with mirrors, at last!—as the three of us lent our star power to luring in donors. Many of the potential investors we approached couldn't truly envision Arthur's dream for a first-class Black dance center, because in 1968, there was absolutely no precedent for such a notion in the elite and deeply prejudiced world of classical ballet. But if the three of us were involved, some came to believe, then the venture had to be solid.

Anything Arthur asked me to do, I did: I cofounded the first board of directors, solicited grants, worked with renowned dressmaker Zelda Wynn on costuming, taught a course about how to tell a story, graceful yet gripping, through dance. Lorenzo James, Arthur's longtime friend, was a critical part of our efforts. And though Arthur eventually brought in his Caucasian teacher Karel Shook, a well-known ballet master, to partner with him in the venture, Shook is often miscredited with having cofounded Arthur's dance company. Frankly, that's no surprise. Since the days when ancient Greeks stole advanced concepts of architecture, philosophy, and mathematics right out of the palms of Africans, whites have been taking credit for Black successes, co-opting our ingenuity at every turn. But to be clear, on the morning when Arthur, Brock, and myself formed the blueprint for the school, Shook was not yet a thought. While he indeed contributed mightily later, it was Arthur, Brock, and I who first lifted Dance Theatre of Harlem off the ground. And in between all the going and the doing and the launching, I served as Arthur's confidante, the friend who, during our nightly phone calls, lent an ear and moral support.

Before long, Arthur had opened his doors to children from the Harlem neighborhood, charging them fifty cents a week for a place in history. At the outset, he had about thirty students.

Arthur pushed every one of them to stand on their toes and reach past mediocrity toward a virtuosity the dance world has seldom witnessed. And in so doing, he defied the notion that Black bodies were not made for classical ballet, that the lines of our figures weren't suited for arabesques and pirouettes. During the summer of 1968, all of Harlem gathered, it seemed, to watch these gifted dancers arch their backs toward excellence. Harry Belafonte and Lena Horne were in attendance. So were Sidney, Ossie, Ruby, Maya, and scores of other notable artists. With every leap and *grand jeté*, their exacting standards became a source of our shared pride.

Dance Theatre of Harlem quickly outgrew its original space, and by 1971, it had moved to its current quarters, a parking garage at 466 West 152nd Street. Arthur renovated the new space with a gift from Alva B. Gimbel. When Lorenzo invited Alva to observe the dancers (by then, classes were being conducted in the basement of Church of the Master in Harlem), Alva declared, "These children should not be in a basement! They need a home of their own." On the spot, she wrote the dance company a check for $50,000. That same year, Arthur prepared his students to present three ballets at the Guggenheim. The mostly white audience applauded and was moved to tears. The group took its talents overseas soon after, performing in the Netherlands. Not only had Arthur, chief ambassador for Black classical dance, preserved Dr. King's dream and made it international, he'd done so in lockstep with the Black Arts Movement—alongside poets and painters and singers and actors who protested not just with picket signs, but through the mastery of their crafts. They believed, as Arthur and I did, in the unique transformative power of the arts. A well-told story, in whichever artistic medium it is delivered, can touch corners of the soul otherwise unreachable.

14

Rebecca

My work on *Sounder* began with a prediction. In the spring of 1971, I was set to fly out to Los Angeles to start work on the film, and as was true with every important moment in my life, I wanted to share this one with Arthur. He'd been overseas on tour with his students, and we hadn't yet connected about my role. So on my way to the airport, I stopped by his place to give him my good news in person. "I'm going out to Hollywood to do my first big movie," I said, joy lifting my cheeks.

"And if you do," Arthur said, "you're going to be nominated for an Oscar."

"And if I am," I told him, "you will be my escort." We hugged and I went on my way.

Even before filming began, skepticism abounded over whether *Sounder* would resonate. The short three-year gap between Dr. King's assassination in 1968 and our first day on set in 1971 felt more like a decade. Throughout the sixties, there'd been a major political shift among young Blacks in particular, some of whom were weary with King's passive resistance and favored forceful rebellion. The change became more pronounced after we lost King—and movies began mirroring the evolving times.

Theatergoers longed for brazen Black characters, heroes willing to take up arms in battling racial violence, in place of conciliatory Negroes serving as white America's moral conscience. This new spirit was, in part, what gave rise to Blaxploitation cinema, the genre that, as I see it, did more to impede our progress than to fuel it. In such an environment, director Marty Ritt made the brave choice to feature a loving Black family in a plot that neither satisfied the thirst for Black rebel characters nor reinforced the stereotype of us as heathenish villains. It was bold. It raised eyebrows and doubts. And even Paul Winfield and I, the principal actors, wondered whether anyone would show up to see the film.

First things first: The story of *Sounder* may have been stolen from a Black man. William H. Armstrong is said to have penned the 1969 children's book upon which the film is based, and he even won the Newbery Medal for it. But while preparing for the film, a young Black author I met insisted he'd written the story during the years he worked for Armstrong. He even gave me a signed copy of his original draft, and it breaks my heart that I no longer have it and cannot track down the man's name. I loaned his draft to Lonne Elder and never got it back. The same thing happened, years later, when I began work on *A Woman Called Moses*. Harriet Tubman's nephew gave me a book of hers, and *poof*, it disappeared.

From the script's opening line, Rebecca crawled under my skin. I could see her, feel her, touch her. Though, as I've told you, I'd initially been asked to play the teacher—a smaller role, but a no less beautiful one—nothing in me stirred when I read that part. Also, it was a role I could've played in my sleep. Rebecca, in contrast, was a character of substance I wasn't sure I could depict. Beneath her placid exterior lived a quiet complexity. I knew who this woman was—a long-suffering wife and mother who brought to mind the woman who reared me, as well as the myriad Black women who've carried our world on their shoulders—which is why I knew it would prove challenging to do her justice on-screen. That I was terrified to take the role was, for me, a sign that I should. Intimidation is a prerequisite to growth as an artist.

At the start of the project, I stopped first in LA to meet with the crew about costuming and hair and then flew on to Baton Rouge, Louisiana, for filming. By the time I stepped on set, Rebecca had already taken me over. I'd of course pored over the script and started in with my usual inquisition: *Why did the writer create the character? Why was she given the name Rebecca? How does her dialogue reinforce her characterization?* Rebecca's purpose, in a word, was *support.* She was the rock sustaining those children while her husband was in jail for the "crime" of ensuring his family could eat. I took all of that in as I read. And once I allowed Rebecca's essence to dislodge my own, she began manifesting in my gestures. One morning when I was cleaning, I began doing everything with my left hand. *What the devil is wrong with me?* I thought. *Rebecca must be left-handed.* Sure enough, one afternoon between takes on set, Kevin Hooks, who portrayed my eldest son, said, "Mama, let's play ball." He picked up the ball with his left hand and threw it. "Kevin, are you left-handed?" I asked. He nodded. It stood to reason that Rebecca's firstborn, like his mother, would be a leftie. So I played Rebecca completely from my left side.

I also got Rebecca's hair right. Just as I'd done in *East Side* and every other film I've been in, I felt determined to bring authenticity to my character. During the 1930s in the South, poor Black women typically cornrowed their hair, as well as wrapped their heads while laboring in fields and kitchens. I called on Omar, the stylist I'd been working with in California, and I asked her to cornrow my hair. She knew how to braid, but because she wasn't a union worker, she couldn't do the job. So I began calling around to see whether I could find someone in my network. Through a friend, I connected with a woman who was married to an African, and when she and her husband had lived on the continent, the women there taught her how to cornrow. She wasn't a union worker either, but somehow, we were able to bring her in. She's the one who gently parted and braided my hair into perfectly spaced rows.

Filming went on for several weeks, and one scene in particular will always be memorable. Near the end of the film, after Jim Crow's injustices have separated Nathan and Rebecca for months, the two run toward each other along a long dirt road and embrace. Everywhere I go, folks ask me about that scene. After we'd filmed the tearful reunion, Marty Ritt, compassionate soul that he was, came over and put his arm around my shoulder. "Cic," he said, "I think we're going to have to do that again." I stared blankly at him, knowing that I'd emptied myself fully into the previous take. "Why?" I asked him. He nodded toward the cinematographer, John Alonzo. "When you were running to meet Nathan," Marty said, "John's eyes filled with tears and he isn't sure he got the shot." *Oh boy.* "You know," I told him, "I don't think I can do that again, Marty."

Once a scene like that is done, it's impossible to repeat. The moment has come and gone. The next take will perhaps give you something equally moving, but it will be different. Acting, at its core, is about surrendering to a moment and allowing it to give whatever it has. I get baffled about people who just won't let things be, onstage and in life. Life is unfolding exactly as it is meant to, exactly as the Spirit intended. Leave it alone and let it play out. Marty understood that, and yet thanks to a weepy cinematographer, he needed the scene again. So I attempted it, and of course, it lacked the pathos of the original. Thank God that John eventually discovered he'd captured the first take. His tears, though they'd obscured his own vision, hadn't blotted the camera lens. As filming wrapped that day, I'll always remember what Marty said to me. "You know, Cic," he said, "this is supposed to be a children's film. But if we're not careful, we're going to make a damn good movie"—one that could transcend its category.

Paul Winfield was slated to be the movie's headliner. I was to receive second billing as his costar. After the movie was complete, Paul called me. "Congratulations, Cic," he said. "For what?" I asked. He explained that the directors and producers had decided, upon viewing the finished work, to make me the star and Paul my costar. I was flummoxed. "Why would you let them do that?" I asked, disturbed to hear that his contract would not be honored. He chuckled. "When you see the movie," he told me, "you will understand." That is how, for the first time in my career, I became a headliner. And it happened not because I'd orchestrated it, but because heaven had.

When the film landed in theaters on September 24, 1972, the outlook seemed bleak. Paul and I were together that day, walking up Broadway. We looked over into a theater we passed and there wasn't a soul at the box office, not even a person in line to buy tickets. We didn't say a word to one another. We just kept walking in silence. I don't care how many shows an actor has played in, a single question hangs over every opening day: *Will this time be good enough?* I went home and cried privately over the disappointment, as I'm sure Paul did. But those tears dried up soon after when the reviews came in. Some praised *Sounder* as a courageous counter to the new wave of Blaxploitation characters, noting how the film portrayed an affectionate and devoted Black couple rarely witnessed on-screen. Others mentioned how it put the Depression-era struggles of Black folks into historical context, all while Nathan and Rebecca put our humanity on full display. Nobody, not even me, expected *Sounder* to receive such strong reviews.

The phenomenal critical reception lit a match under the executives at 20th Century Fox. They realized what they had and launched a media blitzkrieg, pouring more than a million dollars into a massive promotional campaign. They quoted every positive word of every review and organized hundreds of screenings all over the country. Religious and civic organizations endorsed the film, and a study guide was even created. The movie went from struggling at opening weekend to becoming a major box-office success.

I love telling this story because it flies in the face of the notion that Black films don't sell. First of all, the very designation of a movie (or any product) as "Black" smacks of superiority. When a Caucasian actor stars in a film, no one calls it a white film. It is presumed universal. When a film has a Black cast, however, it is immediately sidelined into its own dimly lit corner, disconnected from the broader human experience and believed to be incapable of speaking to a wide cross-section of people. This is utter nonsense. When film companies put their marketing machines behind a movie featuring a Black cast, as 20th Century Fox did with *Sounder* and as Marvel did with *Black Panther* (rest in power, Chadwick Boseman), such films can and do often perform well. Not every project will take off, of course, no matter the racial heritage of its actors. But how can directors and studio heads declare a film a failure when they've put little to no effort into promoting it? As I see it, time is ripe for directors of color to continue what many now are doing: creating and distributing our own content and investing in our genius.

Fox's efforts were fruitful. The film, which was made for less than a million dollars, grossed about $17 million at the box office. In terms of the profit it generated, it landed at number 15 out of the hundreds of films released in 1972. The triumph sent a resounding message to all of our skeptics. And for me, the strong sales and outpouring of applause represented a powerful acknowledgment: that my work could move people, that I had inhabited Rebecca in such a way that her voice, one long silenced, could finally be heard.

The day I learned I'd been nominated for an Oscar, I was filming a small role for a new Black director. Just as I was delivering an important line, I heard laughter on the sidelines of the set. "Don't they know we're shooting in here?" I snapped. "What's the matter with them?" A moment later, a producer walked in. "We've just gotten some good news," he said. I held up my hand. "I don't want to hear anything," I told him. "Whatever it is can wait." When I am working, I show up to do exactly that. All else is a distraction, a disruption to an unfolding moment. The gentleman smiled, shook his head, and left.

The director, who must've heard the news that awaited, gave me a strange look before we resumed. We completed the scene, and even on my way out, I wouldn't let anyone tell me anything. It was upon arriving home, at Haber's place, that my agent gave me the exhilarating announcement: I'd been nominated for an Academy Award for Best Actress. "Really?" I said, the living room suddenly swirling out of focus. "Yes!" he yelped. As tears flooded my face, all I could think about were Arthur's words to me: "You're going to be nominated for an Oscar." My friend's *what-if* had come true. When I called him later that evening, he squealed like a baby boy, as if he'd been the one to receive the nomination. What a jewel that man was. His reaction was no less exuberant when, later on, I told him I'd also been nominated for a Golden Globe.

I don't care what any actor says, that golden statue matters. It is what we're all vying for—the ultimate validation from our peers. You empty yourself into a character, you labor hour upon hour to get every single gesture and sentence precise, and you mean to tell me that such an affirmation means nothing to you? It holds tremendous power. When I was just getting into the business, I'd looked on in awe as Sidney Poitier earned that affirmation for his marvelous work in *Lilies of the Field*, becoming the first Black man to win an Academy Award for Best Actor. That evening as I watched the ceremony on my old black-and-white RCA set, I said to myself, *I'm going to sit in the front at the Oscars one day.* That was my dream. But as my career carried me mostly toward stage and television, that hope seemed unlikely. That is why, long before I did *Sounder*, I'd quietly accepted that the Academy Awards would probably not be part of my path. And yet, lo and behold, here I was, on the verge of taking a seat in that front row I'd envisioned for myself.

My own good news was just the beginning. *Sounder* received a slew of nominations, for Best Picture, Best Writing (Lonne Elder), and Best Actor (I was as delighted for Paul Winfield as I was for myself). The film's message also reverberated beyond our shores, earning a British Academy Film Awards nomination (BAFTA is the English equivalent of an Oscar) for its score, created by Taj Mahal, who also earned a Grammy for his work. Kevin Hooks, who played my son (and who, in real life, is the son of director and actor Robert Hooks), received a Golden Globe nomination. That awards season also became a landmark recognition of Black talent: Diana Ross was nominated for an Oscar for her role in *Lady Sings the Blues*, as was screenplay writer Suzanne de Passe. The 1973 nominations for Diana Ross and myself were the first time Black women had been nominated in the Best Actress category since trailblazer Dorothy Dandridge received the honor in 1954 for her role in *Carmen Jones*.

The morning after the official nomination announcement in Los Angeles, I called my mother in New York. On television, she'd seen how all those white folks had stood and applauded me. "Well?" I said to her.

"Well, what?" she said chuckling.

"You'd better tell me something," I said. The line went silent.

"I am so proud of you, Sister," she finally said. I could feel tears brimming and I let them fall, unable to speak because I was so overcome by what I'd longed to hear. If I had not heard those words from my mother, none of this would have made any difference. If she had not been able to participate in the acclaim I was receiving, all of it would've felt empty to me.

I of course already knew she and my father recognized my work. "Why do you do such *sad* movies?" my dad once joked after he'd seen me in *Brown Girl, Brownstones*. Likewise, Mom would often tell me what her friends were always asking her: "Why is she always wearing rags in her movies? Doesn't she ever dress up?" Though their teasing was an indirect acknowledgment of their pride, I needed my mother, in particular, to voice her validation. She'd implied it on the night she'd seen *Dark of the Moon*, but I craved more. She'd been my greatest source of energy, the reason I'd devoted myself so wholly to my work. She had believed I'd go out and become a slut of some kind, had no idea this Hollywood journey could lead me to play a character as honorable as Rebecca. My nomination did more than just prove my mother wrong. After a childhood during which my mother's opinions drowned out all others, it gave me the last say.

I flew my mother to Los Angeles to attend the screening of

Sounder. We were seated in the mezzanine, and she was one row behind me. In the dark, just as the curtains parted, she tapped me on the shoulder. "Ed Sullivan is sitting behind me," she said, pronouncing his last name *Sulli-wan*, because for whatever reason, West Indians can't say v's. For years, she'd never missed *The Ed Sullivan Show* on Sunday nights. I turned around and whispered to her, "And I am sitting here." We both snickered, she loudly enough to prompt Ed Sulli-wan to smile in my mother's direction.

To celebrate *Sounder*'s cascade of nominations, the studio hosted a splashy New York premiere. I called upon acclaimed fashion designer Bill Whitten to design my dress (years later, Bill would design Michael Jackson's rhinestone glove to cover the singer's early signs of vitiligo). "I want to create the kind of gown that Rebecca might have worn if she'd had money," I told Bill. That sent him in search of the prints and cottons poor colored women would've worn in 1933. Using the fabric remnants he found, he pieced together a treasure. The dress, antebellum in style, came with a fancy apron that served as a flower sack. He filled it with cotton balls he'd sent for from down South. It was the most glorious creation. The same woman who braided my hair for the movie created a crown of beautiful cornrows to complement my look. When I strode into the theater that evening, chin lifted, pride on my brow, I showed up in the name of the ancestors whose sweat and sorrow had carried me there.

In the months leading up to the ceremony, the devil got to work doing what he does best: attempting to pit Black women against each other. In the lead-up to the Oscars, one of Diana Ross's designers tried to keep my dress from being finished by hiring my designer to make suits for the Jackson Five. I don't know whether Diana knew anything about it, but I heard the whispers. The media, for months, had been playing up the narrative that there was some big competition between the two of us. I refused to feed into that story line, which was false. I have never been in competition with anybody but myself, and I wanted no part in such unpleasantness. Just Breathing While Black is trouble enough.

A month before the ceremony, the studio sent me overseas on a promotional tour in Europe, my first time in Paris and London. Months before I left town, I'd rubbed elbows with British royalty. Antony Charles Robert Armstrong-Jones, First Earl of Snowdon, was then husband to Princess Margaret and an avid photographer and filmmaker. Lord Snowdon had taken quite an interest in Arthur's work at Dance Theatre of Harlem. The two began a partnership, with Lord Snowdon investing in the school. Arthur connected me with him, and during one of Lord Snowdon's trips to New York, he and I met for appetizers and a brief conversation. As we awaited our order, he kept glancing over his left shoulder. *How strange*, I thought. *I wonder if he's expecting someone.* As it turned out, he was on the lookout for the paparazzi, who of course had followed him to the restaurant. Later, on another one of his trips to New York, Lord Snowdon photographed me wearing that Bill Whitten masterpiece of a dress. What a memory.

In London, the marveling began with my ride from Heathrow in an enormous black taxi, a Hackney carriage so gargantuan that I could stand up inside of it! In a penthouse suite in the Dorchester Hotel, I spent a half-hour just wandering around the space, gawking at the grandeur of the accommodations, thinking back on those days when I, Emily, and Melrose had all been squished together on a rollaway bed in our parents' living room.

And to think that I now had this sprawling space to myself, in a world where my name was plastered on billboards all over America and Europe. It was nothing short of spectacular. The same was true of my time in the City of Light, where, from my balcony, I gazed in awe at the Eiffel Tower, head held high and preening in the distance.

Back in New York before the ceremony, the surrealism continued. In another head nod to Rebecca, I wanted my hair done in a *croquignole*, the deep-wave style that would've been popular for well-to-do women during the 1930s. "Do you know how to do that style?" I asked Omar. "No," she said, "but my mother can." Can you believe that child's mom came out of retirement just to create my waves? The words *thank you* fell short of expressing the gratitude I felt. Designer Bill Whitten turned up the luxury by creating a white silk-wool fitted dress, with a touch of grey in it, complete with a heart cut-out, lace-trimmed detail across the décolletage. Gracing each sleeve was a glistening row of tiny gold buttons, with the same buttons stretching down the back. It was absolutely stunning. When Arthur arrived, dashing in his tuxedo, he escorted me by the arm to the awaiting limo. The evening, for us, marked two celebrations: the Forty-Fifth Academy Awards, and my dear Arthur's thirty-ninth birthday.

The quintet of hosts—Carol Burnett, Michael Caine, Charlton Heston, and Rock Hudson—took the stage at the Dorothy Chandler Pavilion. As I sat beaming, I absolutely knew I would not win. My dream was to be in the front row, and there I sat, delighted that my fantasy had come to pass. But as for the possibility of garnering the gold statue, I had done my back-of-the-napkin math. I'm logical that way, a pragmatist who is always weighing the odds, and in Hollywood politics, those odds were decidedly not in my favor. That same year, Liza Minnelli had been nominated for her role in *Cabaret*. Her father, Vincente, was a big-time director, which gave her one advantage. *Check*. Her mother was Judy Garland. *Double check*. Neither of them had ever earned an Oscar. *Triple check*. And at the time, Liza was dating Desi Arnaz Jr., son of Desi and Lucille Ball, Hollywood royalty. *Quadruple check*. Common sense told me that I had no chance amid the schmoozing and vote-securing that goes on in back rooms. So as I sat near the stage that evening, I relaxed into the joy of just being there, with Arthur to my left and with Rebecca's spirit dancing on my shoulder. So certain was I that this was Liza's year, when Gene Hackman said, "And the winner is . . . ," I turned to Arthur and said "Liza Minnelli."

Liza made her way up to the stage, tearful and jubilant, and I sat there, palm over my heart, relishing my presence in the arena. This journey of mine, this path so unpredictable, had somehow carried me from 219 East 102nd Street in the slums to the front row of movie magic at Hollywood's most grand affair. As Liza accepted her award, I'd already received the only prize I have ever truly wanted—the affirmation of the dear woman who gave me birth.

Soon after the Oscars, Miles reappeared in my world. His marriage with Betty had lasted just one year, and when it was done in 1969, word of their split of course found its way to my ears. He'd apparently slipped back into heavy drug use after the divorce. Miles began reaching out to me, leaving messages on my answering machine at all hours of the day and night. "I can't live like this anymore, Cic," he said pleadingly in one message. "I'm done with this dope."

I'd seen Miles a few times after he and Betty divorced. He still lived around the corner from my place on the Upper West

Side, and occasionally when I was in town, my sixth sense would send me over to his brownstone to check on him. You may dim love's light, but when you've cared for someone, you never fully switch off the affection. In spite of the emotional lacerations I'd endured at Miles's hand, some part of me still felt concern for him as a human being. It broke my heart that he was back in cocaine's grip.

One morning, my spirit told me to look in on him, and what I found still horrifies me. Particularly when Miles was using heavily, he left his front door unlocked. So when I walked up and found it standing fully ajar, I knew there was trouble. There, in the sitting room on the main floor, Miles and a young woman lay passed out, the room reeking of a foul odor rivaling any I've since smelled. I don't know how long they'd been lying there, but judging by the vomit dried onto their cheeks and foreheads, it had to have been hours. I reached down over Miles and tapped him on his shoulder. His lids flew open. "Cicely?" he sputtered, forcing a drool of white vomit down his chin. I just stared at him. He lifted his head and gazed around, first at the woman, and then back at me. He did not get up from the floor, which is where I left him wallowing in his puke. I walked back to my apartment and called Harold Melvin, the cousin of Miles's longtime housekeeper. "Where is Burlina?" I asked him, after briefly apprising him of the situation. Harold immediately sent his cousin over to clean up the mess. "You always know right when to come, don't you?" Miles said to me a few days later. It was just that binding tie we had, an otherworldly connection. I'd always get this gnawing feeling in my gut when Miles was in deep trouble.

For the most part, however, I gave Miles a wide berth, having no desire to get caught back up in his toxicity. Maintaining my distance wasn't too difficult, given that I was in Los Angeles far more than I was in New York during those years. Out at Haber's place, I'd become the new darling in town, waltzing out on dates with this man and the next, showing up fashionably late to ensure I'd never be the one left waiting. For a brief time during my work on *Sounder*, Paul Winfield and I courted. On-screen romances have a way of spilling over into real life. You get swept up in your costar's persona, which was particularly easy to do with characters as likable as Nathan and Rebecca. During our weeks of filming, Paul and I spent long hours shooting scenes passionate enough to melt even the most frigid heart. Our on-set relationship eventually grew into a personal one. Our affinity for one another is perhaps one reason Paul gave me his spot as *Sounder*'s headliner. The other reason was that I'd earned it.

Paul, unlike his character, was quite shy. So although I could sense his interest when we'd first met during auditions in California, it took him a while to ask me out. He dredged up the courage midway through filming. During a weekend break from the set, we visited a Baton Rouge restaurant that we'd heard had the best gumbo in Louisiana. It didn't. Still, over steaming okra and bouillon, we traded laughs and easy conversation, and from there, our connection slid into an easy sway. Paul was a kind soul, as gentle as the century is long. During quiet evenings indoors, he loved making me spaghetti, doused in his special sauce. Our relationship lasted a year, give or take. A work prospect cut it short.

Berry Gordy Jr., founder of Motown Records, had plans to continue developing his new film and television division following the success of *Lady Sings the Blues*. He approached Paul about lending his talents to the division. According to Paul, Gordy also wanted me to get involved, though he never asked me personally. "Wouldn't it be wonderful to have a steady income, to not have to struggle to pay rent?" Paul asked me. In principle, I agreed. But in fact, my spirit, which has never steered me wrong, nudged me to decline. Although no one can argue Gordy's genius as a record executive—his label, the highest-earning African-American label for decades, launched the careers of The Supremes, Marvin Gaye, and Stevie Wonder, among scores of other greats—I'd heard there was drama behind the scenes. I didn't know what was true and what wasn't, but I did have the sense to follow my instinct, which I voiced to Paul. "But you should still pursue it, if you really want to," I told him. He did for a time, though I don't think much ever came of the collaboration. Yet it was at that juncture that Paul and I naturally moved in different directions, and as we did, neither of us attempted to reverse course—in my case, because our connection, while tender, lacked the intensity I'd shared with Miles.

When Miles began calling me in 1970, I did not respond, nor had we spoken during the filming of *Sounder.* That changed on an afternoon in the spring of 1972, when my press tour for the film took me from the West Coast to New York. I was in my suite near the top floor of the Sherry-Netherland hotel on Fifty-Ninth Street and Fifth Avenue when the phone rang. "Ms. Tyson?" said a woman's voice when I picked up. "This is the front desk. There's a gentleman downstairs who says that you are expecting him."

I paused. "Really?" I said, glancing down at my press itinerary to see whether there was a meeting on the books. There wasn't. "I don't have any appointments," I told her. "What is his name?"

She put me on hold, obviously to check with him. "He says he is Mr. Miles Davis, your husband," she announced. I almost dropped the phone. "My husband?" I said, laughing. "My dear, I don't have a husband, and certainly not one by the name of Mr. Davis." I could hear him pleading in the background, and she asked whether she could send him up. Largely out of curiosity about how Miles had even discovered where I was staying, I allowed her to let him come to my door. Moments later, I heard a knock and I peeped through the hole. Sure enough, it was Miles.

When I opened the door, Miles stumbled toward me, absolutely stoned out of his mind. He was so high he could barely stay on his feet. He reached for me, and with my heart thundering in my chest, I closed the door halfway. "Please, Cic, let me in," he begged. I widened the door slightly, and in he fell, down onto his knees in front of me, with his shirt halfway unbuttoned and saliva dripping from the corners of his mouth. I closed the door behind him, stood him up, led him to the edge of the bed, and lowered him onto it. He sat there for a moment before he tried to get up again, but he fell to his knees once more. He then crawled over to a large window overlooking Fifth Avenue, which was dotted with high-rises. He pointed out to them.

"Cic . . . Cicely," he stammered, "you see all of those apartments?" I stared at him and did not answer. "Every person in those buildings knows who you are," he slurred. He began to cry. "Tell them I'm your boyfriend," he went on. "I'll take ya' any place you wanna go . . . just tell them I'm with you." I stood there dazed, saddened to my core at the state he was in. It was so pitiful. Here was this man, among the most gifted musicians who has ever trod this earth, desperately seeking the validation I had attained on my own.

"Where do you want me to take you?" he muttered, trying but failing to stand again. "I'll get myself a tuxedo and get cleaned up, Cic. Let's get outta here." Even now, decades after that day, envisioning Miles down on that floor fills my eyes with tears. It was wrenching to see him stoop so low, heartbreaking to witness the depth of his brokenness. Millions had hailed him as a living legend, and still, this genius of a man, this master of sound, believed his presence in this life was inconsequential. He had no idea what he meant to the world, because he meant so little to himself.

I had a hell of a time getting him on his feet and back to the door. I called the front desk and asked that a bellman be sent up to help him to a taxi. As I put my hand on the knob to let him out, Miles toppled back to his knees. "Cic, let's get married," he slurred. "I want you with me." I shook my head slowly from side to side and turned the knob.

15

Jane Pittman

During breaks in *Sounder*'s filming in Baton Rouge, I kept my weekend ritual out in California. I'd get up, do some cleaning, and head to my car. I drove a red Ford Pinto wagon then, one lent to me by 20th Century Fox. I eventually asked to keep the car, and the studio heads agreed, which was the least they could've done, given the peanuts they'd paid me to play Rebecca. Every Sunday, I'd get in my Pinto, ride over to Hollywood, and dart in and out of bookstores, browsing for novels that might tie in to future film projects. One afternoon my eyes landed on a book jacket bearing the photograph of an elderly Black woman. She gazed into the distance, as if trying to recall some memory from long ago. The lines in her brow, creased and gently folded, spoke of contentment. I picked up the novel, pulled it close, and read its cover: *The Autobiography of Miss Jane Pittman* by Ernest J. Gaines. Based solely on the arresting face, I purchased the book.

That evening, I read the novel in one sitting. The 110-year-old Miss Pittman, once an enslaved girl, reflects on her long journey from bondage to freedom, and in so doing, she captures the breadth of the struggle of Black Americans from the end of the Civil War through the Civil Rights Movement. The next morning, bleary-eyed but joyous, I called a few friends to tell them about the book and this remarkable woman, Jane Pittman, whom I was convinced was real. "No, she's not real," said one friend, laughing. "It's fiction." "Oh no, darling, this is an actual woman," I insisted. "And Ernest Gaines knows her personally." That's how convincingly Ernest had rendered Jane Pittman. From the first page to the last, I found her story as captivating as I had her cover photo.

Near the end of *Sounder*'s filming in Baton Rouge, Marty Ritt, the director, pulled me aside. "Do you know Ernest Gaines?" he asked. "No, but I just read his latest novel," I said. "Well Ernest sent the book to me some time ago and asked me to read it," he said. He hadn't yet gotten around to reading those galleys, he explained, which made him feel a bit embarrassed when Ernest circled back to ask him to go to lunch. "He's interested in turning it into a film and possibly having you play in it," Marty said. My eyes widened. "Really?" I said. "Yes, and he wants to have lunch with us," he said. "Well I *have* read the book, so I'll go to lunch," I said casually, though the requisite tingle had already made its way up my spine. My sixth sense seemed to be clearing its throat.

The lunch was pleasant, and days later, Ernest, a Louisiana native whose extended family still lived there, warmly welcomed me into the home of one of his relatives. On that afternoon, he'd assembled the glorious bevy of Black women—his mother, cousins, aunts, friends—upon whom he'd based Jane Pittman's story. He'd taken all of the beloved women of his childhood and rolled them into one mesmerizing composite who leaped from the page. On the way out, Ernest said to me, "There's talk about turning the book into a movie, but you know how these people are." He explained that he was going away for a couple of months, but when he returned, he'd be back at his home in San Francisco. "If you're ever up that way," he said, "give me a call and let's have lunch." I smiled and thanked him, but for whatever reason, we did not reconnect that year.

That was around 1971. Sometime between then and 1973, Ernest's novel was turned into a screenplay, one penned by Tracy Keenan Wynn. His script ended up on someone's desk at CBS, and late one Friday evening, a junior producer on his way out happened to spot the screenplay. He picked it up, tucked it in his satchel, and over that weekend, became as taken with Jane Pittman as I had been. On Monday morning, he rushed into his supervisor's office. "We've got to do this," he said breathlessly, flopping the script down on his boss's desk. The head producer flipped briefly through the screenplay and then looked at him. "Who wants to listen to an old Black woman tell her story?" he said. "It won't sell." But this young producer insisted there was something there, and over the next weeks, he channeled his belief into a crusade. I do not recall the producer's name, nor do I know whatever came of him, but I'd give my eye tooth to talk with him now. Because had it not been for that man's passion in championing *Jane Pittman* within CBS, the film may never have been made. Things don't just happen—they happen just.

The producers called me in for a reading, and like with *Sounder*, I could've saved them the appointment. I knew the part was mine and so did Ernest, who was delighted to hear I'd auditioned. The CBS team indeed offered me the role, for more money than I'd made on *Sounder*, though still a pitiful amount. But I would have done Jane Pittman in the basement of a basement, do you hear me? Her story was critical to the cultural moment. Between 1972 and 1973, Blaxploitation had shifted into sixth gear with disgraceful movies like *The Legend of Nigger Charley* and *Trick Baby*. Father, help me.

How is it that we are "sticking it to the man," as some proponents of Blaxploitation cinema argue that these films do, by committing narrative assassination of ourselves? Why would we spend money reinforcing deeply stereotypical depictions of who we are? It pains me. I understood the desire for high-octane fantasy films, just as I understand that deeply flawed Black people exist. But when those are the only characters and plotlines put forward about us, it is disturbing. Crack cocaine exists as well, but its existence is not reason enough for me to take to the pipe. I once declined to play a maid who had five children, each with a different father—a stereotypical two-for-one. When I later ran into the director, a white woman, she seemed perplexed by why I'd turned down the part. I explained my misgivings. "But women like her exist, and in fact, my own maid . . ." I stopped her before she could get the rest of that poppycock off her tongue. "Look," I told her, "I have nothing against such women, and I'm not debating whether they exist. I am simply telling you that I do not wish to project them."

At the heart of Black theatergoers' hunger for Blaxploitation films was, I suspected, a profound sense of our own worthlessness, rooted in ancestral trauma. We'd been taught, time and again in this nation, to see ourselves either as inferior or not at all. Though our minds knew better, our spirits, engraved with that lie over hundreds of years, still bore the scars. A story like Jane Pittman's seemed to me a challenge to that falsehood. In those years, some Blacks scorned films like *Sounder* and *Jane Pittman* for featuring us as downtrodden, for dredging up a painful past we'd just as soon forget. I saw it differently. As a people, we've done what we've had to do to survive, and rather than feeling ashamed of it, we should celebrate it. It is upon Rebecca's and Jane Pittman's broad shoulders that our feet rest.

Resolute as I was to play the role, the enormousness of the

part initially paralyzed me. I retreated under my covers, too frightened to even look at the script, terrified by the responsibility of inhabiting such a monumental character. *How am I supposed to portray this woman from the time she's 19 till she's 110?* I was forty-nine at the time, nearly in the middle of that age span. I felt confident I could play her in her young adult and middle-age years, given that I had my own lived experience of those seasons. What unnerved me most was capturing who she was during the winter of her life. After a few days of cowering, I finally decided I'd better get up and get to work. *The part is yours now*, I thought, *so you had better do something with it.* I never start with memorizing lines. In fact, the dialogue, for me, is usually the last to come. "Please call the producers and tell them that I need to do some research," I told Haber. I'd begin where Ernest had—by sitting and listening to the stories of the elders. Acting, for me, has always been an organic process that involves absorbing my character's reality, allowing her to saturate the cells and fibers of my being.

Well before shooting commenced, I began my preparations. The studio arranged for me to visit a home for the elderly. The three remarkable women I met there, ages 90 to 105, shared freely about their lives, throwing back their heads in laughter at some moments, cupping their faces in agony during others. I'll always remember Pearl Williams, my primary model for Miss Pittman. She was the eldest in the group, and yet she had the best memory, not to mention a quick tongue. "God gave me a good mind," she once quipped, "and I like to tell people what I think." Each of the women had a different take on the times in which they'd been reared. A woman whose name was Eula, I think, reminded me of Beal, the elder who'd become my godmother on that day she spotted my mom approaching with me in her arms and said, "Give me that child." Eula had spent her life as a domestic worker, caring for the two small children of the wealthy woman her family lived with. And yet that servile role—which began when Eula was just six years old, and the woman's children were two and three—hadn't dimmed her light. Her expression still bore the kindness of Beal's. "I didn't know any other life but being the help," she said. "My mother grew up picking cotton out in the fields, so for me, working indoors felt like a step forward. I thought I had a wonderful life." Another woman was clearly wounded by the indignities that came with just growing up colored. She spoke of the day a white woman in a dime store hurled spit in her eye. I spent long hours with these women, visiting many times over several months, allowing their humiliations and their memories to be inscribed upon my heart, recording their speech patterns. I felt that by way of those three, I'd truly glimpsed Jane's interior world. My next challenge became embodying her physically.

I had a few concerns about whether I could authenticate Jane's appearance in her later years, but I felt certain I could capture her voice. During my years at the Red Cross when I was trying to break into modeling, I'd mastered how to fake a scratchy voice in order to get time off for auditions. "Ms. Ruben, I can't come in today," I'd call and claim, straining and reaching deep into my diaphragm for a low pitch. "I can't even talk. I've got a bad throat." That is where Jane's voice came from. Years after the film was released, I heard that CBS had reached out to an older character actor, intending to dub in her voice over mine. They didn't need her because from the first day on set, I had that voice down. When one of the producers heard it, he pulled me aside and said, "That's incredible. How did you do that . . . and can you keep it up?" I smirked and nodded yes.

As for whether I could mimic Jane's other characteristics, I had my worries, starting with my teeth—too white. Then there was my straight body, which bore none of the hallmarks of advanced age. As one gets older, the body naturally hunches forward, and a hump often develops in the upper back. And my eyes? I wondered how I could change them from bright to more yellowish over the course of filming. In the weeks leading up to my first day on set, heaven sent me help in a couple of those departments.

When it came to my teeth, the producers considered staining them with makeup. That became largely unnecessary. One night when I dreamed of Jane, she smiled at me—and I spotted gold around her front tooth. My eyelids flew open at 3 a.m., and I rang a producer, Rick Rosenberg, right then. "I've got it, I've got it!" I shouted.

"Who is this?" he asked.

"It's Cicely," I said. He paused.

"You've got *what*?"

"The tooth! I've got the tooth for Jane Pittman."

"Cicely, would you please call me at nine o'clock?"

I agreed and quickly moved onto my next assignment: finding a local dentist. I recalled I knew a dentist by the name of Valerian Smith, the father to actress Lynn Whitfield. They lived in Baton Rouge, our film location then. I'd met Valerian through my cousin Don Shirley, and I rang Don—who was also less than amused by my early call—to get Valerian's phone number. Later that morning, I dialed him. "Can you make me a tooth with gold around it?" I asked. "Yes, I can," he said. Days later, he'd done exactly as he'd promised, fitting the gilded faux pearl right on top of my front one, as well as creating a row of dental veneers. That's how Jane Pittman's grill came to be.

The hump came next, as Jane Pittman made her presence known in me. I was up early one morning, mopping my floor, when suddenly, my whole left side collapsed. I set aside the mop handle and thought, *What's this?* With my left side still caved in, I walked to the bathroom mirror and studied my reflection. I was hunched over, with a large protruding onion at the very top of my back. *Oh God, I got it*, I thought. *I've got the hump.* By then, the CBS team had ordered a body suit with a hump built into it. "You can send back the fake hump," I called my producer and told him. "I've got a real one." My hump—an actual hump, not one I created by contorting my body—miraculously remained during all five weeks of filming and then just went away. A third gift, realistic old eyes, came courtesy of an ophthalmologist who fitted me with cloudy contact lenses.

On set, the physical transformation continued. I arrived at four o'clock each morning and sat through six hours of special effects makeup, applied by a duo of artists. Stan Winston was then credited for applying my makeup, and he rightfully earned an Emmy for his work. The second artist, Rick Baker, could not be publicly acknowledged at the time because he wasn't in the union (though he was later credited). Rick was the true master. He and Stan divided my face in half, with Rick guiding Stan in creating a masterpiece on the canvas of my face, adding a stroke on my cheekbones here, a swirl or three there, a spin of the brush along my brow line. Once the makeup application was complete, I then spent seven hours in character, delivering take after take, followed by another two hours of removing the liquid layers. I was fortunate to be home by ten on most evenings, only to be up before the chickens the next morning to do it all again.

So many moments in the film send shivers through me, but there's one scene that always makes me tear up. Near the end of the movie, Jane sits alongside a four-hundred-year-old oak tree, recalling what it has seen during its long life, compared to what she has seen during hers. "When you talk to an oak tree that's been here all these years, and knows more than you'll ever know, it's not craziness," she says. "It's just the nobility you respect." During filming as I took my spot near that tree—its arms spread wide, its massive trunk rooted deep in the Louisiana soil, its head adorned with a crown of leaves—that Billie Holiday song from 1939 reeled through my head:

Southern trees bear a strange fruit
Blood on the leaves and blood at the root
Black bodies swingin' in the Southern breeze
Strange fruit hangin' from the poplar trees.

I couldn't help but think of the innocent Black men and women who'd hung from the branches above me, their cries cut short by the pull of a noose, their feet swaying back and forth, the blood draining from their faces along with their unfulfilled dreams. When I remember the thousands who died, many whose stories were never recorded in history, I bow my head. And when my wailing is done, I get up and I carry on, not in my own name, but in theirs.

The film's most climactic scene comes when Jane Pittman makes a long, solitary walk toward a whites-only water fountain and then drinks from it, in defiance of Jim Crow. When she sets out on the walk, an officer tries to stop her, but she moves ahead, with a cane in her right hand, her pocketbook on her left arm, and determination written on her face. "That walk," folks still say to me, smiling and shaking their heads, marveling at how I could capture the gait of a 110-year-old woman. I'm like, "What walk?" I was so divorced from myself in that moment during filming, so completely immersed in Jane, that I had no idea what they were talking about. I did the scene in one take.

As pivotal as Jane's drink from the fountain is, the most memorable part of that scene, for me, is the moment when she pulls away from the family member who's helping her down the sidewalk. It's as if she's saying, "I know how to walk. I'm going down to that fountain, and I don't need nobody holding on to me and ushering me nowhere." That notion is the gift Miss Pittman left me with, the treasure that guides me now. If you're fortunate enough to live as long as I have, you come to realize how others will try to make a cripple out of you. They think you're fragile, and perhaps in certain moments, you are. But rather than waiting for you to reach out, to *ask* for help, they grab on to you. They figure if you're seventy-five or eighty or ninety-six, you're supposed to be decrepit, that you can't even go up the steps anymore. They assume you're unable to function. And before you know it, they're even finishing your sentences for you. Please—let me speak for myself! I'm not addled yet. The minute you hit a number, boy, folks are ready to put you in a box, and Jane Pittman knew that. By making that walk on her own, she was saying what I say now: Let me live. Let me keep going till I can't go no more. Let me walk to that fountain, pocketbook on my arm, and fulfill my purpose here. Don't cripple me.

When *Jane Pittman* aired in January 1974, it ran straight through for 110 minutes, with just one commercial break at the start and another at the end. I will forever be grateful to Xerox, the film's sponsor, for making that possible. Nothing like that had ever been done, which let me know how much the work was respected. Viewers were able to enter Jane Pittman's world and remain there, in rapt attention, as her story unfolded seamlessly. Fifty million people tuned in—nearly a quarter then of the nation.

I was stunned by how swiftly the acclaim poured in, followed by a wave of nominations. The film received nine Emmy nods, all of which were awarded. For my title role, I won not just one Emmy, but a pair of them. The first was for Outstanding Lead Actress in a Miniseries. The second was for Actress of the Year, a specially created Emmy that, up to then, had never been given—nor has it been awarded since. With both awards, I made history as the first Black actress to receive them, and I also earned a British Academy Film Awards nomination. I'll tell you, child, I beamed through that entire awards season, soaking in the joy at every turn, reveling in the many calls and notes I received from others in the business. In the evenings, I'd run myself a warm bath and sink down into it, lost for hours beneath the bubbles and the bliss. On the evening of the Emmys ceremony, I stood backstage afterward wearing a grin as wide as the Nile, clutching my golden statues, feeling like a princess in my flowing spring dress, in awe of my presence there. It may sound unbelievable, but for the first time, I started to think, *Maybe this acting thing isn't a fluke. Maybe I'm here to stay.* Two years earlier, *Sounder* had set the table as my breakout role. *Jane Pittman*, it seemed, served up sweet confirmation—a word, from on high, that I'd earned my spot at the banquet.

Jane Pittman marked the end of my anonymity. Everywhere I went, folks recognized me much more than they had after *Sounder*—a shift I found at once thrilling and a bit strange. It's only after your sense of privacy slips away that you recognize how long you've taken it for granted. As my star rose, so did my number of public appearances. I served as a presenter, alongside Peter Lawford, at the 1974 Oscars. That same year, I cohosted the Tony Awards. I've never been one to cocktail my way around town, so unless I had official business, I happily retreated to my apartment. Yet when I did go out, strolling to the market became not a quick errand, but a circus that drew stares and crowds. I'd think to myself, *What is all this fuss?* I was once speaking to a receptionist when a woman behind me tapped me on the shoulder. "Hello, Ms. Tyson!" she said when I turned around. I chuckled. "How do you know who I am?" I asked her. "Your voice," she said. It was the first time I became aware that my vocal chords alone were enough to give me away.

I enjoyed the adulation, the words from those who approached me, tears in their eyes, to say how Jane Pittman had touched them. It was deeply satisfying. And yet the reticent girl in me still yearned for my space, and I found ways to carve it out. I'd slide into a matinee alone to watch a movie at noon, my way of avoiding the inevitable scene of attending a night show. Even now, I love to disappear into a film house at midday, relishing the stories of Black filmmakers in particular. In 2006, I slipped into a showing of *Saturday Night Life*, the directorial film debut of a young Black woman I knew little about then. Ava DuVernay, the movie's gifted director, is now my friend.

Among family, I was thankfully still just Sis. Neither my parents nor my sister, Emily, got caught up in the fanfare and celebrity. The same was true of my daughter. When Joan and I were with one another, I wasn't Cicely Tyson, the big film star. I was simply her mom, though I'm sure it must've felt bizarre for her to notice others craning their necks to glimpse me. When our large extended family came together during holidays, gathering over fish curry, no one carried on over my film work. My brother was the exception. If Melrose had had his way, he would've paraded me through Times Square while yelling, "This is my sister!" I learned to keep my visits with him indoors.

After the magic carpet ride of *Jane Pittman*, I couldn't imagine what other experience might compare. I said to myself, *That's it. There'll never be another Jane.* I knew I'd continue acting, of course. But since I'd been blessed, back to back, with such substantive characters, I figured Jane and Rebecca were my high-water marks. My agent must have felt the same. After *Pittman*, someone asked Haber what he thought was next for me. "I don't know," he said, chuckling. "She may have acted herself clean out of the business." On stage and off, God alone knew what thunderclaps awaited.

16

Endings and Beginnings

I HAD two peculiar dreams in the fall of 1974 after *Jane Pittman*'s January release. Dance Theatre of Harlem was due to perform for Queen Elizabeth, so I took a red-eye from LA to New York, with plans to eventually fly on to London with Arthur. It was during my red-eye flight that the first dream came about. I was in Harlem, standing on a sidewalk across from Sydenham Hospital on 124th near my godmother's apartment. I looked up and spotted her on her balcony, alongside a young woman with fair skin who looked exactly like Miles's first wife, Frances. When I awakened, I thought, *What is Frances doing in my dream? I wonder if Miles is okay.*

That afternoon, I got in a cab and went over to Casdulan salon to check in with Frenchie, who knew Miles well. "How is Miles?" I asked him. "Oh that bad boy, he's all right," he said, laughing. "I saw him yesterday, and he's acting up as usual." So I knew my dream wasn't about Miles, but I felt tortured by the thought that someone was trying to get a message to me. And no way was I traveling across an ocean until I found out what it was. "Do you know anybody who tells fortunes?" I asked my then-assistant, Susan Siem. She didn't.

So I called Lorenzo James, Arthur's friend, who gave me the number for a retired palm reader. We made an appointment for her to come and see me at the Sherry-Netherland hotel, which is where I was staying while doing some press work for *Jane Pittman*. But before this woman and I could get together, the future revealed itself.

Shortly after I'd booked the reading, I began having strange flashes. I'd be burning up one minute and cold as January the next. When the third heat wave hit, I leaped up from my bed, went into the bathroom, and closed the door. I gazed in the mirror, studying my face from every angle. *Am I going to die?* I thought. Between that and the dream, it was the only explanation I could come up with. That same evening, once I could settle myself down for sleep, I had a second dream, this one more disturbing than the first. In that vision, I was all dressed up, walking down a city street, when I suddenly stumbled to the ground. As I fell, I extended my left arm toward heaven, as if I were reaching out for God's help. I had absolutely no idea what to make of either dream.

A few days later, I'd just emerged from a clothing store on the Upper West Side when I spotted two guys staring at me. The first one, a tall man wearing spectacles, was leaned up against the hood of a Chevy, reading a newspaper that had my photograph on its front page. He looked at the picture and then at me. The other man, short and burly, stood next to him with his arms folded. My instincts told me to flee, so I ducked into Zabar's near Broadway and Eightieth and waited there for thirty minutes, hoping they'd leave. I stepped out and scanned the block and didn't see them, so I quickly hailed a cab to take me back to my hotel on Fifty-Ninth Street. I went up to my room, relaxed for a while, and came down that evening to go out walking. When I entered the lobby, I nearly screamed when

I saw the tall man. I dashed into the hotel's pharmacy, right off the lobby, and approached the clerk. "Can you please call security?" I leaned over the counter and whispered to her. "A man is following me." Just then, the guy wandered into the store and began browsing the shelves. I nodded in his direction to let the clerk know that was him. A security officer soon arrived, questioned the man, and escorted him out of the hotel.

That evening, I called my mother, who in those years was living near Emily in Mount Vernon. I told her about both dreams, as well as about the men who seemed to be stalking me. "You'd better be careful," she said. "Last night, I saw you in a dream—and you were dressed in white." In West Indian culture, white is worn for both weddings and funerals, so the color can be associated with death. When my mother told me that she'd seen me in white, a wave of fear surged through me. *It's not me you saw in your dream*, I thought. *It's you.*

One week later, I was packing my formal wear before the London trip when the phone rang. It was my sister. "How are you?" I asked her. "Not well," Emily said, her voice trembling. "Mother just passed." The phone slipped from my hand as the room blurred. That is the last thing I remember before my world went dark.

My mother had known the end was near. A couple of months before my arrival in New York, Mom had apparently called on my brother's wife, Bernice. The two of them had been separated for years, and my brother was living in Florida then, but Bernice still lived in Harlem. "I'm going home to my mother," my mom had said to Bernice. My sister-in-law stared at her, unnerved by her declaration. "Mama, please don't talk like that," she told her. "I don't like to hear you say things like that." When my mother repeated her assertion, Bernice said to her, "Why don't you wait until Sister comes," probably hoping that seeing me would return Mom's thoughts to her loved ones here on earth. At the time, Bernice did not relay that conversation to me, Emily, or Melrose. I'm sure she must've believed that my mother, reflecting wistfully on her early years in Nevis when her dear mother had held her close, was just missing her mom. Bernice couldn't have realized that my mother's musings meant she'd already placed one foot inside heaven's gates. She'd last seen her mother when she was twenty-three years old, on that day when she'd waved tearfully from a ship deck on her way to America. At age seventy-seven, the time had drawn near for my mother to at long last reunite with her mom.

My mother, a year earlier, had given another sign that her earthly days were numbered. I was out in California when she called me up from her place in Mount Vernon one afternoon. "Come here, I want to talk to you," she said, as if I was around the corner. Now mind you, Emily lived across the street, but it was me she sent for. When I arrived the next week, we sat in her bedroom in front of her television for the longest time, with Mom catching me up on the latest plot twists in *Guiding Light*, as I sat there thinking, *Is this why you called me here from the other side of the country?* As if she'd read my mind, she got up and walked over to a small safe she kept in the corner of her room. She opened it and began pulling out her important records, everything from insurance policies to war bonds to Christmas funds. One document at a time, she laid them out across the bed as I looked on. "Now this is for Melrose," she began. "And this here is for Emily." On it went, with her parceling out the few pennies she'd squirreled away over the years, wanting to ensure that those she loved most were taken care of.

"I don't know what you're doing this for," I said to her. "You ain't goin' no place." She knew different.

For me, my mother left not a teaspoon. Given my success in the film business, she knew I could financially provide for myself. She also knew I could be trusted to carry out her last wishes, just as a stranger in the Bronx had once predicted. "Take care of that child," said the woman, an angel who'd appeared from nowhere and vanished just as quickly on that day in 1925. "She has a sixth sense. She's going to make you very proud one day—and she's going to take care of you in your old age." By 1973, the year my mother called me across the country to see her, both prophecies had come true. She'd put her earthly possessions not in the hands of her eldest, her Heart String, Melrose. Nor did my mother entrust her belongings to her second daughter, her mirror. "I am so proud of Emily," my mother had often said over the years. "She did everything exactly like me. She even had three children like I did, one boy and two girls." Yet in her final days, my mother had placed her faith in me, a mirror of a different sort, the daughter who, at times, had reflected her untended hurts, those shadowy corners of her soul she cringed when staring upon. As God would have it, the child who did the opposite of everything my mother ordered, the one whose out-of-wedlock shame shined a light on her great unspoken one—that daughter turned out to be the child she relied on. I received that trust in the way I believe she intended it, as a final declaration of her forgiveness and love. That she left me nothing mattered not at all to me. Her pardon, alongside her final approval, was treasure enough.

By the time we lost my mother in November 1974, my father had already gone home. He had passed years earlier in the summer of 1961, the year I landed a role in *The Blacks*. Around that time, doctors had discovered my dad had lymphoma, a blood cancer. By then, he'd remarried, much to my mother's aggravation, because despite the heartache Willie Tyson had brought her, she'd never stopped believing he was her soul mate. In the months before his death, Daddy was in and out of the hospital, and much of the time, we didn't even know he was there. On his hospital entry forms, he never listed his children, which I still find curious. Perhaps scrawling our names was a painful reminder of the day our family splintered into two. Or maybe he was just trying to avoid any conflict that may have arisen if my mother had shown up at the hospital, alongside us, to visit him. He was well acquainted with the potential thunderstorm lurking behind Fredericka's placid exterior. Dosha, the quiet church girl from Nevis, was peace like a river. The fiery Fredericka, however, had once stoned the Other Woman in front of a church house. A cross glance from my father's new wife might've been enough to unleash such fury, and Daddy knew it.

Though he clearly preferred otherwise, news of my father's hospitalizations still, at times, made its way around to me and the Tyson crew. On one such occasion, I visited him. Around that same time, his brother, my Uncle Charles, had also been ill and was staying in the same hospital on another floor, which meant my father was grappling with dual heartaches.

Upon entering the room, I walked slowly to his bedside. There he lay in his hospital gown, propped up by pillows, frail and huddled beneath the white sheets, reduced to a fraction of the mighty presence he'd been during my childhood. A few of my cousins and other relatives were already gathered. His face was sallow, the vigor drained from his countenance. I knew he didn't have long. Uncle Charles had passed away that very morning, but no one had yet had the heart to tell my father. He nodded and smiled as I entered, and I leaned over to kiss his forehead. "Hello, String Bean," he whispered, the light returning to his eyes for the briefest of moments. I took a place at his side among the others. No one spoke a word. My father, sensing the palpable heaviness, scanned the faces of those gathered. "My brother died, didn't he?" he said. A few of us traded glances as his wife nodded. The little remaining color in Dad's cheeks faded. He lowered his head and wept like an infant, with a question in his sobs: *Is my turn next?*

The next day I returned to see my father. I took the elevator up to his room, and when the doors parted, there he sat in a wheelchair, with a nurse ready to transfer him to another floor for x-rays. His cheekbones lifted when he glimpsed me, and I held open the door as the nurse wheeled him in. The elevator was somewhat crowded, so a few people scooted to the outer edges to make space for him. Once the doors closed, he peered around and smiled. "This is my daughter," he announced to those around us, with pride in his eyes. "This is my eldest girl, come to see me." He may not have written my name on his intake form, but he clearly wanted the world to know that I was his. He got his x-rays, and during our visit alone, we chatted about this and that, carefully sidestepping, per the Tyson code of silence, what we both knew was imminent. When I kissed him goodbye that afternoon, I sensed I might never see him alive again. I did not.

Two weeks later, I was hanging out at the Orchidian, a bar then near Eighth Street and Second Avenue where a lot of us actors congregated after our shows. A Russian couple owned the spot. Over the loudspeakers every evening, they'd play the Russian national anthem as the wait staff hummed along. On this evening, some old friends, including Sidney Bernstein, one of the producers of *The Blacks*, were with me, and I'd just auditioned for a small role in a production that day. The play was to be directed by my longtime friend and mentor Vinnette

Carroll. Our waiter approached the table. "You have a phone call, Ms. Tyson," he said. I made my way to the phone and took the receiver. It was Vinnette. "Have you talked to your family?" she said. That is all I heard before I passed out. The next thing I knew, I woke up in Sidney Bernstein's living room. He and his wife were standing over me. "What happened?" I muttered. He told me what my spirit had sensed upon hearing Vinnette's question. My father had passed.

Like my mother, my father knew he was near the end. I later learned that, days earlier, he'd called the family to his bedside. I still have a hard time understanding what happened next. My mother and sister, along with Vinnette, had decided that because of my audition, it was best not to tell me that my father was in his last days. They did not want to pull my focus away from my preparation. I'll tell you, boy, there are some things you can never quite pardon others for. This, for me, is one such occurrence. That my family would think that it was more important for me to prep for an audition than to be at my father's bedside—it still puzzles and deeply pains me.

On the day Emily called to tell me our mother was gone, I fainted momentarily. Once I lifted myself from the floor and picked up the phone again, Emily, through tears, explained how my mother had passed. She'd been dressed in her Sunday best, on her way to an appointment in the city. As a precaution while walking the streets of New York, she, like the old-time West Indian woman that she was, always attached her pocketbook to a safety pin and pinned it inside her coat. She'd then carry a decoy pocketbook, an empty one, so that if someone snatched it, the thief would find nothing in it. That's how smart she was. While strolling along the sidewalk, likely scoping out her surroundings, my mother suffered a major stroke. A couple of passersby spotted her and rushed to her side to try to revive her, but she was already gone. She lay sprawled on the pavement, with her left hand stretched toward heaven—in exactly the position I had dreamed. The woman in my second dream had been her.

I never made it to London. Once I hung up the phone, I called my brother in Florida. After he'd left Montclair and his job at the post office, he'd married Bernice. Their union became strained and they eventually separated, but like our parents, they did not immediately divorce. My brother then joined the Merchant Marines, but having inherited our father's temper, he was dismissed for brawling with a fellow mariner who'd provoked him. Melrose, ever the drifter, moved from here to there, and truthfully for a time, we didn't know where he was. But at some point, he called my mother and asked for his papers so that he could apply for reentry into the Merchant Marines. That is how I knew he was living in Florida. And as I see it, it is a miracle that, because he'd called asking for his papers, I even knew where to find him when our mother passed. "Come home," I said when he answered the phone. "What's the matter?" he asked. "Just come home," I repeated. "We need you." I met him at the airport with the news that I am sure, based on the quiver in my voice when I'd called him, he was expecting to hear. My poor brother, Mommy's Heart String, crumpled into a heap of wails.

My mother did not want to be buried in pink. I don't know why, but she disliked the color. For her funeral she'd set aside the silk beige gown she'd worn to my sister's wedding decades earlier. Upon inspecting it, I noticed its frayed edges and stains and decided it was not good enough for my mother's journey through the pearly gates. So I went and bought her a gown that would best complement her figure, and it happened to be rose colored. I've sometimes imagined my mother up in heaven, sitting alongside her own mother, recounting scenes from *Guiding*

Light while fussing, in a deep West Indian accent, about that pink gown and the rebellious last word of her eldest daughter.

After my mother's passing, my brother and I were cleaning out her apartment, a sorrowful duty that, each time I breathed Mom's scent on a piece of her clothing, felt like losing her all over again. We took apart her queen bed frame, and beneath it, I spotted a stationery box. When I pried it open, a slew of envelopes fell out, letters I'd sent to her over the years. Inside them was a stash of money totaling several thousand dollars. Along with my letters I'd always included checks, which she'd cashed but never spent. Instead, she'd tucked the money in the envelopes, perhaps forgetting the stockpile was there. I used the money to send my daughter, Joan, then in her early thirties, on her first trip around the world. "This is your grandmother's gift to you," I said as I pressed an envelope containing a check into her palm. She whispered thank you.

I may never know what my first dream meant, or why the fair-skinned woman resembling Frances appeared. God's ways are indeed a mystery to us mortals, and as the scriptures have proclaimed, we see dimly in this life what we shall one day know in full. And yet my second dream, as well as my mother's own vision, seem undeniable in their message. The woman my mother had envisioned in white had not been me, but her. My instincts had rightly told me that. My mother, in her own way, had foreseen her own passing, as clearly as she'd once known that shards of glass would slice open my forearm. The scar that still runs alongside my right wrist reminds me of her prescience. The pain rippling through me in these times now reminds me of losing her.

You can never predict how you will feel when your parents pass away. You think you know, but you do not. You may believe you'll be too stunned to speak, and perhaps at moments, the grief will indeed render you voiceless. But your silence may also be punctuated with bouts of wailing, of cowering beneath your covers for days, trying to suspend the bleeding, trying to find the ground beneath you again. You may believe that if you have been estranged from or in conflict with your mother and father, you will experience a strange relief upon their passing. None of this or all of this may come to pass. The truth is that, like a great many crises in this life, you cannot truly know how you will respond until you are standing in them. There is no preparing.

Losing my father and mother felt, to me, like walking through the world without arms. Your skin is freshly bruised and exposed. The pain is raw. Through death, you realize that the word *heartache* is not metaphorical but literal. Every part of you throbs and burns. After the rice and peas and plantains have been brought over by caring neighbors, and once the mourners are long gone, you are left only with the silence, the knowing, the realization that you are on your own. Others you hold dear surround you, of course. But when the people who gave you life have departed this earth, you enter a strange new corridor of detachment. You are untethered, disconnected from the two story lines that gave birth to your one.

As much as I adored my father and ached after his passing, I felt the loss of my mother most profoundly. Once our family split apart when I was nine, my mother became the ever-present force in my childhood, the one who wrote most prolifically upon the canvas of who I am. When you bury a parent, you lower his or her casket into the ground, but the history between you lives on. The funeral is an ending, yes, but it is also a beginning—the start of a true reckoning with those hurts between you that must be laid to rest. When we buried my mother, I mourned her then and in the years that followed. As I grieved, I thought I'd long since come to terms with my father—with how he'd both delighted and failed me, with the ways in which he'd unknowingly bruised me just as all parents do, despite their best intentions. But once Miles stumbled back into my world, I learned just how much of a father wound I was still nursing.

17

The Ladder

WITH my spirit still ailing from the loss of my mother, I returned to work. When you're Black in Hollywood, and frankly, when you're Black and doing just about anything in this life, you do not have the luxury of sitting on the sidelines for long. Work beckons amid the reality that when you slow down, so does your income. The wealth gap between Blacks and whites in the United States, created by decades of systematic injustice, was as evident in the 1970s as it is now. That gap has always been more pronounced for Black women. I don't know one Black actress who works with the consistency of a white actress who has the same credentials. That truth holds when it comes to gender. Accomplished artists such as Angela Bassett, Viola Davis, and Halle Berry do not have nearly the same script opportunities as, say, Denzel Washington—and even Denzel, brilliant as he is, has fewer options than white male actors of his caliber. In every aspect of society, we Black women find ourselves on the bottom rung of what I call The Ladder. We are holding on for dear life, I tell you, surviving as our knuckles bleed.

As a Black actress, even when you're at the so-called pinnacle of your career, your choices are severely limited. Characters such as Bree Daniels in *Klute*, the 1971 film role for which Jane Fonda earned an Oscar, come along for a Black artist perhaps once in a career, if at all. How can a Black actress ever become a Meryl Streep or a Glenn Close if she cannot build the illustrious body of work that is generally available to actors of that stature? It's impossible. The opportunities are just not there for us, which is why I so strongly encourage the efforts of Black scriptwriters and directors. If our stories do not exist in the mainstream—in part because, despite evidence to the contrary, the industry's power brokers do not truly believe Black protagonists will resonate with white audiences—we do not have the chance to showcase the full extent of our capabilities. That will change only as we continue bankrolling and scripting our own stories.

Even when Black women are written into a story line, we are often cast as characters with no evident depth or backstory, largely included as scaffolding to hold up narratives centered on whites. I was quite fortunate to have landed two layered and emotionally complex characters in Rebecca and Jane, though as you know, I earned practically nothing for them. The Women's Movement of the sixties and seventies was focused primarily on the needs of middle- and upper-class white women, which meant our unique concerns as Black women were largely overlooked. Ever present was the reality Zora Neale Hurston wrote of when she called Black women "de mule uh de world" in her 1937 novel *Their Eyes Were Watching God*. We are subject to the dual scourges of racism and sexism, a reality articulated by the first Black woman elected to Congress, Shirley Chisholm. In 1972, Shirley made history again as the first sister to launch a presidential bid as a major-party candidate. "In the end," she once said, "anti-Black, anti-female, and all forms of discrimination are equivalent to the same thing: anti-humanism." Shirley understood that we live in a world constantly seeking to reduce us as Black women, be it through racism or sexism. The Women's Movement made its strides, and to be sure, many Black women lifted their voices alongside those of whites. But in our America, precious little shifted.

And then there's the issue of pay. Even with the same competencies, and often stronger ones, Black female artists are routinely paid less than their white colleagues. Out in California, I once ran into renowned actress Alfre Woodard. I was just about to do my daily set of stairs, leading up to the beach in Pacific Palisades, when I spotted her from a distance, exercising with her baby strapped to her chest. She was storming up and down those stairs, boy, as if something had upset her. "Alfre, what's the matter with you?" I called out to her when she drew close. She looked over and smiled when she realized it was me. "I'm so sick of these blankety-blanks not paying me," she said. "I've been in this business a hundred years, and they still don't want to pay me what I'm worth." *Hmm*, I said to myself. *So it's not just me.*

Every Black woman knows that reality. This country has never valued us. Sure, many now take to the streets, declaring that Black Lives Matter, and I believe the murders of George Floyd and Breonna Taylor have at last removed the scales from the eyes of countless whites. I applaud the awakening. Yet in a country that prioritizes commerce above all, a nation where money has always talked louder than rhetoric, the proof of a perception shift will be evidenced in the payment rendered, enough to put us on par, I hope, with less talented whites who've been earning more for decades. It's easy to say Black Lives Matter. The question is, do they matter enough for this nation to treat and compensate them fairly? Historically, the answer has been a resounding no.

In 1972 while promoting *Sounder*, I'd traveled all over the country, speaking to mostly whites, including that journalist who couldn't believe Nathan's son had called him Daddy, just as his own son referred to him. How could that be the case if Nathan, as this nation had taught him to believe, was more animal than human? Once I realized such ignorance abounded, I chose to become an ambassador of sorts, helping whites understand what clearly was not apparent to many: that Black people experience the full spectrum of human emotion. With the success of *The Autobiography of Miss Jane Pittman* in 1974, my platform widened, and I again took to the road. Given that I was turning down roles left and right during the Blaxploitation era, there were long stretches when I did not have enough work or enough money, and often both. Speaking is how I remained solvent. For a full month every year throughout the seventies, I toured on college campuses, talking to young people about the roles I'd played, hoping to wield my microphone as a force for good. It was my way of picketing, my contribution to hastening the fulfillment of Dr. King's dream.

Following a dry spell in film roles after *Jane Pittman*, I did play two characters I am proud of. The first was Coretta Scott King in the NBC miniseries *King*. I reunited with my costar in *Sounder*, Paul Winfield. After our romance had faded, we remained quite fond of one another, a bond that surely bolstered our on-screen chemistry. He took the role of Dr. King, and boy did Paul embody him in both appearance and spirit. I'd never met Dr. King, but by the time I finished the series, I felt like I had. In 1977, Mrs. King, the essence of grace, invited me to stay with her in her Atlanta home while I was researching the role. We spent hours across from each other at her dining room table, covering the terrain of her love story with Martin, whom she'd lost nearly a decade before. He had a wonderful sense of humor, she told me, a lighthearted side the cameras often did not capture. She spoke of the time they traded their well-appointed Georgia home for a much more humble one because Martin, answering his passion's siren call, wanted to live among the impoverished.

"When I was decorating the bathroom," Coretta told me, "I put a simple rug down on the floor in front of the shower, and a matching cover on the toilet seat. When Martin saw the toilet seat cover, he said, 'We've gotta take this off.' I said, 'What are you talking about?' He said, 'Poor people don't have money to buy food. How are they going to buy a rug just to cover the toilet?'" I thought I would die laughing when she told me that story. So committed was Reverend King to the Movement that he wanted every detail of his surroundings to reflect his rallying cry for justice. The same applied to the modest way they dressed their four children.

It's both a challenge and a blessing to portray someone who is still alive. The blessing is that the person is a living, breathing body of research you can tap into. The challenge is that there's pressure to get it exactly right. For me, the process of portraying someone living is not markedly different from the one I usually undertake. I listen. I watch. I smell and taste and touch and inhale. I take in every mannerism, every grimace and head turn, every smile and flutter of the eyelids. My intention was never to completely imitate Coretta, and I couldn't have if I'd tried. As an actor, I am not a puppet, but rather an open vessel—a channel through which a character flows. My portrayals are, in essence, an interpretation. With Coretta, I listened for the emotional truth beneath her words and gestures with the hope of infusing my portrayal with that truth. And as an aside, I initially wore a full head weave for the role. But they brought in a stylist who put in the weave so tight I couldn't even sleep! My head was on fire. It was the first time I'd worn a full weave. It was also the last. "Send that guy back in here to take this stuff outta my head," I told a producer. From then on, I wore a wig.

I asked Coretta about losing Martin. I recall seeing images of her at the funeral at Ebenezer Baptist Church in Atlanta, the way she'd held close in her lap her daughter Bernice, then five, as she stared straight ahead. She did not shed a tear. From afar, she appeared solemn and unflinching, like a soldier just called into battle. When I met her in person, she was the same. I asked her children whether they'd seen her break down during the week of the funeral. They hadn't, which told me a lot about Coretta. Can you imagine what it takes to hear the news that your husband has been murdered, and then to restrain yourself from falling apart? Do you know the strength that must've been required for her to carry on in such circumstances, the kind of fortitude Black women, time and again, have been called upon to demonstrate? During the few weeks that I spent with Coretta in her home, I never once saw her cry, not even when she was talking about losing this man she loved so much. That does not mean she was not devastated. In her private moments, I am sure she wept. But she knew she had to keep it together for the sake of her children and the country that was watching. She had a job to do, and the grieving would have to wait. That is precisely how I felt when I lost my mother. I did not cry when Emily first told me Mom was gone. My initial shock immediately gave way to an urgent sense of responsibility, to carry on with making arrangements. The mourning would come later.

A fresh wave of grief over my mother's passing had flooded me near the end of 1975 while I was in Russia. I'd landed a role in *The Blue Bird*, an American-Soviet children's fantasy film based on the 1908 play *L'Oiseau bleu*. The film had been slated to begin months earlier than it did, but when I lost my mother, shooting was delayed. Liz Taylor, every bit the grande dame in life as she was on-screen, played the lead in the star-studded cast. Jane Fonda and Ava Gardner also had roles. I played Tylette, a cat incarnate. The filming took place in both Leningrad and Moscow. When I arrived in the capital, I was greeted by the sounds of the Russian national anthem, which I knew by heart after all the time I'd spent at that bar in New York, the Orchidian. Even after I'd been in Russia for several weeks—long enough to have gotten past my jet lag—I could not sleep well. I'd awaken in the middle of the night howling, "Momma, Momma, Momma!" One evening, I must've wept for three hours straight. By then, my mother had been gone for a year. And yet it was the first time I'd been able to fully release my sorrow, like exhaling after holding my breath for months.

The Blue Bird was trouble from the beginning. George Cukor, the American director, assembled a Russian crew, most of whom could not speak a lick of English. How is it that you're shooting a film in a foreign country and do not bring in a Russian translator or associate director? It was a mess. And George, who often reverted to sign language to get his point across to the crew, should have known better. The whole process was one big argument after another. At one point, my role required me to fly, leaping into the air toward a passing bird. The crew hoisted me up on ropes, with the (non-English-speaking) cinematographer down below, poised to film the shot. As I swung, he clearly was in the wrong position to capture the scene. He started screaming out directions in Russian, like I could understand him. I was directed to shoot the scene again, so I got back into position. When I heard "Action!" I leaped up . . . and same song, second verse. "I'm not doing this another time," I told the director. "This cameraman has no idea what he's doing." The whole production was lost in translation. In fact, I'm not sure how we even got that film done. It was an absolute disaster.

I later heard that George Cukor—who had been the original director of *Gone with the Wind*, until he was replaced—had wanted to turn *The Blue Bird* into his *Gone with the Wind*. That approach obviously did not work, as the film was critically skewered upon release. And incidentally, I also heard that the movie's soundman had been madly in love with Liz Taylor. During filming, so went the grapevine chatter, the man wandered by Liz's dressing room to give her something. When she opened the door, she was wearing an old frock, like a frumpy housewife, and her hair was all over the place. She wasn't the Liz Taylor of his fantasy, but a mortal just like the rest of us. From that day forward, it seems like everything with the production went south.

Still, there was one bright spot: I got on well with Jane Fonda. She knew I'd lost my mother, and when I arrived in Moscow, she embraced me. "Do you know how worried we were about you?" she said. I will always remember her kindness. On set and off, we talked constantly, and she was as passionate about her causes then as she is now. Through the early 1970s she had been protesting against the Vietnam War, a move that made some people question her patriotism. She is, at her core, a fighter, and a Sagittarian like me. In the United States, protest is our birthright, but when you exercise that right, you are often penalized for it. Jane, by then, had discovered that. I didn't spend much time off set with Ava Gardner or Liz Taylor, who was then Hollywood's darling. My dustup with Liz would come years later on a different project.

Liz and I both took our pets with us to Moscow. She had two dogs (I don't recall what breeds), while I had my Lhasa apso called Stuff, for no reason in particular other than that I liked that name. I'd spotted Stuff on the same day I left for Moscow. From the moment I saw his little nose pressed up against the storefront glass window, I was smitten. In Moscow, Liz turned her dogs over to the caretaker of the property at which we stayed, whereas I let Susan, the assistant traveling with me, care for Stuff. While we were on set working during eighteen-hour days, the caretaker fell in love with Liz's dogs. Near the end of filming, Liz said to me, "I don't have the heart to ask him for them back," and she indeed left them in Russia. I brought Stuff home with me during what turned out to be a thunderbolt of an exit.

George had asked the crew to stay on a while longer to reshoot some scenes that his Russian-speaking crew had failed to capture. I refused. Our film dates, outlined in my contract, had already come and gone, and I was eager to get back to my life in the United States. A contract is a contract. Also, Moscow isn't exactly the tropics, and after weeks layered in every piece of clothing I'd packed, I was frozen. And then there was the bland Russian cuisine, which did little for my West Indian taste buds. I was cold. I was hungry. I was grieving my mother. Plus, I'd already committed to do another movie back in Los Angeles. Filming was to start shortly.

I asked my assistant, Susan, to arrange for my departure. No flights out of Leningrad were immediately available, so she booked me on a train from Leningrad to Zurich, and from there—after a tussle with airport officials, who tried to ban me from traveling with my dog—I flew on to Los Angeles. I told no one in the crew I was leaving. Somehow or another, while I was en route home, word got around to Frank Sinatra that Russia was giving me a hard time crossing its borders with a pet. Frank and I go way back, to the days when we both played in the 1966 film *A Man Called Adam*. Frank called my agent, Haber, and said, "I hear they won't let Cicely Tyson out of Russia. Can I help?" What a gracious offer. But by then, child, I'd already made my own way back to the offices of 20th Century Fox (the distributor of *The Blue Bird*) before anyone on George Cukor's crew even knew I was gone.

While I was at the studio, one of the execs picked up the phone to call George in Russia. "Do you know where Cicely Tyson is?" the exec asked. "She's in her suite," George answered. "No, she isn't," the studio head said, laughing. "She's sitting here at my desk in Beverly Hills." Around the business, I have sometimes been called difficult. The truth is that I insist upon respect. I don't take any tea for the fever, child. Even now, at age ninety-six, I teach folks not to mess with me.

The year after my mother went home to heaven, Miles went missing here on earth. By then he'd taken a hiatus from music, and as he put down his horn, he picked up his drug habit again. Word around town was that he'd sunk to his lowest. I'd gotten to know Miles's eldest daughter, Cheryl, during the years when Miles and I were first together. In 1975, with desperation in her voice, she called me.

"We can't find Father," she said, referring to Miles as she and her siblings always did. I pressed the phone closer to my ear. "What do you mean you can't find him, Cheryl?" I asked. "Nobody has seen or heard from him," she replied. He'd gone out to San Francisco weeks earlier, she told me, but since then, neither his housekeeper, Burlina, nor anyone else in his family had gotten a call. In California, Miles had been staying with a couple he knew well, the same friends who'd breathed life back into him years earlier when he'd overdosed. They were the ones who told her he was missing. "Well I have no idea where he is," I told her. Though I hadn't seen Miles since the day he'd stumbled into my hotel suite stoned, and though we'd certainly had our moments of strife, I of course still regarded him as a friend. And as a friend, I was concerned.

I knew the couple that Miles had stayed with and called them myself. I wish to God I could recall their names, but time has dimmed that from memory. The wife answered when I rang. When they hadn't heard from Miles for a couple of days, her husband had put out the word around town, even asking about him in the dope houses Miles frequented. "We've talked to everybody we know," she told me. "We've gone every place that he hangs out, even asked about him among the dealers. Nobody has seen him."

Over the next week, I checked in with both the woman and Cheryl. "Any luck?" I'd ask. "Dead or alive?" No word. Finally, the following week, a dealer spotted Miles in a street gutter. His face was covered in spit and vomit, his eyes glued shut. He was unconscious, in a drug coma. The man leaned over, took Miles's pulse, and once he realized he was still alive, he called the couple. The husband arrived a short time later, and to avoid unfavorable press attention, he decided against taking Miles to the hospital. Instead, he and the dealer hoisted Miles's limp body into the back seat of the car. He then drove him to his home and called Cheryl, who called me. "We found him," she told me, relief in her voice. "And he's alive."

Barely. The couple did everything they could think of to nurse Miles back to consciousness—including putting cold compresses on his face every hour as he lay in bed—but he would not wake up. The wife called me daily with updates. "He's breathing," she said, "but he's still unconscious." Finally, on the third day, Miles cracked open his lids and stared blankly at her, as if she were a stranger. To spark his memory, she played some of his records and began talking to him about his children, his music, his life in New York. That did the trick. When she mentioned his daughter, Cheryl, Miles lifted his hand toward hers, as if the world had leapt into color. The woman took Miles's hand, cold as clay, and would not let go. Though his eyes were open, he did not speak.

That evening, the husband sat Miles up on the side of his bed. Miles then tried to stand, but as he did, his legs buckled and he collapsed. The couple, each on one side of Miles, lifted him up and led him to the bathroom. "Let's take him to the shower," the husband said, hoping some cool water would hasten his recovery. Miles sat on the tub's edge, looking down at his feet and up at the shower head as a waterfall descended. They dried him off, put him in some pajamas, and helped him back into bed. He was still mute.

That dear couple hovered over Miles as he alternated between the chills, sweats, and nausea brought on by his drug withdrawal. Finally, after three weeks, he was strong enough to fly home to New York. When the couple told him how worried I'd been, he began weeping. Cheryl called me with the news of Miles's recovery and travel plans, saying that when she talked to him, he sounded like himself. Miles and I never spoke directly at that time. Frankly, there was little to say. My concern from afar, an act of friendship born purely of my care for him, had spoken clearly enough.

18

Roots

EVERYWHERE in the world I go, folks still come up to me, palms over their hearts, and whisper, "Roots." Though I've played more than a hundred roles in my time, many of which have fallen from memory, millions will forever know me as Binta, mother of Kunta Kinte, the Gambian man at the center of Alex Haley's epic saga *Roots*. Over eight nights in the winter of 1977, the nation sat in rapt attention as the story of Haley's ancestry, starting with Kinte's birth and winding its way through two continents and seven generations, unfolded on their televisions. It's a testament to God's handiwork that *Roots* came to include my portrayal.

A couple of years earlier, when *Jane Pittman* was complete, I went away to Rancho La Puerta, Mexico, for a two-week vacation. Near the end of it, my agent, Haber, called me. "Hurry up and get back here," he said. "I've got some big things going for you." Soon as I arrived at his place, he gave me a copy of *The Ledger*, a crime-thriller novel by Dorothy Uhnak, and told me to read it. The book's main character, Christie Opara, works as an undercover detective—a white New York City policewoman who prances through town, half-naked with her skirt up to her crotch, as a decoy to ensnare criminals. ABC had adapted the story for the small screen in a series to be called *Get Christie Love!*, featuring a Black female lead. ABC had me in mind to play Christie, Haber explained. The more I read, the lower my heart sank. *He must be crazy if he thinks I'm taking part in this foolishness*, I thought. Surely there had to be a mistake.

The next day, I called Haber at his office. "Are you sure you gave me the right book?" I asked him. "Yes," he said. "What's the matter?" I paused. "I know you don't expect me to do this," I told him. "And if you do," I continued, "I am telling you right now, I will not." It's interesting that when the network heads adapted the novel to the screen, they reimagined it with a Black woman as basically a prostitute—a narrative in line with the many featured in the Blaxploitation films of that era, not to mention a reinforcement of the very stereotype I'd been attempting, with my choice of roles, to counter. That wasn't the surprise. The real stunner was that they thought that I—on the heels of having earned every accolade imaginable for portraying the dignified Jane Pittman—would even consider such a role. Between that and the ignorance I'd witnessed while traveling this country to address outright bigotry against Black people, no way was I about to strip down to play a hooker with a badge. "All right," Haber said. "Let's meet and talk." I had little more to say.

That evening when he arrived at the house, I repeated my misgivings. "Are you sure you won't even consider it?" he said. I nodded and his eyes filled with tears. And in that moment, I said to myself, *Oh boy, he's in trouble.* It occurred to me that he'd already agreed that I would do the role. He did not admit that, nor did he have to. His expression gave it away. As he lowered his gaze to the floor, I knew the truth: if I did not show up on set the following week, his job could be in jeopardy, which is why I relented. "I'll meet with the producers and maybe do just one episode," I told him, "but they'll need to find someone to replace me." The color returned to his face as he thanked me profusely.

The day before I was to show up at ABC, a fungus developed under the big toenail of my left foot. "Take some olive oil, heat it up, and soak your foot in it," a friend told me. "That'll pull the infection right out." I unearthed my glass electric kettle, filled it with water and a touch of oil, and plugged it in. Moments later from the living room, I heard the kettle boiling and rushed to the kitchen to unplug it. I then wrapped a cold wet rag around the glass canister to cool it off. That's when the glass cracked into pieces and shattered onto my foot, along with a flood of scalding water.

I crawled to the phone and called Haber, who rang for an ambulance. Doctors later confirmed what my foot, red and throbbing, had already told me: I'd suffered third-degree burns. The nurses wrapped my foot tightly, urged me to stay off of it for at least three weeks, and sent me home on crutches. "Call ABC and tell them I won't be there," I said to Haber. To this day, he swears I burned myself deliberately, just to get out of the role. "Now I know how serious you are about your work," he told me. Truth is, though it had been an accident, I was relieved. Because the closer I got to the first day of playing a role that turned my stomach, the more conflicted I felt. *This is God's work*, I thought, *and I'm not going to question it*.

As I limped my way through the next few weeks, the producers began auditioning potential replacements. They eventually discovered one in Teresa Graves, the actress who'd played in the long-running TV sketch comedy *Rowan & Martin's Laugh-In*. David Wolper, whose production company produced the series, called me. "We found someone, Ms. Tyson," he said, chuckling, "but you owe me one." Months later he also said to me, "You were right not to do *Christie Love*." As it turned out, that girl was so unhappy in that role that she eventually left the business and became a Jehovah's Witness. Years later, she tragically died in a house fire.

Two years later, in 1976, that same producer, David Wolper, called me again. "I have a role for you," he said. His production company, he explained, had just started work on the TV miniseries *Roots*. "And remember," he said, laughing, "you owe me one." I smirked. "Well I'm not going to do it for nothing," I told him. Like Alfre, I was tired of studios paying me pennies, only to turn around and make a mint. "Of course not," he said. "I'll call your agent and we'll discuss it." One week later, for a sum more respectable than any I'd ever earned up to then, I signed on to play Binta, mother of Kunta Kinte, in a film that would shake the nation to its core.

The book preceded the miniseries, but only by a few months. In the fall of 1976 before the film aired in January 1977, Alex Haley's *Roots: The Saga of an American Family* debuted to critical and commercial fanfare, ultimately spending forty-six weeks on the *New York Times* bestseller list (twenty-two of them at number one) and earning Haley a Pulitzer Prize and a National Book Award special citation. The book went on to sell six million copies. But what appeared to be an overnight success had actually spanned more than a decade. Haley, who'd merited acclaim for his 1965 collaboration *The Autobiography of Malcolm X*, became curious about his own ancestry. In his family's rich oral tradition, Haley's grandmother had passed along stories of their ancestor Kunta Kinte—a young Muslim man who'd been enslaved during his teen years and shipped to America during the treacherous four-month-long Middle Passage. Family lore told that Kinte obstinately refused to trade his given name for Toby, the one forced upon him by his new masters. Haley followed that trail to the shores of West Africa, where, armed only with this oral history and the name Kunta Kinte (portrayed, in his younger years in the film, by LeVar Burton), he began tracing his family's lineage with the help of a Gambian griot, or storyteller. That search, over twelve long years, gave birth to *Roots*.

I met Alex Haley soon after his book had been published. As his story gripped readers around the nation and world, he began hosting forums, town hall gatherings much like those I'd participated in after the release of *Sounder*. I took part in a few of his forums, which is how he and I first became acquainted. I adored him from the first meeting, when our rich conversations weaved and bobbed through the story of how his book came to be. When I find someone who stimulates me intellectually, as he did, that person can never get rid of me. What an extraordinary human being Alex Haley was, both soft-spoken and humble. Over the years of our friendship—and these days, I can hardly recall a time when he wasn't in my life—he rarely raised his voice above a whisper. Few would have guessed that the gale winds unleashed by *Malcolm X* and *Roots* flowed from such an even-tempered soul. Like many talented artists, he let his pen do his picketing.

God began preparing me for *Roots* years before the series was even a thought. I had traveled to Africa for the first time in 1967, to the Kingdom of Dahomey, tucked between Togo and Nigeria in present-day Benin. My work on *The Comedians*, a film costarring Liz Taylor and Richard Burton, is what took me there. The story was set in Haiti, but because of political conflict there, the film was shot in Dahomey. The movie was a forgettable flop, but the vivid colors, aromas, and sounds of

Africa still dance in my memory. Away from filming, I traveled the country with a translator, talking to women who gathered at the shoreline to wash their clothes, witnessing the rich community and uproarious laughter around supper tables, relishing the vibrant flavors of maize, yams, and peanut stew served from their wooden tables. I did not speak their language, but I knew these women. The abiding care that knits together the African-American community, that profound intuitiveness and palpable spirituality that has always been within us—it is present in Mother Africa. In truth, it originated there.

I was studying and didn't know it. The Dahomean women wore their bushels of hair in elaborate braided styles, each parted to perfection and often signaling their tribal affiliations. The Bantu knots I donned in *Roots* are like those I spotted during my travels (and on set with my hairdresser, Omar, I insisted the style be precisely replicated). So much of great acting is about paying attention to the passing world, and every morning while in Africa, I homed in on the details of their grooming habits. The people there never used soap and water on their skin. Rather, they washed their faces with the juice they'd squeezed from leaves. I don't know what was in those leaves, but I hardly ever saw anyone with a pimple. At sunup before the women began their daily work, they'd clean their teeth using bark they'd stripped from a tree—and by the way, they had perfect teeth. When I returned home to New York and walked along 125th Street in Harlem, I chuckled when I spotted African immigrants, street salesmen, doing the same thing: sitting on boxes alongside their wares, using a piece of bark as a homemade toothbrush. Like a great many traditions our ancestors brought to America, they carried that practice with them. I brought those memories with me onto the set of *Roots*.

A few years later, I returned to Africa, this time as part of a tour with the United Nations. On our journey to the remote villages of Senegal, I had the privilege of being present alongside an impoverished woman as she gave birth in a makeshift ward, on the springs of a tattered iron bed with a thin sheet draped over her. She'd lost a baby during childbirth the year before. I was asked to come see her, as a way to ease the anxiety that might clasp shut one's womb following such a tragedy. Between her fluent French and my broken version, we greeted each other as I took a seat near her. She was sweating profusely in a sweltering room with no air conditioner or fan. I pulled out a packet of wipes from my pocketbook and wiped her forehead. She commented on the scent of its perfume. I smiled and nodded, and then folded her hand into mine. I told the few corny French jokes I knew, attempting to distract her from the labor pains. Never once did she scream or cry, not a single sound. I kept thinking, *They gave her something*. But the nurse said she hadn't had an epidural, or any of the other anesthetics we take for granted in the United States. Other than the sweat, I could hardly even tell this woman was having a child.

Next thing I knew, the nurse was shouting, "I see the head!" As doctors directed the woman to push, there wasn't an ounce of strain on her face. Moments later, her baby boy, swaddled and wailing, lay pressed against her bosom. Little did I know I'd one day be called upon to portray the birthing experience of an African woman. On the first day of filming, I asked the director, "Do you want a silent birth?" I told him about the one I'd witnessed in Senegal. The director, it turned out, wanted a conventional labor, complete with moaning and screaming—and I gave him precisely what he requested.

Binta's birthing scene opens the film, just as it does the book. Wrote Haley: "Early in the spring of 1750, in the village of Juffure, four days upriver from the coast of The Gambia, West

Africa, a man-child was born to Omoro and Binta Kinte. Forcing forth from Binta's strong young body, he was Black as she was, flecked and slippery with Binta's blood, and he was bawling." Maya Angelou the almighty, who played my mother, Nyo Boto, joined me in moving that passage from page to screen on our film set in Savannah, Georgia (a location chosen, in part, because the vegetation there resembles that of the Gambia). My character, during that scene, served as my salve. What a blessing it was to just fold myself into Binta, to forget my mourning for a time. My mother, by then, had been gone for two years, but the ache lingered. Stepping into Binta's labor was how I divorced myself from my own grief. Binta's birthing scene was of course imaginary: there I lay, legs open, with a sheet pulled over my lower half and the camera aimed only at the agony on my face. And yet the anguish behind those primal wails could not have been more real. Binta, for me, was more than a character. She was my catharsis.

Portraying Binta also gave me a scorching back. Perched above me on set stood a row of bright lights, as well as some kind of heating instrument, for only God knows what purpose. That equipment set my entire back on fire, from the shoulders down. Initially, I thought the Georgia sun, unforgiving as it is hot, had lit me ablaze. But even once shooting was done, I kept on burning. I finally showed my blistering shoulders to one of the producers and said, "You'd better get me a nurse." The nurse administered a topical treatment that eased the pain well enough for me to continue. Back to shooting we went during eighteen-hour days, with me grunting and screaming while giving birth. We shot that opening scene so many times I'd nearly lost my voice by the end of filming.

As my newborn makes his grand entrance, my mother stands proudly at my rear, wiping sweat from my brow. My husband,

Omoro (played by Thalmus Rasulala), dashes into the villa upon hearing the first cries of our son. "We will give him a very good life," I whisper, to which Omoro replies, "We've given him life, Binta—good or not good. That is for Allah to say." Eight days later, Omoro, in keeping with the African tradition, bestows upon his son a name that will be echoed through the centuries. Soon after, the father cradles his swaddled newborn in the crease of his elbow as he strides into a dark forest. He kneels to the ground, gently unwraps his treasure, and lifts him toward the Maker of the heavens. "Kunta Kinte," he proclaims as he holds the squirming child beneath the starry firmament. "Behold, the only thing greater than yourself." That scene, in all of its rhetorical potency and visual splendor, would come to define *Roots* in the hearts of millions.

Roots felt like a gamble for ABC. The executives there had a gripping historical drama on their hands, based on a book that had already riveted the masses—that much they knew. But above that certainty hung a pair of questions: Would white folks tune in for a generational slave narrative featuring a mostly Black cast? And if they did tune in, would they turn away in guilt, denial, or grief over their foreparents' savage treatment of Blacks? Perhaps with those questions in mind, the series' writers created a white slave captain with a moral compass: Thomas Davies, portrayed by Ed Asner. Such a sympathetic character did not appear in Haley's volume. His inclusion would make the plotline more palatable for Caucasians, or so went the thinking. Still, even after the story line had been softened, there was a whole lot of hand-wringing leading up to airtime. To increase the series' chance of success, ABC had filled the cast with a slew of familiar Black faces, including John Amos, O. J. Simpson, and Louis Gossett Jr.

Ahead of *Roots*' release in January 1977, the studio screened all eight hours of the series for a mostly white Los Angeles audience. The theater was jammed to the rafters. I was in attendance, and when the film ended, you could've heard a hair hit the floor. No one moved or said a word for several minutes. In my mind, viewers' silence likely meant the film's message had reverberated, but it scared the daylights out of the already-nervous network heads. Not only were they not sure how Middle America would respond to the story, but talk soon swirled of what they secretly feared—that Blacks, gazing anew upon the barbarism we've endured in this nation, would riot. The ABC team's initial plan, I heard, had been to roll out the film over eight weeks, with an hour for each episode. And yet doing so would have extended the series into "sweeps," the period when Nielsen surveys television viewership habits and sets advertising rates. The bigger a network's audience during sweeps, the more it can charge advertisers for commercial spots. Some of the ABC heads were terrified they'd lose sweeps by airing *Roots*—which is why they chose to get it on and get it off quick, during eight straight nights.

I'm sure those executives later wished they'd had a crystal ball, because from the opening night to the final credits, Americans were mesmerized by the series. The ratings reached beyond the stunning to the stratospheric: approximately 130 million viewers tuned in to some part of *Roots*, more than half of the US population then (and 85 percent of those with televisions tuned in). With each installment, the viewership rose as people of all stripes canceled plans to huddle in their living rooms. Bars and bistros, theaters and casinos emptied out as folks raced home to witness our fraught history unfold on the small screen.

The final episode, which aired on January 30, 1977, catapulted *Roots* into the record books. That episode, at the time, was the most-watched in television history. Even now, it is still the fifth-most-watched non–Super Bowl show of all time (*Roots* was eventually bested only by the last episode of *M*A*S*H* in 1983, the final episode of *Cheers* in 1993, the "Who Done It?" episode of *Dallas* in 1980, and the *Seinfeld* finale in 1998). It even drew more viewers than the Apollo 11 moon landing in 1969, which was telecast across all networks. *Roots* was more than a prime-time phenomenon set to a soul-stirring soundtrack by the masterful Quincy Jones. It was a national meeting around the village well, the start of a reckoning that bears a resemblance to the one of our current times.

Roots' ratings were eclipsed only by its cultural impact. In the summer of 1976, six months before the series aired, the nation had celebrated the Bicentennial—America's two-hundredth birthday, in which the African-American perspective felt glaringly absent. Haley's tale became a counterpoint. With the airing of *Roots*, the historical record had at last been rendered more complete, with the testimony of the persecuted featured right alongside that of the captors. The bestiality of the slave trade was no longer buried. *Roots* brought slavery's cruelty to life in vivid and searing color, with images capable of haunting even the most coldhearted. ABC had feared that whites might cringe, and some may have. But millions also leaned in to a new social consciousness. Seldom had there been so many kitchen-table conversations about our nation's original sin and our place, as descendants, in that legacy. For whites, the series prompted an awakening to the horrors of a not-so-distant past. Perhaps surprisingly to some, *Roots* also served that purpose for Blacks, many of whom did not know, and still don't, the full extent to which our ancestors were dehumanized. Everyone, it seemed, had been moved by some on-screen moment in *Roots*—whether it was the day Kunta was captured and herded onto the *Lord Ligonier* ship for the voyage to America, or the time, amid lashings from his slave master, he at last relented and took the name Toby. Even the few who hadn't watched the series got swept up in the national obsession, as *Roots* crawled under our collective skin and stayed. The television community acknowledged as much by awarding the series a record-setting thirty-seven Emmy nominations and six wins.

As I see it, *Roots* resonated because it touched a nerve that runs far deeper than race—family identity. The human desire to know where we've come from, and who our foreparents were, is a universal longing that transcends ethnicity. When you know your history, you know your value. You know the price that has been paid for you to be here. You recognize what those who came before you built and sacrificed for you to inhabit the space in which you dwell. In sharing the story of his one tribe, Haley precipitated a curiosity and a question for millions: *What is my own family history?* Like never before, people of all backgrounds began researching their ancestries, wondering how their pasts had given birth to their present lives. Looking into one's heritage became, and still is, a national fascination. Judging by the scores of folks who approached me with tears in their eyes as they spoke of the series, I felt like I'd been part of educating the entire world.

Decades before I portrayed Binta, I'd longed to discover more about my own ancestry. *Roots* deepened that yearning. I knew the few stories my mother and father had passed on to me, the tales of resilience and survival that I've recounted in these pages. But sadly, I never met any of my grandparents in Nevis, never had the opportunity to ask them about their lives or those of their parents and grandparents. For African Americans in particular, genealogical research can be frustrating, with dead-ends around every corner. Records don't often exist for the enslaved, who, when they were even counted, were frequently numbered as chattel rather than as human. When our ancestors were sold away from their homelands, their voices were silenced beneath the crack of their masters' whips. That is why it is so meaningful when we manage, through documentation, to unearth even the tiniest bread crumbs of our past. Knowing your generational story firms the ground upon which you stand. It makes your life, your struggles and triumphs, bigger than your lone existence. It connects you to a grand plotline.

While I was writing this book, I called up Dr. Henry Louis Gates Jr., director of the Hutchins Center for African & African American Research at Harvard University, and host of the award-winning PBS documentary series *Finding Your Roots*. Dr. Gates and I have known each other for years, and each time I saw him, I'd mention eventually wanting to uncover my family tree. He was of course eager to do so as soon as I gave him the word. Finally, in the fall of 2019, I rang him and said, "I'm ready." He and his team began the process of researching my full ancestry, but weeks into their exploration, they encountered a heartbreaking impasse: in Nevis, most of my family's critical records had been lost during a fire, the remnants of my ancestry gone up in flames. I will never know why my mother's mother, Mary Jane Sargent, who was born in Barbados, left there on her own to settle in Nevis, or why she and Charles, my mother's father, never married. I will also never know from where in Africa my ancestors descended.

Perhaps *Roots*' most enduring legacy is that it sparked a conversation around two powerful questions: How will we, as a nation of immigrants, heal the wounds of our painful history? And what personal responsibility does each of us bear in attempting to do so? Whatever our contribution is, you and I are unlikely to see the full picture of that healing during our lifetimes. Social transformation is not measured in weeks or months, but in generations. Our children, and their children and grandchildren, may witness the conclusion of a story that began hundreds of years before they were even conceived.

James Baldwin, in a 1976 piece for the *New York Times*, wrote this of Kunta Kinte and *Roots*: "We are in his skin, and in his darkness, and, presently, we are shackled with him, in his terror, rage, and pain, his stink, and the stink of others, on the ship which brings him here. It can be said that we know the rest of the story—how it turned out, so to speak, but frankly, I don't think that we do know the rest of the story. It *hasn't* turned out yet, which is the rage and pain and danger of this country." The story, stretching back for centuries and extending to this very moment, is for us to continue writing.

Miles had a way of showing up in my world each time my career reached a new pinnacle. He'd done so after the success of *Sounder*, on that day he'd crawled his stoned self into my hotel room, pleading for my hand in marriage. He'd done so again following *Jane Pittman*, when the question over his whereabouts made its way to me. Then in 1978, while still basking in *Roots*' afterglow, I played the formidable abolitionist and Underground Railroad conductor Harriet Tubman in the NBC miniseries *A Woman Called Moses*—a role that, on the heels of Rebecca, Jane Pittman, Coretta, and Binta, fulfilled my mission of portraying the best of who we are as Black women. While I was completing work on that series over the summer, Miles showed up once more. He again had his hand on death's doorknob.

I was in California when Miles called me. In the months leading up to our reconnection, I'd taken two significant wellness strides, both of which helped me restore my balance after losing my mom. Sometime in 1976, I went to a health spa, where patrons were served only whole organic foods, all fruits and vegetables and natural grains, no animal products. When I left there after a week of following that program, the world looked different to me. My head was clear. Colors, smells, and sounds felt more pronounced. My memory improved. I felt energized. So on my own at home, I continued eating that way. I'd begin the day with a cup of fresh celery juice (before any solid food, as a way to cleanse my system), followed by a serving of oatmeal (I enjoy mine whipped, in a blender, like a soufflé) and fruit. For lunch and dinner, I'd make myself some collards and yams, or else I'd fill an enormous wooden salad bowl with every vegetable in the rainbow, topping it off with lentils. Sometimes I'd just climb up into my bed with that bowl and eat my vegetables raw, no dressing to speak of. I eat this way now, four decades later, and these days, I also sometimes have fish and egg whites. The change has agreed with me, it seems. At age ninety-six, I'm still kicking.

Following the alteration in my diet came an addition to my spiritual practice. I began meditating and chanting daily, after connecting with some followers of Nichiren Buddhism (the same form of Buddhism adopted by Tina Turner after she left Ike). The group was just forming a chapter in Los Angeles when I became involved. The leaders and parishioners were walking around the city barefoot, trying to get people to join. I've never been a joiner. Also, my spiritual identity is anchored by my Christian faith, so I was concerned about how this group's beliefs would fit with mine, if at all. That is why, when I was asked to become part of the sect, I declined. And yet I remained open to the meditation practices I learned from the leaders, and as I implemented them, I felt more awake, more in tune with myself. All these years later, I still follow my morning prayer and Bible reading (I love Psalm 91) with the chant *Namu Myōhō Renge Kyō* and a time of stillness. It centers me. My Christian faith and my meditation practice are not conflicting, but rather complementary. Mindfulness is simply about paying attention in a world overflowing with distractions, whereas Christianity is about acknowledging my utter dependence on the Creator of that world. To him alone I bow.

Miles was sober when he rang me. I don't know to what degree he was still using cocaine then, if at all, but the damage he'd inflicted on his body over so many years was clear. His kidneys were shutting down, he told me. His lungs were in horrible shape. He was coughing all the time and could hardly stand up straight. He had trouble keeping any food down. "I'm tired of how I'm living, Cic," he said, wheezing as he spoke. "I don't want to do this no more. Please come back to me. I need you."

I said nothing at first. Every cell in my body screamed for me to put down that receiver, to walk away from this man who'd caused me so much aggravation. And yet I could not turn away. From the day Miles and I had first connected in Riverside Park all those years earlier, I'd felt a profound pull toward him, an attraction that runs counter to logic and leans toward mystery. I knew about the drugs. I'd heard the stories of his philandering, and during my first time around with Miles, I'd experienced the grief of it. Folks were always wondering aloud how the two of us, a church girl and a drug addict, could ever possibly fit together. They couldn't understand why I was so drawn to him, and in my quiet moments, even I sometimes questioned that.

What was dim to me then, at age fifty-three, I see more clearly now. Miles felt desperate for someone to save him from himself, someone who wanted nothing to do with the drugs destroying him. He yearned for someone he could trust to climb down into the gutter and pull him out, while never succumbing to the forces that lured him there. And I, the daughter of a man fueled by a rage as potent as any narcotic, needed someone to save. As a girl, I'd looked on in helpless horror as my father and mother went to war, as my daddy raised his voice and fist to the mother of his children. Try as I did, I could not end the battle. Miles, for me, was a chance to at last provide a remedy, to lend myself to the care of another human being, to help fix a situation badly in need of repair. He had a strong need to be cared for, and that need intersected with my desire to provide care. That is why, when Miles called me that day pleading for my help, I finally whispered yes.

When I saw Miles for the first time back in New York, he looked worse than he'd sounded on the phone. He was fifty-two then but appeared twenty years older. He hobbled across the floor to his front door to greet me, as pain shot through his legs with every step. He'd even bought himself a wheelchair to use around the house. He'd lost a tremendous amount of weight, with loose flesh hanging from his lower jaw. His eyes were dim. He hadn't picked up the trumpet for the longest time, he told me, which was the surest sign of his despondency.

We didn't move in together, nor had I ever given up my place on Seventy-Fourth Street a few blocks from his brownstone (and around this time, in California, I'd finally moved out of Bill Haber's home and into a place I had purchased on Malibu Beach). When I was in New York, I mostly stayed with Miles. Once I saw what bad shape he was in, I did not want to leave him. I was surprised at how quickly we fell back into an easy rhythm, the way you do when you hear a favorite song you haven't heard in years. We'd sit for hours at his kitchen table, laughing and carrying on about all that had happened in the world during our years apart. He teased me about the scratchy voice I'd used in *Jane Pittman*, claiming I'd stolen it from him. I just shook my head and smiled, since we both knew that was nonsense. I didn't have much film work, so that year, I made Miles my project.

I took Miles to see Dr. Shen, a Chinese herbalist I'd heard about. A woman in the business, an actress I won't name, had gone to see Dr. Shen when she was suffering with a major physical ailment. Weeks later, after following his treatment plan, she'd left his office in tears of gratitude because he'd been able to cure her. I'd once overheard this woman's secretary mention that story and Dr. Shen, and I wrote down his name and address, which was on Bayard Street in Chinatown. I found Dr. Shen's number and called him about Miles. "Bring him here," he told me. When we entered his office on a Sunday morning, the waiting room was packed.

Dr. Shen called for Miles, and I went in with him. In silence, the doctor took Miles's pulse and blood pressure. He then checked his eyes, listened to his heart and lungs, and laid him on an exam table. He pressed on his abdomen, asking him if he felt any soreness. Miles's groan provided the answer. As Miles sat up on the side of the table, the doctor drew in a deep breath. "You might have two, maybe three weeks left," he said. Miles stared at him blankly, the blood draining from his face as he absorbed a sentence neither of us had expected to hear. No one spoke for a full minute.

"Let's step outside," I finally said to Miles. In the hall, I asked him whether I could talk with Dr. Shen alone, to hear the details of his full assessment. Miles agreed. Back in the room, I closed the door.

"Please tell me what the problem is," I said to Dr. Shen.

"His vital organs are shot," he explained. "I don't think I can help him. It might be too late."

I stared at him. "You don't know who this man is," I said to him as tears filled my eyes. He of course, like the world, understood who Miles was as a performer, but the shell of a man who'd shown up in his office was irrefutably on his way out of here. "Please, whatever you can do, it is important that we try to help him," I pleaded. "He cannot believe that we've given up on him."

The doctor stared at the floor for a long moment, and then returned his gaze to me. "All right," he said, exhaling. "But he will have to do everything that I tell him to do." I assured him that I'd see to it. In a cab headed back uptown, I shared with Miles what Dr. Shen had requested. With fear in his eyes, he nodded yes.

Thus began the road back for Miles. The doctor had sent me home with a bushel of herbs, a bag so enormous we'd hardly been able to get it into the back of the taxi. His instructions to me were precise: put a portion of it into a massive pot, boil it down for several hours, and have Miles drink eight ounces of the liquid every day. He also gave me a container of concentrated clear gel, and frankly, I don't know what it was—some kind of Chinese remedy. Every morning, Miles was to stir a spoonful of it into whatever he was eating, which, because I was preparing his meals, became whole foods—vegetables only—rich with nutrients. And above all, he could consume no drugs or alcohol of any kind during the course of treatment. On Sundays, Dr. Shen had told me, we were to return to his office so he could monitor Miles's progress and load us down with more herbs.

Praise God that by the time Miles had called on me for help, he was so sick that he'd already given up cocaine, cold turkey. In our earlier years together, I'd watched him wean himself a couple of times. His process was remarkable to me. He'd first let go of all the hard drugs and liquor, then marijuana, then cigarettes, then even beer. He'd close himself off in his room and stay in bed for weeks, sweating and moaning while his system revolted. In the end, he'd be sitting at the table with a cup of water, looking like he'd never been hooked.

When it came to Dr. Shen's prescription, Miles was a willing student. He followed the orders to the letter, and as far as I was concerned, he did not have a choice. I was not going to let this man die. I counted it a miracle that we even made it to the third and fourth appointments, given Dr. Shen's assessment during visit one. In addition to the herbs, the doctor added in an ancient herbal tea for Miles to drink twice daily, to aid in restoring his vital organs. Miles did so dutifully. On a couple of Sundays when Miles's body was riddled with pain, I nonetheless dragged him to that office, wheeling him in there in his wheelchair. Week by week, his condition slowly improved. Even Dr. Shen, upon examining him, seemed surprised at the pace of his recovery. He was still quite sick, still limping and hunched over, but a little at a time, I could see the life returning to his countenance. Six months after Dr. Shen told Miles he had just weeks left in this life, that man picked up his horn again.

In the year after Miles and I got back together, he proposed marriage to me twice more, in his own way. "So when are we going to do this thing?" he'd ask, grinning. I demurred. I felt beyond certain of my love for him, yet I thought our relationship was fine as it was. In my mind, we didn't need to formalize the feelings that had been proved. But the better Miles got to feeling, the louder his chorus of insistence became. During the holidays, around my birthday in 1979, he again asked me to marry him. This time, probably because he'd worn me down, I said yes. His eyes filled with tears as he embraced me. "I'm going to try this shit one more time," he said, laughing. I was to be the third Mrs. Miles Davis. I was also to be the last.

Miles sealed the deal soon after. When I arrived at his place one evening, he met me at the door. "I got you an emerald," he said, beaming. "What do you mean, you got me an emerald?" I asked, wondering why he'd choose a green stone. "Go down to the jeweler tomorrow and see if you like it," he said, scribbling the address on a piece of paper and handing it to me. The next morning, at the shop, the man at the counter pried opened a black velvet box to reveal a sparkling solitaire. He slid it onto my finger as I gasped. "Oh, I guess he must've meant an emerald *cut*," I said, laughing. Turns out Miles had asked a woman in his manager's office what ring he should choose, and she told him, "Get her an emerald cut." Miles, who didn't know a marquise from a princess from a cushion cut, grabbed onto the word he understood: *emerald*.

Following our engagement, I got involved with various film projects, so we took our time setting a wedding date. Meanwhile, Miles would sometimes teasingly say to me, "You're a big movie star. What do you want with an old man like me?" That question had less to do with my desires and more to do with his physical state. Dr. Shen had pulled him back from death's cliff edge, no doubt, but he was still on that cliff. Miles knew he wasn't long for this world, and as grateful as he was that I would commit to him, he couldn't quite understand it. Others echoed his dubiousness. "Why are you marrying him?" someone asked me. "Can't you see he's dying?" But I had no reservations. I was not focused on his exterior, his frame. From the beginning, I'd loved Miles for his innards, for the man that he was even at his most vulnerable. And I knew that if I could just get him standing up straight again, if I could get him back on the stage and reconnected with his purpose, this man wasn't going anyplace.

19

Thanksgiving Day

BY THE fall of 1981, Miles and I still hadn't married. "When are we going to do this thing?" he asked me again that October. Neither of us wanted an elaborate affair, nor did we want to just go down to city hall. "You know, the Cosbys invited us for Thanksgiving dinner at their place in Massachusetts," I reminded him. "Why don't we have a small ceremony there?" Miles loved the idea, and I said I'd ring Bill.

"I am calling to accept the invitation to dinner," I told Bill over the phone that week. "And how about a wedding at your home on Thanksgiving Day?" The line went silent for a moment. "Whoops!" he finally said, I'm sure because he was stunned. "Let me ask my wife," he said. Camille graciously agreed, and soon after, I called Andrew Young, the US ambassador to the United Nations and ordained minister who had just been elected mayor of Atlanta. I'd known and admired Andrew for years and had once said to him, "If I ever marry again, I want you to officiate." I told him about our plans, and like Bill, Andrew suddenly got the hiccups: "Whoops!" Once he picked up his jaw from the ground, he said he'd be honored to marry us a few weeks later. "I'm traveling now," he told me, "and I'd want to stop back through Atlanta and bring my wife to the wedding." I thanked him and assured him we'd be delighted to have Jean there.

I knew exactly who should make my dress. A few months earlier I'd been honored with an award in North Carolina, and George Peter Stavropoulos, a Greek designer in New York, made a dress I adored. I asked him to replicate that very design using gold-tinged lace for the bodice and billowy cream chiffon for the skirt and sleeves. Further in step with the eighties fashion trends, I even had my shoes made with fabric matching the dress. I chose my heel height carefully. At five feet eight inches or so, Miles was a few inches taller than me, but I sensed it bothered him when I wore pumps that brought me to eye level. So I chose one-inch kitten heels.

My hair was still natural then, a medium 'fro, and I don't know what gave me the idea that I should relax it. Perhaps I wanted to make my hairstyle the "something new" on my special day, but it instead turned out to be something disastrous. A week before the wedding, I went to see Ruth Santiago, a hairdresser and friend I'd been going to for years. "I'll relax it one section at a time," she told me—first the back, and then the front. Once I was in her chair, she parted my hair section by section and carefully layered on the creamy white lye to the back half of my hair. She and I got to talking about my forthcoming nuptials, and in the middle of a sentence, she stopped, glanced up at the clock, and shrieked. By the consternation on her face, I knew she'd left the chemicals on my head too long. She rushed me to the sink bowl as she asked, "Is your scalp burning?" For whatever reason, it wasn't. Honey, she turned on that cold water so fast, with tears streaming down her cheeks as quickly as that tap was flowing. She finally got me back into her chair and began combing, with her fingers, through my newly straightened strands, and as she did, handfuls of my wet hair came out into her hands. By the time she got done combing, the whole back half of my hair was completely gone. Thank God she had parted it off, because if she hadn't, I would've been as bald as I was on the day I was born. I didn't say a word.

I'm a strange duck, in that when something goes wrong, I don't cry. Instead, I immediately shift my focus onto how I will get through it. "Listen," I told her amid her panic and apologies. "Let's just slick down my hair in the front over the back, and then put a stocking cap on it," I told her, thinking I could hide it with a wig. After leaving the salon that afternoon, looking like a runaway jailbird, I called my dress designer with an idea. "Can you design me a cap to go with that dress?" I asked him. He said he could. Using the same colored lace he'd sewn into my bodice, he created a crown of gold, customized to fit precisely over my half-'fro, with its bottom edge resting perfectly along my nape. The wedding guests would be none the wiser.

Very few people knew Miles and I were to marry. Even my family, including my daughter and siblings, did not know. I didn't tell them because I didn't want to hear folks' mouths, didn't want anyone to distract me from what I was intent on doing. I'm sure Emily must have had a clue about the marriage when, a week before the wedding, I called to ask whether I could borrow Mom's gold wedding band, which our mother had left to her. Though Miles and I had more rings than we knew what to do with (in addition to my engagement ring, the Cosbys eventually surprised us with gold wedding bands bearing the inscription "My only one"), I still wanted my mother's band near me, adorning one of my fingers. It would be my way of having her with me in spirit, if not in the flesh. Mom had never met Miles up close. In the mid-1960s, during Act One of our love story, Mom had once been with me when I'd stopped by to visit him before an event. But for reasons unknown to me, Mom preferred to wait in the car while I went in, perhaps because her Dosha reticence arose. When Miles peered out of his front window and waved, she politely waved back with a satin-gloved palm. I am not sure what my mother would've made of Miles. I knew only that I wanted her with me, in one way or another, on our wedding day. Emily agreed to lend me the ring, and I sent a messenger for it.

The evening before the wedding Miles and I arrived at the Cosbys' home, a sprawling, tree-filled estate near the Deerfield River in western Massachusetts. We settled into an upstairs suite, one Camille had designated just for us, and I began unpacking. I'd arranged for all of my items to be delivered there ahead of time: the dress, the shoes, the cap, the ring. I laid them all out, enjoyed a lovely dinner with our hosts, and ended the evening with a soak in the tub.

Nerves kept me tossing and turning that night, and at daybreak, my eyes flew open. The wedding was to be at 4 p.m. in the living room, before the holiday meal. Other than Andrew and his wife, none of the Cosbys' twelve or so guests had any idea they would witness our nuptials. That afternoon, I donned my dress and cap and slid on my nylon stockings as Miles steam-ironed his Brooks Brothers suit. When I went over to the dresser where I'd laid my mother's band, it was gone. "Have you seen the ring?" I asked Miles. He hadn't. He and I turned that house upside down looking for that ring. As I searched, my heart hammered away in my chest at the thought that I'd somehow lost such an irreplaceable treasure. At 3:30, I finally had to give up the search so I could gather myself for the vows. Bill and Camille presented us with the gift of their bands to be used for the ceremony.

Camille gathered the guests. Andrew, clutching a Bible, stood near a gorgeous fireplace mantel. A hush fell over the sitting room as I descended, one careful step at a time in my lace-and-chiffon stunner, down a tall marble staircase. Bill escorted me. Miles, who had already taken his place near Andrew, straightened his spine—as much as he could. Still broken and hunched over with illness, he could hardly even stand up. His face, grey and sunken, revealed his physical deterioration. As I drew closer, he fixed his gaze on me and did not once blink. When Bill placed my hands into his, Miles leaned toward me and whispered to me a sentence I will forever remember: "Thank you for saving my life." If I'd had any hair on the back of my head, it would've stood up. Tears filled his eyes as Andrew led us through our traditional vows, promises that Miles's health had already begun to test. As I uttered the phrase "for as long as we both shall live," I hoped, for the second time in my life, the covenant could be kept. I shed tears at both of my weddings, the first time, at age eighteen, because I'd been forced to marry. Nearly four decades later, I cried happy tears as I willingly spoke my vows.

The feast was served at Camille's impeccably set banquet table, with tall candles twinkling in the dusk. Among the guests were some I knew, including the actors Clarence Williams III and Gloria Foster, who were then married. Clarence got into the business because of me. In 1962, I was playing in *Moon on a Rainbow Shawl*, which Vinnette Carroll directed. Vinnette was serious about her rehearsals, do you hear me? If anyone so much as sneezed to interrupt, she'd have a fit. One night Clarence came to the Y to visit his sister who worked there, and while she was finishing up her duties, Clarence began roaming around the facility. He cracked open a door where we were rehearsing, and when he did, light rushed in. "Who is that back there!?" Vinnette yelled out as a sheepish Clarence crawled to a back-row seat.

Vinnette later invited Clarence up to the stage, and after

chastising him with a smile, she turned to me and said, "Miss Cicely, doesn't he look like he could be your brother in the play?" I nodded yes, and on the spot, she offered him a role in our production. Clarence had no theatrical experience, but that didn't matter to Vinnette. That woman could make an actor out of anyone.

At the dinner seated next to Clarence and Gloria were Dick Gregory, the comedian and civil rights pioneer, and his wife, Lillian. I met other longtime personal friends of the Cosbys for the first time. Amidst the clink-clank of silverware and laughter, Bill stood at the head of the table and offered us a toast. Those gathered raised their crystal in congratulations. The entire occasion was absolutely lovely.

Late that evening as I entered our upstairs suite, an object caught my eye on my side of the queen bed. There lay my mother's gold band, atop the folded-down crisp sheets. I gasped as I picked it up and studied it in disbelief. No way could that band have been there during my frantic search. In fact, Miles and I had stripped off and shaken out the duvet and sheets. No one had been into or out of our suite since, Camille later confirmed, and yet mysteriously, our bed had been remade with that ring placed on top of the taut linens. I realize now, decades later, that my mother was attempting to get a message to me. Before the ceremony, she'd hidden that ring because she could not, from her grave, offer her consent on the journey I was undertaking. She knew all too well the painful corridor I was entering. She'd navigated the passageway of my father's infidelity and did not want that for me, her eldest girl. I'll tell you, I hurried up and got that ring back to Emily. The entire occurrence spooked me.

The next afternoon, Miles and I were enjoying our final moments with the Cosbys when an announcement came over the radio. "We interrupt this program with a news bulletin," said the broadcaster. "Jazz musician great Miles Davis married actress Cicely Tyson yesterday at the Massachusetts home of Bill and Camille Cosby. UN ambassador and former congressman Andrew Young officiated the ceremony." Miles and I glanced at each other and then burst into laughter, mostly because we couldn't believe our small private wedding had qualified as breaking news. I mean, you're going to cut into programming on a holiday weekend when people are relaxing with their families? It seemed ridiculous to me. And that was just the start of the nonsense. In the coming days, I can't tell you how many people called me to say how they'd fallen out of their chairs when they'd heard that radio announcement. "Why didn't you tell me?" a few of them said. I'd laugh while thinking to myself, *Because I didn't want you to know.* My business is my business, thank you very much.

Miles and I didn't go on a honeymoon, given that I was set to begin work on a project soon after our wedding. We did, however, enjoy a short trip down to New Orleans. During the plane ride, Miles opened up a newspaper and spotted a Black woman, a professional cheerleader whose name happened to be Mary Sargent, the same as my mother's mother. The woman also strongly favored me. "Is that you?" Miles asked, laughing. I glanced at the photo, and given the similarity of our features, even I did a double-take. We both giggled, and he then set aside the paper and took my hand. "Listen," he said, "the last thing I want to do is ruin your career. I am in this with you and for you. And I will do everything I possibly can to make it right." He'd heard the talk around town that I had no business with a man like him, that his demons would eventually pull me down. He wanted me to know, from his lips to my ears, that he intended, to the best of his ability, to uplift me during our marriage.

In the Big Easy, we visited Dooky Chase, the legendary

restaurant owned by Leah Chase, queen of creole cuisine. Miles frequented the restaurant whenever he was in town, as did countless Black luminaries, including Dr. King himself. That place had gumbo good enough to make you take your shoes off and shout along the aisles. You should've seen Leah's face when Miles and I, arm in arm, walked through her door. She quickly escorted us to a private booth in the back and even had her kitchen crew stir up a meatless version of her gumbo. What a beautiful human being she was. For years after that day, she'd often proudly tell her customers, "You know, Miles and Cicely stopped through here right after their wedding." She, too, had heard the radio announcement of our vows. She couldn't believe her restaurant was our first stop as husband and wife.

Around the time Miles and I married, I had my hands in a trio of projects. The first two—a film with Richard Pryor and a TV movie based on the life of trailblazing educator Marva Collins—were filmed back-to-back. The last, a Broadway show with Liz Taylor, ended in a lawsuit.

I'd never met Richard before we costarred in *Bustin' Loose*, the 1981 comedy featuring Joe Braxton (played by Pryor), a con man with a past as colorful as his mouth. In a chance at both parole and a kind of personal redemption, Braxton agrees to transport, via bus, eight special-needs students and their teacher, Vivian Perry (portrayed by me) from Philadelphia to a farm in Washington, where a fresh start awaits the children.

I have David McCoy Franklin to thank for the project. David, a shrewd entertainment attorney and then husband to Shirley Franklin (who was eventually elected mayor of Atlanta), had brokered major deals for some of the top Black stars, including

Miles, Peabo Bryson, and Roberta Flack. In the early 1980s, he also represented both Richard and me. David and I were riding in the elevator one day when he said to me, "Richard wants to do a movie with you." I stared at him as if he'd suggested I fly to Jupiter, a notion I found no less absurd than me playing opposite the most foul-mouthed performer of that era, however much of a comedic genius he was. "Richard *Pryor*?" I said. "What on earth kind of movie would I ever do with Richard?" Richard, he explained, had been quite fond of a schoolteacher who'd once shifted his trajectory. He wanted to create a movie in tribute to her, and David had me in mind to portray the teacher. I still couldn't fathom it. "Why don't you read the script and tell me what you think?" he said. Crazy as it sounded, the story line pulled me in. It apparently did the same for audiences. Though many had initially scratched their heads upon hearing of my on-screen pairing with Richard, the film hit at the box office, debuting in the top spot on its opening weekend and ultimately grossing $31 million domestically.

On the film set in Washington State, Richard was as painfully shy as I'd heard he was, often disappearing into his trailer. Fragility lived behind all that cursing and ranting, a gentleness. Maya Angelou once told me she'd witnessed that side of him when she delivered a scintillating performance on *The Richard Pryor Special?* in 1977. She never forgot his tenderness toward her, which, it seemed, went hand in hand with his reticence. His gentleness was on full display as he interacted with the children on our set. Those kids just loved Richard, and as he laughed and played around with them, his shyness fell away. His own childhood had been marred with such dysfunction. He was reared in a brothel run by his grandmother, and his mom, an alcoholic, worked as a prostitute. He'd survived sexual abuse. Like Miles and scores of other sensitive souls among us, Richard sought solace from his demons through drugs. But while with the children in our crew, the sober Richard was a complete sweetheart. Perhaps he felt a kinship with those young'uns that he'd missed out on during his own boyhood.

Whenever Richard hadn't stolen away to his trailer, he talked endlessly about his fishing expeditions. He absolutely loved the sport and would often return, between film days, with bags of his fish for the crew. For some reason, I'd always wanted to learn how to fish. Perhaps the idea of solitude on the vast seas is what appealed to both Richard and me. Once, when I had a day off from filming, I stepped into a Seattle sporting goods store and said, "Is there anyone here who can teach me how to fish?" The salesman chuckled. "I'm sure a lot of people could," he said. I had my hair and makeup person with me, and our plan was to rent a boat, set sail on Lake Washington, and cast our lines. Sure enough, the salesman found us an associate who agreed to take us out fishing that morning. He helped me get my line in the water, and all of a sudden, my rod began twisting and turning all over the place. My eyes bulged as I gripped the rod, attempting to keep myself from flying overboard. "You've got a big one!" he shouted as he ran to my side. Turns out it was a six-pound bass.

That was only the beginning. By dusk, I, the neophyte, had managed to catch five more fish, all salmon, every one of them flipping and flopping as much as I did whenever my rod got to moving. Back on set, I proudly handed out my gutted and cleaned fish to my fellow castmates and set aside my largest salmon, in the sink, especially for my costar. "Tell Richard to come here," I said to my assistant. Richard stepped into my trailer soon after and we chatted for a bit, with him wondering the whole time, I'm sure, why I'd called for him. On his way out, he spotted the gigantic fish. "Oh by the way," I told him, "that's yours." A smile spread across his face. "Did you catch this?" he asked. My salmon was twice the size of any he'd ever brought back. "Yes," I smirked. He laughed, snatched it by the tail, and slammed the door on his way out. He didn't speak to me for three days, which I thought was just hilarious. Jealousy is the strangest of the vices.

I moved on from novice fisherwoman to educational trailblazer for my work on the CBS made-for-TV movie *The Marva Collins Story*. Marva, an Alabama native educated in a one-room schoolhouse, had risen from her state's segregated school system to earn her teaching degree from Clark College in Atlanta. She taught in Alabama for a time before moving to Chicago, where she became frustrated with the lack of resources and poor test scores of low-income Black children in the public school system there. In 1975, she parlayed that frustration into a newfound passion. Using her personal savings, she opened Westside Preparatory, a private school housed on the upper floors of her brownstone in West Garfield Park. Students included her son and daughter, as well as a handful of other children, some of whom were thought to be "learning disabled." Within a year under her strict-yet-nurturing tutelage based on a modified Socratic method, every one of her students had scored five or more grades higher on standardized tests, an eye-popping success that eventually caught the attention of President Ronald Reagan (he wanted to nominate her as Secretary of Education, but she declined). The school expanded as force-of-nature Marva welcomed students deemed "unteachable" and turned them into academic stars. In 1981, I had the privilege—and the challenge—of portraying her. Morgan Freeman played Marva's husband, Clarence Collins.

The film shoot was difficult from day one, largely because Marva was there for all of the filming. She had every right to watch from the sidelines, of course, especially given that she'd lived the inspiring story. And yet the distraction of her presence, as well as her frequent input to the production crew, just about drove me crazy. My friend Dr. Walter Leonard, himself an educational pioneer who was then president of Fisk University—and who'd helped engineer Harvard's groundbreaking affirmative action program—once came to visit me on the set. After a full day of observing, he pulled me aside. "I don't know how you do it," he said. I didn't either. Marva wanted to be sure I portrayed her exactly as she wanted to be portrayed. Fair enough. Trouble is, her approach made it nearly impossible for me to relax and do my work, a fact that I mentioned to the director. I don't know whether the director said anything to her about my complaint, but I think it not a coincidence that she pulled back on her comments. Somehow, despite Marva ogling me the whole way through, I turned in a performance good enough to earn me an Emmy nod. I only hope dear Marva, who passed on in 2015, felt I did her life justice. Her legacy is one we should all celebrate. It is proof that our children, when accorded the attention and respect they deserve, are capable of greatness.

Marva's hovering was nothing when compared to Liz Taylor's smirking. In 1983, Liz's production company, in conjunction with Zev Buffman, presented a stage revival of *The Corn Is Green*. I played the main character, Miss Moffat, an English spinster teacher, and was the first Black actress to take on the role. Critics excoriated the show, as well as my performance in it (I never could get down that British accent), but that had nothing to do with the small kerfuffle between Liz and me. Near the end of the show's run, I—someone who had, up to then, never missed a single one of my scheduled performances—requested one night off to attend a tribute to Miles. When the show's director would not grant me the time off, I took it anyway. I was subsequently—and unjustly, I might add—fired and replaced for the remainder of the production. I promptly sued Liz's production company for the earnings they still owed me. We shouldn't have had to go to court. I tried to reason with Liz's team, tried to come to an agreement that would've saved us all a headache. But the show had done poorly, and they seemed intent on recouping at least some of their losses. I heard Liz went through four lawyers in attempting to mount a defense, and she no doubt spent hundreds of thousands in fees. As the court battle played out, many others in the industry stopped speaking to me altogether, simply because I'd dared to sue someone of Liz's caliber. Let me tell you something, my dear: If the situation had been reversed, Liz would've sued my nylons off, do you hear me? I would've been down on Sunset Boulevard, living in a cardboard box and begging for my supper, and no one would've cared. I knew I had a strong case, and I intended to see it through. Once the suit was filed, Liz and I didn't speak directly about it.

That changed years after the verdict. As I entered the Beverly Wilshire Hotel for an engagement, an attendant whispered to me, "James Earl Jones is having dinner in the back." In Hollywood circles, folks knew how much James and I adored one another, ever since those days when we'd both played in *The Blacks* and *Moon on a Rainbow Shawl.* Before meeting my dinner companion, I stopped by James's table to greet him. Not until I walked up did I realize that Liz Taylor was there with him. We exchanged one of those fake double-cheek kisses, and she laughed as she said to James, "You know something? Cicely sued me." She then turned to me and smirked, "And how much money did you get?" I raised my shoulders, thrust my nose heavenward, and announced loudly enough for the room to hear, "I was awarded more than a half-million dollars." She just shook her head and grinned. Liz might've been Hollywood's golden girl—but I claimed the golden egg.

My marriage with Miles was a study in opposites. When our energies were in sync, the partnership was powerfully fulfilling. We played our roles to perfection: he, the ailing soul yearning for a salve, and me, the willing healer, ever ready at his side with the vial of medicine. The good times were never in short supply. Particularly in the early years of our marriage, we laughed far more than we battled. Once Miles straightened his spine and again picked up his horn, we sashayed all over town and beyond, from one fancy dinner and concert to the next, the whole time savoring the limelight and amused by the question written on so many faces: *How on earth did these two get together?*

It did not matter to me what others thought about our union. It still doesn't. I married Miles not because of the world's opinion of either of us, but because of who we were for one another in private. For Miles, I was the Trusted One, the person he'd dared let enter the most troubled corridors of his heart. "I know she'll never leave me," he'd often say to his friends. "Not Cicely. Never." For me, Miles was my opportunity to feel deeply needed in this life, and in the satisfaction of his need, I experienced profound love. That love, however, came mixed with grief.

The better Miles got to feeling, the greater his tendency to backslide. I'll tell you, that man did not have nine lives, but ninety. By 1982, he'd grown strong enough to go on an international tour, his first after five long years away from the stage. By then, and even after I'd dragged him to see Dr. Shen, Miles had already had some slip-ups, dabbling in coke and throwing back shots when he was out with his friends. Though we never talked about his drug use, I knew about it—and he *knew* I knew. I could sense when he was using from the moment he entered the house. He walked differently. He smelled differently. He spoke differently, even when he'd had only one beer. Then when sober, he wore his guilt on his brow and couldn't even look me in the eye after knowing all I'd done to help his behind crawl back to sobriety. Miles could not hide from me, even at his slickest. So when it came time for him to take to the road, I recognized he was too vulnerable to go alone. I set aside a project and joined him for the first half of his tour. He used less when I stayed close. A few weeks into the tour, when my film could no longer be postponed, I flew out to Los Angeles—but not before calling for backup.

Miles had always been quite fond of his nephew, Vince Wilburn Jr., son of Dorothy Mae Davis, Miles's older, and only, sister. The family lived in Chicago, and even during Miles's stretch away from the spotlight, Vince and Miles had remained close. From Vince's earliest years, whenever Miles had come through Chicago for a concert, Dorothy would take her son along to witness the magic from backstage. Vince became so mesmerized with the drums that Uncle Miles, gratified by his nephew's passion and burgeoning talent, purchased his first drum kit for his birthday. He'd often mail him records of the greats he admired, musicians like Al Jackson, Charlie Watts, Buddy Miles, and James Brown. Vince had unknowingly played a part in Miles's return to the trumpet. During that period when Miles had sworn off his horn, young Vince persisted in talking music with his uncle, and when he visited, he'd badger Miles to play alongside him. Miles often refused. But eventually, as his emotional recovery caught up with his physical one, he reached for music again.

A few weeks before I had to leave Miles in Paris, I called Dorothy. Vince, then in his teens, had grown into quite an accomplished percussionist. "What would you think about Vince joining Miles on the road for a few weeks during his summer break?" I asked her. She wholeheartedly agreed—and I exhaled. I didn't expect Vince to watch over Miles the way I did; I would never hoist such a responsibility onto a child's shoulders. And yet I knew that leaving Miles in the presence of loved ones would perhaps dampen his desire for drugs. He'd have someone to tend to, someone who looked up to him like the musical giant that he was. The plan worked. For the rest of the tour, Vince became his uncle's shadow, as hypnotized by the sounds of brilliance as he'd been the first time he'd watched Miles play in the Heartland. Vince eventually joined Miles's band as a drummer and traveled all over the world with him. When either Vince or I was close by, Miles strayed far less. During that trip with his nephew, he never once slipped.

When Miles was on coke or heroin, he did not frighten me. Frankly, even when he abstained he could be crazy as a loon, and he didn't scare me then either. But the one time he did truly unnerve me, he happened to be sober as a judge. The rampage was fueled by his major jealous streak, if it can even be called a streak. That man was envious to the bone. His possessiveness was born of his feeling, deep down, that he was not enough. Not for me. Not for music. Not for himself. When you don't know your true value, you see the world through the lens of how you don't measure up. He was intent on marking his territory, and if he suspected anyone was infringing upon it, he exploded.

Around 1983, I'd traveled to Africa to do a movie with Liz Taylor, sometime before our legal dustup. I don't recall the country or film, but I'll never forget what transpired. While we were away, Liz had won an award in the States and couldn't be there to accept it. Marlon Brando, her costar in the 1967 film *Reflections in a Golden Eye*, had received the award on her behalf. He then flew to the Motherland to personally deliver the award to her. He arranged a dinner gathering for Liz and our film crew, in celebration of her honor. I knew to keep my distance. Marlon and I had met around the business many times, and he had a reputation and a half with women. I wanted no part of his womanizing. I can usually tell when trouble is afoot, and in this case, I was spot on.

In advance of the dinner, I let both Marlon and Liz know I would not be in attendance. On the evening of the event, I returned to my hotel after a tiring day on set and began preparing for sleep. As soon as I got under the covers, the phone rang. "Ms. Tyson, Marlon Brando is in the lobby for you," said the attendant. "He says he's here to pick you up for the dinner."

I paused. "Please tell him that I sent a message that I was not coming to dinner and I'm already in bed."

She placed me on hold and returned a moment later. "He says he'd like to come upstairs to your room."

I sat up in bed and mustered my most stern voice. "Please do not allow him up here, okay?" I said. "I did not invite him here. Please ask him to leave." I can only guess what Marlon had in mind when he tried to push his way up to my room. I turned over, tried to forget it, and drifted off to sleep.

The next day, Marlon came to our film set. He spotted me from behind, before I saw him, and he came up alongside me and put his arms around my waist. "I'm sorry I disturbed you last evening," he said. "I hadn't received your earlier message." Both of us knew that wasn't the case, but we laughed it off and moved on. I explained how exhausted I'd been, apologized for missing the festivities, and thought that was the end of it. How wrong I was.

A couple of months after I'd returned to New York, I opened my mail to find a photo of me with Marlon, his arms around me. Someone on the crew had apparently snapped a photograph of us on set that day. Just as I was studying the photo, Miles walked into our bedroom. "What's that?" he asked. It did not occur to me to hide the picture because I had nothing to hide. Before I could answer, he glanced over my shoulder and saw Marlon hugging me. Miles went absolutely berserk, flailing his arms, shouting obscenities, calling Marlon everything but a child of God. "Give me that!" he said, snatching the picture from my grip. He then ripped it into tiny shreds, the jagged pieces scattering across the hardwood floor.

Fear rippled through me. A half-second later, boy, I bolted from that bedroom, jumped down a whole flight of steps, charged out of his brownstone, ran to the apartment I still had around the corner, locked my door, and yanked down all the shades. A woman should always have a place of her own, some independence, and I'd held on to mine, in part, to keep a canyon between me and Miles's rants. He predictably followed me soon after, raising Cain the whole way there. I could hear him through my windows, pleading with me to let him in, cursing Marlon to hell. I just lay on my bed and cried until he left my stoop, which he eventually did after wearing himself out. If I had let him in, I don't know what might have happened. Yet I did know that Miles's rage, reminiscent of the fury I'd often witnessed in my father, had unleashed a fear in me I hadn't known was there. I didn't even get up and prepare myself for bed that evening. I just lay there fully clothed, my face in my pillow, my thoughts on my mother and that mystical wedding band.

20

Threadbare

RELATIONSHIPS are knitted together by need. When two people connect, the purpose each is serving in the other's life is what holds the union in place, keeps the ragged edges of its hemline sewn. My need to nurse Miles back to health fit perfectly with his need to be nurtured, and for the first few years of our reunion, that dynamic bound us tightly. But as Miles outgrew the desire for a caretaker, and as I became less tolerant of what ailed him, our marriage began unraveling. The loose thread, the one strand threatening to pull apart our entire union, appeared in the summer of 1984.

Long before then, there were signs of fraying. After the Marlon Brando incident came other jealous tirades. One evening when Miles and I attended the opening of one of my films, he spotted playwright Chuck Gordone, author of *No Place to Be Somebody* and the first African American to win a Pulitzer Prize for Drama, talking to me. Miles stormed over and inserted himself between us. "What are you doing in her face, man!?" he shouted, forcefully enough to shower Chuck's nose. "Miles, Miles," I said pulling him away. "It's all right. We're just talking." There I was, dressed to the nines in my sequin gown, and I wasn't about to let Miles ruin my celebration. He seemed convinced that all men were attempting to steal his wife, which reflected not their intentions, but his. Miles's roving eye was proof, in his mind, of everyone else's. Anybody who knows me can tell you that I did not sniff around while I was with Miles, was never even open to others' advances. But Miles wanted to own me. You always seek to control others when you are not in full ownership of yourself.

Other peculiar behavior abounded, particularly when Miles had been using. One afternoon, I spotted him through the front window of his townhouse, strutting toward the front door. Once we married, we lived between his place and mine on the other side of town, an apartment I purchased on the Upper East Side right along Central Park. Now Miles, even if he had his keys in his hand, always rang the doorbell at his place. For whatever reason, he wanted me to come down from upstairs and open the door for him. Yet on this day he entered on his own and left the door ajar. I glanced at his glazed eyes and said to myself, *Uh-oh, he's under.* That's when I took my little whiny behind, as my mom would've called it, and lay down on the couch. I knew not to fool with him when he was high.

I heard him fumbling around in the kitchen for something. He emerged holding three butcher knives. He then scooted a dining room chair near the open front door. While clutching the knives, he sat in that chair for the longest time, like he was waiting for Godot. I tell you, God has taken care of me in this life. I'd never seen anyone behave in such a manner, but I was not frightened, nor did I move. I just lay there taking in the scene, wondering who in the world he thought was coming through that door. Neither of us spoke. I studied Miles's face: the same eyes, same nose, same mouth, same velvety smooth skin and sculpted cheekbones. But those drugs, as they often did, had turned him into a stranger. He sat there so long that the sun went down, and I nodded off. Hours later, I awakened to the sound of his slamming the front door. I guess he decided whomever he was waiting on wasn't ever showing up. Strange.

Another knife incident ended differently. Miles was preparing to host a couple he knew from the business. Before their arrival, I stole away to the kitchen to prepare hors d'oeuvres. At some point he came in there and said something salty to me—I cannot recall what. Moments later, I picked up a serving tray holding our silverware, and as I carried it across the room, a knife toppled to the floor. Fire filled his eyes as he lunged toward me and punched me in my chest. "Oh, you have a temper, do you?" he shouted. I dropped the tray and folded my arms around my upper body. "What is the matter with you?" I squealed. He thought I'd thrown down the knife in anger, as a response to his comment, and he interpreted that as an act of defiance, a push-back on his authority. When I explained, through tears, that the knife had fallen by mistake, Miles pulled me into his arms and squeezed me. "I'm so sorry," he said. "Please forgive me, Cic." I'd of course heard that Miles had laid his hands on Frances and Betty, his first two wives, but up to then, he hadn't raised his fist to me. That incident marked the first and last time Miles ever struck me.

And then there were the women. Miles kept his extramarital exploits mostly out of my sight, yet they were never invisible to my third eye. I always knew when Miles was stepping out on our marriage, just as my mother had known of my dad's unfaithfulness. I didn't need to be in the room to sense that it was occurring. Occasionally, evidence of his infidelity presented itself under the noonday sun, like it had in our first years together when Betty had shown up at his door. Once when I confronted Miles about his womanizing, he had the gumption to say to me, "I wish you'd go out and see somebody." If I lifted my skirt around town, Miles reasoned, he'd feel less guilty about his sexual adventures. I did not respond, not with words anyway. As irrefutable proof of his affairs mounted, I pulled away physically. And on the occasions when we were intimate, I insisted on his using protection. We both knew why.

It is astonishing, even to me, that I did not walk away from Miles at that juncture. In one sense, I pitied him even more than I loved him. How can you be angry at a man so broken, so intent on destroying himself? In another sense, I scorned him, resented that he was doing to me exactly what my own father had done to my mom, that he was brazenly betraying our vows. I was reliving my mother's story, a plotline I realize now that I'd unwittingly set up. When Miles and I had reconnected after years apart, I knew exactly who this man was. He'd demonstrated that during our first time together, and it stood to reason that his behaviors would continue as they did, especially once he'd gotten off his crutches and back on his trumpet.

Love, however, is often not born of logic. It is birthed by need. Our dysfunctional histories drew Miles and me powerfully toward one another in ways inexplicable to us. Rage attracts rage. And though my fury, at times, manifested as brooding hostility in contrast to Miles's blazing inferno, our marriage, for both of us, was about coming to terms with the extraordinary ache of our early years, that impressionable time when life pressed its thumbprints into our flesh. Our union was God's spiritual assignment to us, an opportunity to treat severe wounds that had festered for decades. Neither of us knew how to complete that homework. And as far as I was concerned, my relationship with Miles was not a lesson to be heeded, but a mission to be accomplished. God had put me here to save this man's life, a task I intended to carry out.

That is how I saw it then. And that is why I remained at his side for as long as I did.

When Miles cheated, he resumed the cycle he'd set up during our first go-round. I knew when he'd either snorted drugs or hooked up with some woman, because, as before, he'd come bounding home with diamonds, racks of clothes, and enough flowers to host a funeral, as if those items would somehow erase the damage he'd done to me emotionally and spiritually. Nothing whips anybody's tail like guilt. In place of gifts, I longed for him to respect the promises we'd made. On some evenings when he came in late after being out in the clubs with women, he'd slip through the front door and tiptoe to our bathroom, wiping off the lipstick on his mouth and neck. He'd then shower, put on his bedclothes, and sidle up next to me in bed. I'd lie there saying to myself, *Does this man think I'm stupid? Doesn't he know I'm aware of his behavior?* As he pulled me toward him, I'd pretend to be asleep while fuming inwardly.

The thread that began unspooling our union came just after a lovely spring had given way to summer's first heat. I'd traveled out West to work on a project, and Miles, who was preparing to go on tour, had stayed at the Upper East Side apartment in New York. Though Miles still had his Upper West Side brownstone and I of course had my first apartment around the corner on Seventy-Fourth, we mostly lived between my place on Fifth Avenue and the Malibu Beach house. Just as I was settling in at the beach house, my maid, an elderly Jamaican woman by the name of Jean, called me.

"You know, Ms. Tyson," Jean said, "this is really none of my business . . ." My throat tightened.

"What's none of your business?" I asked.

"Uh, well," she stammered, "I mean . . . I just don't think what Miles is doing is proper."

"Proper? What are you talking about?"

"Well," she went on, "there's a lady who lives in your building. She's married and she has a son. But the minute you leave here to go out of town, she is in this apartment with Miles."

I clutched the phone and pressed it into my ear. "What lady are you talking about?" I asked calmly, though Hades raged within me.

She described someone I'd seen, a white woman with a thick mane of curls sprawled all over her head. I hadn't ever spoken to her, but her husband often smiled and nodded when he saw me.

"Do you mean the woman with the bushy hair?" I pressed.

"Yes," she said. "She comes up here to your place, and sometimes he goes down to hers."

There was more. Every morning at around ten o'clock, revealed Jean, Miles and this woman would meet up right in front of the building and head off for a brief stroll along Madison Avenue. They'd then circle back around to the building, which overlooked Central Park. My maid, the elevator operator, the doorman: all three had been whispering about the liaison, stunned that Miles would risk being seen with another woman in and around my apartment. I thanked my housekeeper, hung up the phone, and booked a flight back to New York.

I planned to arrive at the building at 10 a.m., just as Miles would be exiting to meet this woman for their walk. He froze when he saw me.

"What are you doing back already?" he asked, drawing me toward him for a hug.

I grinned. "The project was postponed," I said breezily. He turned to go back into the building, but I said, "Come on, let's go for a walk. I feel like stretching my legs after the flight."

I gave the doorman my bags, and Miles and I set out on the

route he and the woman had apparently often taken, over to Madison Avenue and then back around onto Central Park East. When we returned fifteen minutes later, there she stood, out in front of the building, I'm sure looking for Miles and wondering why he hadn't met her. You should have seen her face when she spotted the two of us walk up. She and Miles glanced at one another, clearly not wanting me to recognize the exclamation points in their eyes as they exchanged looks. I acted as if I did not notice, just as I'd feigned ignorance all those times when Miles slid into bed after wiping off fresh lipstick. My performance should've earned me an Oscar. Miles looked at her, she looked away, and Miles and I strode right past her and into the building. Once upstairs in our apartment, I didn't say a word to Miles about what the maid had revealed. I hoped, perhaps foolishly in retrospect, that my unexpected return home would be enough to put their tryst on ice. It wasn't.

Miles kept right on messing with this woman when I traveled, and the maid kept right on divulging the details. I was as crushed as I was flabbergasted. The two had the nerve to be hooking up in my bed, on my sheets, in an apartment that my decades of toil in this business had bought and paid for. And they didn't even have the decency or discretion to keep it hidden from my maid and the building's employees. My housekeeper had heard their grunts and screams from behind the bedroom door.

After seething privately for a time, I broached the subject with Miles in a doozy of an argument that shook Fifth Avenue. He predictably denied the affair, claiming that he and this woman were merely professional acquaintances. The maid had misunderstood, he told me. According to Miles, this woman, an artist and sculptor, had been teaching him to paint. Months earlier, Miles had been doodling all over the place. When I'd noticed him sketching directly onto our furniture, I'd gone down to Lee's Art Shop on Fifty-Seventh Street, near Carnegie Hall, and bought him paper and tools. Apparently, he'd turned to this woman for some tutoring. And yet based on the claw marks I noticed on Miles's back and stomach, she was teaching him a lot more than how to wield a paintbrush. During the fracas, I threatened to divorce Miles, and he pleaded for me to stay. Then in typical fashion, over the next few days he presented me with a diamond brooch and another mink coat.

Not long after my brawl with Miles, I spotted the bushy-haired woman as I was entering the building. She was sitting on a couch in the lobby, dressed as if she were about to go out for a jog. She looked me in the eye, pursed her lips, and smiled.

"What are you smiling at me for?" I snapped.

She sat back on the bench and exhaled. "Oh, I'm just being nice," she said. "People smile."

Let me tell you something about myself. If this white woman hadn't dared to grin in my direction, I likely would've stepped right on past her and gone up quietly in the elevator. I'd done exactly that several times before then. But the fact that she had the audacity not only to look me in my Black face and smile, but also to answer flippantly, disturbed me beyond measure. *Please don't do that,* I said to myself. *Please stop acting like I don't know you're sleeping with my husband.*

I stepped toward her, and though she didn't push me, she raised her leg as if she were going to. Well honey, she should not have done that, because the next thing I knew, that woman was on the ground. I'm not entirely sure how she got there. Trauma has a way of clouding one's memory. But on the other side of my momentary blackout, I do recall that both the doorman and the building manager whisked me into the elevator. "Ms. Tyson,

Ms. Tyson . . . come with us," the doorman urged. With that woman still sprawled out on the ground, they escorted me up to my apartment where Miles awaited.

Before I'd had a chance to light into Miles, the doorbell rang. Miles stayed in the bedroom as I flung open the door. There stood the woman's husband, his face the color of cotton. He was dressed in a suit, as if he'd been on his way to work.

"Hello, Ms. Tyson," he said. "I'm so sorry to disturb you. My wife said the two of you had a little problem."

I glared at him through eyes wide as dinner plates. "A problem?" I said. "No sir, I don't have a problem. Your wife is the one with the problem. You tell her that I said she is to stay out of my apartment."

He loosened his tie, dropped his eyes to the floor, and then looked back at me. "She tells me they're working on an art project together," he went on. "I think there's been a misunderstanding . . ."

My laugh cut him short. "Yes, they're working on something all right," I smirked, "and I'm glad that you know that they are." That was my way of revealing to him that, despite whatever his wife had told him, she and Miles had fallen into bed. I straightened my spine and stared at him without flinching. "Now I'm going to say this one more time," I said slowly, emphasizing every syllable. "Please tell your wife to stay out of my apartment." Before he could respond, I closed the door.

Over the next hour, brimstone spewed between Miles and me. Skillets were thrown. Insults were hurled. Empty apologies fell to the ground. The pathos and passion, the cataclysmic energy that fueled both our artistic endeavors, set our living room ablaze. Gone was my instinct to simmer in silence, as I'd done during my first years with Miles. In place of that impulse arose a fury, towering and untamable, unleashed with the velocity with which my mom had often cursed the husband who'd so deeply wounded her.

Our conflict curtailed the affair for a time but did not end it. The disgrace, however, did relocate across town to Miles's brownstone, or else to the woman's apartment when her husband was at work. Our Thrilla in Manila in the building lobby had scared both her and Miles away from my four walls. My maid, who cleaned all of our residences, dutifully continued her field reports, once telling me of the day when this woman had left a stoned Miles just outside of the front door of my apartment, several floors above hers. She apparently didn't want to put him on the elevator in such a state, so she'd led him up the stairwell. She then rang the bell and left him for my maid, who dragged him to the shower and rained water over his head to hasten his return to sobriety.

Human behavior is a mystery, one riddled with contradiction. I don't excuse Miles's conduct any more than I dismiss my willingness, consciously or unknowingly, to indulge it. We mortals breathe incongruity. That I chose to stay with Miles is still, in many ways, confounding to me. And yet I've come to realize that Miles's behavior felt sorely familiar, a song, blaring and dissonant, that I'd learned in my early years. Some part of my spirit recognized that discord, had memorized the haunting notes of its refrain. My father had taught me the music. And my mother, in her own way, had emphasized each measure, hummed along with the clamor even as she railed against it. "Men will be men," she'd sometimes mutter following a feud with my father, her way of rationalizing his adultery. In a hovel at 219 East 102nd Street, I'd absorbed every nuance of that song, its words hovering beneath the floorboards and floating along the ceilings: Willie would be Willie, at turns tender and abrasive, and at tremendous cost to those he loved. And in my

Upper East Side high-rise, a world away from the slum of my girlhood and yet overlapping with it, Miles would be Miles. The question became just how long I'd let the tune repeat.

~

As my marriage stretched apart at the seams, Black Democrats rallied around the Reverend Jesse Jackson, the first African American to run a nationwide primary campaign in pursuit of the presidency. Jesse set his political table on the legacies of Channing E. Phillips, the civil rights leader who, in 1968, made history as the first Black nominated for the presidency by a major political party; Charlene Mitchell, the first African-American woman to run for the nation's highest office, which she did in 1968 as a third-party candidate; and of course the formidable Shirley Chisholm, whose place in the 1972 presidential campaign widened the public's imagination of how power can look and sound. Jesse had been with Dr. King when a bullet, ricocheting across a motel balcony, had killed the Dreamer and threatened to snuff out the Dream. Then a young soldier of the Movement, Jesse eventually emerged as the keeper of Dr. King's flame, as well as the founder of the social justice organizations Operation PUSH and the National Rainbow Coalition. Like no other candidate of color before him, Jesse's campaign galvanized the Black community as we glimpsed, for the first time, a viable candidate for the Oval Office.

Reverend Jackson ran twice, in 1984 and 1988, and his first campaign coincided with my heyday as an actress. This was my era. *Sounder* and *Jane Pittman* had introduced me to the masses, while *King*, *Roots*, and *A Woman Called Moses* had deepened the connection. The scores of roles that followed—

those I played, as well as those I wouldn't touch because they chipped away at our dignity—reinforced my stance as a race warrior. Throughout the late seventies and eighties, my phone rang off the hook with requests for me to speak here or appear there. On the eve of the 1984 Democratic convention in San Francisco, Reverend Jackson came a-calling.

"Ms. Tyson," he said with a smile in his voice, "would you be kind enough to speak at this year's convention?"

I laughed as a shot of nervousness surged through me. "Absolutely," I heard myself telling Jesse. "It would be my honor." I was asked to reenact Sojourner Truth's electrifying "Ain't I a Woman?" speech, which she delivered, with nary a flinch or stutter, at the Ohio Women's Rights Convention in 1851. When Sojourner marched to that podium, few might have guessed that she, an escaped slave who could neither read nor write, would ignite a cultural revolution. For that matter, only the Father could have known that I, once a quiet and lanky girl with my thumb parked on my tongue, would channel Sojourner's fierceness on a stage before millions. God is the Master of the unlikely.

By the time Jesse requested that I speak, we already knew each other. Sometime in the late 1970s, I'd connected with his wife, Jacqueline, and the two of us became close. I'd dined with her and Jesse on several occasions. So when Jackie heard that one of my films would bring me through Chicago to shoot, she graciously invited me to stay in her family's home during my weeks of filming. The year was 1983. Jesse hadn't yet announced his presidential bid, but he was gearing up. The public Jesse, the one I'd marveled at from afar, commanded a room with his soaring rhetoric. The private Jesse, the one I came to know, was, by contrast, markedly reserved. On many evenings, Jesse, Jacqueline, and their children gathered around the dinner table. I often joined them. While the group of us laughed and recounted the happenings of the day, Jesse listened intently but said little. When he did speak, there wasn't a hint of flamboyance in his voice and manner. Perhaps he was saving his charisma for the spotlight he'd soon inhabit. On November 3, weeks after I'd departed Chicago, Reverend Jesse Jackson, then forty-two years old, declared his quest to unseat President Ronald Reagan.

The following year as I arrived at the convention, my hands got to trembling. They trembled even more when, backstage, Jesse's team ushered me around like I was a queen. I rarely get nervous before taking a stage, but this was no ordinary event. I'd never even attended a political convention, much less spoken at one, and judging by the way my poor heart palpitated, it frightened me. I whispered a prayer before walking out to the roar of spectators, hundreds of them, waving banners for Reverend Jackson and Walter Mondale and Gary Hart. Upon taking the podium, dressed head to toe in white as my nod to the suffragists, I paused, overcome by the notion that I was standing there. My palms felt as cold as clay.

I'll tell you, boy, Sojourner's spirit carried me through that speech. I drew in a breath, squared my shoulders the way she must've, and imagined the bravery she'd had to summon. Calling on her courage, I began. "Well children," I said into the microphone, "where there is so much racket there must be something out of kilter. I think that betwixt the Negroes of the South and the women at the North all talking 'bout rights, these white men gonna be in a fix pretty soon." The stadium erupted into whoops and shouts, which gave me a moment to further compose myself. "But what's all this here talking about?" I went on. "That man over there says that women need to be helped into carriages, and lifted over ditches, and to have the best place everywhere. Nobody ever helps me into carriages, or over mud puddles, or gives me any best place. And ain't I a woman?"

Thunderous applause ascended to the rafters, while I, exhaling with every refrain, gave myself over to the experience. Nerves have a way of disappearing when you think less about your performance and more about your purpose in speaking. By the end, I'd moved from reticent to rapturous, lifting my arms each time I repeated "And ain't I a woman?!" What a fire Sojourner had lit! And what a privilege it was for me, the daughter of her legacy, to stoke the blaze. Jesse, of course, did not become the nominee that year. Former vice president Walter Mondale claimed the challenge of taking on Reagan, who ultimately triumphed in securing his second term. But Reverend Jackson, in both his 1984 bid and the one to follow, had made his statement. He'd also made space, just as Sojourner once had. Reverend Jackson's candidacy cleared the path that Barack Obama, then just twenty-three and fresh out of Columbia University, would one day navigate.

Jesse's campaign came bearing additional treasures, one for me personally. Backstage at the convention, I met a young lady by the name of Minyon Moore, who was then on Reverend Jackson's team. She'd been the one to arrange my appearance, and in so doing, the two of us struck up a friendship that extends to this day. Following her work on Jesse's campaign, the brilliant Minyon went on to become a political powerhouse, overseeing the Democratic Party as chief executive officer of the Democratic National Committee; advising the campaigns of Michael Dukakis, both Clintons, and a long list of other Democratic luminaries; and serving as a principal political adviser to President Bill Clinton and then–First Lady Hillary Clinton. She's part of that tribe of mighty sisters known as the "Colored Girls," five unstoppable truth-tellers who answered the call to political service (Donna Brazile, Yolanda Caraway, Tina Flournoy, Leah Daughtry, and my dear Minyon: I see and celebrate each of you).

During the years when Minyon worked in the Clinton administration, she'd invite me to various White House events, including the elaborate 1994 state dinner for Nelson Mandela, then president of South Africa, and the man who pushed apartheid down onto its knees. Not long after Mandela's release from prison in 1990, I'd met him and the vibrant Winnie in South Africa. I'd even stood in the eight-by-seven-foot concrete cell at Robben Island where Nelson spent eighteen of his twenty-seven years in captivity. That was an experience and a half. On the day of my visit, an iron bed sat in a corner of the cell. "That was never there while Mr. Mandela was imprisoned," the guard told me. Nelson slept on the hard floor for all his years in prison. There, during long nights down on that unforgiving pavement, Nelson secretly handwrote the first drafts of what would become his internationally acclaimed 1994 autobiography, *Long Walk to Freedom*. What a testament to the resilience of the human spirit.

Before the state dinner, Minyon welcomed me to stay with her, and child, why did she do that? Because now, decades later, she cannot get me out of there! Her home has become my haven away from New York. Anytime I'm in the area or just in the mood, I show up at her doorstep, pull off my wig stocking cap, and settle into the upstairs bedroom she keeps ready for me. What a beautiful human being, that Minyon, so full of warmth and exuberance. I cherish that woman. And I don't have to lift a fingernail when I'm at her place. Sometimes I sleep. Other times my daughter comes with me, and the three of us just sit around, cackling over *Love & Hip Hop: Atlanta*, with me trying to keep up with all the young folks' lingo. Occasionally one of my old films will pop up on Turner Classic Movies (TCM). That's my cue to leave the room. "No, you're going to sit right here and see this!" Minyon always teases. It was on Minyon's couch that I, for the first time, sat through *The Autobiography of Miss Jane Pittman* from start to finish. I've never gotten used to seeing myself on-screen. I hope I never do.

A few years after I first met Minyon, another blessing flowed my way. In the fall of 1987, Pope John Paul II visited the United States, with a stop at the Registry Hotel in Los Angeles. I, along with dozens of other artists and leaders, was invited. My seat was on the aisle, along the right side of the large hall. When the pontiff entered, silence blanketed the room as all eyes turned toward him. Then just as I was shifting my focus to the front of the hall to see what was happening there, I felt a hand on my head. It was his. I froze, not sure what he would do next. He didn't utter a sound as others around us looked on, probably wondering what was happening. He just stood there with his warm palm cradled over my skull.

Finally, after a long moment, he lifted his hand, met my eyes, and then made his way to the front of the hall. On his slow walk to the podium, he did not touch another soul. He delivered his remarks, none of which I can recall. All I could think of was that day, decades ago in Nevis, when a white dove had landed on my young mother's head. She'd been marked. She'd been consecrated. She'd been anointed and appointed to make the journey to America. I do not understand why the Pope singled me out, but God did. He knew that, like my mother before me, I'd need God's favor for the thorny terrain ahead.

21

Lesson Before Dying

MILES carried on constantly about white folks. "These mothafuckas don't even see me," he'd often say. "And when they do, all they see is a nigga." Racism, as it does, sat down on Miles's spine during his boyhood, and over decades, its sheer enormity and weight cracked his back. He'd absorbed the injury, endured the indignities that come with being a brother—the more Black, the more invisible. But once your spine has been broken, you can never quite straighten it again. You navigate the world with a hunch and a limp. Miles's spirit, hobbled and fractured in a million places, bore such injuries.

Miles didn't even want to live among whites, or so he claimed. When I first bought my apartment along Fifth Avenue on the East Side, a stretch known more for its pretension than for its diversity, I didn't even tell him about it until two years after I had purchased it, mostly because I did not want to hear his rants, and also because I craved a respite away from his escapades. "Why would you want to move over there with all those white folks?" he predictably said when I finally mentioned the apartment. The Upper West Side where we'd lived, while not exactly Atlanta, was more integrated. Then one day a few months later when we were speeding up Fifth Avenue, he looked over at me and grinned. "Don't you have an apartment over here someplace?" he asked. I nodded, which marked the end of my safe haven. Soon after, Miles brought his antsy rump over there. Lord, that man could never sit still; he barreled restlessly toward the next experience, the next high, both in music and in life. The impulses that made him a genius innovator perhaps also fueled his promiscuity. Miles hadn't been in my East Side apartment but five minutes before he'd hooked up with the bushy-haired married woman I eventually taught a lesson.

For someone who supposedly couldn't stand whites, Miles sure kept a rotating cast of them in his bed. The woman in my building was one. There were many others—women he carried on with when he was on tour in Europe. Word of his liaison with a young French woman of course got back to me, because with Miles, a secret never stayed that way for long. His body language, his guilty behavior always told on him, and when his gestures weren't speaking, my sixth sense was. During those years, I had traveled to Africa on a tour with the United Nations, and when I returned, Miles surprised me with a Rolls-Royce—a sure sign that he was still skirt-chasing. Sure enough, a few weeks later, the woman he'd been seeing in Paris started calling day and night, demanding that he return there to visit her. He didn't go, nor did he succeed in hiding from me the whispered phone calls. I heard it all, even as I delivered my finest performance in pretending I was plumb deaf.

Miles and I had spoken our promises in 1981, and by 1985, I knew the marriage was over. One day I spotted a cluster of small red bumps just above his right lip. "What is that?" I asked him. "I don't know," he said, shrugging. "It's just a rash." He eventually admitted it was herpes, which I knew nothing about. I looked it up and then called my physician. "Be careful," the doctor warned me, explaining that the sexually transmitted disease had no cure. "You must always use protection." I'd already been doing so for years by then, but at that juncture, I altogether ended our physical intimacy—a lagging indication of our emotional distance. Still, Miles would often reach for me in the middle of the night, with scratch marks all over his stomach and groin after having carried on with his various women. I did not reach back. Jesus clearly lives in my back bedroom. It is only because he hovered so close by that Miles never passed herpes or any other disease on to me.

The final unraveling of our vows came not long after the Pope had cupped his hand over my head. Miles's insistence on sleeping with a woman right under my nose became too much for me. There'd always been women, of course, as far back as when Miles had been fooling with Betty the first time we were together. The difference, at this point, was that she lived in my building. I spotted her often, prancing her tail in and out of the front door like she owned Fifth Avenue. I'd somehow been able to tolerate the stench of Miles's philandering from afar, but up close, its intense odor choked me. And the fact that she was a white woman, one twenty-five years younger than Miles, made the smell of the adultery all the more pungent. I knew I had to escape, and one afternoon in late 1987, an exit door appeared.

Miles was in our bedroom getting dressed to go out and meet with some business colleagues, he'd told me. He stared in the mirror at himself, primping over that hair of his, or at least someone's. His own hairline had been receding for years, and Miles, then in his early sixties, had taken to getting weaves. He'd spend hours having his hairdresser, Finney, install them, and he insisted that every strand be in place. That hair meant the world to him. Just as he left the bedroom and rounded his way into the living room, a piece of paper fell from his pocket. He didn't notice it. When he went back into the bedroom, I reached down and picked it up. It was a note from the woman in my building. In it, she asked Miles to meet her at such-and-such address at such-and-such time that evening. I folded the paper in half, slid it under the lamp, and sat down on the sofa to gather myself. Moments later, Miles rounded the corner back into the living room.

"Cic, did you happen to see a paper I dropped?" he asked. I stared at him without blinking. "I have that business meeting tonight," he went on, "and the folks I'm supposed to meet wrote down their address for me. I can't find it." I remained mute. "Cic, if you've seen it," Miles continued, his voice rising by the syllable, "I really need it."

I finally shook my head from left to right. "No," I said, "I haven't seen any note."

"Are you sure?" he pressed. "I mean, I think it fell on the floor over here, and I need to have it." I stood up from the couch.

"Miles Davis, don't bother me tonight," I snapped. "I don't have any note. And if I did have it, I would be foolish to give it to you."

That's what started the tussle. "Give me the damn note," he shouted, lunging toward me. I backed up.

"I'm not giving you anything," I sneered. "Why don't you go out and meet your woman? You know where to meet her. Y'all been meeting up all of this time, haven't you? Why do you suddenly need an address? If you want to go out and have the woman, then go out and have the woman. That's your choice. But please do not treat me like I'm too dumb to know what's happening!"

I charged into the bedroom, put on my shoes and coat, and reached for my pocketbook, intending to step outside and wedge some air between us. When I opened the front door, Miles grabbed my wrist. "Where do you think you're going?!"

he yelled. I wrenched my wrist free and put my hand back on the knob.

"That's none of your business," I spat. "You've got your date, I've got mine."

He reached for me again, and this time, I snatched him by the back of his hair weave. "Don't touch me!" I shouted. Well honey, he got to twisting and turning, and the more he tugged his head back and forth, trying to pry himself loose, the tighter I held on. By the time he struggled free, I was holding a whole bushel of his weave in my right hand. I hurled it onto the ground, marched out the door, and slammed it shut.

I'm not sure whether Miles met up with the woman that evening, but I suspect that he didn't. Vanity likely kept him indoors, because let me tell you, that man was preoccupied with his appearance in every regard. No way would he allow himself to be spotted around town with a big bald spot in the back of his head. By the time I returned home after a long, tearful walk up Fifth Avenue, those five tracks of weave were still strewn on the floor. Miles was sitting in the kitchen, waiting to kick up more dust. He stood from his chair when I entered. "You pulled out my hair!" he shouted. I gazed at him as a mischievous grin spread over my face. "Oh, I did?" is all I said, although what I wanted to shout was, "Well you can go out and buy yourself some more!" Neither of us said anything else about the incident or the state of our relationship. I felt no need to drape words on the hanger of inevitability. The marriage had long since been over. That was obvious. All that had to be sorted was when we'd make it official.

A few days following Weave-gate, Miles told some journalist that I'd pulled out his hair, while he of course left out the details of what stirred the skirmish. He sought sympathy. He wanted the world to know that this woman, this Cicely Tyson that some perhaps deemed an innocent lady, had attacked him. What nonsense. Because if Miles hadn't tried to block me in that doorway, I never would've touched a strand of his precious locks. By grabbing my wrist, and then by writhing himself all around, he'd pulled out his own hair, just like he'd unspooled the final fibers of our vows. And also, he should've kept his mouth shut. Why would you go around telling folks you've got a plug in your head, prompting them to try and spot it? At one point, I heard Miles saying to someone on the phone, "Do you know how much I paid for that weave? And she just *snatched* it right off of my head!" I didn't know whether to laugh or to cringe, which is why I did both.

At the start of 1988, a month or so after our literal tug of war, I still hadn't fully left Miles. That changed on one morning when, as I was entering the kitchen at Miles's brownstone to blend up my greens, he said something snarky to me. I don't remember what devilishness tumbled off his tongue, and frankly, I don't care to recall. Without a word, I made my way upstairs, picked up my pocketbook, went out to Miles's guilt gift of a Rolls-Royce, and drove to a friend's place. I never returned to Miles's home. That same year, I filed for divorce. Miles, who'd foolishly convinced himself that nothing he could do would wrench me from his side, reeled upon receiving the papers, or so I heard from his friend Finney. Miles eventually rang me.

"Cic, I need to see you," he said with more rasp in his voice than usual. "Can you meet me?" I reluctantly agreed, though I refused to have him at my place. We met instead in a dimly lit café, in a private booth at the rear. Miles leaned in over the table and spoke softly. "Cic, I don't want a divorce," he whispered. My gaze dropped to the table and then traveled back up to his hollow expression. "I want us to stay together—but just no sex," he said. I sat all the way back in the booth, the brute force of his words striking me in my chest. In the months since I'd last seen Miles, I'd heard the talk of his health status. Word at the salon was that he'd contracted HIV. In fact, though the US press hadn't broadcast that news widely, it was all over Europe that he'd sought treatment there. He'd apparently begun a course of AZT, the antiretroviral drug then used to treat HIV and AIDS.

Rumors also swirled that Miles and his longtime male hairdresser, Finney, were lovers. Frankly, I'd heard that gossip for years and had tuned it out for just as many, in hindsight because believing it would've crushed me beyond repair. Denial became my iron shield, the breastplate I kept securely over my heart. As Miles sat there across from me, with sunken eyes and a skeletal frame, I didn't quite know what to believe. Two things, however, were certain. First, if Miles was asking for us to be together minus all physical intimacy—and as I see it, a union without lovemaking does not a marriage make—he must've believed he was infected with something lethal. And second, he clearly respected me enough to protect me from whatever that was. I stared at him as I squelched tears, though one escaped down my cheek. Before the floodgates could swing open, I stood, retrieved my pocketbook, and walked swiftly from the restaurant without a word. That was the last time I ever saw Miles Davis.

Barbara Warren, a friend so close to me that folks thought we were sisters, happened to know the transcriber who was working on Miles's autobiography. For months before our final meeting, Miles had been relaying his life story on tape, speaking in glowing terms about how I'd resurrected him to life, how I'd nursed him back onto his horn and kept him from annihilating himself. According to Miles, said the transcriber to Barbara, I was the greatest woman who'd ever walked across the planet, a towering beacon of compassion and warmth. Well honey, the day after I met with Miles in that café, I became Cruella de Vil.

He apparently tore up his initial transcripts and dramatically altered his characterization of me. It pained him that I would not reverse the divorce process, that I'd refused the pitiful pact he'd extended. He absolutely did not think I'd ever leave him. The truth is, years before I ended our vows, he'd long since given up on both our union and himself. The divorce papers simply formalized his betrayal.

When Miles's book was published in 1989, I never read it, though I heard that, unsurprisingly, he had some not-so-pleasant words to say about me. Miles was clearly concerned about how I'd react to what we both knew were lies, because the second that volume hit bookstores, he started calling my friend Barbara, who also knew him well. For weeks, he rang her morning, noon, and night, leaving messages asking whether I'd read the book. He even called me. I did not answer, nor did Barbara. I had said everything I needed to say since that day, in 1965, when I'd first spotted him on a bench in Riverside Park. Twenty-three years is plenty long enough to clear one's throat and speak. Soon after the memoir's publication, Miles's daughter, Cheryl, came backstage to see me following one of my performances. "Have you read Father's book?" she asked. "Why would I do that?" I said. I didn't need to read a book to know what was true. I lived it. And no written account could fully capture what I know happened between the two of us.

And I know this: I loved Miles and he loved me. At age ninety-six I still have many questions about this life, but of that fact I am certain. In the same imperfect way that my father and mother cared for one another, in the same lopsided manner in which hostility and devotion can live side by side, Miles and I found deep connection, however flawed our union was. The final declaration of Miles's care for me came in the shadows of a café neither of us had ever frequented, in a conversation he'd never dreamed we'd have. "I want us to stay together—but just no sex," his gravelly voice had whispered. And though his words had pierced me on that evening, they also strangely became my salve in the following years. When all was said and done in our marriage, Miles thought enough of me to shield me from the malevolent forces that had taken him under. I think now that it wasn't Miles who'd protected me. Rather, it was the Savior, by way of a pontiff's warm palm, who kept me safe in his care.

In 1991, Quincy Jones, a dear longtime friend to both Miles and me, told me that Miles was near the end. "I didn't know he was so sick," Quincy repeated over the phone, his voice quivering. "I just didn't know." Miles's vital organs were wrecked, just as they'd been in the months before I took him to Dr. Shen. His children and his nephew Vince, along with other close family members, were eventually called to his bedside in Santa Monica. Though I was in California at the time, I had no desire to see Miles in that state, emaciated and struggling for oxygen. That would have tortured me. Barbara went to visit. Just as she was leaving, he motioned for her to draw near him. She leaned down close so she could hear him over the hum of the breathing machines. "Tell Cicely I'm sorry," he whispered through labored breaths. "Tell her I'm very, very sorry." Days later, in the fall of 1991, Miles slipped from this life and into the next.

On the day the world lost Miles, I was at the beauty parlor in New York. While seated in the lobby, waiting for my appointment, a bulletin came over the radio. "We interrupt this broadcast with the news that jazz legend Miles Davis has passed away at St. John's Hospital near his home in Santa Monica. He was sixty-five." In silence, I got up and walked out of the salon, which was near my Upper East Side apartment. Just as I was crossing Madison Avenue, I somehow found myself flat out in the middle of the street. I had not tripped or missed a step. And yet there I was, down on the gravel with my heart galloping away. I quickly gathered myself and stumbled to my feet, shaken by what might have been if a car had sped through there. *Oh no, Miles Davis, I'm not going with you*, I thought as I stood. *I wanted you in life, not in death. You chose to leave this place, but I'm not going anywhere.* I believed then, as I do now, that Miles aimed to take me with him. And yet three decades later, I am, by God's mercy, still right here.

While mourning the Last Act between Miles and me, I poured myself into work. In 1988, the year I filed for divorce, I had met Oprah Winfrey. The premiere of Oprah's national talk show, two years earlier in 1986, had irrevocably altered television's landscape. The shift came literally overnight. The microphone-wielding Phil Donahue had created the template for talk television, moving hot topics from the couch to the studio stage. Who can forget how Phil raced around his set, eliciting input from his audience, while intermittently shouting, "Caller, are you there?" to those who phoned in. His show, syndicated nationally in 1970, had established a seemingly immovable foothold in the ratings. Well darling, God had another foot in mind, a brown one. Enter Oprah Winfrey, Mississippi born and Spirit led, who took Phil's blueprint and made it sing soprano. From her very first episode, Oprah bested Donahue in the ratings, welcoming her viewers to a shoes-off, Kleenex-required, purpose-filled conversation that ultimately revolutionized the culture. She grabbed the number one spot in the ratings and held on to it for twenty-five seasons.

The year Oprah and I first connected, her production company, Harpo, had begun filming *The Women of Brewster Place*, an ABC miniseries based on the National Book Award–winning novel by Gloria Naylor. The story showcases the nuanced experiences of seven Black women in a dilapidated tenement. Oprah, who played Mattie Michael, the main character, had gathered an ensemble cast of other gifted actors, including Lynn Whitfield, Jackée, Robin Givens, Mary Alice, and Olivia Cole. She asked me to portray Mrs. Browne, the dignified, well-to-do mother of Melanie, Robin Givens's character. Having read the book, which few could do without weeping, I wholeheartedly said yes.

It makes me smile now, given the global force for good that Oprah has become, but her body language told me she was a little nervous the first time she saw me on set. By then, she'd delivered a pair of hankie-lifting performances in *The Color Purple* and *Native Son*, yet alongside an old-timer like me, she was then a relative neophyte of the stage. When I noticed her slight fidgeting, I chuckled to myself, thinking, *I'm the one who oughta be intimidated!* Like her daily talk show, the award-winning *Brewster* resonated with viewers, and it eventually even led to a weekly series. Though I played in the original series, I of course did not view it at the time. Two decades later, I happened to catch it one evening on BET, and mesmerized by the plotline, I cried from start to finish. I called Oprah afterward. "Boy, that *Women of Brewster Place* was *something*!" I exclaimed. "What a fabulous piece of work!" The phone line went silent for a moment.

"You mean you've never seen it?" she asked in disbelief.

"No," I told her, "but I finally caught the rerun."

"Oh, Cicely!" she said, cracking up. What can I tell you? Twenty years late is still better than never.

My work with Oprah on *Brewster* was just the start of what

has become a cherished sisterhood. For her fiftieth birthday in 2004, I knitted Oprah a special gift, a tapestry rug, with no idea how my creation would spawn one more priceless. Upon receiving my present, Oprah thanked me, while inwardly chiding herself that she'd forgotten to invite me to her birthday luncheon that year. That gave her the idea to ask me over for our own tête-à-tête, a thought that soon prompted another: *Why not invite Ruby Dee as well?* Next thing Oprah knew, her inkling had flourished into the Legends Weekend, a grand three-day celebration of twenty-five African-American women whose legacies have served as a bridge from past to present. She also invited forty-five "young'uns," those with the privilege of navigating that overpass. In May 2005, we all gathered at the breathtaking Montecito estate Oprah aptly calls the Promised Land.

My heart just about burst open with joy that weekend as I reveled in the company of longtime friends—including Diahann Carroll, Ruby Dee, Coretta Scott King, Maya Angelou, and renowned *Essence* editor in chief Susan L. Taylor—while soaking in the tributes of the young'uns who, in unison, read to us the Pearl Cleage poem "We Speak Your Names." That Sunday morning on Oprah's lawn, at a gospel brunch like none I've ever attended, BeBe Winans handed the mic to Shirley Caesar, first lady of gospel, and the Holy Ghost showed up and cut a step. Throughout the weekend, Gayle King and Stedman Graham, Oprah's two mightiest oaks, teased me. "This is all your fault!" they kept saying, laughing as they recounted how my gift had given birth to the grandmama of soirees. For Oprah's sixtieth a decade later, I moved on from knit work and sent an enormous bouquet of roses, with stems nearly as tall as she is. That blew her away, so much so that she posted a photo on Twitter. "I've never *seen* roses that tall!" she told me.

Not too long ago, I ran into her and Stedman, Oprah's rock

of nearly four decades, her gentle giant. I tell you, boy, that man must be seven feet tall. "What do you *dooooo*!?" Stedman said when he saw me, sweeping me up in his wide arms, baffled that I never seemed to age. It's all about the greens, my dear—thrice daily, blended if you prefer, taken with a side of temerity. That, along with bar pull-ups in my apartment and walks all over Manhattan, keeps my body strong. My bar is right in the doorway of my master bedroom. Soon as I get up in the morning, I do three sets of twenty pull-ups.

As for preserving my mind, continuing to take roles, well into my nineties, has been my sustaining force. Folks "retire" so they can sit on the couch and watch television while they wait to die. I've known several people—six months after they stopped working, so did their hearts. Some form of occupation is necessary for survival. For years, you get up, get dressed, eat breakfast, and work all day. It's an exercise. What makes you think you can suddenly cease that routine without slipping into senility? You can't just stop or that'll be the end of you. I aim to live. Purpose courses through my veins just as surely as artistry does. It's what gets me out of bed, eager to do my pull-ups, and curious to discover the world anew.

Following the airing of Oprah's *Brewster* in 1989, other roles came my way, though still never with the same frequency with which they flowed for my white contemporaries. But you take what you can get, and sometimes, what you can get is a delightful character like Sipsey in the 1991 classic *Fried Green Tomatoes*. Sipsey, a family cook dressed in a head wrap and an apron, lacks in glamour what she makes up for in guts. Still, some of my mother's old friends, those who'd been murmuring since the day I showed up on-screen in *Sounder* donning a do-rag, piped up with their chorus of complaints. Asked one, "Why are you always looking like a *ton-a-lodgin*?"—the West Indian expression for a ragamuffin. I don't write the roles, sweetheart, I simply authenticate them. And why on earth would a home cook be made up in lipstick and heels? Anyway, I loved that Sipsey because she was ballsy. In the film, Sipsey stirs up some trouble for a certain wife beater, and that maverick act leads to her best line: "The secret's in the sauce!" To this day, when folks come up to me and utter that phrase, I know they've reveled in Sipsey's chutzpah as much as I do. Madame Queen, another audacious character I portrayed, in the 1997 crime drama *Hoodlum*, had twice Sipsey's moxie. You talking about feisty, boy. That woman was something, a gangster through and through. She brought the numbers racket to Harlem. Oh, how I loved playing her.

The mid-nineties, for me, is a misty watercolored blur of films that could put me fast to sleep right now, save for my star turn in the 1994 CBS miniseries *The Oldest Living Confederate Widow Tells All*, which chronicles the life of a ninety-nine-year-old woman once married to a Civil War veteran. I can tolerate playing a maid and a former slave when doing so shines a light on an important chapter in history, and when the role just might earn me an Emmy, which this one did. The tail end of the decade brought me another cinematic gem. In 1999, I joined the cast of *A Lesson Before Dying*, a made-for-TV film based on the number one *New York Times* bestselling novel by my friend Ernest Gaines, who of course also wrote *The Autobiography of Miss Jane Pittman*. The story centers on Jefferson (Mekhi Phifer), a young man who has been wrongfully convicted of murdering a white man and thus sentenced to death. Enter Grant Wiggins (Don Cheadle), my godson in the film and a teacher tapped by God to come alongside Jefferson. The spiritually devout Tante Lou, my character, worked herself into my pores the way Rebecca and Jane once had, so much so that when I look now at photos from my time on set, I don't see my own face, but hers.

I knew the soul of that woman. She embodies the scores of steadfast, faithful Black women who have always surrounded me. I channeled them into Tante Lou, who feels determined that if young Jefferson must die, he do so with dignity.

A lesson before dying—that is what Miles, in his passing, left for me. We don't have long here, children. Our hopes and aspirations may feel limitless, but our days are finite, our experiences fading in the twinkling of an eye. Death is a love note to the living, to regard every day, every breath, as sacred. "What is your life?" the scriptures ask us. "You are a mist that appears for a little while and then vanishes" (James 4:14, NIV). The Spirit is ever beckoning us to heed that wisdom, to get on with what we've been put here to do. And whatever that calling looks like, however it may seemingly vary from one person or season to the next, at its core, it is simply this: cherish one another. That is all. That is our purpose in its entirety, to bestow God's care onto others. "Do you think Miles knew just how loved he was?" a friend asked me after his passing. Sadly, he did not. That awareness is why now, in these times today, I hold my dear ones ever closer.

In the years immediately after Miles's passing, I grieved in the way that I always have, between the crevices of my art. Stepping into another's reality gives me shelter from my own. Slowly, as I become a conduit for someone else's anguish, the raw pain of my own throbs less. Healing, as I see it, is not the absence of pain. Rather, it is a gradual reduction in the ache. The lessening of that hurt eventually makes room for fond memories to surface. Miles has been gone for three decades now, and to this day, when I see a photo of him, or else recall one of his crazy sayings ("Can't no one monkey stop a show," he'd quip when someone attempted to block his path), it can take me right back to our years together. At the start of this journey called grief, I teared up upon remembering him. These days, I do more smiling than weeping. Though Miles is long gone, he is right here with me. Our love story will never be finished. After his passing, I went out with other men, some of them in the industry, none of whom I care to name. Nothing serious ever came of it. We're fortunate, in this life, if we've known true love once. I have and I relished it.

About eight years after Miles's death, sometime around 1999, God showered me with a fresh round of his mercies. I turned seventy-five in 1999, though I still allowed the world to believe I was a decade younger. While on a red-eye flight from Los Angeles to New York, I spotted an advertisement about a new vegetarian restaurant in the Village. I took a cab to the restaurant, which turned out to be the size of a teaspoon, with just four tables and a counter. I ordered my meal to go. Then, given that it was a bright Sunday morning, I felt like going to church. I'd been wanting to attend Harlem's Abyssinian Baptist Church, the internationally renowned congregation headed by the Reverend Dr. Calvin O. Butts. I arrived late, after the service was already well on its way.

The sanctuary was packed to the gills. An usher directed me downstairs to an overflow area, where I stood alongside a wall. A woman by the name of Cheryl Washington, the news anchor who has since become my friend, recognized my face and noticed me holding up that wall. "What are you doing down here?" she asked me.

"Well, I wanted to go to church," I told her. She laughed and took me by the hand.

"You don't stand nowhere, Ms. Tyson," she said. "Please come with me." She led me upstairs and found me a seat in a pew on the main floor. She must've also sent word to Reverend Butts that I was in attendance, because not long after, he called my name from the pulpit. "I hear there's a young lady here today that I have long respected and admired," he said, beaming. He went on to explain that, as part of his cherished music collection, he still owned Miles's 1967 album *Sorcerer*, the one bearing my profile. "If you're here, Ms. Tyson," he went on, "I am extremely grateful that you chose to visit us today. Please stand if you are present." I sheepishly rose as he and the congregants applauded. That day marked my first visit to Abyssinian. Today, more than twenty years later, it is still my spiritual home.

Many summers ago at the church, I dedicated a third-row pew to my mother's memory. The plaque bears the inscription, "To mother—Blessed Assurance," a reference to the hymn that anchored her. In 2019, when Annie Leibovitz photographed me for *Vanity Fair*'s Hollywood issue, she captured me right there in that pew, humming the song that carried my mother through this life's toils and triumphs. On Sundays when I take my seat near her name, I think of all she endured, the many times she surely wanted to give up but pressed onward. I recall her swaying, eyes tightly shut, as the words of that hymn washed through her. "This is my story, this is my song," she'd belt out during the refrain. "Praising my Savior, all the day long." Her powerful testimony, grounded in grace and nourished in glory, has since become my own.

PART THREE

BOUNTIFUL

We are each other's harvest:
we are each other's business:
we are each other's magnitude and bond.

—GWENDOLYN BROOKS

22

A Strong Harvest

FOR everything there is a season, the Bible teaches us. There's a time to mourn, as I did greatly after Miles's death, and a time to laugh, a habit that has always been my sanity. There's a time to sow, as my dear parents once did into the soil of my young life, and a time to pluck the harvest. In these years now, my crop is plentiful. I marvel daily at its abundance. The yield, sweet and ripe, has brought unexpected fruit, riches I never dreamed would come my way. Among them is a school in New Jersey.

I never set out to have a school. Sometime around 1994, a sweet woman by the name of Laura Trimmings called my agent. Mrs. Trimmings was then serving as principal of Vernon L. Davey Middle School in East Orange, New Jersey. District officials wanted to rename the school, as well as to expand it into a high school at a new location. Their bold vision: to eventually demolish the vacant East Orange High School and, in its place, construct a three-hundred-thousand-square-foot campus with state-of-the-art facilities—a school where students could rigorously pursue the arts while also undertaking traditional academic disciplines. The new campus, cradled between Walnut and Winans Streets, would include a television studio, an eight-hundred-seat theater, and music rehearsal rooms. The school's name had not yet been chosen, which is what prompted Mrs. Trimmings's call. "The board would like to name the school after Ms. Tyson," she told my agent. By this time I'd moved on from Bill Haber and was working with Erwin Moore. When Erwin relayed her proposition, my jaw grazed the floor. "Why on earth would anyone want to name a New Jersey school after me?" I said. I'd never lived there, nor did I know anything about partnering with a school. I told him to thank Mrs. Trimmings for her kind offer but to decline it.

That Mrs. Trimmings, she was persistent. Over the next year, she rang my agent time and again, pleading to talk directly with me. I finally relented, mostly to get her off our backs. On the phone, she passionately made her case. I paused and drew in a breath. "You know," I told her, "Dionne Warwick went to school in East Orange. So did John Amos. Why don't you ask one of them?" She chuckled. "Ms. Tyson, the board has voted unanimously, more than once, that they want the school to bear your name," she said. "That's why you haven't been able to get rid of me!" I told her I'd give it some more thought and get back with her that week. I did—and the answer, for all the initial reasons, remained no.

Around that time, I had lunch with my cousin, Emily, the one my sister is named after. She's a professor at Montclair State University and the daughter of my father's eldest brother, George. I told her this principal had been badgering me for months. When I mentioned the school's location, she put down her water glass. "Listen," she said, "you really oughta let them go ahead with that." "Why?" I asked. She explained that when my father had first arrived in the United States from Nevis in 1919, he'd moved in with my Uncle George and his family in East Orange—a fact I hadn't known up to then. "And you want to hear something else?" she went on. "The home they lived in was six houses down from that campus." I stared at Emily, stunned that this piece of family history had somehow escaped my ear. An awareness rippled through me. *Oh my Lord, I'm supposed to complete the cycle*, I said to myself. *I'm meant to pour back into the community that nourished my father.* I instantly knew that I had to get involved, just as I've always known when I should take a role. My skin tingles. My pulse quickens. My soul just says amen.

That very afternoon, with goose pimples all over my neck, I got Mrs. Trimmings on the phone again. She was of course surprised to hear from me so soon after I'd given her my regrets. "I humbly accept your invitation with one stipulation," I told her. "If the school will have my name on it, I want to be actively involved with the students." She laughed. "Of course, Ms. Tyson," she said. "That's what we'd hoped would happen."

Thus began a divine assignment that, to this moment, continues. On November 5, 1995, the Cicely L. Tyson Community School of Performing and Fine Arts flung open its doors. Then fourteen years later, when the state-of-the-art campus was at last completed, Mrs. Trimmings and I hosted a gala that felt like a family reunion. So many of my longtime friends, my extended family, joined me in celebrating. Oprah attended. "Please let me know exactly when it is because I want to be there," she'd been telling me for months, and true to her word, she was there with bells on. Angela Bassett and Lynn Whitfield also honored me with their presence, as did Nick Ashford and Valerie Simpson, Susan L. Taylor, Soledad O'Brien, BeBe Winans, and too many other dear ones to list. Jon Corzine, then the New Jersey governor, was on site, along with David Dinkins, the former New York City mayor. The grand unveiling of the new campus, complete with a ribbon-cutting ceremony, set the table for a feast I'm still savoring.

From the beginning, the school's motto hoisted the bar heavenward: "We aim high, we soar high" is our creed. My intention is to have every student who strides our halls, every one of the more than seven hundred lives we have the privilege of imprinting, surpass all limitations, real and perceived. There is nothing our children cannot achieve when they're given the proper tools and nurturing, starting with a belief in their own brilliance despite social messages to the contrary. I don't simply want to teach these young folks to reach for excellence; I want them to breathe excellence, wallow in it, allow it to saturate their beings. With that goal in mind, our administrators and teachers are carefully chosen. We bring in only those who see our children through the lens of their full potential.

I love visiting campus. Some semesters, I teach a master class in acting, which is why I know there's a pipeline of stage warriors set for Broadway. Other times, I just drop in and surprise the students, who gather 'round excitedly to show me their art pieces, their vibrantly colored wall murals, their newest A grades. And let me tell you about our award-winning choir. They are nothing short of sensational. They've enchanted audiences everywhere, including at the United Nations and, in 2019, at the McDonald's Gospelfest held at Newark's Prudential Center. Those singers not only raised the roof with their spine-tingling rendition of the Negro spiritual "I Know I've Been Changed," but they also bested ten thousand international competitors to garner the top prize.

Graduation has become my annual can't-miss affair. The ceremony feels like a church revival, and given that it spans three hours, it's nearly as long as one. Song, dance, and poetry drift skyward. In 2018, two seniors gave me chills when they played "The Star-Spangled Banner" on their saxophones. Maya Angelou once served as our graduation speaker. All of New Jersey turned out, with parents and community members lined up against the walls. The same was true when civil rights pioneer Rosa Parks graced the stage. What a wonderful woman she was, soft-spoken and humble, yet fierce enough to shake our nation awake. "The only tired I was, was tired of giving in," she said of the day in 1955, on a Montgomery bus, when she refused to give up her seat to a white patron. That Rosa was a sturdy oak, with strong roots stretching far beneath the soil. I gloried in witnessing my students, in rapt attention, soaking in Miss Rosa's wisdom.

In the twenty-five years since we enrolled our first class of artists on the rise, our seniors have consistently been admitted to our nation's finest institutions of higher education, from Spelman College to Boston University. Many of them earn academic scholarships. I'm so proud of these young folks, I hardly know what to do with myself. I wake up in the mornings thinking about what else we can offer them, how we can sow more powerfully into their lives the way my own village once did for me. I smile when I recall my third-grade teacher, Miss Sullivan, prancing by my desk singing "You oughta be in pictures!" In her own way, she made me feel seen, lifted my eyes toward a future I couldn't have known was coming. We may never realize the extent to which our behaviors impact our children, how they seek validation in our every word and smile, gaze and gesture. That awareness guides how I connect with my students. I'll tell you, boy, this work just lights me up. That's how service operates: it blesses the giver more than it gifts the recipient.

I'll forever remember Darryl, a delightful young man with a warm smile. He was as sharp as a jackknife, an honor roll student respected by his peers, and yet there was not a trace of arrogance in his manner. In the months leading up to graduation, he applied to multiple schools and was accepted by all of them, including the number one historically Black men's college, Morehouse. Though he was admitted and yearned to attend, he didn't receive a scholarship. "Let me tell you something," I said to Carl Foster, my assistant then. "That young man is going to Morehouse, do you hear me? That's all there is to it."

Over that weekend, we both made calls to everyone we knew who was affiliated with Morehouse. The admissions team asked for more of his particulars, and within a week, we received word. "This is the kind of young man we want here," an administrator told us, explaining that he'd be awarded a scholarship. Yet another challenge soon emerged. Darryl's mother wasn't keen on his moving to Atlanta. I never heard what his father thought. But particularly since Darryl was his mom's eldest, her Heart String, she wanted him to study locally. "You'd better talk to her, Carl," I said, laughing. "That woman does not want me to knock on her door." Obviously, it was the parents' choice where to send their child, not mine, and that had to be respected. Yet with everything in me, I longed to see Darryl take flight. I knew attending Morehouse would raise his shoulders as it broadened his horizons. To soar toward what's possible, you must leave behind what's comfortable.

Thanks to Carl's persuasive lobby, the parents ultimately agreed to send Darryl to Morehouse. Carl even became his mentor. In fact, because Darryl's mother and father weren't able to make the trip to Atlanta, Carl accompanied Darryl to campus, helped him settle in, and introduced him to some top administrators. Four years later, Darryl graduated with honors, and I flew down to celebrate his accomplishment. Squelching tears, I embraced him like he was my son, as he has come to feel like to me. And you want to know what else? Darryl's younger siblings were so inspired by his achievement that they made plans to attend college. Even his mother went back to school and earned her diploma! That's the power of education. It expands one's field of vision, and in so doing, it lifts entire families and communities. When you witness better, you often want better.

I have Mrs. Trimmings to thank for such a mighty yield. Had she not been so persistent, I might've missed out on what has become one of the single greatest bounties of my years now. Sadly, Mrs. Trimmings passed away in 2015. And yet I've kept her memory alive in a photograph that sits atop my dresser. The two of us stand arm in arm, elation on our faces at the school's gala. When my eyes fall upon that photo, I whisper gratitude for her life. "Carve your name on hearts, not tombstones," author Shannon L. Alder once wrote. Dr. Martin Luther King Jr. put it another way: "Use me, God. Show me how to take who I am, who I want to be, and what I can do, and use it for a purpose greater than myself." That is my aspiration. It is also Mrs. Trimmings's abiding legacy.

Tyler Perry is another of my jewels. Hardly a week goes by that the two of us aren't on the phone, cackling about one thing or another, swapping stories and scuttlebutt. Let me tell you something about Tyler. Long before he arrived in 1969 New Orleans, providence had already hewn his path. Born into poverty and abuse but refusing to be defined by either, Tyler struggled through his early years. Around 1990, he moved to Atlanta with the hope of becoming a playwright, but he instead found himself living in his car after being evicted from his apartment on Sylvan Road. Still, he kept on dreaming.

While watching Oprah's show in 1991, Tyler heard that journaling could be cathartic. That epiphany wrapped his fingers around a pen, and before long, he'd filled a diary with letters to himself, creating a compendium that eventually became the basis for the play *I Know I've Been Changed*. He poured both his spirit and his life savings into that maiden production and soon ended up on the streets again. But Tyler, though broke, was unbroken by the defeat. He revised his play over and over, and by 1998, folks were swarming to experience it, elbowing their way toward the best seats. Other successes followed, including his introduction of the razor-tongued, bosom-drooping, pistol-packing, make-you-laugh-'til-you-cry Madea, the Southern matriarch who first appeared in Tyler's 1999 play *I Can Do Bad All by Myself*.

A lot has since changed for Tyler, all of it for a higher purpose. In 2006 when he opened Tyler Perry Studios, he became the first African American to ever own a major film production company. Then in 2019, he took another giant leap forward when he reopened his studio as a fifteen-thousand-square-foot symbol of fortitude on 330 acres in southwest Atlanta. Along Georgia State Route 66, a green exit sign now bears his studio's name, alongside another sign for Sylvan Road—the street on which he was once evicted. I'll tell you, boy, every aspect of Tyler's journey shouts destiny. "The studio was once a Confederate army base," Tyler has said, "which meant that there were Confederate soldiers on that base, plotting and planning on how to keep 3.9 million Negroes enslaved. Now that land is owned by one Negro." If we are ever to prosper as a people, the path to the Promised Land runs through self-ownership. Tyler astutely retained full rights to his intellectual property, a move that catapulted him to billionaire status. As Billie Holliday once musically testified, "God bless the child that's got his own."

At the studio's majestic opening gala, Tyler named one of his twelve soundstages after me, an honor I cherish as much as I do him. Though his sprawling complex and his platform dwarf those of his contemporaries, Hollywood's white power brokers have always dismissed him. That's how he got into the great habit of ignoring the naysayers early on. "If they don't give you a seat at the table," Shirley Chisholm once said, "bring a folding chair." Tyler did one better and built his own dining set, complete with all he needs to finance his storytelling. It is precisely what I've spent much of my career hoping for: that we, as a people, would one day be able to reflect our own varied experiences on the screen, rather than accepting this nation's one-dimensional, erroneous depictions of who we're not. Tyler shares the stories he knows best. Yet that leaves room for other Black scriptwriters to sharpen their pencils and render their takes. Directors such as Ava DuVernay, Steve McQueen, Issa Rae, Lee Daniels, Barry Jenkins, Ryan Coogler, and Jordan Peele are doing just that. Viola Davis and her husband, Julius Tennon, are creating content through their own JuVee Productions. Decades-long directors such as Denzel Washington, Spike Lee, and Kasi Lemmons continue to delight and challenge us, while Angela Bassett, Regina King, Halle Berry, and others are now rightfully seated in directors' chairs. As someone who has been in the industry for as long as Moses was old, I applaud every one of these efforts. What some white folks never seem to understand is that we're not a monolithic group. While there are certainly rich cultural traditions that bind us together, there is no singular "African-American perspective," just as there is no one way to be Black. There are as many viewpoints as there are glorious Black faces.

Tyler and I first worked together on 2005's *Diary of a Mad Black Woman.* He now tells me he had the shakes before asking me to play Myrtle, mother of Helen, portrayed by the gifted Kimberly Elise. (And incidentally, many moviegoers began believing Kimberly was my real-life daughter. She isn't, but even I see our resemblance.) When Kimberly was first cast, she said to Tyler, "Miss Cicely and I have always wanted to work together. What do you think about having her playing Myrtle?" Tyler loved the idea, but it intimidated him. He mentioned it to Reuben Cannon, the producer. "I don't think she'll do it," Reuben told him. "She's very selective." But he pushed past his nerves and called me anyway, and I asked him to send me the script. To his astonishment—and in line with my goose pimples—I answered yes.

After filming wrapped, Tyler and I stayed in touch. In 2006, he invited Sidney Poitier and me on a (long!) transatlantic flight to Johannesburg, South Africa, to attend the splendorous unveiling of the Oprah Winfrey Leadership Academy for Girls. That gave us plenty of time to kick off our shoes and connect. I shared some of my best stories as a wide-eyed Tyler listened, laughing hardest at my skirmish with Liz Taylor. Our friendship has blossomed from there, and so far, we've done six films together. And he's the world's greatest tipper. When he heard how little I was paid for *Sounder* and *The Autobiography of Miss Jane Pittman*, his mouth fell open. From then on, he decided to double, and sometimes even triple or quadruple, my asking price for any role he requested that I play. He padded my pay in 2012 when he hired me to portray his mother in the crime drama *Alex Cross*. In one scene, his character turns his back on me and walks away, and faster than you can spell *pivot*, I grabbed him by the arm and spun him back around. He tells that story all the time. He can't get over the fact that I, this little bitty woman, could set a strapping six-foot-five-inch man back on his heels. A few years following that collaboration, Tyler placed another crown on my head when he asked me to become the godmother to his son, Aman. You should see that child and me down on the carpet together, doing handstands, with a nervous Tyler standing by to be sure I don't crack my neck. What a joy.

And speaking of godchildren, my cup runneth over with too many to name, though I will share one other who fills me with pride. Years ago while I was walking down the street, minding my own business as I am prone to do, this rather handsome young man approached me. "Good afternoon, Ms. Tyson. My name is Denzel Washington," he said, flashing a wide grin. "Oh," I said, thinking, *I guess I'm supposed to know who he is.* "I was once in a movie with you," he said. I lifted my brows. "You were?" I asked, flipping through my mental Rolodex to recall which one. "Yes," he said, reminding me that we'd both played in the 1977 television film *Wilma* about iconic track sprinter Wilma Rudolph, who rose above physical handicaps to earn three gold medals in the 1960 Olympics. "I also met my wife on that film set," he told me. My conversation with Denzel that day flourished into a decades-long friendship, one I hold dear. He and sweet Pauletta thought enough of me to name me the godmother of their first daughter, Katia. How time goes. The little Katia I once bounced on my knee has now grown into an independent young woman, a Yale graduate who has lent her production talents to films such as *Django Unchained* and *Fences*. What a treasure she is, as precious to me as Tyler's babe.

One of my fondest Tyler memories came in December 2018. "Would you consider doing a role for just one day?" he asked me. "Of course," I told him. "Send me the script." I read it and immediately called him back with a question: "When do we begin?" "Let me discuss it with your team," he told me. I later received word from my current manager, Larry Thompson, of the start date. When I arrived, Tyler's entourage escorted me through his fortress to a studio upstairs. I just about fainted when I rounded the corner. There, under a massive banner that read "Happy Birthday, Cicely Tyson!" the entire production crew had gathered to surprise me. The "one-day role" had been a ploy to get me down there, though I did end up playing Alice in *A Fall from Grace*, the script he'd sent me. His crew had wanted to scream "Surprise!" when I came around that corner, but Tyler had altered their plan. "We've gotta be careful," he told his team. "She's over ninety. We don't want her falling out." Even minus the shout, my heart toppled out of my chest. He got me good. That Tyler is the devil.

The 2011 film *The Help* brought me a gem of a role, however tiny the part. For me, the work is never about the size of the portrayal. It's about the passion I pour into it. If I decide to take on a project, it is because I feel there is something in it that may move viewers. I immediately felt that about Constantine, the elderly maid and nanny I play. Though I will always have my misgivings about portraying domestics, I sensed this character had a deeper emotional backstory than is usually evident in such characters. That is why I agreed to take the part. The script, based on Kathryn Stockett's novel of the same name, chronicles the experiences of four Black maids in 1960s Mississippi. The illustrious cast includes Viola Davis, Octavia Spencer, Sissy Spacek, Emma Stone, and Jessica Chastain.

The role came along a couple of years after my school's new campus had opened. I met several times with the director, and if memory serves me as well as it typically does, Viola had not yet been cast. When she and I later spotted one another on the Mississippi set, which marked our first time in each other's presence, she embraced me. Through tears, she conveyed how she'd watched me in *Jane Pittman* in 1974, when she was a child with stardust in her gaze. That day on set, sweet Viola fell right into my arms and heart, which is where she is still. Sometimes, I can't even believe just how old I've gotten to be. I was eighty-seven when I met Viola, feeling as spry as a fifty-year-old. And yet there she stood, this dynamo of an artist in her prime, recalling how, at age seven, I'd inspired her. I never take such gifts for granted or feign modesty. When the harvest flows, honey, you've got to let it tumble forth.

I prepared as I always do, by reading and rereading the lines until they jumped off the page and slapped me in the face. Then on set, even between takes, I stayed in character, insisting that the crew refer to me only as Constantine and never as Ms. Tyson. That's the only way I can remain in someone else's skin, and that is also why I choose to stay in my own place while I'm working. That used to drive Miles crazy. Even if I was in town, I'd lock myself in my own apartment and away from him, often for long stretches. Anyway, I'd allowed Constantine's spirit to crawl inside of mine, which is what comes through during her most pivotal moment in the story. She has loyally served a white family for much of her life, and in one intense scene, she is suddenly sent away, with no chance to say goodbye to a child she has come to love as her own. She'd reared that girl from infancy, charted her growth with pencil markings on a wall whenever the girl visited her place. As Constantine packs to leave Mississippi, she runs her weathered, trembling hands along those markings as she chokes back tears. While filming that scene, I stayed right in the emotion of what any woman would've been feeling if she suddenly had her child and livelihood wrenched away. When Constantine sees those markings, she doesn't just see lines. Rather, she sees that girl, standing right there with her. Her hands quiver because she's reliving the memories.

I of course never watched the film, but when it premiered,

everybody seemed to be talking about my portrayal. After Viola and her husband, Julius, saw a screening, Julius said to me, with his hand over his heart, "And *you* . . . oh my God." I kept asking myself, *What is all the fuss?* I'm still asking myself that. If I was on that set for three minutes, I was there plenty. That's how brief my appearance was.

Viola, beacon of brilliance that she is, delivered a performance that earned her a well-deserved Oscar for Best Supporting Actress. She has since said that although she will always cherish her experience on the set and her relationships with her castmates, she feels, in hindsight, that the voices and perspectives of the maids weren't fully represented. In short, the story line doesn't have the nerve to utter the ugly truth, to speak of what it actually must've felt like for those Black women to eke out an existence in the Jim Crow South. I concur, particularly in light of our times now, as well as with the knowledge of how our stories have historically been diluted to make white audiences feel comfortable. The scarcity of work for Black actors has much to do with why we even consider certain roles. As artists and as a people, we've come this far by faith—and yet, up ahead, we've got many more seeds to plant.

A few years after Viola and I embraced on the set of *The Help*, we reunited on the television series *How to Get Away with Murder*, created by Shonda Rhimes, otherwise known as the most powerful woman in television. I'd received a call from the ABC team, asking me to play Ophelia, mother to Viola's character, Annalise. Without hesitation, I accepted. When I later heard that Viola had personally requested that I play her on-screen life force, my mouth fell open and my eyes moistened, which is how they remained during our six-season run.

I have such respect for Viola's instrument. Few living actors can so convincingly capture what it means to live a life, how it feels to truly ache. Her depth of emotion has no floor. On set one day, she recounted a memory from her childhood, one sprinkled with joys and difficulties. I cannot recall the story, but I will forever remember that she spoke with such feeling. "You know," I told her, "that is what makes you the great actress that you are." That child's roots run deep. During our final episodes of filming together, I refused to bid either her or her character farewell, though I knew I'd miss them both terribly, which I have. I hate endings, which is why it has taken me decades to get around to writing this book. Thankfully, though the curtain has closed on the groundbreaking series, my friendship with Viola will never take a final bow.

A strong harvest is meant to be shared. During these years, as I stand in awe of my abundance, I'm always looking for ways to resow its seeds in the rich earth of others. My school is one. My stage work is another. And my camaraderie with a vast network of soror sisters keeps me grounded in what matters in this life—service.

I never intended to join a sorority, just as I never set out to have a school or pen this autobiography. I'm grateful that God often laughs at our plans and substitutes his better ones. My close friend Jeanne Noble, an education pioneer, served as the national president of Delta Sigma Theta sorority for several years. Long ago, I vowed I'd never join a sorority because I have great friends in all of them. I wanted to remain neutral. But when Jeanne fell quite ill in 2002, she whispered her dying wish: she wanted me to become a Delta. Given how dearly I loved Jeanne, it was a request I could not refuse. That year, I became an honorary member, and I'm now delighted that I did.

I stepped into an organization steeped in the activism I so cherish. Among my sisters are political powerhouses such as Shirley Chisholm, Barbara Jordan, and Mary McLeod Bethune. "If the time is not ripe," said civil rights trailblazer Dorothy Height, the longest-serving Delta president, "we have to ripen the time." Her words perfectly capture the spirit of the Deltas, as well as serve as a rallying call for elevating our community.

My lifelong friend Ruby Dee was a Delta. Following a journey defined by her pioneering work on stage and off, she passed away in 2014. My heart still weeps at the loss. Several years later in 2019, I received the Ruby Dee Renaissance Award for Artist Activism, an honor given to me by Ruby and Ossie's daughter, Hasna Muhammad. The ceremony was organized by the New York Alumnae Chapter of the Deltas, a number of whom that day donned the sorority's splendorous colors, crimson and cream. (Civil rights activist Betty Shabazz, wife of Malcolm X, was also once a member of the New York chapter.) During my remarks, I mentioned my friend Jeanne Noble. As soon as I spoke her name, everyone in that room stood and applauded loudly for a full thirty seconds! The outpouring of exuberance reflected just how many lives she pressed her thumbprints into, how many paths she altered. When you give yourself away, when you surrender yourself as a divine vessel, as my beloved Jeanne did, you impact lives eternally.

23

Trip to Bount

ONE Sunday way back in 1985, I
Hollywood when I passed a marqu
to Bountiful, which Horton Foote had
play. I stopped, studied the poster, ar
Geraldine Page, an actress I've long ad
for the matinee, slid into a seat in the
From the first scene, Geraldine was mes
Watts, a feisty elderly widow who yea
ful, her rural, fictitious hometown in T
and daughter-in-law, however, aim to l
stirred was I by Geraldine's performan
and took a cab straight to the office of
then working for my manager, Larry T
my *Trip to Bountiful*," I told him after c
role. "I just want one more great chara
I went on, "and then I could retire." H
since we both knew I'd likely never qu

During the months after that conv
Erwin brought me a role that made my
and say to him, "I'm still waiting on r

beca
seri
stan
Jane
furt
Ger
to m
othe
S
"Va
desi
with
and
proc
The
me t
you
"
"
"
of y
in 2
wou
agre
I
I'd s
this
mati
arou
I don
run
hope

ne our running joke, only in my case, I was 100 percent ıs. Over my career, I'd been blessed with far more subive roles than the average Black actress, from Rebecca and Pittman, to Binta and Harriet Tubman. And yet I longed to er sharpen my instrument, to stretch myself in new ways. ldine's performance, for which she earned an Oscar, spoke :. It moved me to tears. It transported me. And like every actor I know, I'm in the transportation business.

metime in 2012, my phone rang. It was my assistant, Carl. Ramsey is looking for you," he told me. Van, a costume ner I'd worked with many times, wanted to connect me a friend of his to speak about a possible project. I agreed, day later, this friend called me. She explained she was ıcing one of her father's plays with a mostly Black cast. how, she said, was *The Trip to Bountiful*, and she wanted play Carrie Watts. My heartbeat quickened. "What did ay your name was?" I asked her.

[allie Foote," she said.

nd what is your father's name?" I asked.

[orton Foote," she told me. "My dad was such an admirer ur work," she went on, explaining that she'd lost him 09, when he was ninety-two years old. "And I know he ln't want anyone else to play the role. In fact, if you don't to play the lead, I'm not sure that we'll do the production."

:arly fell out of my chair. More than twenty-five years after :n *Bountiful* and declared my intention aloud, here came roject, dropping right into my lap. God heard my proclan as a prayer, and a quarter century later, he finally got d to answering. If you don't believe in miracles, my dear, t know why, because this is exactly how my last Broadway egan. The revival production of *Bountiful*, Hallie then l, would feature a talent-rich cast. She got her wish: Cuba

Gooding Jr., Vanessa Williams, and Condola Rashad eventually joined the ensemble.

I of course accepted the role and began making plans to visit Texas so I could sink into the research. As you know, I approach every role as if it will be my only, and I'd never even visited the Lone Star State. Before my trip in the spring of 2013, someone overheard me talking about my upcoming tour. "I've gotta experience the smells, the tastes, the feeling of where Mrs. Watts lived," I said to a friend. "How can you project a character if you don't know where she's from?" Next thing I knew, CBS had contacted me about capturing my journey on film. I laughed, astonished that my offhand comment had spurred such a request.

I'd yearned to go alone. I simply wanted to walk around in silence, hear folks talk, visit the market, breathe the air. That plan went south. In the end, I did allow the CBS crew to accompany me to Wharton, Texas, Horton Foote's birthplace and his inspiration for *Bountiful*. Hallie walked me around the grounds of her father's homestead, giving me the particulars of the family history. I also ventured over to East Gate Baptist Church and took my place alongside the locals, who sang the old hymns I grew up on. Later, I wedged my hand down into the soil of a cornfield, just to get a feel of the earth. I even put a handful of that dirt in a Ziploc bag so I could carry it home and remember the smell. By the time I left Wharton, I understood exactly why Mrs. Carrie so longed to return. Magic lives in that place, in the arms of the oaks and in the whisper of the cool breeze off the Gulf of Mexico.

With much study, I came to know Carrie Watts through and through. At my age now, I understand her all the better. Do you have any idea how many elders find themselves in her position? They suddenly lose their spouses, their faculties, or both. They're then often living with their grown children, even as they crave an autonomy that has slipped away. Praise God I still have my independence and my mind, but I do know how it feels to grow vulnerable. No matter the measure of fortitude you carry, a certain anxiety arises. You know you cannot control all you once could, so you hold fast to the little you can still govern. In the case of Mrs. Carrie, that is her one last journey home.

As opening night drew nigh in the spring of 2013, I became more nervous than I usually get. I'd been away from stage acting for nearly three decades. There's a rigor to performing live, a muscle that atrophies without use. You don't get a second or seventh take. You're completely in the moment, gaffes and all. Every single night, you've got to bring your best, because despite how well you might've performed the evening before, this audience has never experienced the story. The last big show I'd played in was *The Corn Is Green*, that short-lived Liz Taylor production that ended in a legal brouhaha. Upon my return, I didn't know upstage from downstage from around stage. And at age eighty-eight, I was also substantially older than I'd been in *Corn*. I worried that my voice, which had lost some robustness over the years, wouldn't project well enough for the audience members in the back row of the balcony to hear me. Day and night, I practiced vocal exercises meant to move my voice from my head into my diaphragm. A little at a time over weeks of rehearsals, I made progress.

Another concern I had was whether I'd remember my lines. I probably own two dozen digital recorders, most of them junk, not to mention too fancy for my preference. Why do they make these machines so complicated, huh? I unearthed the one I could tolerate and carried it in my pocketbook, speaking my lines into the microphone and then listening back every chance I got. By the time I showed up for our first previews at the Stephen Sondheim Theater just off Times Square, I had my part down, do you hear me? I also had my prayer beads draped around my neck. I used them to quiet my mind before each performance, moving along each bead with my thumb as I recited my mantra. Hallie gave me that set, which she'd purchased in Japan. It got me through 187 performances.

The show resonated with theatergoers even during previews, so much so that the audience took part in a pivotal scene. Near the start of the Second Act, Mrs. Carrie—on the run from her son and daughter-in-law—awaits on a bus station bench, alongside Thelma (Condola Rashad), a young woman she has just befriended. Mrs. Carrie bursts into song, lifting her arms heavenward while delivering the rapturous refrain of "Blessed Assurance," the hymn that is written on my soul. "This is my story, this is my song!" she belts out. "Praising my Savior, all the day long!" Spontaneously, the audience, filled with people of all stripes, with a heavier-than-usual smattering of brown faces, joined in, their collective voices echoing through the theater. Let me tell you something about Black folks: we love to interact. Whether we're in the house of the Lord or gathered in our living rooms, we talk back. It's part of that call-and-response tradition birthed in the pews of the Black church. Initially, I didn't notice folks singing along. That's how focused I was on channeling Mrs. Carrie, to the exclusion of all else. But after the first preview, when a journalist pointed out the audience participation, I began taking note—and it was absolutely thrilling. That hymn was Horton Foote's favorite, just as it was my mother's. Can you imagine? God's handprints were all over this experience.

Though I remembered my lines and projected quite well, there was of course the occasional disturbance—including one behind the scenes that annoyed me to no end. An actor I won't name was a bit of a troublemaker. Just before I'd stride onto the stage, he'd pop up in my face and say, "Hoop-dee-do-dee-do!" He thought it was amusing. I did not share his sense of pleasure. Anyone who has ever worked with me can tell that, while I have a well-developed sense of humor away from the stage, I approach my work with a clear-eyed seriousness. I told our director, Michael Wilson, that if he didn't put an end to this man's antics, I'd leave the production. That straightened everyone right up.

The revival was such a hit that it was extended once. Then again. Then a third time. We even took the show on the road, performing in Boston and Los Angeles. Over two years, ancient as I was, I never missed a single performance. The show was later turned into a Lifetime film, released in 2014. Vanessa Williams and I played in that version as well, along with Blair Underwood and Keke Palmer. The accolades poured in, a harvest as unexpected as the call I'd first received from Hallie. The Broadway production received four Tony nominations, including one for me as Outstanding Actress in a Play. I was also nominated for a Drama Desk Award, as well as an Emmy for my Lifetime performance.

Before the Tonys, the distinguished designer and my beloved longtime friend B Michael created my haute couture masterpiece, an indigo trumpet-silhouette gown with hand-draped ruffle seams in silk Mikado. I'd worked with B Michael for the first time before Oprah's Legends Weekend in 2005. Boy, was he a nervous wreck! He couldn't get over the fact that he was making a gown for Cicely Tyson, for a ball at Oprah's house, for a once-in-a-lifetime affair. He took my measurements and spun up a work of art, and though it was a little big in a couple of places, I pinned it here and tucked it there until it was a stunner. I never know what that man is going to create. Nor does he, I'm sure, like most of the greats. He works best under pressure, and though his creations often reach me at the nail-biting last moment, I rarely use any other designer. His talent is unparalleled. For the 2013 Tonys held at Radio City Music Hall, he aimed to make me feel like royalty. On that evening and a great many others, he succeeded.

I did not prepare an acceptance speech. That is obvious by the astonishment on my face when my name was called as the winner. I think it's presumptuous to write remarks ahead of time, when you're in competition with four others, all of them supremely gifted. You have no idea who will win, and though I hoped I might, I did not arrive with that expectation. As my mother so often reminded me, if you expect nothing, you will never be disappointed. And what is the point of preparing anyway? If you're chosen, the room begins spinning, so you might as well stay in the moment and speak from the heart, which is exactly what I did.

"It's been thirty years since I stood on the stage," I said. "I really didn't think it would happen again in my lifetime, and I was pretty comfortable with that. Except that I had this burning desire to do just *one* more great role . . . just one more! And it came to me through no effort on my part." Before I could get through the names of the many I aimed to thank, the music began to play, with the intent of hastening me from the stage. Right then, a message flashed on the teleprompter. "'Please wrap it up,' it says!" I read as the audience laughed. "Well that's exactly what you did with me," I concluded. "You wrapped me up in your arms after thirty years. Now I can go home with a Tony! God bless you all, and thank you."

Throughout that entire evening, I smiled so much that my cheeks ached for several days afterward. The award, for me, felt like a pinnacle. Over six decades, I'd earned an Oscar nomination, two Drama Desk Awards, three Emmys, and now I could add a Tony to my mantel. I'd gotten my *Trip to Bountiful* all right, and though I still wasn't ready to retire, I felt as if I could. But rather than placing my feet on an exit ramp toward retirement, God put me on a bridge to another production.

In the fall of 2015, James Earl Jones and I costarred in the Broadway revival of *The Gin Game*, our first onstage reunion since we played in 1966's *A Hand Is on the Gate*. At the start of the production, I was ninety, and James was eighty-four. While age and experience had sharpened our instruments, they hadn't altered our core tendencies. James, who by then had earned Tonys for *Fences* and *The Great White Hope*, was nearly as shy as he'd been years earlier, and still far more reticent than I ever was. He seems to draw his energy from silence, the kind of quiet one wouldn't expect from a man with such a burly baritone. Backstage and between takes, he spoke so little that, at times, I'd look over at him with a question in my eyes: "Are you all right?" He'd glance at me and smile before again retreating inward. But when that curtain lifted, boy, we both fluttered to life. The show is about two friends who shuffle cards and emotions on the front porch of their nursing home. What it's truly about, I understand more clearly as I grow older, is two elders coming to terms with their choices, their mistakes, their joys, their disappointments. Amid the pair's laughs and testy exchanges, they seek solace and a space in which to be heard. That is, in this life, who we are for one another—fellow sojourners and witnesses. We are here to see and hear one another.

A couple of years following my Tony triumph for *Bountiful*, two more riches arrived in relatively quick succession. The first prompted me to lift the curtain on my real age. The second left me blushing. Both involved a certain history-making president.

When Barack Obama was sworn in as president of the United States on a frigid January morning in 2009, I had never thought I'd see a Black president in my lifetime, just as Jane Pittman had never believed she'd drink from that whites-only fountain. And yet there he stood, both a manifestation of Dr. King's dream and an extension of it. He rested his palm on that Lincoln Bible as Michelle, as steady with the Good Book in her hands as she'd be at her husband's side, gazed on with pride. I didn't know whether to shout or weep, and from my seat in the audience, I did both. There is a time to rally, to raise our collective voices in protest. There is also a season to celebrate, to set aside all crusading and just stand in awe of the harvest. For me and for millions, Barack Obama's inauguration was such a moment. I get choked up talking about it even now. And what I love is that, during Barack and Michelle's eight years in the White House, there wasn't a whiff of a scandal. What an honorable legacy. Who knows whether another Black leader will ever inhabit the Oval Office, but I can leave here joyous that I witnessed the first.

In 2015, near the end of Obama's second term, another gift came my way. "You've been chosen as an honoree at the Kennedy Center Honors," my manager, Larry Thompson, told me. I pressed the phone to my ear. "The *what*?" I asked, not sure I'd heard him right. Once he repeated himself, I did not go speechless—I went breathless. After a long pause, I said to myself, *My dear, you had better start breathing if you want to be here to accept this award.* The festivities were to be held in a matter of weeks.

I'd of course heard of the prestigious awards, which recognize achievements by Americans in the arts. But I never imagined I'd stand among the chosen. For the ceremony that year, Larry explained, the songwriter Carole King would be honored, as would filmmaker George Lucas; actress Rita Moreno; the rock band the Eagles; and conductor Seiji Ozawa. The president and the first lady, as per tradition, would be in attendance.

For decades up to then, folks had been trying, and largely failing, to guess how old I was. When I'd starred in *Bountiful*, most news outlets erroneously reported me to be in my late seventies, when in fact, I was on my way out of the eighties. The *New York Times* got it right, and yet the younger age had already taken hold in much of the press. The truth is, I've always been quietly proud of my real age. Why wouldn't I want to celebrate every crease in my brow, all that hard-earned wisdom that lives between the folds? If my first manager, Warren Coleman, hadn't been so insistent that I age myself down—he feared, and perhaps rightfully so, that an industry rife with female age discrimination would count me out of a lot of roles—I may have just omitted my age, rather than changing it. It's nobody's business. But when the Kennedy Center honor came around, I felt it was important to at last set the public record straight. Months before I learned I was to receive the award, I'd celebrated my ninetieth birthday. During the press blitzkrieg surrounding the Kennedy Center ceremony, I spoke that number aloud with nary a quake in my voice. "When were you born?" one reporter asked me. "December 19, 1924," I answered. For me, it was not a matter to be ashamed of. It was a journey to delight in. When the news of my age got around, many couldn't believe that I'd been eighty-eight when I'd done *Bountiful* a couple of years before, and that I was ninety at the Kennedy Center Honors. "If that woman is ninety," one social media poster joked, "then I need names and numbers! How is it that she's still working?" That comment, though made in jest, goes to show the limits we place on ourselves. Why *wouldn't* I be working? The alternative is to sit around making butt prints.

One of my favorite memories of that evening came before the ceremony even began. I'd invited my great-nephew, Devin, to join me at the awards show. He came on his own, and when he arrived, he set out to find me in the crowd. "Aunt Boo Boo!" I suddenly heard ring out over the lobby. "Where are you?" I cupped my hand over my mouth in embarrassment, squelching laughter as I scanned the room to find him. I knew it had to be Devin. Because since the day, all those decades ago, when Emily's daughter, Verna, began calling me Aunt Boo Boo, the family had joined the chorus. Devin and I finally located one another, and when we did, I threatened to pop him in his mouth. "Why on earth would you be shouting 'Aunt Boo Boo!' when I'm about to receive one of the most distinguished awards of my career?" I said to him. When I recall what he did, I grin and shake my head.

During the ceremony, Aretha Franklin, whom I'd adored for years, tore up the house. She'd been an honoree herself back in 1994, and she returned to pay tribute to Carole King with a soul-opening rendition of "(You Make Me Feel like) A Natural Woman," a song Carole penned. With her fur coat dragging across the stage floor, honey, she brought Pentecost to that building. The audience, rising to its feet, erupted in shouts and applause. Once she was done, there wasn't a dry eye on the premises. Even President Obama, who was seated in the box next to mine, shed tears. As Aretha made her way up an aisle carrying a bouquet of flowers, an audience member teased, "Oh, thank you, those must be for me." Aretha smiled. "No," she said, chuckling, "these are for my lady." She later placed the flowers in my arms.

The true Everest of the evening came when my beloved students, the sensational choir from my school, paid tribute to me by singing—what else?—"Blessed Assurance." CeCe Winans and Terence Blanchard led the selection as I, with one hand over my heart and another raised skyward, wept like a newborn. The delightful Kerry Washington, gifted as she is gracious, added magic to the affair with her spirited introduction of me. She'd been just as generous when, in 2010, she'd introduced me as I received the Spingarn Medal—the most distinguished honor the NAACP bestows. Thank you, my dear Kerry. Thank you, NAACP.

Several months after the Kennedy Center high note, I received yet another shock. "Ms. Tyson," said a woman's voice on the line, "I am calling you at the request of President Obama." She paused for a moment, perhaps waiting for a reply, but all I could do was sit there thinking, *Is this a joke?*

"Who is this?" I asked. She gave me her name, which I now cannot remember.

"The President has asked me to call and let you know that he is awarding you with the Medal of Freedom"—as in the highest civilian award in the land.

"Oh please," I said laughing, feeling sure it was a prankster talking some foolishness. "How did you even get this number?" She tried to persuade me that her declaration was true, but I wouldn't hear of it.

"But the president wants you to have the award," she went on. Finally, just as I was about to hang up on that poor woman, she blurted out, "I'll tell him you said yes." *Click.*

Years earlier in 1996, I'd looked on in admiration as President Bill Clinton draped the Medal of Freedom around the neck of Rosa Parks. She was and is an icon, one whose remarkable courage served as a lightning rod during the Civil Rights Movement. Though I'm proud of the work I've done, I certainly did not put myself in Rosa's category. Such a monumental honor was surely reserved for the nation's most esteemed trailblazers, the Dr. Kings of the world. That's what had me so convinced this had to be a hoax. But just in case it wasn't, I called a friend who'd once worked on President Obama's campaign. When I told her the name of the woman who rang me, she started laughing. "Yes, I know exactly who she is!" she said. "She definitely works in the White House." "Come on," I said. "No way." "Congratulations, Ms. Tyson," she told me. "You've earned the award. The only thing left to do is graciously accept it"—a reminder we could all use in this life. My manager, of course, immediately got the White House on the phone and confirmed my attendance at the celebration.

On the day of the ceremony, President Obama stood at the podium and gave some kind remarks about me, most of which I don't recall. That is because there's one line he spoke that I still haven't gotten over. Near the end of his speech, with his stunning wife, Michelle, sitting right there opposite him in the audience, he smiled broadly as he said of me, "And she's just *gorgeous*!" I nearly fainted. Lord, have mercy! After the ceremony, someone said to me, "Do you realize you were the last person he put that medal on during his presidency?" I hadn't—and upon hearing it, I beamed. Just when I think God has outdone himself, he surprises me. The lesson, I know now, is to relish the ride.

24

When Great Trees Fall

My feast of blessings continued in fall 2018, when Robert Endara, who works alongside my manager, Larry, called me. "I have some good news," he said. My ears perked up. I assumed I'd been nominated for an Emmy for a segment in *How to Get Away with Murder*. I'd been nominated four times. *I guess they're going to go ahead and give me one*, I thought upon hearing from Robert. "I have someone on the line who wants to speak to you," he told me. Before I could respond, I heard another male voice. "Ms. Tyson, this is John Bailey," he said, "and I am the president of the Academy of Motion Picture Arts and Sciences. It gives me great joy to tell you that yesterday, the Board of Governors, all fifty-four of them, decided to give you an honorary Oscar."

Well, child, I went to water. For a full thirty seconds I could not utter a single word as Niagara gushed from my eyes. "Really?" I finally managed to get out. "Yes," he said, chuckling. I was so overcome with emotion that after I got off the phone, I realized I hadn't even thanked the gentleman. I later heard that it was my longtime friend Whoopi Goldberg, herself an "EGOT"—Emmy, Grammy, Oscar, and Tony—winner, who'd submitted my name for consideration. God bless that child.

For the next week, I wandered around Manhattan in a happiness high, dazed and bewildered at the news, wondering whether I'd dreamed it during my sleep rather than experiencing it wide awake. I had my Tony. My three Emmys. My Drama Desk Awards. My Oscar nomination. My life's Christmas tree, tall and mighty, had already been fully decorated, its branches heavy with accolades. The pair of glistening stars on top, I reckoned, had been the Kennedy Center Honors and the Presidential Medal of Freedom. And back in 1972, after I'd been nominated for an Oscar for *Sounder*, I'd truly made peace with the fact that the current of my career had swept me more forcefully toward stage and television than it had the big screen. Though like most actors, I yearned for an Oscar, I never expected to get one. And yet here I was, at age ninety-three, on the verge of receiving the industry's most cherished prize. My name would also be carved into Academy history as the first African-American actor to be chosen for an honorary Oscar. I could cry right now.

That September soon after I heard the news, I stopped by to visit my lifelong friend Arthur Mitchell. He of course once escorted me to the Academy Awards, and I wanted to ask him to do the honor again—this time with me receiving the golden statue. He wasn't there, so I later rang him and left a message, sharing my good news on his voice mail, reminding him of his prediction four and a half decades earlier. "This time," I said into the receiver, "I have the Oscar—and this time, I am asking you to repeat your performance and escort me to accept the incredible honor." Arthur did not answer, which puzzled me, because it was very unlike him not to immediately return my calls. I rang again, and then once more, until a family member at last picked up his phone. "Arthur's not well," she said slowly, with sadness between each word. "He's in the hospital." My heart stopped.

"What's the matter with him?" I asked.

She paused. "No diagnosis has been given," she told me. "That's all I can tell you."

For the previous two years, on and off, Arthur had been undergoing kidney dialysis. Through that ordeal, I'd been at his bedside, squeezing his hand, and at no point had we ever lost touch. I reasoned that this hospitalization must somehow be connected to his kidney condition, and I pressed his loved ones to share his location with me. Strangely, they would not. I called his family over and over, urging them to at least give me a number where I could reach him directly. My request went unmet.

A few days later, just after midnight, my dear friend passed on. "Call Cicely," he'd whispered to his family during his last moments, when he knew he was fading. "We can't call her at this hour," his family told him. "We'll ring her tomorrow." Shortly after, he breathed his last breath. He'd never heard my voice message. By the time I called, he'd already been on his way home.

Oh, how I wept at Arthur's passing, howling in disbelief that I hadn't been able to share his final days. I now know that Arthur, weak and emaciated from kidney failure, hadn't wanted anyone, especially me, to see him in such a frail state. He knew it would break me, and indeed it may have, though not being able to speak to or see him has, in its own way, shattered me. He was such a gentleman to the end, my beloved Arthur, as proud as he was generous. If that man had just one hair left in his nostrils, he'd give it away. He strode through this world with the posture of a king, and he loved with the soul of a lamb. Even in his last weeks, he thought more of how his deterioration might impact me than he did of himself. At his most vulnerable, he remained intent on protecting me, of serving as my steady shoulder, just as he'd been all those years ago when he escorted me, proud and beaming, to the front row of the Oscar ceremony. He'd been the one to direct his family not to share his hospital phone number or exact whereabouts. His family knew how close he and I were, and they considered overriding his instruction. But feeling caught between the devil and the deep blue sea, they ultimately honored his request.

I moved through that fall with a heavy heart, even as I made preparations for the ceremony. B Michael, of course, got right to work on my dress, and boy did he outdo himself, with a showpiece worthy of his designation as the first African American to design a gown for an Oscar winner. He created a dazzling haute couture two-piece gown ensemble in vintage silk brocade. The gown, with its cropped bolero and single bias train, was constructed using ninety-two pattern pieces. He completed the look with silver metallic leather gloves. When I entered the ceremony, donning his work of art, I didn't know whether I was there to claim my statue or model as one. That dress stole my breath.

Much of Hollywood, it seemed, showed up. Oprah flew in all the way from South Africa, where she'd been visiting her school. Quincy Jones and Shonda Rhimes were there, seated at my table. Ava DuVernay and Kerry Washington blessed me with tributes I will always hold close. "She is the seed for so many of us," said Ava, "the rose that we adore." Tyler Perry spoke glowingly of me as well, as did Quincy, all while I sat there feeling sheepish. Grateful as I am for their kind words, there comes a point when you start thinking, *Now who in the world are they talking about?* Even here during this last stretch of my life and career, I still feel like the child at my mother's kitchen table, sucking her thumb and quietly absorbing the world. That such a girl ended up in a silver ball gown, with folks carrying on about her work upon a stage, is a conundrum to me. I felt the same when, earlier that year, I appeared on the cover of *TIME* magazine. Ava guest-edited the issue, one all about optimism, and Lord knows I must have plenty to still be here.

At last, it was my turn to take the podium. "Forty-five years ago, I was offered a movie entitled *Sounder*—it was the first major movie that I would have done in my career," I began. I recounted the story of the spring afternoon in 1971 when I'd stopped by to share my news with Arthur, who'd predicted I'd be nominated for an Oscar. "I was nominated," I went on, "and he flew out to be my escort." With the agony of his loss still fresh, I revealed how, just two days after I'd left him a voice mail, telling him I'd finally receive an Oscar, he had passed. "Arthur," I said, clutching my prize, "wherever you are, this is what you were promising me—and I want to thank you." I concluded as I'd began, with my heart in my throat and tears in my eyes. "Next month," I said, "I will be ninety-four. And I don't know that I would cherish a better gift than this." In Arthur's memory, I relish my treasure, and whenever I glance at it atop my mantel, I pause and think of him. For fifty-eight years, we stood together in this life. For infinity, our bond remains.

I am the sole remaining member of my immediate family. After my parents went on home, my brother, Melrose, who developed a blood cancer like my father's, passed in 1991. Emily, who was also stricken with cancer, followed in 1999. Both died near my birthday. Each year when I celebrate my birth, I likewise commemorate their lives.

My season of harvest runs parallel to one of tremendous loss. On many days, I feel as if I have no space left in my heart for another grief, no holding pen for the overflow of tears. So many of my loved ones have left here. Maya Angelou and Ruby Dee both passed in 2014. Diahann Carroll went home in 2019, just before many of us gathered at the opening of Tyler's new studio. My sixth sense told me she was near the end. "You know, I'm worried about Diahann," I kept telling my daughter. "I need to go out and see her."

Around that time, my work on *Cherish the Day*, the series created by Ava DuVernay and produced by Oprah's network, took me to California. I decided to stop in and see my friend, and I called her daughter, Suzanne, to arrange it. "Please tell me when I can come," I said. "Come now," she told me. When I arrived that afternoon, Diahann was asleep. I sat in the living room and caught up with Suzanne, whom I hadn't seen for years. When Diahann awakened, Suzanne propped her up and made her comfortable so we could connect. I wasn't sure she'd still know who I was, given how fragile she appeared, but a light of recognition filled her eyes when I entered the room. "Hi, Cic," she said in a whisper that was hardly audible. I sat on the edge of the bed and began telling stories of those years when she and I bicycled all over New York, cracking ourselves up along the path. She smiled and nodded but did not speak. It took all the energy she could muster just to sit up. When I left there, I knew she didn't have long. Two days later, she was gone.

A year before I lost Diahann, Aretha went to be with Jesus after a battle with pancreatic cancer. In a televised homegoing service that felt like a Baptist revival, the world united in grief at her passing. Aretha and I go so far back that I can hardly recall a time when I did not know her. "If I ever do a movie of my life," she'd say every time she saw me, "you're going to play my mother." Her plans to star in her own biopic sadly never came together, and yet her music, her extraordinary body of work, is a heritage in itself.

When I received word of her passing, I began making plans to attend the memorial, held at Detroit's Greater Grace Temple—the church where Aretha sang at Rosa Park's funeral in 2005. My dress was a simple black sheath that I would adorn with a strand of pearls. But B Michael had an idea for a bold accessory. "Try this on," he said, handing me a black hat—one with a brim the circumference of the equator. I stared at him, and then at the hat, and then back at him. "I can't wear this," I said, laughing. "Nobody behind me will be able to *see*!" My daughter, who was with me that day, urged me on. "Just try it, Mom!" she said. I reluctantly did so, and somehow or another, I let those two devils persuade me to wear it to the service.

Well honey, you would've thought that hat had worn *me*! For weeks after that service, when folks would recount their memories of Aretha, many would end with, "And did you see Cicely's *hat*?" That stunner stole the show. In fact, it was so enormous that Oprah later had a custom box made for me to store it in. During the service, I took to that podium, with that brim flapping all over the place, and delivered a tribute to my friend—an adaptation of Paul Laurence Dunbar's poem "When Malindy Sings." I called it "When Aretha Sings," because oh, when that sister blessed us with her voice, the soul of the world fell open. As with Miles, her agony lived in every note. What a gem that Aretha was.

Several years before Maya went home to heaven, she penned the poem popularly known as "When Great Trees Fall," but properly titled "Ailey, Baldwin, Floyd, Killens, and Mayfield," a lyrical ode she ends this way:

And when great souls die,
after a period peace blooms,
slowly and always
irregularly. . . .

Our senses, restored, never
to be the same, whisper to us.
They existed. They existed.
We can be. Be and be
better. For they existed.

Her sentiments, so often repeated, powerfully sum up what loss does to the human heart, how it lowers our heads and deepens our sorrows, and yet how, in the end, it miraculously restores us. When great trees fall, we weep in unity with the forest—and we rejoice at the legacy that lingers.

25

Just as I Am

I NEVER leave home without my cayenne pepper. I either stash a bottle of the liquid extract in my pocketbook, or I stick it in the shopping cart I pull around with me all over Manhattan. When it comes to staying right-side up in this world, a Black woman needs at least three things. The first is a quiet spot of her own, a place away from the nonsense. The second is a stash of money, like the cash my mother kept hidden in the slit of her mattress. The last is several drops of cayenne pepper, always at the ready. Sprinkle that on your food before you eat it, and it'll kill any lurking bacteria. The powder does the trick as well, but I prefer the liquid because it hits the bloodstream quickly. Particularly when eating out, I won't touch a morsel to my lips 'til it's speckled with cayenne.

That's just one way I take care of my temple. Aside from preparing my daily greens, certain other habits have carried me toward the century mark. First thing I do every morning is drink four glasses of water. People think this water business is a joke, but I'm here to tell you that it's not. I've known two elderly people who died of dehydration, one of whom fell from his bed in the middle of the night and couldn't stand up because he was so parched. Following my water, I drink eight ounces of fresh celery juice, blended in my Vitamix. The juice cleanses the system and reduces inflammation. My biggest meal is my first one: oatmeal. I soak my oats overnight so that when I get up, all I have to do is turn on the burner. Sometimes I enjoy them with warm almond milk. Other times, I add grated almonds and berries, put the mixture in my tumbler, and shake it until it's so smooth I can drink it. In any form, oats do the heart good.

Throughout the day, I eat sweet potatoes (which are filled with fiber), beets (sprinkled with a little olive oil), and vegetables of every variety. I also still enjoy plenty of salad, though I stopped adding so many carrots. Too much sugar. But I will do celery, cucumbers, seaweed grass, and other greens. God's fresh bounty doesn't need a lot of dressing up, which is why I usually eat my salad plain. From time to time, I do drizzle it with garlic oil. I love the taste. I also love lychee nuts. I put them in the freezer so that when I bite into them, cold juice comes flooding out. As terrific as they are, I buy them only once in a while. I recently bit into an especially sweet one, and then I stuck it right back in the freezer. *Not today, Suze-ay*, I said to myself. Full of glucose. I try never to eat late, and certainly not after 9 p.m. Our organs need a chance to rest. And before bed, of course, I have a final glass of water. I don't mess around with my hydration.

I live right around the corner from my doctor—and he and I fight all the time. "When people talk about how good you look," he teases, "I take credit." I can't imagine why. Just about all I ever let that man do is examine me. "Tell me what the issue is," I say to him, "and I will take care of it myself." These US doctors are trained to cut you and write prescriptions. That is all. They don't know a thing about healing you. They treat symptoms, not causes. Like other professionals, they're working to buy their homes and send their kids to Harvard. That doesn't mean they don't care about your wellness, or that they're not good at diagnosing, and some of their treatments are excellent and should be followed. But before you let anyone go sticking a knife or needle in you, you've got to investigate. You've got to be sure you know what's happening with your body. You've got to advocate for yourself and your loved ones.

For someone who doesn't like to visit the doctor, my daughter teases, I seem to darken my physician's door quite frequently. I'll go to him over something as small as a hangnail, or anything else that strikes me as odd. "Why is this here?" I once asked him about a tiny patch of flaky skin on my arm. He examined it closely. "It's just dry skin," he concluded. "Do you feel fine otherwise?" I nodded yes. "I'll get you some cream to put on it," he said, pulling out his Rx pad. "I don't know why I even bother," he said, chuckling as he scribbled. "You're not gonna have the prescription filled, let alone use it." He was right. Beyond my basic physical exams, the most I've ever let him do is draw my blood and order chest x-rays. I'm not taking any drugs or using any creams, do you hear me? I haven't had an aspirin in so long, I don't even recall what it feels like on my tongue. If you're having pain, you don't want to simply kill it. You want to get to the bottom of what's causing it. That is why, in addition to my primary care physician, I stay in touch with a naturopathic doctor trained in Eastern medicine. I also keep close a copy of *The Juicing Bible*, a compendium of recipes meant to address various ailments. And once a month, I see my masseuse and an acupuncturist—or at least I did before this pandemic hit.

I never expected to live as long as I have. Up in heaven, my mother must be laughing and shaking her head, in between watching reruns of *Guiding Light*. Of her three young'uns, I was the one who wasn't supposed to make it. I was the child who came here with a bald head and murmuring heart, the scrawny babe she and my father hovered over. And yet here I am, perched on the doorstep of one hundred years, the last remaining member of the Tyson five. Nowadays, I do wonder about when I'm going, about how many sunrises I have left. In 2019, I dreamed I was shopping for a white dress, and since white can stand for funerals in my culture, I took that as a sign that my time was near. But the dream wasn't about me. Soon after my vision, fashion designer Arthur McGee, my friend for many decades, passed on, and may he rest in peace. I don't know when my day is coming. None of us does. Which is why, as soon as my lids slide open each morning, I say thank you. Thank you, Father, for the gift of another day. Thank you for just one more breath. Thank you for the sacred opportunity to live this life.

The way I see it, I'm still here because God isn't finished with me. And when I've completed my job, he'll take me. Until then, I've got plenty to do. I glimpse my purpose every time I'm in the presence of my darling daughter, whom I see frequently. Joan and I continue to work on our relationship, as fragile as it is precious, and even as I write of her in my story, I leave space for her to one day share her own. I see my purpose in the faces of my students. I also recognize it in my characters, in their heartaches and victories. I am the sum total of the women I've portrayed. Each has endowed me with an invaluable gift. From Rebecca, I learned grace. From Jane, I gleaned determination. From Coretta, Harriet, Binta, and others, I borrowed courage. That these Black women were able to survive what they did, in the manner in which they did, has allowed me to believe that I, too, can hold steady. My existence is tied up in theirs.

My remaining purpose is also connected to this surreal season in our world. I'm here, as we all are, to meet this moment. Like you, I can feel the times shifting even as we're standing in them, can sense history stirring and moaning. I've lived through sixteen presidents, witnessed movements come and go. Seldom have I felt so strongly that our nation is at a turning point. The COVID pandemic has claimed hundreds of thousands of lives, far too many of them Black. The disease has laid bare the structural inequalities that have always existed for us. It's not by accident that we always find ourselves languishing near the bottom of the social caste system. Our communities have been exploited and overpoliced. Discriminatory economic policies have relegated large swaths of us to low wages and crowded neighborhoods. More often than not, we are the essential workers. We are the ones who lack access to quality health care. We are the group that suffers when jobs vanish and schools shut down amid infection.

During a good year, to be Black is to live with an ongoing hum of anxiety, a static ever present beneath life's high notes. During a plague and a racial revolution, to be Black is to be rendered deaf by the uproar, knowing that if this virus doesn't take you down, a blue knee on your neck or bullets in your back just might. When you leave your house, you're never quite sure whether you'll make it back alive, and that is no exaggeration. In this country, Blacks don't have to go looking for trouble. It finds us. Ahmaud Arbery was murdered in cold blood while out for a jog. Botham Jean was sitting in his own apartment, enjoying a bowl of ice cream and watching television, when a white police officer exploded through his door and snuffed out his life. As bullets rained down on Breonna Taylor, that child was asleep in her bed. All of these young people were under the age of twenty-seven. Stop and take that in. If you've been fortunate enough to surpass that milestone, think back on what your life was like at that point, on what your aspirations were.

Can you imagine how many years these babies might've had

ahead of them, how their dreams were cut short by the roar of gunfire, how their families have been left reeling? And then folks have the nerve to bring up Black rage. Wouldn't you be seething if, for centuries, the world placed such little value on your existence? Wouldn't you feel wounded if your ancestors had been treated like beasts, your features and your culture disparaged, your families wrested apart on auction blocks? Wouldn't you cry out in anguish if your country's leaders, rather than renouncing and rectifying such injustice, stoked the flames of it? We're not even allowed our humanity when it comes to expressing the full spectrum of our emotions. Whether we're sitting quietly in a corner or forthrightly stating our concerns, many are quick to label us as "angry," which goes right along with the age-old narrative that we're dangerous savages, recklessly spewing vitriol. And even as they brand us, they dismiss the abuse that first lit the smoldering embers. The youth, exhausted with the criminalizing of our bodies, are taking to the streets like no time in recent memory.

For years, I've been quietly concerned that my generation, the one led by Dr. King, gave our young people too much. It seemed they had little idea about the price that had been paid for them to vote, to attend integrated schools, to improve their prospects through higher education, to drink from any water fountain. When we were fighting for civil rights, we did so with the hope that our children would never have to suffer the humiliations we'd endured. We wanted to free them to use all their talents to further lift themselves. Over this past year, my worry has been allayed. I am heartened by the response from our young people, by how they've risen up en masse to demand more, by how they've organized to make our voices heard at the ballot box. They are impassioned and knowledgeable and fierce. They are linking arms with those who want to join us on the front lines. And to my delight, they are taking on Dr. King's mantle and soldiering forward.

This recent racial reckoning is but a comma in a centuries-long sentence, a pause during which many, for the first time, have awakened to the horror of Black genocide—and I choose that word intentionally, because over and over throughout history, attempts have been made to extinguish us in one way or another. That Americans of all races are now focused on the massacre is indeed progress, just as it was when Emmett Till's heinous lynching, his mutilated body in that open casket, shook the nation from its slumber in 1955. In our current times, I see the outcry as an opportunity for us to unite in action, to move from demonstration to legislation, from picketing to building economic parity. If history and human nature are reliable measures, this window won't be open for long. And as it closes, I find myself wondering, *What will become of Black people, and of Black women in particular?* That, as it has been for all of my career, is my chief concern.

"Sit down here and let me talk to you," my mother would say when she wanted to get my attention. If I heard that sentence, I knew she was about to speak some sense to me, as she did on that day when she told me, despondent after an audition, "What's for you in this life, you will get. And what is not for you, you will never get. Do you hear me?" I did hear her, and that wisdom has buoyed me through the decades. It is in my mother's name, in her spirit and memory, that I ask you, Black women, to gather 'round. Sit down here and let me talk to you—just us.

I often ponder what has happened to us as a people. I know the overarching plotline. I understand that our existence stretches back to the Nile River Valley, when our ancestors erected vast kingdoms, advanced civilizations the Europeans wrenched from our palms. I understand how our story eventually floated its way across the Atlantic, on Middle Passage ships where Black corpses—so-called cargo—were hurled overboard for sharks to devour. I'm aware of the many ways in which two hundred–plus years of enslavement maimed us, and of the countless other ways it never could. I understand that any time we sought to rise—as sharecroppers struggling to earn our way to freedom in an unjust system, as workers laboring in the long shadow of Jim Crow, as aspiring homeowners locked into redlined ghettos and, thus, locked out of wealth for generations—we've been repeatedly shoved onto our knees. What I find most troubling nowadays, given this history, is how little we seem to value ourselves. Centuries of abuse have taught us to regard one another with disdain, to treat ourselves with the same contempt plantation owners once held for us. What else can explain why some of us still use terms like *nigger* and *whore* when referring to each other, why we partake in narrative homicide of ourselves in films, in music, in books, in culture? It pains me. It also makes me aware of just how acute our wound is.

And make no mistake, my dear children: whether or not we recognize it, you and I were born into a legacy of trauma, just as surely as we've inherited our foreparents' resilience. The wound, festering for centuries, morphs frequently in appearance. It has traversed through woods and swamps, navigated in darkness from the South to the North, and presented itself right here in the present. Upon arrival, it looked a whole lot like fortitude, which it is. But beneath that brave face is another, one bruised and ailing, bloodied by the indignities of the journey. That wound, in our times now, manifests as self-injury. It shows up in behaviors, conscious and unconscious, that demean us. It appears in the form of sharp-tongued mothers more apt to take up their switches than to display tenderness toward their young'uns. It rises to the surface as hypertension and anxiety and depression. It looks like Miles Davis, trying to deaden a lifetime of agony with a cocaine high. It has revealed itself in my life over and over, priming me to tolerate an abuse so achingly familiar in both my own story and that of my mother. No amount of Black Girl Magic, no repeated proclamations of our worth, can fully treat the wound, although acknowledging its persistence is a beginning. The ultimate remedy, as I see it, is supernatural. I look daily toward heaven for restoration, for spiritual healing. My true identity isn't rooted in our history, grievous and glorious as it is. It is grounded in my designation as a child of God, the daughter of the Great Physician. In his care, I find my cure.

My hope for you is the same one I carry for myself. I pray that, amid the heartache of our ancestry, you can grant yourself the grace so seldom extended to us. I pray that you can pass that compassion on to your children, and to their children, so that it slathers comfort on our sore spots. I pray that, as a people, we can give ourselves a soft place to land. I pray, even as we rightly express our fury at being regarded as subhuman, that we don't dwell in that space, that we don't allow anger to poison our spirits, that we embrace love as our one true antidote. I hope, too, that you recognize your specialness, the distinctiveness the Creator has imbued us with. I see you as clearly as history has, and in unison with it, I nod. I know that swivel in your hips, that fervor in your testimony, that ebullience in your stride, that flair in your song. The fact that others are constantly trying to diminish you, ever attempting to dismiss your talents even as they mimic them, is proof of your uniqueness. No one bothers to undermine you unless they recognize your brilliance.

More than anything, I pray that you can carve out a purpose for yourself, a calling beyond your own survival, a sweet offering to the world. You gain a life by giving yours away. Not everyone is meant to raise a picket sign. And yet each of us can choose a path of impact. Rearing your children with affection and warmth is a form of activism. Honoring your word impeccably is a way to raise your voice. Performing your job with excellence—with your chin high and your standards higher—is as powerful as any protest march. Sowing into the lives of young people is a worthy crusade. That is what it means to leave this world of ours more lit up than we found it. It's also what it means to lead a magnificent life, even if an unlikely one. The Father has a way of choosing the flawed to attempt what many deem improbable. My journey upon the stage, and every moment in between, is a testament to the mystery in God's choosing.

Here in my twilight years, as my Christmas tree towers and glistens, folks are always asking me what legacy I want to leave—what roots beneath my soil I most hope will outlive me. I want to go home knowing that I loved generously, even if imperfectly. I want to feel as if I embodied our humanity so fully that it made us laugh and weep, that it reminded us of our shared frailties. I want to be recalled as one who squared my shoulders in the service of Black women, as one who made us walk taller and envision greater for ourselves. I want to know that I did the very best that I could with what God gave me—just as I am.

ACKNOWLEDGMENTS

This book is a special gift to my mama, Fredericka Theodosia Huggins Tyson; my daddy, William Augustine Tyson; my brother, Melrose Emmanuel Tyson; and my baby sister—although she thought I was her baby sister!—Emily Rebecca Tyson-Henry. Each of you, in your own way, molded me into the woman I have become.

I've loved flowers all my life. At daybreak before my father went to work, he'd walk me over to Central Park so that I, his frail child, his firstborn girl, could breathe in fresh air amid the lush gardens. It was our special time together. My father would spread a blanket on the grass for us to sit, close as we could, and watch the world stir awake. We'd be out there for an hour or more, the dew settling on our cheeks, the day's newness filling our lungs. I must've been around five when, near our blanket one morning, I spotted a patch of yellow daisies. I reached over and began plucking them. Just then, a white lady stopped and smiled at me.

"Little girl," she said, "you don't like flowers?" With three daisies clutched in my palm, I stared at her, studying her face for what she meant. She laughed. "I'm sure you do like flowers," she went on, "and I do too. But you know, if you pick them, they won't be around for other people to enjoy."

I've never forgotten that kind woman or the awareness she left me with. Flowers, she understood, were meant to be savored, but most of all to be shared. They are God's gift to humankind, his bounty springing up in sidewalk cracks and manicured gardens alike. It is for us to relish the beauty, even as we leave it for others to delight in. My path to writing this book has been lined with such flowers—those who have gifted me with their skills, their passions, their partnership. I offer them to you here, my bouquet of blessings, for us to appreciate together.

My family is my most cherished blossom, my source of strength. I might be the only remaining member of my immediate tribe, but the powerful Tyson spirit lives on in my daughter, in my nieces and nephews, in my cousins, and in their children and grandchildren. Thank you for giving me roots. I am grounded by your love and nourished by your devotion.

Were it not for my manager, Larry Thompson, you would not be holding this book. Our relationship spans four decades, and at every juncture, he has encouraged me to share my story, on my terms, before others could rush in with their erroneous versions. Larry, thank you for your insistence that I be the sole author of my memories, now committed to paper for eternity. I could not ask for a more ardent advocate. Your partnership means so much to me, as do you and your family. To Robert G. Endara II, who has worked alongside Larry for more than two decades: Thank you for your diligent service over so many years—for the late nights, the long hours, and your extraordinary attention to even the smallest of details. I am deeply grateful for your patience, dedication, and dependability. And to my literary agent, Jan Miller, and her team at Dupree Miller & Associates: I sincerely appreciate your phenomenal efforts and publishing expertise in bringing *Just as I Am* to the world. Your advice and judgment have been invaluable to me. Thank you for your outstanding work on my behalf.

To Michelle Burford, my collaborative writer: Thank you for lending me the poetry of your pen and the openness of your heart. During my six decades on the stage, I have always been divinely guided, and the spirit once again led me well in prompting me to choose you. Our intimate conversations over many months are a sacred gift I hold dear. Thank you for gathering the scattered pieces of my memories and arranging them into a powerful, cohesive whole. Your excellence shines through in every passage.

Tracy Sherrod, from the moment we met, I knew my life story was best entrusted in your capable hands. My confidence in you has been well placed. You are a true visionary, a beacon in the publishing community. Thank you for acquiring my book and for championing its publication at every turn. Thank you as well for your strong management and unflappable calm at the helm of Amistad Press, and as a leader within HarperCollins. I am also grateful to the HarperCollins team members—those behind the scenes and those out front—for investing their time and talents in *Just as I Am*. To Judith Curr, president and publisher at HarperCollins: Your enthusiasm for this book has cleared the path for its publication. I am thankful for your unwavering support. To Paul Olsewski, senior director of publicity, and to Stephen Brayda, art director and cover designer: Thank you for your exceptional work, and for going the extra mile. And to Terri Leonard, Suzanne Quist, Yvonne Chan, Marta Durkin, Lucy Albanese, John Jusino, and Anna Brower—thank you for the love and care you put into the production, photo insert, and packaging of the book.

Maxine Grandison, my niece, you are not only the keeper

of our family's rich culinary tradition, you're also the guardian of the family tree. Thank you for researching the Tyson and Huggins ancestries and contributing your findings to this book. You are a glorious demonstration of both legacies. Your mother, Emily, would be as proud of you as I am.

A special thank you to Viola Davis, Minyon Moore, and Tyler Perry—each of whom so graciously gave of their time during the completion of *Just as I Am.* Viola, I appreciate your beautiful foreword, and even more than that, your warm spirit. Minyon and Tyler, thank you for recalling colorful stories that now live on these pages. Thank you, too, for blessing me with your light and laughter. I adore you.

Carol Wiggins, you have been a loyal confidante to me, as well as a dear friend to our beloved Arthur Mitchell. You shared with me that Arthur Mitchell, on his deathbed, told you "Take care of Cicely"—and you have honored his wish. Thank you for the countless hours you've spent at my side, and for the years you stood at his. Also, thank you for your assistance in reviewing drafts of this book.

B Michael, the words "thank you" fall short in conveying my gratitude to you. You are more than a masterful designer, the couturier I've relied on for more than fifteen years. You're also a trusted escort. Thank you for your hands-on caring, and for your assistance with this book. You and Mark-Anthony Edwards are my extended family.

Bill Haber, I will forever be grateful that you and your wife, Carole, welcomed me into your home and hearts all those years ago. You were with me from the beginning, watching this marvelous path unfold, encouraging me at every turn. It is because of your generosity that my career on the West Coast took root. Thank you for investing in me over many decades, both as an agent and as a dear friend.

To my attorney, Glenn Goldstein: You have been my saving grace since the start of my career. I don't know what I would do without you. God bless you.

Lois Harris, there are moments in our relationship that I will never forget. Thank you.

Debra Lee, although we rarely see each other, for you to announce to the world that Cicely Tyson is your new best friend—I believe you. Thank you so much for all of your years of support. It's invaluable to me.

To CiCi in Dr. Orsher's office: I am grateful for your willingness to do whatever task was needed. Every time you looked in my face and considered what had to be done, you said, "I'll do it." That was always manna for my ears. To Arthur Hicks at London Town Car: Thank you for safely driving me all over New York City and beyond. You've been a marvelous traveling companion. And to Carl Foster, who served faithfully as my assistant for many years: Thank you for sharing your recollections for this book.

Dr. Henry Louis Gates Jr., director of the Hutchins Center for African and African-American Research at Harvard University, and host of the award-winning PBS documentary series *Finding Your Roots*: I appreciate your willingness to research my family's ancestry, and though we encountered an impasse, I am grateful to your team for offering its findings as reference material for this book.

To the staff and students at Cicely L. Tyson Community School of Performing and Fine Arts: I cannot tell you how much you mean to me, every one of you. I was mesmerized to see the first graduating class, marching across that stage to receive your diplomas, and I've been no less in awe during each successive ceremony. I am so proud of you. You've added joy to my days and years to my life. Your love is a priceless gift. And to the school's first principal, Mrs. Laura Trimmings, may you rest in peace: It is only because of your persistence that a school now bears my name. I am grateful for your passion and determination. You are a rose among roses, a treasure to me and to the scores of students you touched during your career. Thank you for using your life in service to a higher call.

To the Reverend Dr. Calvin O. Butts, pastor of Abyssinian Baptist Church in Harlem: Over many decades, your encouragement is what has helped me to carry on. Thank you for providing me with a spiritual home. When I'm in town, I do not miss Sunday service, which you've often commented upon from the pulpit. Despite whatever is happening in my life, gathering with the saints always gives me strength, as does sitting in the pew on which my mother's name is engraved. Her spirit lives there.

As far back as I can recall, E.A.T. restaurant on New York's Upper East Side has been my home away from home—my supper table on the go. To Eli Zabar, the owner, thank you for the years of hot soup and warm service, as well as for lending me your upstairs space to conduct interviews for this book. You and your entire waitstaff have always made me feel welcome.

Each of you, my dear readers and viewers, has surrounded me with the sweet scent of your presence. When I made the choice to devote my life to the stage, I did so with the hope that I might change one person—just one. God heard my quiet prayer and granted it a hundredfold, with grace beyond measure over all these decades. Thank you for your abundant love to me during my journey. In your care, I have flourished.

"Can a woman's tender care cease toward the child she bare?
Yes, she may forgetful be, yet I will remember thee."

—FROM THE HYMN "HARK, MY SOUL, IT IS THE LORD,"
BASED ON ISAIAH 49:15

To the one who has paid the greatest price for this gift to all—*Just as I Am* is dedicated to Joan.

Love, Mom

INDEX

Page numbers of photographs appear in italics.
Key to abbreviations: CT = Cicely Tyson; NYC = New York City

ABOUT THE AUTHORS

Ms. Cicely Tyson—legendary actress, advocate, and humanitarian—is renowned for her portrayals of strong female characters on stage, screen, and television, from her stunning initial stage appearance as Barbara Allen in *Dark of the Moon*, to her triumphant 2013 return to Broadway as Mrs. Carrie Watts in Horton Foote's *The Trip to Bountiful*. For that portrayal, she received rave reviews and the triple crown of theater awards: the Tony, Drama Desk, and Outer Critics Circle awards for Best Actress in a Play.

Best known for her double Emmy performance (Best Lead Actress in a Drama, and a special, unprecedented Emmy for Actress of the Year) as Jane in *The Autobiography of Miss Jane Pittman*, Ms. Tyson was also nominated for an Emmy in 2015, 2017, 2019, and 2020, for her recurring guest role as Ophelia, Annalise's mother (Viola Davis) in ABC's *How to Get Away with Murder*. She received her third Emmy for *The Oldest Living Confederate Widow Tells All* and was nominated for her performances in *Roots*, *King*, *Sweet Justice*, *The Marva Collins Story*, and *A Lesson Before Dying*.

In January 2020, Ms. Tyson was inducted into the Television Academy Hall of Fame. She is among the elite number of entertainers honored with a star on the Hollywood Boulevard Walk of Fame. Ms. Tyson was recognized for her contribution to the performing arts at the 2015 Kennedy Center Honors. In addition, she is the recipient of the NAACP's highest honor, the prestigious Spingarn Medal. In 2016, she received the Presidential Medal of Freedom, the highest civilian award of the United States.

Ms. Tyson was nominated for an Academy Award for *Sounder*. Her film credits include *The Heart Is a Lonely Hunter*, *Fried Green Tomatoes*, *Because of Winn-Dixie*, *Hoodlum*, *Diary of a Mad Black Woman*, *Madea's Family Reunion*, *Why Did I Get Married Too?*, *The Help*, *Alex Cross*, *Last Flag Flying*, and in 2020, *A Fall from Grace* directed by Tyler Perry. On November 18, 2018, Ms. Tyson received an Honorary Oscar at the Motion Picture Academy's Governors Awards.

Since 1995, Ms. Tyson has served as the guiding force of the Cicely L. Tyson Community School of Performing and Fine Arts. This $143 million institution of academic and creative expression in East Orange, New Jersey, serves twelve hundred students from kindergarten through twelfth grade. As both a screen legend and a cultural icon, Ms. Tyson continues to develop her art by taking on new roles and opportunities.

Michelle Burford served as Ms. Cicely Tyson's collaborative writer. She is a number one *New York Times* bestselling author who has collaborated on ten memoirs. She is also a founding editor of O, *The Oprah Magazine* and a former *Essence* magazine editor. A native of Phoenix, she resides in New York City.